D1439104

THE **ABC** OF BRITISH LOCOMOTIVES

PART 1

1-9999

STEAM LOCOMOTIVES :
WESTERN REGION

LONDON :

Ian Allan Ltd

1948

INTRODUCTION TO THE SERIES

BRITISH MOTIVE POWER OF THE FUTURE

By CECIL J. ALLEN, M.Inst.T., A.I.Loco.E.

FROM the beginning of 1948 the railways of Great Britain lost their separate identity, and became merged in one national system. As a result, the process of locomotive standardisation is certain to be carried further than ever before, and the number of independent locomotive classes, which has been in course of reduction ever since the railway grouping of 1923, eventually will become fewer still. Fortunately it is impossible, on economy grounds alone, to scrap relatively new locomotives, so that this process of elimination is bound to take a very long time, and the large locomotive classes of the four main line railways that had become standard will remain with us for a long while to come.

Before we review these classes, it is of interest to speculate as to the direction in which future standard design is likely to trend. The appointments to the Railway Executive, in connection with motive power, have been significant. The full-time member responsible for locomotives, carriages and wagons is Mr. R. A. Riddles, C.B.E., at one time Personal Assistant to Mr. W. A. Stanier—later Sir William Stanier—when the latter was Chief Mechanical Engineer of the L.M.S.R. After that, Mr. Riddles became Mechanical Engineer for Scotland, L.M.S.R., and after the war the Vice-President of that company in charge of motive power. The Executive Officer for Design, Mr. E. S. Cox, and the Chief Officer for Locomotive Construction and Maintenance, Mr. R. C. Bond, were both on Sir William Stanier's staff. The locomotive influence at the executive level of British Railways is thus predominantly that of the late L.M.S.R.

For the present, however, there seems to be no hurry to impose L.M.S.R. standards on the rest of the country. The first step taken, under executive direction, has been the highly interesting series of locomotive exchanges which took place during the months of May, June and July, when the wildest dreams of railway enthusiasts as to the possibility of their favourite locomotive classes showing off their paces on rival lines were far more than realised. The aim of the tests was to examine the behaviour of the leading locomotive classes, with their own crews, equal loads, and the same quality of coal in all cases, in every possible variety of running conditions, as represented by the main lines of the four previous railways.

Right : Ex-Taff Vale Rly. 0-6-2T No. 381

Below : Ex-Rhymney Rly. 0-6-2T No. 63

[P. L. Melvill

Ex - Alexandra (Newport & S. Wales) Docks Rly. 2-6-2T No. 1205

[P. L. Melvill

Right : Ex-Swansea Harbour Trust 0-4-0T No. 701

[*A. B. Crompton*

Below : "1101" Class 0-4-0T No. 1105

[*H. C. Casserley*

Right : Ex-Swansea Harbour Trust 0-4-0T No. 1098

[*H. C. Casserley*

Right: Ex-Cardiff Rly. 0-4-0T No. 1338

[*B. V. Franey*

Below : Ex-Powlesland & Mason 0 - 4 - 0T No. 942

[*A. B. Crompton*

Left: Ex-Llanelly & Mynydd Mawr Rly. 0 - 6 - 0T, No. 359 *Hilda*

[*H. C. Casserlev*

Ex-Swansea Harbour Trust 0-6-0T No. 1085 [*A. B. Crompton*

Ex-Burry Port & Gwendraeth Valley Rly. 0-6-0T No. 2197 *Pioneer* [*A. B. Crompton*

Ex-Burry Port & Gwendraeth Valley Rly. 0-6-0T No. 2167 [*H. C. Casserley*

In particular, it was desired to measure the power output of representative engines of each class, and to relate it to coal and water consumption, so that relative efficiency as well as tractive power might both be under observation. For this purpose the dynamometer cars of the late L.M.S., L.N.E. and G.W. Railways were all in use, on the test trips proper. Though the trainloads were all made up to the maximum loads normally worked single-headed over the various test routes, the easy post-war schedules and the numerous track speed restrictions took much of the sparkle out of this contest of the giants by ruling out high speeds at the pre-war level, with certain notable exceptions.

It is interesting to review the classes that were tested against one another, as indicating possible future trends. In the express passenger group there were three Pacifics. The London Midland Region was represented by a " Duchess " Pacific of Stanier's design ; on the Eastern Region a tribute was paid to the late Sir Nigel Gresley by the choice of the streamlined " A4 " Pacifics, an undiluted Gresley design ; while the Southern selection, needless to say, was a Bulleid " Merchant Navy " Pacific. The Western Region, having no Pacifics, produced a 4-6-0 Collett " King "—a design by now 21 years old. Competing with these, and the smallest and lightest type in this group, was one of the highly efficient London Midland rebuilt " Royal Scot " 4-6-0's, which on two of the four test routes—those from King's Cross and Waterloo—was called on to handle the same loads as the considerably more powerful Pacifics, and did so with complete competence.

The second group consisted of engines of " general purpose " types, with smaller driving wheels. Of mixed traffic 4-6-0's there were the ubiquitous Class " 5's " of the late L.M.S.R., the Thompson " B1's " to represent the late L.N.E.R., and a " Hall " of the late G.W.R. Against these was pitted a much more powerful class in the shape of the Southern " West Country " Pacifics, which covered themselves with glory on every route over which they were tested. But constructional and maintenance costs of each type must be considered equally with times and speeds, and coal and water consumption, so that it must not be assumed that the engines which made the best times and speeds in the tests necessarily will be the types on which ultimate standardisation will be based.

In the freight locomotive tests there was no representative of the Southern Region. The London Midland selection was obvious—one of the standard Class " 8 " 2-8-0's built in such large numbers during the war. For the Eastern Region the choice fell on a design which was standardised for war service during the First World War—the Robinson 2-8-0 of the one-time Great Central Railway—as modernised and fitted during the L.N.E.R. Thompson *regime* with a boiler carrying 225 lb. pressure. The Western Region provided a " 38XX " 2-8-0, a practically unaltered Churchward design in its proportions and details. Against these were tried two classes which originated outside the four main line railways, and for which Mr. Riddles of the Railway Executive was himself partly responsible —the 2-8-0 and 2-10-0 locomotives built for the Ministry of Supply during the late war.

From the ranks of these contestants there were some significant omissions. In the express passenger category, apart from the London Midland rebuilt "Royal Scot," there were no examples of the intermediate types used for the secondary duties. There was no need to include the London Midland "5XP" 4-6-0's, for ultimately these are all to be rebuilt with the larger boilers and to become generally uniform with the "Royal Scots." The Class "B17" 4-6-0's of the late L.N.E.R. also seem destined for conversion to a two-cylinder type very similar to the "B1" 4-6-0's that figured in the "general purpose" tests, in all respects other than their larger driving wheels. There seems no likelihood of any ultimate perpetuation of the Southern "Lord Nelson" and "King Arthur" 4-6-0's, building of which ceased many years ago. But a curious omission was that of the Western Region "Castle" 4-6-0's, which are still being turned out, even though the design is now a quarter-of-a-century old. The absence of this class from the tests is the more surprising in view of the outstanding success of these locomotives in the famous locomotive exchanges of 1925 and 1926, which so strongly influenced later British locomotive design.

In the "general purpose" category the omission of the ex-London & North Eastern Class "V2" 2-6-2 locomotives is readily understandable by the fact that their dimensions and weight exclude them from the almost unrestricted radius of action of the other classes under test. A "Green Arrow" could not have been used, for example, over the Highland main line of the Scottish Region between Perth and Inverness. But the Great Western "County" 4-6-0, a modern design which is showing itself capable of some first-class performance on the road, was, perhaps, a more eligible competitor in the "general purpose" group than the "Hall," though equally restricted as to route.

In the freight group, the exclusion of any of the Gresley 3-cylinder 2-8-0's of the late L.N.E.R. seems to foreshadow a concentration on the simplicity of two-cylinder propulsion for future freight work, as all the engines compared were of two-cylinder types. No comparative tests were made of locomotives for light branch work, but it may be added that engines of the latest London Midland light Mogul type have been loaned to the Eastern Region for trial. In this connection it should be noted that up to the time of nationalisation no railway other than the L.M.S.R. had prepared new designs for locomotives intended specifically for routes over which severe weight restrictions obtain, so that it will not be surprising if the types just mentioned are among the first to come into general use in other parts of the country.

There have been no tests, either, of tank engines, though standard London Midand 2-6-4 tanks have been loaned to the Southern Region for trial purposes. In this category the competition seems to lie between the Thompson 2-6-4 tank of the late L.N.E.R. —most recent of all the bigger tank designs—and the ex-L.M.S.R 2-6-4 type just referred to ; both are still being built in large numbers. Elsewhere, except for the light 2-6-2 type introduced by the L.M.S.R. shortly before the onset of nationalisation, no new passenger tank designs have emerged in Great Britain for some years past, and no new types of shunting tank, either, apart from the Hawksworth taper boiler version of the Western Region 0-6-0 pannier tanks, which also is being turned out on an extensive scale at the present time.

For the present, each Region is continuing to build its own designs, as some of the preceding paragraphs have indicated. Recently, the London Midland Region has been building Class " 5 " 4-6-0's, the latest ultra-modern Class " 4 " 2-6-0's, 2-6-4 tanks, Class " 2 " 2-6-2 tanks, and an occasional Pacific ; the Eastern and North Eastern Regions have been concentrating on Class " A1 " and " A2 " Pacifics, " B1 " 4-6-0's, and " L1 " 2-6-4 tanks ; on the Western Region the building has been of " Castle " and " Hall " 4-6-0's and the new 0-6-0 pannier tanks ; and on the Southern Region of " Battle of Britain " and " Merchant Navy " Pacifics.

Mr. Bulleid of the Southern Region also is proceeding with his revolutionary double-end " Leader " class design, of which little is yet known ; and this is a welcome sign, as it shows that in the new set-up a good deal is being left for the time being to individual initiative. Much more will be done by pooling the technical resources of all four pre-nationalisation railways than by any attempt to impose the standards of one of them on all the remainder.

Certain main lines of development, however, emerge fairly clearly. For the heaviest express passenger work Pacifics will be the standard practice. For the secondary work the performance of the ex-L.M.S.R. " Royal Scots " would appear to indicate that a thoroughly modern 4-6-0 design is adequate, and is even a substitute for a Pacific when occasion requires. For " general purpose " or " mixed traffic " work it is not quite so easy to foresee what will be the future preference. Both the ex-L.N.E.R. Thompson Pacifics and the Southern " West Country " Pacifics, with their 6 ft. 2 in. wheels, have shown the value of the 4-6-2 wheel arrangement for work of this description, with the ability to take over front rank express passenger service if necessary. Like the London Midland Class " 5 " 4-6-0's, the Thompson " B1's," and other similar types, they are an even greater necessity as locomotives which have an almost universal radius of action without restriction ; and for mixed traffic it is an engine of this type which is certain to be built on the most extensive scale. For main line freight service the two-cylinder 2-8-0 for the heavy work, and the 2-6-0 for the lighter duties, seem marked out as the wheel arrangements of the future.

Certain wheel arrangements appear doomed to disappear altogether. Among them is the 4-4-0 for passenger service ; of the last remaining 4-4-0 classes which still exist on a large scale—the ex-L.M.S.R. Midland compounds and the Class " 2 " 4-4-0's—the first examples are now being scrapped. It is unlikely that any further 0-6-0's will be built, though those still in service are so numerous that their extinction is bound to be a lengthy process. No more 0-4-4, 2-4-2, or 0-6-2 tanks will be turned out ; nor, indeed, any more engines with less than three axles coupled. The handy 0-6-0 tank will continue to be popular for shunting, but it is questionable whether various larger and more complicated wheel arrangements for special marshalling yard use are likely to survive, in view of the arrival of a new competitor in the form of the diesel-electric locomotive.

Another notable move has been the building by the London Midland Region of the first diesel-electric express passenger locomotives, which already have proved themselves to be highly competent and reliable machines. But for the meteoric rise in the price of coal, and the decline in its quality, such a competitor might not have been seen in Great Britain for many years ; but the die has now been cast, and it is difficult to forecast the ultimate result of the throw. In brief, we are at an extremely interesting stage in British locomotive development, and as yet no one can foresee with any precision what line it is likely to take during the next few years.

LOCOMOTIVE SUPERINTENDENTS AND CHIEF MECHANICAL ENGINEERS OF THE G.W.R.

Sir Daniel Gooch	1837—1864
Joseph Armstrong	1854—1864* 1864—1877
George Armstrong ... ... *(Bro. of J. Armstrong)*	1864— * 1877—1892*
William Dean	—1877* 1877—1902
G. J. Churchward	1902—1921
Charles B. Collett	1922—1941
F. W. Hawksworth	1941—1947

* In charge of standard gauge locomotives at Stafford Road Works, Wolverhampton, with wide powers in design and construction. The exact dates of Geo. Armstrong's and Dean's terms of service there cannot be definitely ascertained from existing records.

NOTES ON THE USE OF THIS BOOK

1. This booklet lists British Railways locomotives numbered between 1 and 9999 in service at August 31st, 1948. This range of numbers covers Western Region (ex-G.W.R.) engines with the following exceptions :

(i) Diesel and forthcoming gas turbine locomotives, which are dealt with in the ABC OF BRITISH RAILWAYS LOCOMOTIVES NOS. 10000-39999.

(ii) " Austerity " 2-8-0 locomotives on loan to Western Region from the Ministry of Supply. These are listed in the ABC OF BRITISH RAILWAYS LOCOMOTIVES Part 4—60000-79999.

2. With the exception of Diesel locomotives, Western Region locomotives retain their original Great Western numbers. Where locomotives have been renumbered under the continued Great Western schemes involving a partial renumbering of former South Wales companies' engines, and renumbering in new series of engines converted to oil-burning, the former numbers of locomotives affected are shown in brackets in the following lists.

3. Throughout the book the dimensions shown for each class are only typical examples and should not be taken as applying to every engine of the class.

4. ¶ indicates loco fitted for burning oil fuel.

5. The following is a list of abbreviations used to indicate the pre-grouping owners of certain Western Region locomotives :

AD	Alexandra (Newport and South Wales) Docks & Railway
BR	Barry Railway
BM	Brecon and Merthyr Railway
BPGV	Burry Port & Gwendraeth Valley Rly.
Cam.R.	Cambrian Railways
Car.R.	Cardiff Railway
CMDP	Cleobury Mortimer and Ditton Priors Light Railway
Cor.R.	Corris Railway
LMM	Llanelly & Mynydd Mawr Railway
MSWJ	Midland and South Western Junction Railway
NB	Neath and Brecon Railway
PM	Powlesland & Mason (Contractor)
PT	Port Talbot Rly.
RR	Rhymney Railway
SHT	Swansea Harbour Trust
TV	Taff Vale Railway
V of R	Cambrian Railways (Vale of Rheidol)
WCPR	Weston, Clevedon & Portishead Rly.
W & C	Whitland & Cardigan
W & L	Cambrian Railways (Welshpool and Llanfair)

NUMERICAL LIST OF LOCOMOTIVES

The tables on these pages show engine number, wheel arrangement and pre-grouping owner or Western Region Class. For abbreviations see page 11. Where no initials are shown, the loco is of G.W.R. origin.

1 0-6-0T‡
3 0-4-2T* Cor. R.
4 0-4-2T* Cor. R.
5 Portishead 0-6-0T W.C. & P.R.
7 2-6-2T V.of R.†
8 2-6-2T V.of R.†
11 0-6-2T BM
28 0-6-0T CMDP
29 0-6-0T CMDP
30 0-6-2T RR
31 0-6-2T RR
32 0-6-2T RR
33 0-6-2T RR
34 0-6-2T RR
35 0-6-2T RR
36 0-6-2T RR
37 0-6-2T RR
38 0-6-2T RR
39 0-6-2T RR
40 0-6-2T RR
41 0-6-2T RR
42 0-6-2T RR
43 0-6-2T RR
44 0-6-2T RR
46 0-6-2T RR
47 0-6-2T RR
51 0-6-2T RR
52 0-6-2T RR
53 0-6-2T RR
55 0-6-2T RR
56 0-6-2T RR
57 0-6-2T RR
58 0-6-2T RR
59 0-6-2T RR
60 0-6-2T RR
61 0-6-2T RR
62 0-6-2T RR
63 0-6-2T RR
64 0-6-2T RR
65 0-6-2T RR
66 0-6-2T RR
67 0-6-2T RR
68 0-6-2T RR
69 0-6-2T RR
70 0-6-2T RR
71 0-6-2T RR
72 0-6-2T RR
73 0-6-2T RR
74 0-6-2T RR
75 0-6-2T RR
76 0-6-2T RR
77 0-6-2T RR
78 0-6-2T RR
79 0-6-2T RR
80 0-6-2T RR
81 0-6-2T RR
82 0-6-2T RR
82 0-6-2T RR
83 0-6-2T RR
90 0-6-0T RR (604)
91 0-6-0T RR (605)
92 0-6-0T RR (606)
93 0-6-0T RR (608)
94 0-6-0T RR (609)
100 A1¶ 4-6-0 4073 Class
111 4-6-0 4073 Class
155 0-6-2T Car. R.
184 0-6-2T PT
193 0-6-0T TV (792)
204 0-6-2T TV (311)
205 0-6-2T TV (313)
207 0-6-2T TV (315)
208 0-6-2T TV (317)
209 0-6-2T TV (318)
210 0-6-2T TV (319)
213 0-6-2T BR
215 0-6-2T TV (321)
216 0-6-2T TV (324)
231 0-6-2T BR
236 0-6-2T TV
240 0-6-2T BR
246 0-6-2T BR
258 0-6-2T BR
262 0-6-2T BR
263 0-6-2T BR
265 0-6-2T BR
267 0-6-2T BR
269 0-6-2T BR
270 0-6-2T BR
271 0-6-2T BR
272 0-6-2T BR
274 0-6-2T BR
276 0-6-2T BR
277 0-6-2T BR
278 0-6-2T TV
279 0-6-2T TV
280 0-6-2T TV
281 0-6-2T TV
282 0-6-2T TV
283 0-6-2T TV
284 0-6-2T TV
285 0-6-2T TV
286 0-6-2T TV
287 0-6-2T TV
288 0-6-2T TV
289 0-6-2T TV
290 0-6-2T TV
291 0-6-2T TV
292 0-6-2T TV
293 0-6-2T TV
294 0-6-2T TV

* 2′ 3″ gauge. † Built to V. of R. design by G.W.R., 1923. 1′ 11½″ gauge
‡ Purchased by British Railways from Ystalyfera Tin Works.

295 0-6-2T TV
296 0-6-2T TV
297 0-6-2T TV
299 0-6-2T TV
301 0-6-2T TV
303 0-6-2T TV (401)
304 0-6-2T TV (402)
305 0-6-2T TV (403)
310 0-6-2T TV
314 0-6-2T TV
320 0-6-2T TV
322 0-6-2T TV (441)
332 0-6-2T BM
333 0-6-2T TV
335 0-6-2T TV
337 0-6-2T TV
343 0-6-2T TV
344 0-6-2T TV
345 0-6-2T TV
346 0-6-2T TV
347 0-6-2T TV
348 0-6-2T TV
349 0-6-2T TV
351 0-6-2T TV
352 0-6-2T TV
356 0-6-2T TV
357 0-6-2T TV
359 Hilda 0-6-0T LMM
360 0-6-2T TV
361 0-6-2T TV
362 0-6-2T TV
364 0-6-2T TV
365 0-6-2T TV
366 0-6-2T TV
367 0-6-2T TV
368 0-6-2T TV
370 0-6-2T TV
371 0-6-2T TV
372 0-6-2T TV
373 0-6-2T TV
374 0-6-2T TV
375 0-6-2T TV
376 0-6-2T TV
377 0-6-2T TV
378 0-6-2T TV
379 0-6-2T TV
380 0-6-2T TV
381 0-6-2T TV
382 0-6-2T TV
383 0-6-2T TV
384 0-6-2T TV
385 0-6-2T TV
386 0-6-2T TV
387 0-6-2T TV
388 0-6-2T TV
389 0-6-2T TV
390 0-6-2T TV
391 0-6-2T TV
393 0-6-2T TV
394 0-6-2T TV
397 0-6-2T TV
398 0-6-2T TV
399 0-6-2T TV
404 0-6-2T TV
406 0-6-2T TV
408 0-6-2T TV
409 0-6-2T TV
414 0-6-2T TV
420 0-6-2T TV
422 0-6-2T BM (21)
425 0-6-2T BM (698)
426 0-6-2T BM (888)
428 0-6-2T BM (1113)
433 0-6-2T BM (1374)
438 0-6-2T TV
439 0-6-2T TV
440 0-6-2T TV
610 0-6-0T RR
611 0-6-0T RR
666 0-6-0T AD
667 0-6-0T AD
680 0-6-0T AD
681 0-6-0T Car. R.
682 0-6-0T Car. R.
683 0-6-0T Car. R.
684 0-6-0T Car. R.
696 0-4-0T PM
779 0-4-0T PM
784 0-6-0T BR
793 0-6-0T TV
794 0-6-0T TV
803 0-6-0T LMM
822 The Earl 0-6-0T* W. & L.
823 Countess 0-6-0T* W. & L.
844 0-6-0 Cam. R.
849 0-6-0 Cam. R.
855 0-6-0 Cam. R.
864 0-6-0 Cam. R.
873 0-6-0 Cam. R.
887 0-6-0 Cam. R.
892 0-6-0 Cam. R.
893 0-6-0 Cam. R.
894 0-6-0 Cam. R.
895 0-6-0 Cam. R.
896 0-6-0 Cam. R.
907 0-6-0T 1701 Class
935 0-4-0T PM
942 0-4-0T PM
943 0-4-0T SHT
968 0-4-0T SHT
974 0-4-0T SHT
992 0-6-0T 1901 Class

* Narrow gauge.

"County" Class

4-6-0 1000 Class

Introduced 1945.
Weights: Loco. 76 tons 17 cwt.
Tender 49 tons 0 cwt.
Pressure: 280 lb. Cyls.: 18½″ × 30″
Driving Wheels: 6′ 3″. T.E.: 32,580 lb.

1000 County of Middlesex
1001 County of Bucks
1002 County of Berks
1003 County of Wilts
1004 County of Somerset
1005 County of Devon

Built Swindon 1896.

1006-1373

1006 County of Cornwall
1007 County of Brecknock
1008 County of Cardigan
1009 County of Carmarthen
1010 County of Carnarvon
1011 County of Chester
1012 County of Denbigh
1013 County of Dorset
1014 County of Glamorgan
1015 County of Gloucester
1016 County of Hants
1017 County of Hereford
1018 County of Leicester
1019 County of Merioneth
1020 County of Monmouth
1021 County of Montgomery
1022 County of Northampton
1023 County of Oxford
1024 County of Pembroke
1025 County of Radnor
1026 County of Salop
1027 County of Stafford
1028 County of Warwick
1029 County of Worcester

Total 30

1084 0-6-2T BM
1085 0-6-0T SHT
1086 0-6-0T SHT
1098 0-4-0T SHT
1101 0-4-0T 1101 Class
1102 0-4-0T 1101 Class
1103 0-4-0T 1101 Class
1104 0-4-0T 1101 Class
1105 0-4-0T 1101 Class
1106 0-4-0T 1101 Class
1140 0-4-0T SHT (701)
1141 0-4-0T SHT (929)
1205 2-6-2T AD
1206 2-6-2T AD
1213 2-6-2T*V. of R.
1331 0-6-0T W. & C.
1334 2-4-0 MSWJ
1335 2-4-0 MSWJ
1336 2-4-0 MSWJ

* 1' 11½" gauge.

1338 0-4-0T Car. R.
1361 0-6-0T 1361 Class
1362 0-6-0T 1361 Class
1363 0-6-0T 1361 Class
1364 0-6-0T 1361 Class
1365 0-6-0T 1361 Class
1366 0-6-0T 1366 Class
1367 0-6-0T 1366 Class
1368 0-6-0T 1366 Class
1369 0-6-0T 1366 Class
1370 0-6-0T 1366 Class
1371 0-6-0T 1366 Class
1372 0-6-2T BM
1373 0-6-2T BM

Totals :

AD 0-6-0T	**3**
AD 2-6-2T	**2**
BR 0-6-0T	**1**
BR 0-6-2T	**16**
BM 0-6-2T	**11**
Cam. R. 0-6-0	**11**
Car. R. 0-4-0T	**1**
Car. R. 0-6-0T	**4**
Car. R. 0-6-2T	**1**
CMDP 0-6-0T	**2**
Cor. R. 0-4-2T	**2**
LMM 0-6-0T	**2**
MSWJ 2-4-0	**3**
PM 0-4-0T	**4**
PT 0-6-2T	**1**
RR 0-6-0T	**7**
RR 0-6-2T	**49**
SHT 0-4-0T	**6**
SHT 0-6-0T	**3**
TV 0-6-0T	**3**
TV 0-6-2T	**95**
V. of R. 2-6-2T	**3**
WCPR 0-6-0T	**1**
W & L 0-6-0T	**2**
W & C 0-6-0T	**1**
1101 Class	**6**
1361 Class	**5**
1366 Class	**6**
1701 Class	**1**
1901 Class	**1**

0-4-2T 1400 Class

Introduced 1932.
Weight : 41 tons 6 cwt.
Pressure : 165 lb. Cyls.: 16"×24"
Driving Wheels: 5' 2". T.E.: 13,900 lb.
FITTED FOR AUTO-TRAIN WORKING

1400	1419	1438	1457
1401	1420	1439	1458
1402	1421	1440	1459
1403	1422	1441	1460
1404	1423	1442	1461
1405	1424	1443	1462
1406	1425	1444	1463
1407	1426	1445	1464
1408	1427	1446	1465
1409	1428	1447	1466
1410	1429	1448	1467
1411	1430	1449	1468
1412	1431	1450	1469
1413	1432	1451	1470
1414	1433	1452	1471
1415	1434	1453	1472
1416	1435	1454	1473
1417	1436	1455	1474
1418	1437	1456	

(*Class continued with No. 5800*)

NOTE : Locomotives numbered between 1531-2186 except Nos. 1668/70, 2162/5-8/76, are pannier tanks converted from saddle tanks.

0-6-2T 1501 Class

(Built at Wolverhampton, 1879-80)

1531 | 1538 | 1542

(*Class continued with No. 1742*)

0-6-2T BM Rly.

1668 | 1670

Total 13

0-6-0T 1701 Class

(*Class continued from No. 907*)
(Built at Swindon, 1891-2)

1705	1715*	1720	1731
1709			

(*Class continued with No. 1752*)

0-6-0T 1501 Class

(*Class continued from No. 1542*)
(Built at Wolverhampton, 1892)

1742 | 1747 | 1749

(*Class continued with No. 1773*)

0-6-0T 1701 Class

(*Class continued from No. 1731*)
(Built at Swindon, 1892-3)

1752	1758	1760	1764
1754			

(*Class continued with No. 1799*)

0-6-0T 1501 Class

(*Class continued from No. 1749*)
(Built at Wolverhampton, 1893-4)

1773 | 1782 | 1789

Total 9

0-6-0T 1701 Class

(*Class continued from No. 1764*)
(Built at Swindon, 1895)

1799

(*Class continued with No. 1855*)

0-6-0T 1813 Class

(Built at Swindon, 1883, as a side-tank and later converted to saddle-tank)

1835

Total 1

* Standard G.W. locomotive, sold out of stock to the Neath & Brecon Rly., and later reinstated.

0-6-0T 1701 Class

(Class continued from No. 1799)

(Built at Swindon, 1890-5)

1855	1863	1884	1894
1858	1867	1888	1896
1861	1870	1889	1897
1862	1878	1891	

Total 27

0-6-0T 1901 Class

(Class continued from No. 992)

(Built at Wolverhampton, 1881-95)

1903	1945	1990	2009
1907	1949	1991	2010
1909	1957	1993	2011
1912	1964	1996	2012
1917	1965	2000	2013
1919	1967	2001	2014
1925	1968	2002	2016
1930	1969	2004	2017
1935	1973	2006	2018
1941	1979	2007	2019
1943	1989	2008	

Total 44

0-6-0T 2021 Class

(Built at Wolverhampton, 1897-1905)

2021	2040	2061	2081
2022	2042	2063	2082
2023	2043	2064	2083
2025	2044	2065	2085
2026	2045	2066	2086
2027	2047	2067	2088
2029	2048	2068	2089
2030	2050	2069	2090
2031	2051	2070	2091
2032	2052	2071	2092
2033	2053	2072	2093
2034	2054	2073	2094
2035	2055	2075	2095
2037	2056	2076	2096
2038	2059	2079	2097
2039	2060	2080	2098

2099	2113	2131	2148
2100	2114	2132	2150
2101	2115	2134	2151
2102	2117	2135	2152
2104	2121	2136	2153
2106	2122	2137	2154
2107	2123	2138	2155
2108	2124	2140	2156
2109	2126	2141	2159
2110	2127	2144	2160
2111	2129	2146	
2112	2130	2147	

Total 110

0-6-0T BPGV Rly.

2162	2166	2168	2176
2165	2167		

(Class continued with No. 2192)

0-6-0T 2181 Class

(Built at Wolverhampton, 1899-1905)

2181	2184	2187	2189
2182	2185	2188	2190
2183	2186		

Total 10

0-6-0T BPGV Rly.

(Class continued from No. 2176)

2192 Ashburnham
2193 Burry Port
2194 Kidwelly
2195 Cym Mawr
2196 Gwendraeth
2197 Pioneer
2198

Total 13

0-6-0 2251 Class

Introduced 1930.
Weights : Loco. 43 tons 8 cwt.
Tender 36 tons 15 cwt.
Pressure : 200 lb. Cyls.: $17\frac{1}{2}'' \times 24''$
Driving Wheels: 5′ 2″ T.E.: 20,155 lb.

2200	2206	2212	2218
2201	2207	2213	2219
2202	2208	2214	2220
2203	2209	2215	2221
2204	2210	2216	2222
2205	2211	2217	2223

2224	2243	2262	2281
2225	2244	2263	2282
2226	2245	2264	2283
2227	2246	2265	2284
2228	2247	2266	2285
2229	2248	2267	2286
2230	2249	2268	2287
2231	2250	2269	2288
2232	2251	2270	2289
2233	2252	2271	2290
2234	2253	2272	2291
2235	2254	2273	2292
2236	2255	2274	2293
2237	2256	2275	2294
2238	2257	2276	2295
2239	2258	2277	2296
2240	2259	2278	2297
2241	2260	2279	2298
2242	2261	2280	2299

(*Class continued with No. 3200*)

0-6-0 2301 Class*

Introduced 1883.
Weights : Loco. 36 tons 16 cwt.
Tender 34 tons 5 cwt.
Pressure : 180 lb. Cyls.: { 17″ × 24″ / 17½″ × 24″ }
Driving Wheels : 5′ 2″
T.E.: { 17,120 lb. / 18,140 lb. }

2322	2407	2464	2541
2323	2408	2468	2543
2327	2409	2474	2551
2339	2411	2482	2556
2340	2414	2483	2568
2343	2426	2484	2569
2349	2431	2513	2570
2350	2444	2515	2572
2351	2445	2516	2573
2354	2449	2523	2578
2382	2452	2532	2579
2385	2458	2534	
2386	2460	2537	
2401	2462	2538	

Total 53

* Built at Wolverhampton.

"Aberdare" Class
2-6-0 2600 Class

Introduced 1900.
Weights : Loco. 56 tons 15 cwt.
Tender 47 tons 14 cwt.
Pressure : 200 lb. Cyls.: 18″ × 26″
Driving Wheels: 4′ 7½″ T.E.: 25,800 lb.

2620	2651	2655	2667

Total 4

0-6-0T 2700 Class

Introduced 1896.
Weight : 45 tons 13 cwt.
Pressure : 180 lb. Cyls.: 17½″ × 24″
Driving Wheels: 4′ 7½″ T.E.: 20,260 lb

2702*	2717*	2754	2786
2704*	2719*	2756	2787
2706*	2721	2757	2789
2707*	2722	2760	2790
2708*	2724	2761	2791
2709*	2738	2767	2792
2712*	2743	2769	2794
2713*	2744	2771	2795
2715*	2745	2772	2798
2716*	2753	2780	2799

Total 40

2-8-0 2800 Class

Introduced 1903.
Weights : Loco. { 75 tons 10 cwt. / 76 tons 5 cwt.† }
Tender 40 tons 0 cwt.
Pressure : 225 lb. Cyls.: 18½″ × 30″
Driving Wheels: 4′ 7½″ T.E.: 35,380 lb.

(*For engines of 2800 class converted to oil-burning, see 48XX, p. 32*)

2800	2810	2820	2830
2801	2811	2821	2831
2802	2812	2822	2833
2803	2813	2823	2835
2804	2814	2824	2836
2805	2815	2825	2837
2806	2816	2826	2838
2807	2817	2827	2840
2808	2818	2828	2841
2809	2819	2829	2842

† Nos. 2884-99 and 38XX series.

2843	2861	2876	2889
2844	2864	2877	2890
2846	2865	2878	2891
2850	2866	2879	2892
2851	2867	2880	2893
2852	2868	2881	2894
2855	2869	2882	2895
2856	2870	2883	2896
2857	2871	2884	2897
2858	2873	2885	2898
2859	2874	2886	2899
2860	2875	2887	

(Class continued with No. 3800)

"Saint" Class

4-6-0 2900 Class

Introduced 1902.
Weights : Loco. 72 tons 0 cwt.
Tender 40 tons 0 cwt.
Pressure : 225 lb. Cyls.: $18\frac{1}{2}'' \times 30''$
Driving Wheels: 6' $8\frac{1}{2}''$ T.E.: 24,395 lb.

2902 Lady of the Lake
2903 Lady of Lyons
2906 Lady of Lynn
2908 Lady of Quality
2912 Saint Ambrose
2915 Saint Bartholomew
2920 Saint David
2924 Saint Helena
2926 Saint Nicholas
2927 Saint Patrick
2929 Saint Stephen
2930 Saint Vincent
2931 Arlington Court
2932 Ashton Court
2933 Bibury Court
2934 Butleigh Court
2935 Caynham Court
2936 Cefntilla Court
2937 Clevedon Court
2938 Corsham Court
2939 Croome Court
2940 Dorney Court
2941 Easton Court
2942 Fawley Court
2943 Hampton Court
2944 Highnam Court
2945 Hillingdon Court
2946 Langford Court
2947 Madresfield Court
2948 Stackpole Court
2949 Stanford Court
2950 Taplow Court
2951 Tawstock Court
2952 Twineham Court
2953 Titley Court
2954 Tockenham Court
2955 Tortworth Court
2979*Quentin Durward
2981*Ivanhoe
2987*Bride of Lammermoor
2989*Talisman

Total 41

* Converted from 4-4-2.

2-8-0 R.O.D. Class

Purchased from Govt. 1919.
Weights : Loco. 73 tons 11 cwt.
Tender 47 tons 14 cwt.
Pressure : 185 lb. Cyls.: $21'' \times 26''$
Driving Wheels: 4' 8" T.E.: 32,200 lb.

3008	3017	3028	3040
3010	3018	3029	3041
3011	3020	3031	3042
3012	3022	3032	3043
3013	3023	3033	3044
3014	3024	3034	3047
3015	3025	3036	3048
3016	3026	3038	3049

Total 32

2-6-2T 3100 Class

Introduced 1938. Rebuilt from 3150 Class (Nos. 3173/56/81/55/79 respectively).
Weight : 81 tons 9 cwt.
Pressure : 225 lb. Cyls.: $18\frac{1}{2}'' \times 30''$
Driving Wheels: 5' 3" T.E.: 31,170 lb.

3100	3102	3103	3104
3101			

Total 5

2-6-2T 3150 Class

Introduced 1907.
Weight : 81 tons 12 cwt.
Pressure : 200 lb. Cyls.: 18½"×30"
Driving Wheels: 5' 8" T.E.: 25,670 lb.

3150	3163	3174	3185
3151	3164	3175	3186
3153	3167	3176	3187
3154	3168	3177	3188
3157	3169	3178	3189
3159	3170	3180	3190
3160	3171	3182	
3161	3172	3183	

Total 30

0-6-0 2251 Class

(*Class continued from 2299*)

3200	3205	3210	3215
3201	3206	3211	3216
3202	3207	3212	3217
3203	3208	3213	3218
3204	3209	3214	3219

Total 120

"Bulldog" Class
4-4-0 3300 Class

Introduced 1898.
Weights : Loco. 51 tons 16 cwt.
Tender 40 tons 0 cwt.
Pressure : 200 lb. Cyls.: 18"×26"
Driving Wheels: 5' 8" T.E.: 21,060 lb.

3335
3341 Blasius
3363 Alfred Baldwin
3364 Frank Bibby
3376 River Plym
3377
3382
3383
3386
3393 Australia
3400 Winnipeg
3401 Vancouver
3406 Calcutta
3407 Madras
3418 Sir Arthur Yorke
3419
3426
3430 Inchcape
3431
3432
3438
3441 Blackbird
3443 Chaffinch
3444 Cormorant
3445 Flamingo
3446 Goldfinch
3447 Jackdaw
3448 Kingfisher
3449 Nightingale
3450 Peacock
3451 Pelican
3453 Seagull
3454 Skylark
3455 Starling

Total 34

0-4-2T 517 Class

3574 | 3575 | 3577

Total 3

2-4-0T 3500 Class

3561	3582	3588	3599
3562	3586	3592	

Total 7

0-6-0T 5700 Class

Introduced 1929.
Weight : 49 tons 0 cwt.
Pressure : 200 lb. Cyls.: 17½"×24"
Driving Wheels: 4' 7½" T.E.: 22,515 lb.

3600	3615	3630	3645
3601	3616	3631	3646
3602	3617	3632	3647
3603	3618	3633	3648
3604	3619	3634	3649
3605	3620	3635	3650
3606	3621	3636	3651
3607	3622	3637	3652
3608	3623	3638	3653
3609	3624	3639	3654
3610	3625	3640	3655
3611	3626	3641	3656
3612	3627	3642	3657
3613	3628	3643	3658
3614	3629	3644	3659

5700 Class—*continued*

3660	3695	3730	3765
3661	3696	3731	3766
3662	3697	3732	3767
3663	3698	3733	3768
3664	3699	3734	3769
3665	3700	3735	3770
3666	3701	3736	3771
3667	3702	3737	3772
3668	3703	3738	3773
3669	3704	3739	3774
3670	3705	3740	3775
3671	3706	3741	3776
3672	3707	3742	3777
3673	3708	3743	3778
3674	3709	3744	3779
3675	3710	3745	3780
3676	3711	3746	3781
3677	3712	3747	3782
3678	3713	3748	3783
3679	3714	3749	3784
3680	3715	3750	3785
3681	3716	3751	3786
3682	3717	3752	3787
3683	3718	3753	3788
3684	3719	3754	3789
3685	3720	3755	3790
3686	3721	3756	3791
3687	3722	3757	3792
3688	3723	3758	3793
3689	3724	3759	3794
3690	3725	3760	3795
3691	3726	3761	3796
3692	3727	3762	3797
3693	3728	3763	3798
3694	3729	3764	3799

(*Class continued with No. 4600*)

2-8-0 2800 Class

(*Class continued from 2899*)

3800	3807	3815	3824
3801	3808	3816	3825
3802	3809	3817	3826
3803	3810	3819	3827
3804	3811	3821	3828
3805	3812	3822	3829
3806	3814	3823	3830

3832	3842	3850	3858
3833	3843	3851	3859
3834	3844	3852	3860
3835	3845	3853	3861
3836	3846	3854	3862
3838	3847	3855	3863
3840	3848	3856	3864
3841	3849	3857	3866

(*Class continued with No. 4800*)

"Hall" Class
4-6-0 4900 Class

FITTED FOR OIL BURNING¶

The numbers in italics have been listed to enable the reader to enter against them the old numbers and names of engines as they are converted to oil-buring and renumbered in the 39XX series.

3900 (4968) Shotton Hall
3901 (4971) Stanway Hall
3902 (4948) Northwick Hall
3903 (4907) Broughton Hall
3904 (4972) Saint Brides Hall
3905
3906
3907
3908
3909
3910
3911
3912
3913
3914
3915
3916
3917
3918
3919
3920
3921
3922
3923
3924
3925
3926

4900 Class—*continued*

3927
3928
3929
3930
3931
3932
3933
3934
3935
3936
3937
3938
3939
3940
3941
3942
3943
3944
3945
3946
3947
3948
3949
3950 (5955) Garth Hall
3951 (5976) Ashwicke Hall
3952 (6957) Norcliffe Hall
3953 (6953) Leighton Hall
3954 (5986) Arbury Hall
3955 (6949) Haberfield Hall
3956
3957
3958
3959
3960
3961
3962
3963
3964
3965
3966
3967
3968
3969
3970
3971
3972
3973
3974
3975
3976
3977
3978
3979
3980
3981
3982
3983
3984
3985
3986
3987
3988
3989
3990
3991
3992
3993
3994
3995
3996
3997
3998
3999

(*Class continued with No.* 4900)

"Star" Class
4-6-0 (4 Cyl.) 4000 Class

Introduced 1907 (based on 4-4-2 prototype built 1906)
Weights: Loco. 75 tons 12 cwt.
Tender 46 tons 14 cwt.
Pressure: 225 lb. Cyls.: 15″ × 26″
Driving Wheels: 6′ 8½″ T.E.: 27,800 lb.

4003 Lode Star
4007 Swallowfield Park
4012 Knight of the Thistle
4013 Knight of St. Patrick
4015 Knight of St. John
4017 Knight of Liége
4018 Knight of the Grand Cross
4019 Knight Templar
4020 Knight Commander
4021 British Monarch

4022	4025	4028
4023	4026	4030

4000 Class—*continued*

4031 Queen Mary
4033 Queen Victoria
4034 Queen Adelaide
4035 Queen Charlotte
4036 Queen Elizabeth
4038 Queen Berengaria
4039 Queen Matilda
4040 Queen Boadicea
4041 Prince of Wales
4042 Prince Albert
4043 Prince Henry
4044 Prince George
4045 Prince John
4046 Princess Mary
4047 Princess Louise
4048 Princess Victoria
4049 Princess Maud
4050 Princess Alice
4051 Princess Helena
4052 Princess Beatrice
4053 Princess Alexandra
4054 Princess Charlotte
4055 Princess Sophia
4056 Princess Margaret
4057 Princess Elizabeth
4058 Princess Augusta
4059 Princess Patricia
4060 Princess Eugénie
4061 Glastonbury Abbey
4062 Malmesbury Abbey

Total 46

"Castle" Class

4-6-0 (4 Cyl.) 4073 Class

Introduced 1923.
Weights : Loco. 79 tons 17 cwt.
Tender 46 tons 14 cwt.
Pressure : 225 lb. Cyls.: 16″×26″
Driving Wheels: 6′ 8½″ T.E.: 31,625 lb.

100 A1 ¶Lloyds
111 Viscount Churchill
4000 North Star
4016 The Somerset Light Infantry (Prince Albert's)
4032 Queen Alexandra
4037 The South Wales Borderers
4073 Caerphilly Castle
4074 Caldicot Castle
4075 Cardiff Castle
4076 Carmarthen Castle
4077 Chepstow Castle
4078 Pembroke Castle
4079 Pendennis Castle
4080 Powderham Castle
4081 Warwick Castle
4082 Windsor Castle
4083 Abbotsbury Castle
4084 Aberystwyth Castle
4085 Berkeley Castle
4086 Builth Castle
4087 Cardigan Castle
4088 Dartmouth Castle
4089 Donnington Castle
4090 Dorchester Castle
4091 Dudley Castle
4092 Dunraven Castle
4093 Dunster Castle
4094 Dynevor Castle
4095 Harlech Castle
4096 Highclere Castle
4097 Kenilworth Castle
4098 Kidwelly Castle
4099 Kilgerran Castle

(*Class continued with No. 5000*)

2-6-2T 5100 Class

4100	4115	4130	4145
4101	4116	4131	4146
4102	4117	4132	4147
4103	4118	4133	4148
4104	4119	4134	4149
4105	4120	4135	4150
4106	4121	4136	4151
4107	4122	4137	4152
4108	4123	4138	4153
4109	4124	4139	4154
4110	4125	4140	4155
4111	4126	4141	4156
4112	4127	4142	4157
4113	4128	4143	4158
4114	4129	4144	4159

Nos. 4160-79 to be constructed.

(*Class continued with No. 5100*)

Above: Class "4300" 2-6-0 No. 5327

[*B. V. Franey*

Right: "Bulldog" Class 4-4-0 No. 3443 *Chaffinch*

[*B. V. Franey*

Below: "Grange" Class 4-6-0 No. 6877 *Llanfair Grange*

[*M. W. Earley*

" Hall " Class 4-6-0 No. 4942 *Maindy Hall* [*H. C. Casserley*

Modified Hall " Class 4-6-0 No. 6977 *Grundisburgh Hall* [*B. V. Franey*

" Manor " Class 4-6-0 No. 7805 *Broome Manor* [*H. C. Casserley*

" County " Class 4-6-0 No. 1028 *County of Warwick* [M. W. Earley

" Saint " Class 4-6-0 No. 2920 *Saint David* [C. R. L. Coles

Above : "Star" Class 4-6-0 No. 4052 *Princess Beatrice* passes Cholsey with an up Birmingham express

Below : The "Castle" Class was virtually an enlarged "Star." No. 5017 *St. Donats Castle* heads an up Worcester express near Maidenhead

THE CHURCHWARD-COLLETT TRIO

[*Photographs by M. W. Earley*]

Above : From the " Castles " were developed the " Kings," most powerful 4-6-0's in Britain. Speeding through Sonning cutting with the up 8.30 a.m. Plymouth express is No. 6019 *King Henry V*

Above: "4700" Class 2-8-0 No. 4700
[*R. Delves*

Left: "2800" Class 2-8-0 No. 2866
[*R. Tourret*

Below: "2800" Class 2-8-0 No. 4857 (oil-burning)
[*B. V. Franey*

Above : "7200" Class 2-8-2T No. 7240
[*H. C. Casserley*

Right : "4200" Class 2-8-0T No. 4254
[*G. O. P. Pearce*

Below : "6100" Class 2-6-2T No. 6112
[*B. V. Franey*

" 4400 " Class 2-6-2T No. 4406 [H. C. Casserley

" 4500 " Class 2-6-2T No. 5542 [B. V. Franey

2-8-0T 4200 Class

Introduced 1910.
Weight : 82 tons 2 cwt.
Pressure : 200 lb. Cyls.: 19″×30″
Driving Wheels: 4′ 7½″ T.E.: 33,170 lb.

4200	4230	4258	4280
4201	4231	4259	4281
4203	4232	4260	4282
4206	4233	4261	4283
4207	4235	4262	4284
4208	4236	4263	4285
4211	4237	4264	4286
4212	4238	4265	4287
4213	4241	4266	4288
4214	4242	4267	4289
4215	4243	4268	4290
4217	4246	4269	4291
4218	4247	4270	4292
4221	4248	4271	4293
4222	4250	4272	4294
4223	4251	4273	4295
4224	4252	4274	4296
4225	4253	4275	4297
4226	4254	4276	4298
4227	4255	4277	4299
4228	4256	4278	
4229	4257	4279	

(*Class continued with No. 5200*)

2-6-0 4300 Class

Introduced 1911.
Weights : Loco. { 65 tons 6 cwt.* / 62 tons 0 cwt.
Tender 40 tons 0 cwt.
Pressure : 200 lb. Cyls.: 18½″×30″
Driving Wheels: 5′ 8″ T.E.: 25,670 lb.

4303	4326	4358	4377
4318	4337	4375	4381
4320	4353		

(*Class continued with No. 5300*)
* " 93XX " series.

2-6-2T 4400 Class

Introduced 1904.
Weight : 56 tons 13 cwt.
Pressure : 180 lb. Cyls.: 17″×24″
Driving Wheels: 4′ 1½″ T.E.: 21,440 lb.

4400	4403	4406	4409
4401	4404	4407	4410
4402	4405	4408	

Total 11

2-6-2T 4500 Class

Introduced 1906.
Weight : { 57 tons.† / 61 tons 0 cwt.
Pressure : 200 lb. Cyls.: 17″×24″
Driving Wheels: 4′ 7½″ T.E.: 21,250 lb.

4500	4525	4550	4575
4501	4526	4551	4576
4502	4527	4552	4577
4503	4528	4553	4578
4504	4529	4554	4579
4505	4530	4555	4580
4506	4531	4556	4581
4507	4532	4557	4582
4508	4533	4558	4583
4509	4534	4559	4584
4510	4535	4560	4585
4511	4536	4561	4586
4512	4537	4562	4587
4513	4538	4563	4588
4514	4539	4564	4589
4515	4540	4565	4590
4516	4541	4566	4591
4517	4542	4567	4592
4518	4543	4568	4593
4519	4544	4569	4594
4520	4545	4570	4595
4521	4546	4571	4596
4522	4547	4572	4597
4523	4548	4573	4598
4524	4549	4574	4599

(*Class continued with No. 5500*)
† Nos. 4500-4574.

0-6-0T 5700 Class

(*Class continued from 3799*)

4600	4612	4624	4636
4601	4613	4625	4637
4602	4614	4626	4638
4603	4615	4627	4639
4604	4616	4628	4640
4605	4617	4629	4641
4606	4618	4630	4642
4607	4619	4631	4643
4608	4620	4632	4644
4609	4621	4633	4645
4610	4622	4634	4646
4611	4623	4635	4647

5700 Class– *continued*

4648	4661	4674	4687
4649	4662	4675	4688
4650	4663	4676	4689
4651	4664	4677	4690
4652	4665	4678	4691
4653	4666	4679	4692
4654	4667	4680	4693
4655	4668	4681	4694
4656	4669	4682	4695
4657	4670	4683	4696
4658	4671	4684	4697
4659	4672	4685	4698
4660	4673	4686	4699

(*Class continued with No. 5700*)

2-8-0 4700 Class

Introduced 1919.
Weights : Loco. 82 tons 0 cwt.
Tender 16 tons 14 cwt.
Pressure : 225 lb. Cyls.: 19" × 30"
Driving Wheels: 5' 8" T.E.: 30,460 lb.

4700	4703	4705	4707
4701	4704	4706	4708
4702			

Total 9

2-8-0 2800 Class

¶ FITTED FOR OIL-BURNING

(*Renumbered from* 28XX *and* 38XX *series, which see pp.* 17 *and* 20)

The numbers in italics have been set out so that the reader may enter against them the appropriate old number of each engine newly converted to oil burning and renumbered in the 48XX series.

4800 (2872)
4801 (2854)
4802 (2862)
4803 (2849)
4804 (2839)
4805 (2863)
4806 (2832)
4807 (2848)
4808 (2834)
4809 (2845)
4810 (2853)
4811 (2847)
4812
4813
4814
4815
4816
4817
4818
4819
4820
4821
4822
4823
4824
4825
4826
4827
4828
4829
4830
4831
4832
4833
4834
4835
4836
4837
4838
4839
4840
4841
4842
4843
4844
4845
4846
4847
4848
4849
4850 (2888)
4851 (3865)
4852 (3818)
4853 (3839)
4854 (3837)
4855 (3813)
4856 (3820)
4857 (3831)
4858
4859
4860
4861
4862
4863
4864
4865
4866
4867
4868
4869
4870
4871
4872
4873
4874
4875
4876
4877
4878
4879
4880
4881
4882
4883
4884
4885
4886
4887
4888
4889
4890
4891
4892
4893
4894
4895
4896
4897
4898
4899

Total 167

Throughout this book the dimensions shown at the head of each class are only typical examples and should not be taken as applying to every engine.

"Hall" Class

4-6-0 4900 Class

Introduced 1928.
Weights: Loco. 75 tons 0 cwt.
Tender 46 tons 14 cwt.
Pressure: 225 lb. Cyls.: 18½" × 30"
Driving Wheels: 6' 0" T.E.: 27,275 lb.
(For engines of "Hall" class converted to oil-burning, see 39XX, p. 20)
(Class continued from 3955)

4900 Saint Martin
4901 Adderley Hall
4902 Aldenham Hall
4903 Astley Hall
4904 Binnegar Hall
4905 Barton Hall
4906 Bradfield Hall
4908 Broome Hall
4909 Blakesley Hall
4910 Blaisdon Hall
4912 Berrington Hall
4913 Baglan Hall
4914 Cranmore Hall
4915 Condover Hall
4916 Crumlin Hall
4917 Crosswood Hall
4918 Dartington Hall
4919 Donnington Hall
4920 Dumbleton Hall
4921 Eaton Hall
4922 Enville Hall
4923 Evenley Hall
4924 Eydon Hall
4925 Eynsham Hall
4926 Fairleigh Hall
4927 Farnborough Hall
4928 Gatacre Hall
4929 Goytrey Hall
4930 Hagley Hall
4931 Hanbury Hall
4932 Hatherton Hall
4933 Himley Hall
4934 Hindlip Hall
4935 Ketley Hall
4936 Kinlet Hall
4937 Lanelay Hall
4938 Liddington Hall
4939 Littleton Hall
4940 Ludford Hall
4941 Llangedwyn Hall
4942 Maindy Hall
4943 Marrington Hall
4944 Middleton Hall
4945 Milligan Hall
4946 Moseley Hall
4947 Nanhoran Hall
4949 Packwood Hall
4950 Patshull Hall
4951 Pendeford Hall
4952 Peplow Hall
4953 Pitchford Hall
4954 Plaish Hall
4955 Plaspower Hall
4956 Plowden Hall
4957 Postlip Hall
4958 Priory Hall
4959 Purley Hall
4960 Pyle Hall
4961 Pyrland Hall
4962 Ragley Hall
4963 Rignall Hall
4964 Rodwell Hall
4965 Rood Ashton Hall
4966 Shakenhurst Hall
4967 Shirenewton Hall
4969 Shrugborough Hall
4970 Sketty Hall
4973 Sweeney Hall
4974 Talgarth Hall
4975 Umberslade Hall
4976 Warfield Hall
4977 Watcombe Hall
4978 Westwood Hall
4979 Wootton Hall
4980 Wrottesley Hall
4981 Abberley Hall
4982 Acton Hall
4983 Albert Hall
4984 Albrighton Hall
4985 Allesley Hall
4986 Aston Hall
4987 Brockley Hall
4988 Bulwell Hall
4989 Cherwell Hall
4990 Clifton Hall
4991 Cobham Hall
4992 Crosby Hall

4900 Class—*continued*

4993 Dalton Hall
4994 Downton Hall
4995 Easton Hall
4996 Eden Hall
4997 Elton Hall
4998 Eyton Hall
4999 Gopsal Hall

(*Class continued with No. 5900*)

THROUGHOUT THIS BOOK
¶ Denotes oil - burning locomotive.

"Castle" Class
4-6-0 (4 Cyl.) 4073 Class

(*Continued from 4099*)

5000 Launceston Castle
5001 Llandovery Castle
5002 Ludlow Castle
5003 Lulworth Castle
5004 Llanstephan Castle
5005 Manorbier Castle
5006 Tregenna Castle
5007 Rougemont Castle
5008 Raglan Castle
5009 Shrewsbury Castle
5010 Restormel Castle
5011 Tintagel Castle
5012 Berry Pomeroy Castle
5013 Abergavenny Castle
5014 Goodrich Castle
5015 Kingswear Castle
5016 Montgomery Castle
5017 St. Donats Castle
5018 St. Mawes Castle
5019 Treago Castle
5020 Trematon Castle
5021 Whittington Castle
5022 Wigmore Castle
5023 Brecon Castle
5024 Carew Castle
5025 Chirk Castle
5026 Criccieth Castle
5027 Farleigh Castle
5028 Llantilio Castle
5029 Nunney Castle
5030 Shirburn Castle
5031 Totnes Castle
5032 Usk Castle
5033 Broughton Castle
5034 Corfe Castle
5035 Coity Castle
5036 Lyonshall Castle
5037 Monmouth Castle
5038 Morlais Castle
5039¶Rhuddlan Castle
5040 Stokesay Castle
5041 Tiverton Castle
5042 Winchester Castle
5043 Earl of Mount Edgcumbe
5044 Earl of Dunraven
5045 Earl of Dudley
5046 Earl Cawdor
5047 Earl of Dartmouth
5048 Earl of Devon
5049 Earl of Plymouth
5050 Earl of St. Germans
5051 Earl Bathurst
5052 Earl of Radnor
5053 Earl Cairns
5054 Earl of Ducie
5055 Earl of Eldon
5056 Earl of Powis
5057 Earl Waldegrave
5058 Earl of Clancarty
5059 Earl St. Aldwyn
5060 Earl of Berkeley
5061 Earl of Birkenhead
5062 Earl of Shaftesbury
5063 Earl Baldwin
5064 Bishop's Castle
5065 Newport Castle
5066 Wardour Castle
5067 St. Fagans Castle
5068 Beverston Castle
5069 Isambard Kingdom Brunel
5070 Sir Daniel Gooch
5071 Spitfire
5072 Hurricane
5073 Blenheim
5074 Hampden
5075 Wellington
5076 Gladiator
5077 Fairey Battle

4073 Class—*continued*

5078 Beaufort
5079¶Lysander
5080 Defiant
5081 Lockheed-Hudson
5082 Swordfish
5083¶Bath Abbey
5084 Reading Abbey
5085 Evesham Abbey
5086 Viscount Horne
5087 Tintern Abbey
5088 Llanthony Abbey
5089 Westminster Abbey
5090 Neath Abbey
5091¶Cleeve Abbey
5092 Tresco Abbey
5093 Upton Castle
5094 Tretower Castle
5095 Barbury Castle
5096 Bridgwater Castle
5097 Sarum Castle
5098 Clifford Castle
5099 Compton Castle

(*Class continued with No. 7000*)

2-6-2T 5100 Class

Introduced 1929*
Weight : 78 tons 9 cwt.
Pressure : 200 lb. Cyls.: 18″×30″
Driving Wheels: 5′ 8″ T.E.: 24,300 lb.

(*Continued from 4159*)

5101	5114	5138	5155
5102	5117	5139	5156
5103	5121	5140	5157
5104	5122	5141	5158
5105	5125	5142	5159
5106	5128	5143	5160
5107	5129	5144	5161
5108	5131	5147	5162
5109	5132	5150	5163
5110	5134	5151	5164
5111	5135	5152	5165
5112	5136	5153	5166
5113	5137	5154	5167
5168	5176	5184	5192
5169	5177	5185	5193
5170	5178	5186	5194
5171	5179	5187	5195
5172	5180	5188	5196
5173	5181	5189	5197
5174	5182	5190	5198
5175	5183	5191	5199

Total 148

2-8-0T 4200 Class

(*Continued from 4299*)

5200	5217	5234	5251
5201	5218	5235	5252
5202	5219	5236	5253
5203	5220	5237	5254
5204	5221	5238	5255
5205	5222	5239	5256
5206	5223	5240	5257
5207	5224	5241	5258
5208	5225	5242	5259
5209	5226	5243	5260
5210	5227	5244	5261
5211	5228	5245	5262
5212	5229	5246	5263
5213	5230	5247	5264
5214	5231	5248	
5215	5232	5249	
5216	5233	5250	

Total 151

2-6-0 4300 Class

(*Continued from 4381*)

5300	5311	5318	5325
5303	5312	5319	5326
5305	5313	5320	5327
5306	3514	5321	5328
5307	5315	5322	5330
5309	5316	5323	5331
5310	5317	5324	5332

* No. 5100 (originally No. 99, late No. 3100) built 1903, Nos. 5111-48 rebuilt from locos. Nos. 3111-48 built 1905-6.

† Including 10 to be constructed.

4300 Class—*continued*

5333	5351	5370	5388
5334	5353	5371	5390
5335	5355	5372	5391
5336	5356	5373	5392
5337	5357	5375	5393
5338	5358	5376	5394
5339	5359	5377	5395
5340	5360	5378	5396
5341	5361	5379	5397
5344	5362	5380	5398
5345	5364	5381	5399
5346	5365	5382	
5347	5367	5384	
5348	5368	5385	
5350	5369	5386	

(*Class continued with No. 6300*)

0-6-0T 5400 Class

Introduced 1931.
Weight : 46 tons 12 cwt.
Pressure : 165 lb. Cyls.: 16½″ × 24″
Driving Wheels: 5′ 2″ T.E.: 14,780 lb.

FITTED FOR AUTO TRAIN WORKING

5400	5407	5413	5419
5401	5408	5414	5420
5402	5409	5415	5421
5403	5410	5416	5422
5404	5411	5417	5423
5405	5412	5418	5424
5406			

Total 25

2-6-2T 4500 Class

(*Continued from* 4599)

5500	5512	5524	5536
5501	5513	5525	5537
5502	5514	5526	5538
5503	5515	5527	5539
5504	5516	5528	5540
5505	5517	5529	5541
5506	5518	5530	5542
5507	5519	5531	5543
5508	5520	5532	5544
5509	5521	5533	5545
5510	5522	5534	5546
5511	5523	5535	5547

5548	5555	5562	5569
5549	5556	5563	5570
5550	5557	5564	5571
5551	5558	5565	5572
5552	5559	5566	5573
5553	5560	5567	5574
5554	5561	5568	

Total 175

0-6-2T 5600 Class

Introduced 1924.
Weight : 68 tons 12 cwt.
Pressure : 200 lb. Cyls.: 18″ × 26″
Driving Wheels: 4′ 7½″ T.E.: 25,800 lb.

5600	5625	5650	5675
5601	5626	5651	5676
5602	5627	5652	5677
5603	5628	5653	5678
5604	5629	5654	5679
5605	5630	5655	5680
5606	5631	5656	5681
5607	5632	5657	5682
5608	5633	5658	5683
5609	5634	5659	5684
5610	5635	5660	5685
5611	5636	5661	5686
5612	5637	5662	5687
5613	5638	5663	5688
5614	5639	5664	5689
5615	5640	5665	5690
5616	5641	5666	5691
5617	5642	5667	5692
5618	5643	5668	5693
5619	5644	5669	5694
5620	5645	5670	5695
5621	5646	5671	5696
5622	5647	5672	5697
5623	5648	5673	5698
5624	5649	5674	5699

(*Class continued with No. 6600*)

0-6-0T 5700 Class

Introduced 1929.
Weight: 49 tons 0 cwt.
Pressure: 200 lb. Cyls.: $17\frac{1}{2}'' \times 24''$
Driving Wheels: $4' 7\frac{1}{2}''$ T.E.: 22,515 lb.

(*Continued from* 4699)

5700	5725	5750	5775
5701	5726	5751	5776
5702	5727	5752	5777
5703	5728	5753	5778
5704	5729	5754	5779
5705	5730	5755	5780
5706	5731	5756	5781
5707	5732	5757	5782
5708	5733	5758	5783
5709	5734	5759	5784
5710	5735	5760	5785
5711	5736	5761	5786
5712	5737	5762	5787
5713	5738	5763	5788
5714	5739	5764	5789
5715	5740	5765	5790
5716	5741	5766	5791
5717	5742	5767	5792
5718	5743	5768	5793
5719	5744	5769	5794
5720	5745	5770	5795
5721	5746	5771	5796
5722	5747	5772	5797
5723	5748	5773	5798
5724	5749	5774	5799

(*Class continued with No.* 6700)

0-4-2T 1400 Class

NOT FITTED FOR AUTO TRAIN WORKING

(*Continued from* 1474)

5800	5805	5810	5815
5801	5806	5811	5816
5802	5807	5812	5817
5803	5808	5813	5818
5804	5809	5814	5819

Total 95

"Hall" Class
4-6-0 4900 Class

(*For engines converted to oil-burning, see* 39XX, *p.* 20)

(*Continued from* 4999)

5900 Hinderton Hall
5901 Hazel Hall
5902 Howick Hall
5903 Keele Hall
5904 Kelham Hall
5905 Knowsley Hall
5906 Lawton Hall
5907 Marble Hall
5908 Moreton Hall
5909 Newton Hall
5910 Park Hall
5911 Preston Hall
5912 Queen's Hall
5913 Rushton Hall
5914 Ripon Hall
5915 Trentham Hall
5916 Trinity Hall
5917 Westminster Hall
5918 Walton Hall
5919 Worsley Hall
5920 Wycliffe Hall
5921 Bingley Hall
5922 Caxton Hall
5923 Colston Hall
5924 Dinton Hall
5925 Eastcote Hall
5926 Grotrian Hall
5927 Guild Hall
5928 Haddon Hall
5929 Hanham Hall
5930 Hannington Hall
5931 Hatherley Hall
5932 Haydon Hall
5933 Kingsway Hall
5934 Kneller Hall
5935 Norton Hall
5936 Oakley Hall
5937 Stanford Hall
5938 Stanley Hall
5939 Tangley Hall
5940 Whitbourne Hall
5941 Campion Hall

4900 Class—*continued*

5942 Doldowlod Hall
5943 Elmdon Hall
5944 Ickenham Hall
5945 Leckhampton Hall
5946 Marwell Hall
5947 Saint Benet's Hall
5948 Siddington Hall
5949 Trematon Hall
5950 Yardley Hall
5951 Clyffe Hall
5952 Cogan Hall
5953 Dunley Hall
5954 Faendre Hall
5956 Horsley Hall
5957 Hutton Hall
5958 Knolton Hall
5959 Mawley Hall
5960 Saint Edmund Hall
5961 Toynbee Hall
5962 Wantage Hall
5963 Wimpole Hall
5964 Wolseley Hall
5965 Woollas Hall
5966 Ashford Hall
5967 Bickmarsh Hall
5968 Cory Hall
5969 Honington Hall
5970 Hengrave Hall
5971 Merevale Hall
5972 Olton Hall
5973 Rolleston Hall
5974 Wallsworth Hall
5975 Winslow Hall
5977 Beckford Hall
5978 Bodinnick Hall
5979 Cruckton Hall
5980 Dingley Hall
5981 Frensham Hall
5982 Harrington Hall
5983 Henley Hall
5984 Linden Hall
5985 Mostyn Hall
5987 Brocket Hall
5988 Bostock Hall
5989 Cransley Hall
5990 Durford Hall
5991 Grosham Hall
5992 Horton Hall
5993 Kirby Hall
5994 Roydon Hall
5995 Wick Hall
5996 Mytton Hall
5997 Sparkford Hall
5998 Trevor Hall
5999 Wollaton Hall

(*Class continued with No. 6900*)

"King" Class

4-6-0 (4 Cyl.) 6000 Class

Introduced 1927.
Weights: Loco. 89 tons 0 cwt.
Tender 46 tons 14 cwt.
Pressure: 250 lb. Cyls.: $16\frac{1}{4}'' \times 28''$
Driving Wheels: 6′ 6″ T.E.: 40,300 lb.

6000 King George V
6001 King Edward VII
6002 King William IV
6003 King George IV
6004 King George III
6005 King George II
6006 King George I
6007 King William III
6008 King James II
6009 King Charles II
6010 King Charles I
6011 King James I
6012 King Edward VI
6013 King Henry VIII
6014 King Henry VII
6015 King Richard III
6016 King Edward V
6017 King Edward IV
6018 King Henry VI
6019 King Henry V
6020 King Henry IV
6021 King Richard II
6022 King Edward III
6023 King Edward II
6024 King Edward I
6025 King Henry III
6026 King John
6027 King Richard I
6028 King George VI
6029 King Edward VIII

Total 30

2-6-2T 6100 Class

Introduced 1931.
Weight : 78 tons 9 cwt.
Pressure : 225 lb. Cyls.: 18″×30″
Driving Wheels: 5′ 8″ T.E.: 27,340 lb.

6100	6118	6136	6153
6101	6119	6137	6154
6102	6120	6138	6155
6103	6121	6139	6156
6104	6122	6140	6157
6105	6123	6141	6158
6106	6124	6142	6159
6107	6125	6143	6160
6108	6126	6144	6161
6109	6127	6145	6162
6110	6128	6146	6163
6111	6129	6147	6164
6112	6130	6148	6165
6113	6131	6149	6166
6114	6132	6150	6167
6115	6133	6151	6168
6116	6134	6152	6169
6117	6135		

Total 70

2-6-0 4300 Class

(*Continued from 5399*)

6300	6320¶	6339	6358
6301	6321	6340	6359
6302	6322	6341	6360
6303	6323	6342	6361
6304	6324	6343	6362
6305	6325	6344	6363
6306	6326	6345	6364
6307	6327	6346	6365
6308	6328	6347	6366
6309	6329	6348	6367
6310	6330	6349	6368
6311	6331	6350	6369
6312	6332	6351	6370
6313	6333	6352	6371
6314	6334	6353	6372
6316	6335	6354	6373
6317	6336	6355	6374
6318	6337	6356	6375
6319	6338	6357	6376

6377	6383	6389	6395
6378	6384	6390	6396
6379	6385	6391	6397
6380	6386	6392	6398
6381	6387	6393	6399
6382	6388	6394	

(*Class continued with No. 7300*)

0-6-0T 6400 Class

Introduced 1931.
Weight : 45 tons 12 cwt.
Pressure : 165 lb. Cyls.: 16½″×24″
Driving Wheels: 4′ 7½″ T.E.: 16,510 lb.

FITTED FOR AUTO TRAIN WORKING

6400	6410	6420	6430
6401	6411	6421	6431
6402	6412	6422	6432
6403	6413	6423	6433
6404	6414	6424	6434
6405	6415	6425	6435
6406	6416	6426	6436
6407	6417	6427	6437
6408	6418	6428	6438
6409	6419	6429	6439

Total 40

0-6-2T 5600 Class

(*Continued from 5699*)

6600	6612	6624	6636
6601	6613	6625	6637
6602	6614	6626	6638
6603	6615	6627	6639
6604	6616	6628	6640
6605	6617	6629	6641
6606	6618	6630	6642
6607	6619	6631	6643
6608	6620	6632	6644
6609	6621	6633	6645
6610	6622	6634	6646
6611	6623	6635	6647

6648	6661	6674	6687
6649	6662	6675	6688
6650	6663	6676	6689
6651	6664	6677	6690
6652	6665	6678	6691
6653	6666	6679	6692
6654	6667	6680	6693
6655	6668	6681	6694
6656	6669	6682	6695
6657	6670	6683	6696
6658	6671	6684	6697
6659	6672	6685	6698
6660	6673	6686	6699

Total 200

0-6-0T 5700 Class

(*Continued from* 5799)

6700	6715	6730	6745
6701	6716	6731	6746
6702	6717	6732	6747
6703	6718	6733	6748
6704	6719	6734	6749
6705	6720	6735	6750
6706	6721	6736	6751
6707	6722	6737	6752
6708	6723	6738	6753
6709	6724	6739	6754
6710	6725	6740	6755
6711	6726	6741	6756
6712	6727	6742	6757
6713	6728	6743	6758
6714	6729	6744	6759

(*Class continued with No.* 7700)

(Additional locomo·ives Nos. 6760-9 to be constructed)

"Grange" Class
4-6-0 6800 Class

Introduced 1936.
Weights: Loco. 74 tons 0 cwt.
Tender 40 tons 0 cwt.
Pressure: 225 lb. Cyls.: $18\frac{1}{2}'' \times 30''$
Driving Wheels: 5' 8" T.E. 28,875 lb.

6800 Arlington Grange
6801 Aylburton Grange
6802 Bampton Grange
6803 Bucklebury Grange
6804 Brockington Grange
6805 Broughton Grange
6806 Blackwell Grange
6807 Birchwood Grange
6808 Beenham Grange
6809 Burghclere Grange
6810 Blakemere Grange
6811 Cranbourne Grange
6812 Chesford Grange
6813 Eastbury Grange
6814 Enbourne Grange
6815 Frilford Grange
6816 Frankton Grange
6817 Gwenddwr Grange
6818 Hardwick Grange
6819 Highnam Grange
6820 Kingstone Grange
6821 Leaton Grange
6822 Manton Grange
6823 Oakley Grange
6824 Ashley Grange
6825 Llanvair Grange
6826 Nannerth Grange
6827 Llanfrechfa Grange
6828 Trellech Grange
6829 Burmington Grange
6830 Buckenhill Grange
6831 Bearley Grange
6832 Brockton Grange
6833 Calcot Grange
6834 Dummer Grange
6835 Eastham Grange
6836 Estevarney Grange
6837 Forthampton Grange
6838 Goodmoor Grange
6839 Hewell Grange
6840 Hazeley Grange
6841 Marlas Grange
6842 Nunhold Grange
6843 Poulton Grange
6844 Penydd Grange
6845 Paviland Grange
6846 Ruckley Grange
6847 Tidmarsh Grange
6848 Toddington Grange
6849 Walton Grange

6800 Class—*continued*

6850 Cleeve Grange
6851 Hurst Grange
6852 Headbourne Grange
6853 Morehampton Grange
6854 Roundhill Grange
6855 Saighton Grange
6856 Stowe Grange
6857 Tudor Grange
6858 Woolston Grange
6859 Yiewsley Grange
6860 Aberporth Grange
6861 Crynant Grange
6862 Derwent Grange
6863 Dolhywel Grange
6864 Dymock Grange
6865 Hopton Grange
6866 Morfa Grange
6867 Peterston Grange
6868 Penrhos Grange
6869 Resolven Grange
6870 Bodicote Grange
6871 Bourton Grange
6872 Crawley Grange
6873 Caradoc Grange
6874 Haughton Grange
6875 Hindford Grange
6876 Kingsland Grange
6877 Llanfair Grange
6878 Longford Grange
6879 Overton Grange

Total 80

"Hall" Class

4-6-0 4900 Class

(Continued from 5999)

(For oil-burning locomotives of this class see 39XX series, page 20)

6900 Abney Hall
6901 Arley Hall
6902 Butlers Hall
6903 Belmont Hall
6904 Charfield Hall
6905 Claughton Hall
6906 Chicheley Hall
6907 Davenham Hall
6908 Downham Hall
6909 Frewin Hall
6910 Gossington Hall
6911 Holker Hall
6912 Helmster Hall
6913 Levens Hall
6914 Langton Hall
6915 Mursley Hall
6916 Misterton Hall
6917 Oldlands Hall
6918 Sandon Hall
6919 Tylney Hall
6920 Barningham Hall
6921 Borwick Hall
6922 Burton Hall
6923 Croxteth Hall
6924 Grantley Hall
6925 Hackness Hall
6926 Holkham Hall
6927 Lilford Hall
6928 Underley Hall
6929 Whorlton Hall
6930 Aldersey Hall
6931 Aldborough Hall
6932 Burwarton Hall
6933 Birtles Hall
6934 Beachamwell Hall
6935 Browsholme Hall
6936 Breccles Hall
6937 Conyngham Hall
6938 Corndean Hall
6939 Calveley Hall
6940 Didlington Hall
6941 Fillongley Hall
6942 Eshton Hall
6943 Farnley Hall
6944 Fledborough Hall
6945 Glasfryn Hall
6946 Heatherden Hall
6947 Helmingham Hall
6948 Holbrooke Hall
6950 Kingsthorpe Hall
6951 Impney Hall
6952 Kimberley Hall
6954 Lotherton Hall
6955 Lydcott Hall

4900 Class—*continued*

6956 Mottram Hall
6958 Oxburgh Hall

Total 258

"Modified Hall" Class*

4-6-0 6959 Class

Introduced 1944.
Weights: Loco. 75 tons 16 cwt.
Tender 46 tons 14 cwt.
Pressure: 225 lb. Cyls.: 18½" × 30"
Driving Wheels: 6' 0" T.E.: 27,275 lb.

6959 Peatling Hall
6960 Raveningham Hall
6961 Stedham Hall
6962 Soughton Hall
6963 Throwley Hall
6964 Thornbridge Hall
6965 Thirlestaine Hall
6966 Witchingham Hall
6967 Willesley Hall
6968 Woodcock Hall
6969 Wraysbury Hall
6970 Whaddon Hall
6971 Athelhampton Hall
6972 Beningbrough Hall
6973 Bricklehampton Hall
6974 Bryngwyn Hall
6975 Capesthorne Hall
6976 Graythwaite Hall
6977 Grundisburgh Hall
6978 Haroldstone Hall
6979 Helperly Hall
6980 Llanrumney Hall
6981 Marbury Hall
6982 Melmerby Hall
6983 Otterington Hall
6984 Owsden Hall
6985 Parwick Hall
6986 Rydal Hall
6987 Sherrington Hall
6988 Swithland Hall
6989 Wightwick Hall
6990 Witherslack Hall
6991
6992
6993
6994
6995
6996
6997
6998
6999

Total 41

NOTE: The above space has been left to enable the reader to enter the names of Nos. 6991-9 as they are delivered. An additional series, Nos. 7900-19, is to be constructed.

"Castle" Class

4-6-0 7000 Class

(Fitted with mechanical lubricators)
(*Continued from* 5099)

7000 Viscount Portal
7001 Sir James Milne
7002 Devizes Castle
7003 Elmley Castle
7004 Eastnor Castle
7005 Lamphey Castle
7006 Lydford Castle
7007 Great Western
7008 Swansea Castle
7009 Athelney Castle
7010 Avondale Castle
7011 Banbury Castle
7012 Barry Castle
7013 Bristol Castle
7014 Caerhays Castle
7015 Carn Brea Castle
7016 Chester Castle
7017 G. J. Churchward
7018 Drysllwyn Castle
7019 Fowey Castle
7020 Gloucester Castle
7021 Haverfordwest Castle
7022 Hereford Castle

* With redesigned boiler, increased superheating surface, "one-piece" main frame, plate-frame bogie and cylinders individually cast.

Class 7000—*continued*

7023 Penrice Castle
7024 Powis Castle
7025 Sudeley Castle
7026 Tenby Castle
7027 Thornbury Castle

Total 161

(*Note*: Not all this series yet in service; No. 7017 latest at Aug. 31st, 1948; an additional series, Nos. 7028-37, is to be constructed).

2-8-2T 7200 Class

Introduced 1934, rebuilt from 4200 class 2-8-0T.
Weight: 92 tons 2 cwt.
Pressure: 200 lb. Cyls.: 19"×30"
Driving Wheels: 4' 7½" T.E.: 33,170 lb.

7200	7214	7228	7242
7201	7215	7229	7243
7202	7216	7230	7244
7203	7217	7231	7245
7204	7218	7232	7246
7205	7219	7233	7247
7206	7220	7234	7248
7207	7221	7235	7249
7208	7222	7236	7250
7209	7223	7237	7251
7210	7224	7238	7252
7211	7225	7239	7253
7212	7226	7240	
7213	7227	7241	

2-6-0 4300 Class

(*Continued from 6399*)

7300	7306	7312	7318
7301	7307	7313	7319
7302	7308	7314	7320
7303	7309	7315	7321
7304	7310	7316	
7305	7311	7317	

(*Class continued with No. 9300*)

0-6-0T 7400 Class

Introduced 1936.
Weight: 45 tons 9 cwt.
Pressure: 180 lb. Cyls.: 16½"×24"
Driving Wheels: 4' 7½" T.E.: 18,010 lb.

7400	7413	7426	7438
7401	7414	7427	7439
7402	7415	7428	7440
7403	7416	7429	7441
7404	7417	7430	7442
7405	7418	7431	7443
7406	7419	7432	7444
7407	7420	7433	7445
7408	7421	7434	7446
7409	7422	7435	7447
7410	7423	7436	7448
7411	7424	7437	7449
7412	7425		

Total 50†

0-6-0T 5700 Class

(*Continued from 6759*)

7700	7725	7750	7775
7701	7726	7751	7776
7702	7727	7752	7777
7703	7728	7753	7778
7704	7729	7754	7779
7705	7730	7755	7780
7706	7731	7756	7781
7707	7732	7757	7782
7708	7733	7758	7783
7709	7734	7759	7784
7710	7735	7760	7785
7711	7736	7761	7786
7712	7737	7762	7787
7713	7738	7763	7788
7714	7739	7764	7789
7715	7740	7765	7790
7716	7741	7766	7791
7717	7742	7767	7792
7718	7743	7768	7793
7719	7744	7769	7794
7720	7745	7770	7795
7721	7746	7771	7796
7722	7747	7772	7797
7723	7748	7773	7798
7724	7749	7774	7799

(*Class continued with No. 8700*)

† **Note: Not all this Class are yet in service. No. 7434 latest at Aug. 31st, 1948.**

"Manor" Class

4-6-0 7800 Class

Introduced 1938.
Weights: Loco. 68 tons 18 cwt.
Tender 40 tons 0 cwt.
Pressure: 225 lb. Cyls.: 18"×30"
Driving Wheels: 5' 8" T.E.: 27,340 lb.

7800 Torquay Manor
7801 Anthony Manor
7802 Bradley Manor
7803 Barcote Manor
7804 Baydon Manor
7805 Broome Manor
7806 Cockington Manor
7807 Compton Manor
7808 Cookham Manor
7809 Childrey Manor
7810 Draycott Manor
7811 Dunley Manor
7812 Erlestoke Manor
7813 Freshford Manor
7814 Fringford Manor
7815 Fritwell Manor
7816 Frilsham Manor
7817 Garsington Manor
7818 Granville Manor
7819 Hinton Manor

Total 20

(*Note:* An additional series, Nos. 7820-9, is to be constructed)

2-6-2T 8100 Class

Introduced 1938, rebuilt from 5100 class
Weight: 76 tons 11 cwt.
Pressure: 225 lb. Cyls.: 18"×30"
Driving Wheels: 5' 6" T.E.: 28,165 lb.

8100	8103	8106	8108
8101	8104	8107	8109
8102	8105		

Total 10

0-6-0T 5700 Class

(*Continued from 7799*)

8700	8706	8712	8718
8701	8707	8713	8719
8702	8708	8714	8720
8703	8709	8715	8721
8704	8710	8716	8722
8705	8711	8717	8723

8724	8743	8762	8781
8725	8744	8763	8782
8726	8745	8764	8783
8727	8746	8765	8784
8728	8747	8766	8785
8729	8748	8767	8786
8730	8749	8768	8787
8731	8750	8769	8788
8732	8751	8770	8789
8733	8752	8771	8790
8734	8753	8772	8791
8735	8754	8773	8792
8736	8755	8774	8793
8737	8756	8775	8794
8738	8757	8776	8795
8739	8758	8777	8796
8740	8759	8778	8797
8741	8760	8779	8798
8742	8761	8780	8799

(*Class continued with No. 9600*)

4-4-0 9000 Class

Introduced 1936.
Weights: Loco. 49 tons 0 cwt.
Tender 40 tons 0 cwt.
Pressure: 180 lb. Cyls.: 18"×26"
Driving Wheels: 5' 8" T.E.: 18,955 lb.

9000	9009	9016	9023
9001	9010	9017	9024
9002	9011	9018	9025
9003	9012	9019	9026
9004	9013	9020	9027
9005	9014	9021	9028
9008	9015	9022	

Total 27

(Nos. 3200-3228 until 1946)

"Duke" Class

4-4-0 3252 Class

Introduced 1895 by William Dean
Weights: Loco. 47 tons 6 cwt.
Tender 34 tons 5 cwt.
Pressure: 180 lb. Cyls.: 18"×26"
Driving Wheels: 5' 8" T.E.: 18,955 lb.

9054 Cornubia
9064 Trevithick
9065 Tre Pol and Pen

3252 Class—*continued*

9072
9073 Mounts Bay
9076
9083 Comet
9084 Isle of Jersey
9087 Mercury
9089
9091 Thames

Total 11

2-6-0 4300 Class

(*Continued from 7321*)

9300	9305	9310	9315
9301	9306	9311	9316
9302	9307	9312	9317
9303	9308	9313	9318
9304	9309	9314	9319

Total 235

0-6-0T 9400 Class

Introduced 1947.
Weight : 55 tons 7 cwt.
Pressure : 200 lb. Cyls.: $17\frac{1}{2}'' \times 24''$
Driving Wheels: $4' 7\frac{1}{2}''$ T.E.: 22,515 lb.

9400	9403	9406	9409
9401	9404	9407	
9402	9405	9408	

Total 10

0-6-0T 5700 Class

(*Continued from 8799*)

9600	9609	9618	9627
9601	9610	9619	9628
9602	9611	9620	9629
9603	9612	9621	9630
9604	9613	9622	9631
9605	9614	9623	9632
9606	9615	9624	9633
9607	9616	9625	9634
9608	9617	9626	9635

9636	9673†	9726	9763
9637	9674†	9727	9764
9638	9675†	9728	9765
9639	9676†	9729	9766
9640	9677†	9730	9767
9641	9678†	9731	9768
9642	9679†	9732	9769
9643	9680†	9733	9770
9644	9681†	9734	9771
9645	9681†	9735	9772
9646	9682†	9736	9773
9647	9700*	9737	9774
9648	9701*	9738	9775
9649	9702*	9739	9776
9650	9703*	9740	9777
9651	9704*	9741	9778
9652	9705*	9742	9779
9653	9706*	9743	9780
9654	9707*	9744	9781
9655	9708*	9745	9782
9656	9709*	9746	9783
9657	9710*	9747	9784
9658	9711	9748	9785
9659	9712	9749	9786
9660	9713	9750	9787
9661	9714	9751	9788
9662	9715	9752	9789
9663	9716	9753	9790
9664	9717	9754	9791
9665	9718	9755	9792
9666	9719	9756	9793
9667	9720	9757	9794
9668	9721	9758	9795
9669	9722	9759	9796
9670	9723	9760	9797
9671	9724	9761	9798
9672	9725	9762	9799

Total 842

* Fitted with condensing apparatus.
† To be constructed.

STREAM-LINED DIESEL RAIL-CARS

Car No.	*Date*	*Engines*	*Total b.h.p.*	*Seats*
1	1934	1	121	69
2-4*	1934	2	242	44
5-7	1935	2	242	70
8, 9	1936	2	242	70
10-12†	1936	2	242	63
13-16	1936	2	242	70
17‡	1936	2	242	—

Car No.	*Date*	*Engines*	*Total b.h.p.*	*Seats*
18§	1937	2	242	70
19-32	1940	2	210	48
33	1941	2	210	48
34‡	1941	2	210	—
35-36‖	1941	4	420	104
37-38‖	1942	4	420	104

* Buffet and lavatory facilities.
† Lavatory facilities.
‡ Parcels cars.
§ Experimentally geared to haul trailer car, became prototype of subsequent designs.

‖ Twin-coach units with buffet and lavatory facilities. Adjoining statistics apply per 2-car unit. When new, some of these units worked as 3-car rakes by the addition of an ordinary 70 ft. corridor coach.

1	**6**	**12**	**17**	**22**	**27**	**32**	**37**
2	**7**	**13**	**18**	**23**	**28**	**33**	**38**
3	**8**	**14**	**19**	**24**	**29**	**34**	
4	**10**	**15**	**20**	**25**	**30**	**35**	
5	**11**	**16**	**21**	**26**	**31**	**36**	

SERVICE LOCOS.

Petrol

0-4-0 : 23, 24, 26 and 27

Total 4

POWER AND WEIGHT CLASSIFICATION

Since 1920 Western Region locomotives have been classified for power and weight by a letter on a coloured disc on the cab side. The letter represents the power of the locomotive, and is approximately proportional to the tractive effort as under :

Power class	*Tractive effort—lb.*	*Power class*	*Tractive effort—lb.*
Special	Over 38,000	B	18,501-20,500
E	33,001-38,000	A	16,500-18,500
D	25,001-33,000	Ungrouped	Below 16,500
C	20,501-25,000		

The colour of the circle represents the routes over which the engine may work. Red engines are limited to the main lines and lines capable of carrying the heaviest locomotives ; blue engines are allowed over additional routes, yellow engines over nearly the whole system and uncoloured engines are more or less unrestricted. The double red circles on the " King " class represent special restrictions for these engines.

Right "1701" Class 0-6-0PT No. 905

[*R. Tourret*

Above : "5600" Class 0-6-2T No. 5680

[*H. C. Casserley*

Right : Ex-Rhymney Rly. 0-6-2T, G.W.R. No. 44

[*H. C. Casserley*

Above : "9400" Class 0-6-0T No. 9406
[*B. V. Franey*

Left : "1400" Class 0-4-2T No. 1425
[*B. V. Franey*

Below : "1901" Class 0-6-0T No. 1957
[*H. C. Casserley*

Above : " 5700 " Class 0-6-0T No. 8773
[B. V. Franey

Right : " 2021 " Class 0-6-0T No. 2035
[P. L. Melvill

Below : " 6400 " Class 0-6-0T No. 6400
[L. Elsey

Above : " 2251 " Class 0-6-0 No. 2274

[*L. Elsey*

Left: Ex-Midland & South Western Junction Railway 2-4-0 No. 1336

Below : Diesel Rail Car No. 4

[*H. C. Casserley*

PRINCIPAL DIMENSIONS OF WESTERN REGION ENGINES

(Tractive Effort calculated to nearest 5lb.)

Class	Type	Designer	Intro-duced	Weight (full) Loco. T. Cwt.	Weight (full) Tender T. Cwt.	Press-ure Lb. per sq. in.	Cylinders (2 unless otherwise shown)	Driving Wheels	T.E. at 85% lb.	Power Class	Route Restriction Colour
517*	0-4-2T	G. Armstrong	1868	35 4	—	165	16″ × 24″	5′ 2″	13.900	—	—
1000	4-6-0	Hawksworth	1945	76 17	19 0	280	18½″ × 30″	6′ 3″	32,580	D	Red
1101	0-4-0T	Collett	1926	38 4	—	170	16″ × 24″	3′ 9½″	19,510	B	Red
1361	0-6-0ST	Churchward	1910	35 4	—	150	16″ × 20″	3′ 8″	14,835	—	—
1366	0-6-0PT	Collett	1934	35 15	—	165	16″ × 20″	3′ 8″	16,320	—	—
1400 (late 4800)	0-4-2T	Collett	1932	41 6	—	165	16″ × 24″	5′ 2″	13,900	—	—
1501	0-6-0PT	Dean & G. Armstrong (Wolv'n.)	1878	42 17	—	165	17″ × 24″	4′ 7½″	17,525	A	Blue**
1701	0-6-0PT	Dean (Swindon)	1891††	46 13	—	180	17″ × 24″	4′ 7½″	19,120	A	Blue
1813	0-6-0PT	Dean (Swindon)	1882	44 8	—	165	17″ × 24″	4′ 7½″	17,525	A	Blue
1901	0-6-0PT	Dean & G. Armstrong (Wolv'n.)	1881	36 3	—	165	16″ × 24″	4′ 1½″	17,410	—	—
2021 / 2181 §	0-6-0PT	Dean (Wolv'n.)	1897	39 15	—	165	16½″ × 24″	4′ 1½″	18,515	A	—
2251	0-6-0	Collett	1930	43 8	36 15	200	17½″ × 24″	5′ 2″	20.155	B	Yellow
2301	0-6-0	Dean	1883	36 16	34 5	180	17″ × 24″ / 17½″ × 24″	5′ 2″ / 5′ 2″	17.120 / 18,140	A	—
2600	2-6-0	Dean	1900	56 15	47 14	200	18″ × 26″	4′ 7½″	25,800	D	Blue
2700	0-6-0PT	Dean†	1896	45 13	—	180	17½″ × 24″	4′ 7½″	20,260	A	Blue
2800	2-8-0	Churchward	1903	75 10 / 76 5	40 0	225	18½″ × 30″	4′ 7½″	35,380	E	Blue
2900	4-6-0	Churchward‡	1902	72 0	40 0	225	18½″ × 30″	6′ 8½″	24,395	C	Red
3100	2-6-2T	Collett	1938	81 9	—	225	18½″ × 30″	5′ 3″	31,170	E	Red
3150	2-6-2T	Churchward	1907	81 12	—	200	18½″ × 30″	5′ 8″	25,670	D	Red
3252	4-4-0	Dean	1895	47 6	34 5	180	18″ × 26″	5′ 8″	18.955	B	Yellow

* Wolverhampton-built in 1895-7.

† Nos. 2701-20 built at Wolverhampton, 1896-7.

‡ Pioneer engine No. 2900 (originally No. 100) designed by Dean, built 1902.

§ 2021 Class with altered brake gear.

** Nos. 1742/5/7/9/73/80/2/9 bear colour "Yellow."

†† Embodying earlier engines.

Class	Type	Designer	Intro-duced	Weight (full) Loco. T. Cwt.	Weight (full) Tender T. Cwt.	Pressure Lb. per sq. in.	Cylinders (2 unless otherwise shown)	Driving Wheels	T.E. at 85% Lb.	Power Class	Route Restriction Colour
3300	4-4-0	Dean	1898	51 16	40 0	200	18″ × 26″	5′ 8″	21,060	B	Blue
3500	2-4-0T	Dean	1899	41 7	—	165	16″ × 24″	5′ 2″	13,900	—	Yellow
4000	4-6-0	Churchward	1906	75 12	46 14	225	15″ × 26″ (4)	6′ 8½″	27,800	D	Red
4073	4-6-0	Collett	1923	79 17	46 14	225	16″ × 26″ (4)	6′ 8½″	31,625	D	Red
4200	2-8-0T	Churchward	1910	82 2	—	200	19″ × 30″	4′ 7½″	33,170	E	Red
4300	2-6-0	Churchward	1911	{ 62 0 65 6 }	40 0	200	18½″ × 30″	5′ 8″	25,670	D	{ Blue Red§
4400	2-6-2T	Churchward*	1904	56 13	—	180	17″ × 24″	4′ 1½″	21,440	C	—
4500	2-6-2T	Churchward†	1906	61 0	—	200	17″ × 24″	4′ 7½″	21,250	C	Yellow
4700	2-8-0	Churchward	1919	82 0	46 14	225	19″ × 30″	5′ 8″	30,460	D	Red
4900	4-6-0	Collett	1928	75 0	46 14	225	18½″ × 30″	6′ 0″	27,275	D	Red
5100	2-6-2T	Collett	1929	78 9	—	200	18″ × 30″	5′ 8″	24,300	D	Blue
5400	0-6-0PT	Collett	1931	46 12	—	165	16½″ × 24″	5′ 2″	14,780	—	Yellow
5600	0-6-2T	Collett	1924	68 12	—	200	18″ × 26″	4′ 7½″	25,800	D	Red
5700	0-6-0PT	Collett	1929	49 0	—	200	17½″ × 24″	4′ 7½″	22,515	C	Blue
6000	4-6-0	Collett	1927	89 0	46 14	250	16¼″ × 28″ (4)	6′ 6″	40,300	Spcl.	Double Red
6100	2-6-2T	Collett	1931	78 9	—	225	18″ × 30″	5′ 8″	27,340	D	Blue
6400	0-6-0PT	Collett	1931	45 12	—	165	16½″ × 24″	4′ 7½″	16,510	A	Yellow
6800	4-6-0	Collett	1936	74 0	40 0	225	18½″ × 30″	5′ 8″	28,875	D	Red
7200	2-8-2T	Collett	1934	92 12	—	200	19″ × 30″	4′ 7½″	33,170	E	Red
7400	0-6-0PT	Collett	1936	45 9	—	180	16½″ × 24″	4′ 7½″	18,010	A	Yellow
7800	4-6-0	Collett	1938	68 18	40 0	225	18″ × 30″	5′ 8″	27,340	D	Blue
8100	2-6-2T	Collett	1938	76 11	—	225	18″ × 30″	5′ 6″	28,165	D	Blue
9000 (late 3200)	4-4-0	Collett‡	1936	49 0	40 0	180	18″ × 26″	5′ 8″	18,955	B	Yellow
9400	0-6-0T	Hawksworth	1947	55 7	—	200	17½″ × 24″	4′ 7½″	22,515	C	Red
R.O.O.	2-8-0	Robinson, G.C.R.	1917**	73 11	48 6	185	21″ × 26″	4′ 8″	32,200	D	Blue

* Nos. 4401-10 built at Wolverhampton, 1905.

† Nos. 4500-19, last engines built at Wolverhampton, 1906-8.

‡ New class rebuilt from obsolescent Dean engines.

§ Engines numbered in 93XX series.

** Date of initial wartime contract for Railway Operating Division. The design originated with G.C.R., 1911.

THE ABC OF BRITISH LOCOMOTIVES

PART 2—10000-39999

STEAM LOCOMOTIVES:
SOUTHERN REGION

DIESEL and ELECTRIC LOCOS:
ALL REGIONS

LONDON:
Ian Allan Ltd
1949

FOREWORD

This booklet lists all British Railways locomotives numbered between 10000 and 39999. This series of numbers includes the following groups of locomotives :

All British Railways diesel and diesel-electric locomotives.

All British Railways Gas Turbine locomotives.

All British Railways Electric locomotives.

All steam locomotives of the Southern Region, British Railways, i.e. former Southern Railway steam locomotives, with the exception of Ministry of Supply "Austerity" 2-8-0 locomotives on loan to the S.R. and classified "AY," details of which will be found in the ABC OF BRITISH RAILWAYS LOCOMOTIVES Nos. 60000-79999.

Under the general British Railways scheme, all diesel, diesel-electric and electric locomotives have been renumbered between 10000 and 29999, all former Southern Railway steam locomotives between 30000 and 39999, the latter by the addition of 30000 to their former numbers (with certain exceptions).

Renumbering is being carried out only as locomotives visit main works for repairs, and thus it will be some time before all locomotives bear the numbers shown in this book.

NOTES ON THE USE OF THIS BOOK

1. The owning Region and pre-nationalisation numbers of all non-steam locomotives are indicated, with the exception of L.M.R. No. 10000, which retains its L.M.S.R. number.
2. Where former S.R. steam locomotives have been renumbered other than by the simple addition of 30000 to their previous numbers, details of their former S.R. numbering are given.
3. Throughout the book details of class continuation are given to enable the reader to trace all the locomotives of a particular class easily. Where the mixture of classes makes the normal method impracticable, e.g. as between Nos. 30134-75, the details are given *en bloc* at the foot of the numbers under the heading "CLASS CONTINUATION." Under the sub-heading "From" will be found the last number of the preceding batch of the class, under "To" the first number of any succeeding batch. If no more batches follow the class total is given.
4. Throughout this book :

   † indicates locomotive fitted for auto-train working.
5. In the lists of dimensions, all steam locomotives are fitted with two cylinders unless otherwise indicated, i.e. (3) : 3 cylinders. Numbers shown against "tender types" refer to Table, p. 46.
6. The locomotives listed have been checked to October 31st, 1948.

BRITISH RAILWAYS DIESEL ELECTRIC and DIESEL MECHANICAL LOCOMOTIVES

0-6-6-0 Diesel Electric

LONDON MIDLAND REGION

Introduced: English Electric Co. and H. A. Ivatt, 1947.
Weight: 121 tons 10 cwt.
Engine: English Electric Co. Type 16 S.V.T.
Cyls. (16): 10″ × 12″. H.P.: 1,600
Max. Eng. Revs.: 750 r.p.m.
T.E.: 41,400 lb.

10000 10001 Total 2

0-6-0 Diesel Electric

LONDON MIDLAND REGION

Introduced: English Electric—Hawthorn Leslie 1936.
Motors: Two nose-suspended motors, single reduction gear drive.
Weight: 51 tons (Nos. 12000/1). 47 tons (No. 12002).
Driving Wheels: 4′ 0½″. H.P.: 350.
T.E.: 30,000 lb.

(Former L.M.S.R. numbers in brackets)

12000 (7074)	12002 (7079)
12001 (7076)	**Total 3**

0-6-0 Diesel Electric

LONDON MIDLAND REGION

Introduced: English Electric—L.M.S.R., 1939.
Motors: Single motor; jackshaft drive
Weight: 54 tons 16 cwt.
Driving Wheels: 4′ 3″. H.P.: 350.
T.E.: 33,000 lb.

(Former L.M.S.R. numbers in brackets)

12003 (7080)	12018 (7095)
12004 (7081)	12019 (7096)
12005 (7082)	12020 (7097)
12006 (7083)	12021 (7098)
12007 (7084)	12022 (7099)
12008 (7085)	12023 (7110)
12009 (7086)	12024 (7111)
12010 (7087)	12025 (7112)
12011 (7088)	12026 (7113)
12012 (7089)	12027 (7114)
12013 (7090)	12028 (7115)
12014 (7091)	12029 (7116)
12015 (7092)	12030 (7117)
12016 (7093)	12031 (7118)
12017 (7094)	12032 (7119)

Total 30

0-6-0 Diesel Electric

LONDON MIDLAND REGION

Built: English Electric—L.M.S., 1945.
Engine: Two nose-suspended motors, double reduction gear drive.
Weight: 50 tons.
Driving Wheels: 4′ 0½″. H.P.: 350.
T.E.: 33,000 lb.

(Former L.M.S.R. numbers in brackets)

12033 (7120)	12051
12034 (7121)	12052
12035 (7122)	12053
12036 (7123)	12054
12037 (7124)	12055
12038 (7125)	12056
12039 (7126)	12057
12040 (7127)	12058
12041 (7128)	12059
12042 (7129)	12060
12043 (7130)	12061
12044 (7131)	12062
12045	12063
12046	12064
12047	12065
12048	12066
12049	12067
12050	12068

(NOTE: Nos. 12047-68 are not yet in service.)

Total (planned) 36

0-6-0 Diesel Electric

LONDON MIDLAND REGION

Introduced: Armstrong-Whitworth, 1934.
Motors: Single motor, jackshaft drive
Weight: 40 tons 10 cwt.
Driving Wheels: 3′ 6″. H.P.: 250.
T.E.: 24,000 lb.

(Former L.M.S.R. number in brackets)

13000 (7058) Total 1

0-6-0 Diesel Electric

EASTERN REGION

Introduced : English Electric—L.N.E.R. 1944.
Motors : Two nose-suspended motors, double reduction gear.
Weight : 51 tons.
Driving Wheels : 4′ 0″. H.P.: 350.
T.E.: 32,000 lb.

(Former L.N.E.R. numbers in brackets)

15000 (8000)	15002 (8002)
15001 (8001)	15003 (8003)

Total 4

0-6-0 Diesel Electric

WESTERN REGION

Introduced : Hawthorn Leslie—English Electric, 1936 (No. 15100) and W.R.—English Electric, 1948 (remainder).
Motors : Two nose-suspended motors, single reduction gear.
Weight : 51 tons 10 cwt. (No. 15100); 46 tons 9 cwt. (remainder)
Driving Wheels : 4′ 1″ (No. 15100); 4′ 0½″ (remainder)
H.P.: 350.
T.E.: 30,000 lb. (No. 15100). 33,500 lb. (remainder)

(Former G.W.R. number in brackets)

15100 (2)	15103	15105
15101	15104	15106
15102		

Total 7

0-6-0 Diesel Electric

SOUTHERN REGION

Introduced : Eng. Elec.—S.R., 1937.
Motors : Two nose-suspended motors, single reduction gear.
Weight : 55 tons 5 cwt.
Driving Wheels : 4′ 6″. H.P.: 350.
T.E.: 30,000 lb.

(Former S.R. numbers in brackets)

15201 (1) | 15202 (2) | 15203 (3)

Total 3

LOCOMOTIVES NOT YET IN SERVICE

L.M.R. Diesel Mechanical, 1,600 h.p.
To be numbered from 10100.
S.R. Diesel Electric, 1,600 h.p.
To be numbered from 10200.
L.M.R. Diesel Electic, 800 h.p.
To be numbered from 10800.
Diesel Mechanical, 400 h.p.
To be numbered from 11000.
W.R. Gas Turbine.
To be numbered from 18000.

BRITISH RAILWAYS ELECTRIC LOCOS.

(Former numbers in brackets)

Co+Co Class CC

SOUTHERN REGION

Introduced : Raworth & Bulleid—S.R., 1941.
Weight : 99 tons 14 cwt. (20001/2); 104 tons 14 cwt. (20003)
Voltage : 600 D.C. T.E.: 40,000 lb.

20001 (CC1)	20002 (CC2)
20003	

Total 3

Bo+Bo Class EM1

EASTERN & NORTH-EASTERN REGIONS

Built : Met. Vick—L.N.E.R., 1941.
Weight : 87 tons 18 cwt.
Voltage : 1,500 D.C. T.E.: 45,000 lb.

26000 (6000) **Total 1**

Bo+Bo Class EB1

NORTH-EASTERN REGION

Built : N.E.R., 1914.
Weight : 74 tons 8 cwt.
Voltage : 1,500 D.C. T.E.: 28,000 lb.

26490 (6490)	26495 (6495)
26491 (6491)	26496 (6496)
26492 (6492)	26497 (6497)
26493 (6493)	26498 (6498)
26494 (6494)	26499 (6499)

Total 10

Bo+Bo Class ES1

NORTH-EASTERN REGION

Built : Brush & Thomson-Houston, 1905.
Weight : 56 tons.
Voltage : 600 D.C. T.E.: 25,000 lb.

26500 (6480) | 26501 (6481)

Total 2

2-Co-2 Class EE1

NORTH-EASTERN REGION

Built : Met. Vick.—N.E.R., 1922.
Weight : 110 tons 1 cwt.
Voltage : 1,500 D.C. T.E.: 28,000 lb.

26999 (6999) **Total 1**

Right : L.M. Region 1,600 h.p. Diesel - Electric Locomotive No. 10000

[*Photo : W. S. Garth*

Below : L.M. Region 350 h.p. Diesel - Electric Shunter No. 7117 (new No. 12030)

[*Photo: H.C.Casserley*

Right : Western Region 350 h.p. Diesel - Electric Shunter No. 15104

[*Photo: B. V. Franey*

Above: Class " D15 " 4-4-0 No. 464 (new No. 30464)
[*Photo : F. F. Moss*

Left : Class " T9 " 4-4-0 No. 30119
[*Photo: S. C. Townroe*

Below: Class "L12" 4-4-0 No. 433 (new No. 30433)
[*Photo : A. F. Cook*

Above: Class "D1" 4-4-0 No. 31470

[*Photo: P. Ransome-Wallis*

Right: Class "D" 4-4-0 No. 1748 (new No. 31748)

[*Photo: H. C. Casserley*

Below: Class "K10" 4-4-0 No. 142 (new No. 30142)

Photo: C. C. B. Herbert

I. O. W. LOCOS.

Above : Class "E1" 0-6-0T No. 4 *Wroxall*
[*Photo : A. F. Cook*

Left : Class "A1X" 0-6-0T No. 8 *Freshwater*

Below : Class "O2" 0-4-4T No. 28 *Ashey*
[*Photos : E. R. Wethersett*

SOUTHERN REGION STEAM LOCOMOTIVES

WESTERN SECTION

0-4-4T Class T1

Introduced 1888
Weight: 57 tons 2 cwt.
Pressure: 160 lb., Cyls. 18"×26"
Driving Wheels 5' 7". T.E. 17,100 lb.

30001	30005	30008	30020
30002	30007	30013	

(*Class continued No.* 30361)

0-4-4T Class M7

Introduced 1897
Weight: {*60 tons 4 cwt. †62 tons 0 cwt. / *Others*: 60 tons 3 cwt.
Pressure: 175 lb. Cyls. 18½"×26"
Driving Wheels: 5' 7". T.E.: 19,755 lb.

30021†	30031	30041	30051†
30022	30032	30042	30052†
30023	30033	40043	30053†
30024	30034	30044	30054†
30025	30035	30045†	30055†
30026	30036	30046†	30056†
30027†	30037	30047†	30057†
30028†	30038	30048†	30058†
30029†	30039	30049†	30059†
30030*	30040	30050†	30060†

(*Class continued No.* 30104)

*†With long front overhang and steam reverse. Remainder with short front overhang and lever reverse.

0-6-0T Class USA

Introduced 1942
Weight: 46 tons 10 cwt.
Pressure: 210 lb. Cyls. 16½"×24"
Driving Wheels: 4' 6". T.E.: 21,600 lb.

30061	30065	30069	30072
30062	30066	30070	30073
30063	30067	30071	30074
30064	30068		

Total 14

0-4-0T Class B4

Introduced 1891.
Weight: {33 tons 9 cwt. / 32 tons 18 cwt.*
Pressure: 140 lb. Cyls. 16"×22"
Driving Wheels: 3' 9¾". T.E.: 14,650 lb.

30081 Jersey
30082*
30083*
30084*
30085 Alderney
30086 Havre
30087
30088
30089 Trouville
30092
30093 St. Malo
30094
30095 Honfleur
30096 Normandy
30097 Brittany
30098 Cherbourg
30099
30100
30101* Dinan
30102 Granville
30103

(*Class continued No.* 30147)

* Built Drummond, with small diameter boiler. Also No. 30147, *q.v.*

0-4-4T Class M7

Class continued from No. 30060)

30104†	30107†	30109†	30111†
30105†	30108†	30110†	30112
30106†			

(*Class continued No.* 30123)

4-4-0 Class T9

Rbt. from engines Introduced 1899.
Weight: Loco. 51 tons 16 cwt. (307XX series)
51 tons 18 cwt. (301XX, 302XX series)
51 tons 7 cwt. (303XX series)
Tender types: 17, 18, 28.
Pressure: 175 lb. Cyls. 19"×26"
Driving Wheels: 6' 7". T.E.: 17,675 lb.

30113	30116	30119	30121
30114	30117	30120	30122
30115	30118		

(*Class continued No.* 30280)

0-4-4T Class M7

(*Class continued from No. 30112*)

30123	30127	30130	30132
30124	30128†	30131†	30133
30125†	30129†		

(*Class continued No. 30241*)

0-4-0T Class B4
4-4-0 Class L11
4-4-0 Class K10
0-6-0T Class G6

	L11 4-4-0	K10 4-4-0	G6 0-6-0T
Intro.	1903	1901	1894
W'hts	tons cwt.	tons cwt.	tons cwt.
Loco.	50 11	46 14	47 13
Tend'r Types	18, 28, 32	18, 20, 28	— —
Press.	175 lb.	175 lb.	160 lb.
Cyls.	18½"x 26"	18½"x 26"	17½"x 24"
D.W.	5'7"	5'7"	4'10"
T.E.	19,755 lb.	19,755 lb.	17,235 lb.

No.	Class	No.	Class
30134	L11	30159	L11
30135	K10	30160	G6
30137	K10	30161	L11
30140	K10	30162	G6
30141	K10	30163	L11
30142	K10	30164	L11
30144	K10	30165	L11
30147	Dinard B4	30166	L11
		30167	L11
30148	L11	30168	L11
30151	K10	30169	L11
30152	K10	30170	L11
30153	K10	30171	L11
30154	L11	30172	L11
30155	L11	30173	L11
30156	L11	30174	L11
30157	L11	30175	L11
30158	L11		

Class Continuation

Class	From	To	Total
B4	30103	—	22
K10	—	30329	—
G6	—	30237	—
L11	—	30405	—

0-4-4T Class O2

Introduced 1889-95
Weight : 46 tons 18 cwt. / 48 tons 8 cwt. (I.O.W. Locos.)
Pressure : 160 lb. Cyls. 17½" × 24"
Driving Wheels : 4'10". T.E. 17,235 lb.

30177	30197	30212	30229
30179	30198	30213	30230
30181	30199	30216	30231
30182	30200	30221	30232
30183	30203	30223	30233
30192	30204	30224	30236
30193	30207	30225	

(*Class continued p.38, I.O.W. locomotives*)

0-6-0T Class G6

(*Class continued from No. 30162*)

30237 | 30238 | 30240

(*Class continued No. 30257*)

0-4-4T Class M7

(*Class continued from No. 30133*)

30241	30245	30249	30253
30242	30246	30250	30254
30243	30247	30251	30255
30244	30248	30252	30256

(*Class continued No. 30318*)

0-6-0T Class G6

(*Class continued from No. 30240*)

30257	30263	30269	30276
30258	30264	30270	30277
30259	30265	30272	30278
30260	30266	30273	30279
30261	30267	30274	
30262	30268	30275	

(*Class continued No. 30348*)

NOTE: To facilitate arrangement the entries between Nos. 30280 and 30328 are not in strict numerical order.

4-4-0 Class T9

(Class continued from No. 30122)

30280	30286	30302	30311
30281	30287	30303	30312
30282	30288	30304	30313
30283	30289	30305	30314
30284	30300	30307	
30285	30301	30310	

(Class continued No. 30336)

0-6-0 Class 700

Rbt. from engines introduced 1897
Weights: Loco. 46 tons 14 cwt.
Tender types: 17, 18
Pressure: 180 lbs. Cyls. 19" x 26".
Driving Wheels: 5' 1". T.E.: 23,540 lb.

30306	30309	30316	30317
30308	30315		

(Class continued No. 30325)

0-4-4T Class M7

(Class continued from No. 30256)

30318	30320	30322	30324
30319	30321	30323	30328†

(Class continued No. 30356)

0-6-0 Class 700

(Class continued from No. 30317)

30325 | 30326 | 30327

(Class continued No. 30339)

4-4-0 Class K10

(Class continued from No. 30153)

30329

(Class continued No. 30341)

4-6-0 Class H15

(Dimensions below applicable only to this series)

Introduced 1914
Weights: Loco. { 80 tons 11 cwt.* / 82 tons 1 cwt.* (No. 30335) }
Tender types: 29, 31
Pressure: 175 lb. Cyls. 21" × 28"
Driving Wheels: 6' 0". T.E.: 25,510 lb.

30330	30332	30334	30335
30331	30333		

(Class continued No. 30473)

4-4-0 Class T9

(Class continued from No. 30314)

30336 | 30337 | 30338

(Class continued No. 30702)

0-6-0 Class 700
4-4-0 Class K10
0-6-0T Class G6
0-4-4T Class M7
0-4-4T Class T1

No.	Class	No.	Class
30339	700	30374	M7
30341	K10	30375	M7
30345	K10	30376	M7
30346	700	30377	M7
30348	G6	30378	M7
30349	G6	30379†	M7
30350	700	30380	K10
30351	G6	30382	K10
30352	700	30383	K10
30353	G6	30384	K10
30354	G6	30385	K10
30355	700	30386	K10
30356	M7	30389	K10
30357	M7	30390	K10
30361	T1	30391	K10
30367	T1	30393	K10
30368	700	30394	K10

Class Continuations

Class	From	To	Total
700	30327	30687	—
K10	30329	—	23
G6	30279	—	32
M7	30328	30479	—
T1	30020	—	9

* Rebuilt from Drummond 4-cyl. 4-6-0's.

4-4-0 Class S11

Rbt. from engines introduced 1903
Weights: Loco. 53 tons 15 cwt.
Tender types : 17, 28
Pressure : 175 lb. Cyls. 19"×26"
Driving Wheels: 6' 0". T.E.: 19,390 lb.

30395	30398	30401	30403
30396	30399	30402	30404
30397	30400		

Total 10

4-4-0 Class L11

(Class continued from No. 30175)

30405	30408	30411	30413
30406	30409	30412	30414
30407	30410		

(Class continued No. 30435)

4-4-0 Class L12

Rbt. from engines introduced 1904
Weights : Loco. 55 tons 5 cwt.
Tender types : 18, 28
Pressure : 175 lb. Cyls. 19"×26"
Driving Wheels: 6' 7". T.E.: 17,670 lb.

30415	30420	30425	30430
30416	30421	30426	30431
30417	30422	30427	30432
30418	30423	30428	30433
30419	30424	30429	30434

Total 20

4-4-0 Class L11

(Class continued from No. 30414)

30435	30437	30439	30441
30436	30438	30440	30442

Total 40

4-6-0 Class T14

Rebuilt from Drummond engines introduced 1911.
Weights : Loco. 76 tons 10 cwt.
Tender type : 40
Pressure : 175 lb. Cyls. (4) 15"×26"
Driving Wheels: 6' 7". T.E.: 22,030 lb.

30443	30445	30446	30447
30444			

(Class continued No. 30459)

4-6-0 Class N15

(Dimensions applicable only to this series)

Built 1925, assimilated to Class N15 introduced 1918
Weights : Loco. { 80 tons 19 cwt. (Nos. 30448-52) 79 tons 18 cwt. (Nos. 30452-7)
Tender type : 29
Pressure : 200 lb. Cyls. $20\frac{1}{2}$"×28"
Driving Wheels: 6' 7". T.E.: 25,320 lb.

30448 Sir Tristram
30449 Sir Torre
30450 Sir Kay
30451 Sir Lamorak
30452 Sir Meliagrance
30453 King Arthur
30454 Queen Guinevere
30455 Sir Launcelot
30456 Sir Galahad
30457 Sir Bedivere

(Class continued No. 30736)

0-4-0ST Class 0458

Introduced 1890
Weight : 21 tons 2 cwt.
Pressure : 120 lb. Cyls. 12"×20"
Driving Wheels : 3' 2". T.E.: 7,730 lb.

30458 Ironside

Total 1

4-6-0 Class T14

(Class continued from No. 30447)

30459	30460	30461	30462

Total 9

4-4-0 Class D15

Rebt. from engines introduced 1912
Weights : Loco. 61 tons 11 cwt.
Tender type : 17
Pressure : 180 lb. Cyls. 20"×26"
Driving Wheels: 6' 7". T.E.: 20,140lb.

30463	30466	30469	30471
30464	30467	30470	30472
30465	30468		

Total 10

4-6-0 Class H15

(Class continued from No. 30335. Dimensions below applicable only to this series and Nos. 30491, 30521-4)

Introduced 1914
Weights : Loco. 79 tons 19 cwt.
Tender type : 36
Pressure : 180 lb. Cyls. 21" × 28"
Driving Wheels: 6' 0". T.E.: 26,240 lb.

30473	30475	30477	30478
30474	30476		

(Class continued No. 30482)

0-4-4T Class M7

(Class continued from No. 30379)

30479 | 30480† | 30481†

(Class continued No. 30667)

4-6-0 Class H15

(Class continued from No. 30478. Dimensions below applicable only to this series, except No. 30491)

Introduced 1914
Weights : Loco. 81 tons 5 cwt.
Tender type : 39
Pressure : 180 lb. Cyls. 21" × 28"
Driving Wheels : 6' 0". T.E. 26,240 lb.

30482	30485	30488	30490
30483	30486	30489	30491*
30484	30487		

(Class continued No. 30521)

* Dimensions as 30473-30478 series.

4-8-0T Class G16

Introduced 1921
Weight : 95 tons 2 cwt.
Pressure : 180 lb. Cyls. 22" × 28"
Driving Wheels: 5' 1". T.E.: 33,990lb.

30492 | 30493 | 30494 | 30495

Total 4

4-6-0 Class S15

(Dimensions below applicable to this series only)

Introduced 1920
Weights : Loco. 79 tons 16 cwt.
Tender types : 28, 37
Pressure : 180 lb. Cyls. 21" × 28"
Driving Wheels: 5' 7". T.E.: 28,200 lb.

30496	30501	30506	30511
30497	30502	30507	30512
30498	30503	30508	30513
30499	30504	30509	30514
30500	30505	30510	30515

(Class continued No. 30823)

4-6-2T Class H16

Introduced 1921
Weight : 96 tons 8 cwt.
Pressure : 180 lb. Cyls. 21" × 28"
Driving Wheels : 5'7". T.E. 28,200 lb.

30516	30518	30519	30520
30517			

Total 5

4-6-0 Class H15

(Class continued from No. 30491. For dimensions see 30473-30478 series)

30521 | 30522 | 30523 | 30524

Total 26

0-6-0 Class Q

Introduced 1938
Weights : Loco. 49 tons 10 cwt.
Tender type : 19
Pressure : 200 lb. Cyls. 19" × 26"
Driving Wheels: 5' 1". T.E.: 26,160 lb.

(All except Nos. 30545/9 fitted with multiple-jet blast pipe and large diameter chimney)

30530	30535	30540	30545
30531	30536	30541	30546
30532	30537	30542	30547
30533	30538	30543	30548
30534	30539	30544	30549

Total 20

0-6-0 Class 0395

Introduced 1881
Weights: Loco. {37 tons 12 cwt. / 38 tons 14 cwt.‡}
Tender types : 2, 9
Pressure : {140 lb. / 150 lb.‡} Cyls. 17½"×26"
Driving Wheels : 5' 1".
T.E. {15,535 lb. / 16,645 lb.‡}

(Former S.R. numbers in brackets)

30564 (3029)‡	30573 (3433)*
30565 (3083)‡*	30574 (3436)
30566 (3101)‡	30575 (3439)
30567 (3154)	30576 (3440)
30568 (3155)	30577 (3441)
30569 (3163)	30578 (3442)
30570 (3167)	30579 (3496)‡
30571 (3397)	30580 (3506)‡
30572 (3400)	30581 (3509)‡

Total 18

*Rebuilt with ex-SECR Class M3 boilers
‡ With longer front overhang

4-4-2T Class 0415

Introduced 1882
Weight : 55 tons 2 cwt.
Pressure : 160 lb. Cyls. 17½"×24"
Driving Wheels: 5' 7". T.E.: 14,920 lb.

(Former S.R. Nos. in brackets)

30582 (3125)	30584 (3520)
30583 (3488)	

Total 3

2-4-0WT Class 0298

Introduced 1874
Weight : 37 tons 16 cwt.
Pressure : 160 lb. Cyls. 16½" × 20"
Driving Wheels: 5' 7". T.E.: 11,050 lb.

(Former S.R. Nos. in brackets)

30585 (3314)	30587 (3298)
30586 (3329)	

Total 3

0-4-0T Class C14

Introduced 1906 as 2-2-0T
Weight : 25 tons 15 cwt.
Pressure : 150 lb. Cyls. 14"×14"
Driving Wheels : 3' 0". T.E. 9,720 lb.

(Former S.R. Nos. in brackets)

30588 (3741)	30589 (3744)

2
Service Locos 1

Total 3

0-4-2 Class A12

Introduced 1887
Weights : Loco. 42 tons 7 cwts.
Tender 33 tons 4 cwt.
Pressure : 160 lb. Cyls. 18"×26"
Driving Wheels : 6' 0". T.E. : 15,900 lb.

30627	30629

Total 2

0-4-4T Class M7

(Class continued from No. 30481)

30667	30670	30673	30675
30668	30671	30674	30676
30669			

Total 103

0-6-0 Class 700

(Class continued from No. 30368)

30687	30691	30695	30699
30688	30692	30696	30700
30689	30693	30697	30701
30690	30694	30698	

Total 30

4-4-0 Class T9

(Class continued from No. 30338)

30702	30710	30718	30727
30703	30711	30719	30728
30704	30712	30721	30729
30705	30713	30722	30730
30706	30714	30723	30731
30707	30715	30724	30732
30708	30716	30725	30733
30709	30717	30726	

Total 66

4-6-0 Class N15

(Class continued from No. 30457. Dimensions below applicable only to this series)

Introduced 1918
Weights : Loco. 80 tons 7 cwt.
Tender type : 37
Pressure: 180 lb. Cyls. { 21" × 28" / 22" × 28" (No. 30755)
Driving Wheels: 6' 7".
T.E. : { 23,915 lb. / 26,245 lb. (No. 30755)

30736‡ Excalibur
30737‡ King Uther
30738 King Pellinore
30739 King Leodegrance
30740 Merlin
30741‡ Joyous Gard
30742 Camelot
30743 Lyonnesse
30744 Maid of Astolat
30745 Tintagel
30746 Pendragon
30747 Elaine
30748 Vivien
30749 Iseult
30750 Morgan le Fay
30751 Etarre
30752‡ Linette
30753 Melisande
30754 The Green Knight
30755‡ The Red Knight

(Class continued No. 30763)

‡ Fitted with multiple jet blast pipe and large diameter chimney.

0-6-0T Class 756

Introduced 1907
Weight : 35 tons 15 cwt.
Pressure : 170 lb. Cyls. 14" × 22"
Driving Wheels: 3' 10". T.E.: 13,545 lb.

30756 A. S. Harris **Total 1**

0-6-2T Class 757

Introduced 1907
Weight : 49 tons 19 cwt.
Pressure : 170 lb. Cyls. 16" × 24"
Driving Wheels: 4' 0". T.E.: 18,495 lb.

30757 Earl of Mount Edgcumbe
30758 Lord St. Levan

Total 2

4-6-0 Class N15

(Class continued from No. 30755. Dimensions below applicable only to this series)

Introduced 1925 (Nos. 30763-92), 1926 (Nos. 30793-30806).
Weights : Loco. { 80 tons 19 cwt. (Nos. 30763-92) / 81 tons 17 cwt. (Nos. 30793-806)
Tender types : { 36 (Nos. 30763-92) / 21 (Nos. 30793-806)
Pressure : 200 lb. Cyls. $20\frac{1}{2}$" × 28"
Driving Wheels : 6' 7". T.E.: 25,320 lb.

30763 Sir Bors de Ganis
30764 Sir Gawain
30765 Sir Gareth
30766 Sir Geraint
30767 Sir Valence
30768 Sir Balin
30769 Sir Balan
30770 Sir Prianius
30771 Sir Sagramore
30772 Sir Percivale
30773 Sir Lavaine
30774 Sir Gaheris
30775 Sir Agravaine
30776 Sir Galagars
30777 Sir Lamiel
30778 Sir Pelleas
30779 Sir Colgrevance
30780 Sir Persant
30781 Sir Aglovale
30782 Sir Brian
30783 Sir Gillemere
30784 Sir Nerovens
30785 Sir Mador de la Porte
30786 Sir Lionel
30787 Sir Menadeuke
30788 Sir Urre of the Mount
30789 Sir Guy
30790 Sir Villiars
30791 Sir Uwaine
30792 Sir Hervis de Revel
30793 Sir Ontzlake
30794 Sir Ector de Maris
30795 Sir Dinadan
30796 Sir Dodinas le Savage
30797 Sir Blamor de Ganis
30798 Sir Hectimere
30799 Sir Ironside

30800 Sir Meleaus de Lile
30801 Sir Meliot de Logres
30802 Sir Durnore
30803 Sir Harry le Fise Lake
30804 Sir Cador of Cornwall
30805 Sir Constantine
30806 Sir Galleron **Total 74**

4-6-0 Class S15

(Class continued from No. 30515. Dimensions below applicable only to this series)
Introduced 1927
Weights : Loco. 80 tons 14 cwt. (Nos. 30823-37)
79 tons 5 cwt. (Nos. 30838-47)
Tender types : 35 (Nos. 30823-32/8-47)
26 (Nos. 30833-7)
Pressure : 200 lb. Cyls $20\frac{1}{2}'' \times 28''$
Driving Wheels: 5′ 7″. T.E.: 29,855 lb.

30823	30830	30837	30843
30824	30831	30838	30844
30825	30832	30839	30845
30826	30833	30840	30846
30827	30834	30841	30847
30828	30835	30842	
30829	30836		

Total 45

4-6-0 Class LN

Introduced 1926
Weights: Loco. { 83 tons 10 cwt. / 84 tons 16 cwt. No. 30860)
Tender type : 38
Pressure : 220 lb. Cyls. (4) $16\frac{1}{2}'' \times 26''$
Driving Wheels: { 6′ 7″. / 6′ 3″ (30859)
T.E.: { 33,510 lb. / 33,300 lb. (30859)

30850 Lord Nelson
30851 Sir Francis Drake
30852 Sir Walter Raleigh
30853 Sir Richard Grenville
30854 Howard of Effingham
30855 Robert Blake
30856 Lord St. Vincent
30857 Lord Howe
30858 Lord Duncan
30859 Lord Hood
30860 Lord Hawke
30861 Lord Anson
30862 Lord Collin wood
30863 Lord Rodney
30864 Sir Martin Frobisher
30865 Sir John Hawkins

Total 16

4-4-0 Class V

Introduced 1930
Weights : Loco. 67 tons 2 cwt.
Tender type : 27
Pressure : 220 lb. Cyls. (3) $16\frac{1}{2}'' \times 26''$
Driving Wheels: 6′ 7″. T.E.: 25,135 lb.

30900* Eton
30901* Winchester
30902 Wellington
30903 Charterhouse
30904 Lancing
30905 Tonbridge
30906 Sherborne
30907* Dulwich
30908 Westminster
30909* St. Paul's
30910 Merchant Taylors
30911 Dover
30912 Downside
30913 Christ's Hospital
30914* Eastbourne
30915* Brighton
30916 Whitgift
30917* Ardingly
30918* Hurstpierpoint
30919* Harrow
30920* Rugby
30921* Shrewsbury
30922 Marlborough
30923 Bradfield
30924* Haileybury
30925 Cheltenham
30926 Repton
30927 Clifton
30928 Stowe
30929* Malvern
30930* Radley
30931* King's Wimbledon
30932 Blundells
30933* King's Canterbury
30934* St. Lawrence
30935 Sevenoaks

* With multiple jet blast-pipe and large diameter chimney.

30936 Cranleigh
30937* Epsom
30938* St. Olave's
30939* Leatherhead

Total 40

* Fitted with multiple jet blast pipe and large diameter chimney.

0-6-0T Ex-E. Kent Rly.

Introduced 1917
Weight : 40 tons 0 cwt.
Pressure : 160 lb. Cyls. : 17" x 24"
Driving Wheels: 5' 7". T.E.: 14,080 lb.

30948 (E.K.R. No. 4)

Total 1

0-8-0T Class KES

Introduced 1905
Weight : 47 tons 10 cwt.
Pressure : 160 lb. Cyls. 16"×24"
Driving Wheels: 4' 3". T.E.: 16,385 lb.

30949 Hecate **Total 1**

0-8-0T Class Z

Introduced 1929
Weight : 71 tons 12 cwt.
Pressure : 180 lb. Cyls (3) 19"×26"
Driving Wheels: 4' 8". T.E.:29,375 lb.

30950	30952	30954	30956
30951	30953	30955	30957

Total 8

SOUTHERN RAILWAY LOCOMOTIVE SUPERINTENDENTS AND CHIEF MECHANICAL ENGINEERS OF CONSTITUENT COMPANIES

LONDON & SOUTH WESTERN RAILWAY

J. Woods	1835–1841
J. V. Gooch	1841–1850
J. Beattie	1850–1871
W. G. Beattie	1871–1878
W. Adams	1878–1895
D. Drummond	1895–1912
R. W. Urie	1912–1922

LONDON, BRIGHTON AND SOUTH COAST RAILWAY

—. Statham	? –1845
J. Gray	1845–1847
S. Kirtley	1847
J. C. Craven	1847–1869
W. Stroudley	1870–1889
R. J. Billinton	1890–1904
D. Earle Marsh	1905–1911
L. B. Billinton	1911–1922

SOUTH EASTERN RAILWAY

B. Cubitt	? –1845
J. Cudworth	1845–1876
A. M. Watkin	1876
R. Mansell	1877–1878
J. Stirling	1878–1898

LONDON, CHATHAM AND DOVER RAILWAY

W. Cubitt	? –1860
W. Martley	1860–1874
W. Kirtley	1874–1898

SOUTH EASTERN AND CHATHAM RAILWAY

H. S. Wainwright ...	1899–1913
R. E. L. Maunsell ...	1913–1922

SOUTHERN RAILWAY

R. E. L. Maunsell ...	1923–1937
O. V. Bullied	1937–1947

SOUTHERN LOCOMOTIVES PRESERVED

Invicta, Canterbury & Whitstable Rly., 0-4-0, built 1830. On pedestal in Dane John Gardens, Canterbury.

Gladstone, L.B.S.C.R. 0-4-2 (Class B1) No. 214, built 1882, at Brighton by W. Stroudley. In York Museum.

Boxhill, L.B.S.C.R. 0-6-0T (Class A1) No. 82, Stroudley "Terrier," built 1880 at Brighton. Until 1946. No. 380S, Works Shunter‡.

No. 563, L.S.W.R., Adams T3 Class 4-4-0, built 1893 at Nine Elms‡.

‡ Housed on Southern Region system.

EASTERN SECTION

4-4-0	Class FI	4-4-0	Class EI
0-6-0	Class OI	0-6-0T	Class P
0-6-0	Class C	4-4-0	Class E
0-4-4T	Class H	4-4-0	Class D
0-6-0T	Class RI	4-4-0	Class DI
4-4-0	Class BI	0-4-0CT	Class 1302

Class	FI 4-4-0	OI 0-6-0	C 0-6-0	H 0-4-4T	RI 0-6-0T	BI 4-4-0
Intro. ...	1903 *	1903‡	1900	1904	1910‖	1910§
Wts. ...	tons cwt.	tons cwt.	tons cwt.	tons cwt.	tons cwt.	tons cwt.
Loco....	45 2	41 1*	43 16	54 8	{46 8¶ 46 15	45 2
Tender type	3	1, 42	10	—	—	6
Press. ...	170 lb.	150 lb.	160 lb.	160 lb.	160 lb.	170 lb.
Cyls. ...	18″×26″	18″×26″	18½″×26″	18″×26″	18″×26″	18″×26″
D.W. ...	7′ 0″	{5′ 1″ 5′ 2″	5′ 2″	5′ 6″	{5′ 1″ 5′ 2″	7′ 0″
T.E. ...	14,490 lb.	{17,610lb. 17,325lb.	19,520 lb.	17,360 lb.	{18,780lb. 18,480lb.	14,490 lb.

Class	EI 4-4-0	P 0-6-0T	E 4-4-0	D 4-4-0	DI 4-4-0	1302 0-4-0CT
Intro. ...	1919	1909	1905	1901	1921	1881
Wts. ...	tons cwt.	tons cwt.	tons cwt.	tons cwt.	tons cwt.	tons cwt.
Loco....	53 9	28 10	{52 5 53 10**	50 0	52 4	17 17
Tender type	12	—	13	13	11	—
Press. ...	180 lb.	160 lb.	{180 lb. 160 lb.**	175 lb.	180 lb.	120 lb.
Cyls. ...	19″×26″	12″×18″	{19½″×26″ 20½″×26″**	19″×26″	19″×26″	11″×20″
D.W. ...	6′ 6″	3′ 9⅛″	6′ 6″	6′ 8″	6′ 8″	3′ 3″
T.E. ...	18,410 lb.	7,810 lb.	{18,410 lb. 19,050 lb.**	17,450 lb.	17,950lb.	6,330 lb.

No.	*Class*	*No.*	*Class*	*No.*	*Class*	*No.*	*Class*
31003	O1	31007	O1	31018	C	31033	C
31004	C	31010	R1	31019	E1	31036	E
31005	H	31016	H	31027	P	31037	C

*Rebuilt with domed boilers from Stirling " F " Class, built 1883-98.

‡Rebuilt from Stirling " O " Class, built 1891-8.

‖Rebuilt from Stirling " R " Class, built 1888-98.

§Rebuilt from Stirling " B " Class, built 1898-9.

** Superheated engine, Nos. 31036, 31275.

¶Nos. 31010/69, 31147, 31339, modified 1938-42 by Bulleid for Whitstable branch.

No.	Class
31038	C
31039	O1
31041	O1
31044	O1
31047	R1
31048	O1
31054	C
31057	D
31059	C
31061	C
31063	C
31064	O1
31065	O1
31066	O1
31067	E1
31068	C
31069	R1
31071	C
31075	D
31078	F1
31080	O1
31086	C
31090	C
31092	D
31093	O1
31102	C
31105	F1
31106	O1
31107	R1
31108	O1
31109	O1
31112	C
31113	C
31123	O1

No	Class
31127	R1
31128	R1
31145	D1
31147	R1
31150	C
31151	F1
31154	R1
31157	E
31158	H
31159	E
31160	E1
31161	H
31162	H
31163	E1
31164	H
31165	E1
31166	E
31174	R1
31175	E
31176	E
31177	H
31178	P
31179	E1
31182	H
31184	H
31191	C
31193	H
31217	B1
31218	C
31219	C
31221	C
31223	C
31225	C
31227	C

No.	Class
31229	C
31231	F1
31234	C
31238	O1
31239	H
31242	C
31243	C
31244	C
31245	C
31246	D1
31247	D1
31248	O1
31252	C
31253	C
31255	C
31256	C
31257	C
31258	O1
31259	H
31260	C
31261	H
31263	H
31265	H
31266	H
31267	C
31268	C
31269	H
31270	C
31271	C
31272	C
31273	E
31274	H
31275	E
31276	H
31277	C
31278	H

Class F1 : Total 4

No.	Class
31279	H
31280	C
31287	C
31291	C
31293	C
31294	C
31295	H
31297	C
31298	C
31302	1302
31305	H
31306	H
31307	H
31308	H
31309	H
31310	H
31311	H
31315	E
31316	O1
31317	C
31319	H
31320	H
31321	H
31322	H
31323	P
31324	H
31325	P
31326	H
31327	H
31328	H
31329	H
31335	R1
31337	R1
31339	R1
31340	R1

Class R1 : Total 13

(*Class* D *continued No.* 31477)
(*Class* E1 *continued No.* 31497)
(*Class* B1 *continued No.* 31440)
(*Class* D1 *continued No.* 31487)
(*Class* E *continued No.* 31491)
(*Class* O1 *continued No.* 31369)
(*Class* C *continued No.* 31460)
(*Class* P *continued No.* 31555)
(*Class* H *continued No.* 31500)

0-6-0 Class O1

(*Class continued from No. 31316*)

31369	31374	31381	31390
31370	31377	31383*	31391
31371*	31378	31384	31395
31372*	31379	31385	31398
31373	31380	31389	

(*Class continued No. 31425*)

*Nos. 31383, 31372 and 31371 formerly East Kent Rly. locomotives Nos. 2, 6 and 1371 respectively.

2-6-0 Class N

Introduced 1917
Weights : Loco. 61 tons 4 cwt.
Tender type : 16, 25
Pressure : 200 lb. Cyls. 19" × 28"
Driving Wheels: 5' 6". T.E.: 26,035 lb.

31400	31404	31408	31412
31401	31405	31409	31413
31402	31406	31410	31414
31403	31407	31411	

(*Class continued No. 31810*)

0-6-0 Class O1

(*Class continued from No. 31398*)

31425	31429	31432	31438
31428	31430	31434	31439

Total 46

4-4-0 Class B1

(*Class continued from No. 31217*)

31440	31448	31452	31455
31443	31449	31454	31457
31446	31451		

Total 11

0-6-0 Class C
4-4-0 Class D1
4-4-0 Class D
4-4-0 Class E
4-4-0 Class E1
0-4-4T Class H

31460	C	31498	C
31461	C	31500	H
31470	D1	31501	D
31477	D	31502	D1
31480	C	31503	H
31481	C	31504	E1
31486	C	31505	D1
31487	D1	31506	E1
31488	D	31507	E1
31489	D1	31508	C
31490	D	31509	D1
31491	E	31510	C
31492	D1	31511	E1
31493	D	31512	H
31494	D1	31513	C
31495	C	31514	E
31496	D	31515	E
31497	E1	31516	E

CLASS CONTINUATIONS

Class	*From*	*To*	*Total*
C	31317	31572	—
D1	31247	31545	—
D	31092	31549	—
E	31315	31547	—
E1	31179	—	11
H	31329	31517	—

NOTE : To facilitate arrangement the entries between 31517 and 31554 are not in strict numerical order.

0-4-4T Class H

(*Class continued from No. 31512*)

31517	31523	31541	31550
31518	31530	31542	31551
31519	31531	31543	31552
31520	31532	31544	31553
31521	31533	31546	31554
31522	31540	31548	

Total 63

4-4-0 Class D1
4-4-0 Class E
4-4-0 Class D

31545 D1 31547 E 31549 D

CLASS CONTINUATIONS

Class	From	To	Total
D1	31509	31727	—
E	31516	31587	—
D	31501	31574	—

0-6-0T Class P

(Class continued from No. 31325)

31555 | 31556 | 31557 | 31558

Total 8

0-6-0 Class C
4-4-0 Class D
4-4-0 Class E

No.	Class	No.	Class
31572	C	31583	C
31573	C	31584	C
31574	D	31585	C
31575	C	31586	D
31576	C	31587	E
31577	D	31588	C
31578	C	31589	C
31579	C	31590	C
31580	C	31591	D
31581	C	31592	C
31582	C	31593	C

CLASS CONTINUATIONS

Class	From	To	Totals
C	31513	31681	—
D	31501	31728	—
E	31547		15

0-6-4T Class J

Introduced 1913
Weight : 70 tons 14 cwt.
Pressure : 160 lb. Cyls. 19½"×26"
Driving Wheels: 5' 6". T.E.: 20,370 lb

31595	31597	31598	31599
31596			

Total 5

0-6-0T Class T

Introduced 1879
Weight : 40 tons 15 cwt.
Pressure : 160 lb. Cyls. 17½"×24"
Driving Wheels: 4' 6". T.E.: 18,510 lb.

31602 | 31604 — 2

Service Loco — 1

Total 3

2-6-0 Class U

Introduced 1928 (Nos. 31790-31809 rebuilt from "River" Class ("K") 2-6-4T, introduced 1917)

Weights: Loco. { 62 tons 6 cwt. / 63 tons (Nos. 31790-31809)

Tender types : 19, 25

Pressure : 200 lb. Cyls. 19"×28"
Driving Wheels: 6' 0". T.E.: 23,865 lb.

31610	31618	31626	31634
31611	31619	31627	31635
31612	31620	31628	31636
31613	31621	31629	31637
31614	31622	31630	31638
31615	31623	31631	31639
31616	31624	31632	
31617	31625	31633	

(Class continued No. 31790)

0-4-4T Class R

Introduced 1891
Weight : 48 tons 15 cwt.
Pressure : 160 lb. Cyls. 17½"×24"
Driving Wheels: 5' 6". T.E.: 15,145 lb.

31658†	31662†	31667	31673
31659†	31663†	31670†	31674
31660†	31665†	31671†	31675
31661	31666†	31672†	

Total 15

0-6-0 Class C

(Class continued from No. 31593)

31681 | 31682 | 31683 | 31684

(Class continued No. 31686)

0-6-0ST Class S

Introduced 1917. Rebuilt from "C" Class.
Weight: 53 tons 10 cwt.
Pressure: 160 lb. Cyls. 18½"×26"
Driving Wheels: 5' 2". T.E.: 19,520 lb.

31685 **Total 1**

0-6-0 Class C

(Class continued from No. 31684)

31686	31689	31692	31695
31687	31690	31693	
31688	31691	31694	

(Class continued No. 31711)

0-4-4T Class R1

Introduced 1900
Weight: 52 tons 3 cwt.
Pressure: 160 lb. Cyls. 17½"×24"
Driving Wheels: 5' 6". T.E. 15,145 lb.

31696	31700†	31705	31708
31697†	31703†	31706†	31709
31698	31704†	31707†	31710†
31699			

Total 13

0-6-0 Class C

(Class continued from No. 31695)

31711	31715	31719	31723
31712	31716	31720	31724
31713	31717	31721	31725
31714	31718	31722	

Total 106

4-4-0 Class D

(Class continued from No. 31591)

4-4-0 Class D1

(Class continued from No. 31545)

No.	Class	No.	Class	No.	Class
31727	D1	31735	D1	31743	D1
31728	D	31736	D1	31744	D
31729	D	31737	D	31745	D1
31730	D	31738	D	31746	D
31731	D	31739	D1	31748	D
31732	D	31740	D	31749	D1
31733	D	31741	D1	31750	D
31734	D				

Class D: Total 28
Class D1: Total 20

4-4-0 Class L1

Introduced 1926
Weights: Loco. 57 tons 16 cwt.
Tender type: 19
Pressure: 180 lb. Cyls. 19½"×26"
Driving Wheels: 6' 8". T.E.: 18,910 lb.

31753	31755	31757	31759
31754	31756	31758	

(Class continued No. 31782)

4-4-0 Class L

Introduced 1914
Weights: Loco. 57 tons 9 cwt.
Tender type: 14
Pressure: 180 lb. Cyls. 19½"×26"
Driving Wheels: 6' 8". T.E.: 18,910 lb.

31760	31766	31772	31778
31761	31767	31773	31779
31762	31768	31774	31780
31763	31769	31775	31781
31764	31770	31776	
31765	31771	31777	

Total 22

4-4-0 Class L1

(Class continued from No. 31759)

31782	31784	31786	31788
31783	31785	31787	31789

Total 15

2-6-0 Class U

(Class continued from No. 31639)

31790	31795	31800	31805
31791	31796	31801	31806
31792	31797	31802	31807
31793	31798	31803	31808
31794	31799	31804	31809

Total 50

2-6-0 Class N

(Class continued from No. 31414)

31810	31813	31816	31819
31811	31814	31817	31820
31812	31815	31818	31821

(Class continued No. 31823)

2-6-0 Class N1

Introduced 1922
Weights: Loco. 64 tons 5 cwt.
Tender type: 25
Pressure: 200 lbs. Cyls. (3) 16" × 28"
Driving Wheels: 5' 6". T.E.: 27,695 lb.

31822

(*Class continued No.* 31876)

2-6-0 Class N

(*Class continued from No.* 31821)

31823	31837	31851	31864
31824	31838	31852	31865
31825	31839	31853	31866
31826	31840	31854	31867
31827	31841	31855	31868
31828	31842	31856	31869
31829	31843	31857	31870
31830	31844	31858	31871
31831	31845	31859	31872
31832	31846	31860	31873
31833	31847	31861	31874
31834	31848	31862	31875
31835	31849	31863	
31836	31850		

Total 80

2-6-0 Class N1

(*Class continued from No.* 31822)

31876	31878	31879	31880
31877			

Total 6

2-6-0 Class U1

Introduced 1925 (No. 31890 rebuilt from "K1" Class 2-6-4T built 1925)
Weights: Loco. 65 tons 6 cwt.
Tender types: 19, 25
Pressure: 200 lb. Cyls. (3) 16" × 28"
Driving Wheels: 6' 0". T.E.: 25,385 lb.

31890	31892	31894	31896
31891	31893	31895	31897
31898	31902	31906	31910
31899	31903	31907	
31900	31904	31908	
31901	31905	31909	

Total 21

NOTE

Throughout this book the information given against the heading "Tender type" in the details of locomotive dimensions refers to the table of S.R. tenders on pages 46/7, where each type of tender is described and numbered; information is also given as to the allocation of tenders to respective engines in a class shown as equipped with more than one type of tender.

2-6-4T Class W

Introduced 1931
Weight: 90 tons 14 cwt.
Pressure: 200 lb. Cyls. (3) 16½" × 28"
Driving Wheels: 5' 6". T.E.: 29,450 lb.

31911	31915	31919	31923
31912	31916	31920	31924
31913	31917	31921	31925
31914	31918	31922	

Total 15

CENTRAL SECTION

4-4-2T Class I1X

Rbt. class introduced 1925
Weight: 71 tons 18 cwt.
Pressure: 180 lb. Cyls. 17½" × 26"
Driving Wheels: 5' 6". T.E.: 18,450 lb.

32002	32005	32008	32009
32004			

(*Class continued No.* 32595)

4-4-2T Class I3

Introduced: 1907 (No. 32021); 1908 (Nos. 32022-30/75-81); 1912 (Remainder)
Weights: 75 tons 10 cwt. (No. 32021); 76 tons (Remainder)
Pressure: 180 lb.
Cyls.: 19" × 26" (No. 32021); 20" × 26" (1908 type); 21" × 26" (1912 type)
Driving Wheels: 6' 9" (No. 32021); 6' 7½" (Remainder)
T.E.: 17,730 lb. (No. 32021); 20,015 lb. (1908 type); 22,065 lb. (1912 type)

32021	32025	32027	32029
32022	32026	32028	32030
32023			

(*Class continued No.* 32075)

4-4-2 Class H1

Introduced 1905
Weights : Loco. 68 tons 5 cwt.
Tender type : 15
Pressure : 200 lb. Cyls. 19" × 26"
Driving Wheels : 6' 7½". T.E.: 20,070 lb.

32037 Selsey Bill
32038 Portland Bill
32039* Hartland Point

Total 3

4-4-0 Classes B4 & B4X

	B4	B4X (Rebuilt from B4)
Introduced ...	1899	1922
Weights :	*tons cwt.*	*tons cwt.*
Loco. ...	51 10	58 1
Tender type...	7	22
Pressure ...	180 lb.	180 lb.
Cyls.	19"×26"	20"×26"
Driving Wheels	6' 9"	6' 9"
T.E.	17,730 lb.	19,645 lb.

32043 B4X
32045 B4X
32050 B4X
32051 B4
32052 B4X
32054 B4
32055 B4X
32056 B4X
32060 B4X
32062 B4
32063 B4
32067 B4X
32068 B4
32070 B4X
32071 B4X
32072 B4X
32073 B4X
32074 B4

Class B4 : Total 6
Class B4X : Total 12

4-4-2T Class I3

(Class continued from No. 32030)

32075, 32076, 32077, 32078, 32079, 32080, 32081, 32082, 32083, 32084, 32085, 32086, 32087, 32088, 32089, 32090, 32091

Total 26

*Modified 1947 with sleeve valves for experimental purposes.

0-6-2T Class E1/R

Introduced 1927 (Rebuilt from Class E1)
Weight : 50 tons 5 cwt.
Pressure : 170 lb. Cyls. 17" × 24"
Driving Wheels : 4' 6". T.E.: 18,560 lb.

32094 | 32095 | 32096

(Class continued No. 32124)

0-6-0T Class E1

Introduced 1874
Weight : 44 tons 3 cwt.
Pressure : 170 lb. Cyls. 17" × 24"
Driving Wheels : 4' 6". T.E.: 18,600 lb.

32097

(Class continued No. 32112)

0-6-0T Class E2

Introduced 1913
Weight { 52tons 15cwt. (Nos. 32100-4) / 53tons 10cwt. (Nos. 32105-9‡)
Pressure : 170 lb. Cyls. 17½" × 26"
Driving Wheels : 4' 6". T.E.: 21,305 lb.

32100, 32101, 32102, 32103, 32104, 32105, 32106, 32107, 32108, 32109

Total 10

0-6-0T Class E1

(Class continued from No. 32097)

0-6-2T Class E1/R

(Class continued from No. 32096)

32112 E1
32113 E1
32124 E1/R
32127 E1
32128 E1
32129 E1
32133 E1
32135 E1/R
32138 E1
32139 E1
32141 E1
32142 E1
32145 E1
32147 E1
32151 E1
32153 E1
32156 E1
32160 E1
32162 E1

(Class E1 continued No. 32689)
(Class E1/R continued No. 32608)

‡With 1,256 gallon tanks. Others with 1,090 gallon tanks.

Left: "Lord Nelson" Class 4-6-0 No. 30864 *Sir Martin Frobisher*

[*Photo : W. Gilbert*

Right: Class "N15X" 4-6-0 No. 2330 *Cudworth* (new No. 32330)

[*Photo : F. F. Moss*

Above: Class " N15 " 4-6-0 No. s453 *King Arthur* (new No. 30453)
[*Photo : B. V. Franey*

Left : Class " T14 " 4-6-0 No. 461 (new No. 30461)
[*Photo : G. L. Hoare*

Below: Class " S15 " 4-6-0 No. 828 (new No. 30828)
[*Photo: H. C. Casserley*

Above: Class "H2" 4-4-2 No. 2421 *South Foreland* (new No. 32421)
[*Photo* :
C. C. B. Herbert

Right : Class "H1" 4-4-2 No. 2038 *Portland Bill* (new No. 32038)

Below : Class "V" 4-4-0 No. 937 *Epsom* (new No. 30937)
[*Photos: F. F. Moss*

Above : " West Country " 4-6-2 No. 21C138 (new No. 34038) heads an up evening Continental express through Sydenham Hill

[*Photo : E. R. Wethersett*

BULLEID

Below : " Merchant Navy " Class 4-6-2 No. 21C15 *Rotterdam Lloyd* Bournemouth stage of her journey

Above : "Battle of Britain" Class 4-6-2 No. 21C154 *Lord Beaverbrook* (new No. 34054) passes Shorncliffe with an up Continental express

[*Photo : Rev. A. C. Cawston*

ACIFICS

w No. 35015) crossing Redbridge Causeway on the Southampton- the down "Bournemouth Belle"

[*Photo : F. F. Moss*

Class " Q1 " 0-6-0 No. C26 (new No. 33026) [Photo : A R. Venning

[Photo : P. Ransome-Wallis

Class " 0395 " 0-6-0 No. 30576 and Class " R1 " 0-6-0T No. 31069

Class " C " 0-6-0 No. s1245 (new No. 31245) [Photo : B. V. Franey

Class " Z " 0-8-0T No. s953 (new No. 30953) [*Photo P. L. Melvill*

Class " I3 " 4-4-2T No. 2028 (new No. 32028) [*Photo : H. C. Casserley*

Class " 0415 " 4-4-2T No. 3520 (new No. 30584) [*Photo : A. F. Cook*

Left : Class " K " 2-6-0 No. 2351 (new No. 32351)

[*Photo : F. Burtt*

Right: Class " N " 2-6-0 No. s1858 (new No. 31858)

Photo : M. W. Earley

0-6-2T Class E3

Introduced 1894
Weight : 56 tons 15 cwt.
Pressure : { 160 lb. (Nos. 32453-62) / 170 lb. (Nos. 32165-70) }
Cyls.: $17\frac{1}{2}$" × 26"
Driving Wheels : 4' 6"
T.E. { 20,055 lb. (Nos. 32453-62) / 21,305 lb. (Nos. 32165-70) }

32165	32167	32169	32170
32166	32168		

(*Class continued No. 32453*)

0-4-2T Class D1

Introduced 1873
Weight : 43 tons 10 cwt.
Pressure : 170 lb. Cyls. 17" × 24"
Driving Wheels : 5' 6". T.E.: 15,185 lb.

32215†	32235†	32253†	32283†
32234†	32252†	32274	32299†

(*Class continued No. 32358*)

0-6-0 Class C3

Introduced 1906
Weights : Loco. 47 tons 10 cwt.
Tender type : 5, 8.
Pressure : 170 lb. Cyls. $17\frac{1}{2}$" × 26"
Driving Wheels : 5' 0". T.E.: 19,200 lb.

32300	32302	32306	32308
32301	32303	32307	32309

Total 8

4-6-2T Classes J1 & J2

Introduced { 1910 (J1, No. 2325) / 1912 (J2, No. 2326) }
Weight : 89 tons
Pressure : 170 lb. Cyls. 21" × 26"
Driving Wheels: 6' $7\frac{1}{2}$". T.E.: 20,840 lb.

No. Class	No. Class
32325 J1	32326 J2

Class J1 : Total 1
Class J2 : Total 1

4-6-0 Class N15X

Rbt. (1934-6) from 4-6-4T introduced 1914
Weights : Loco. 73 tons 2 cwt.
Tender type : 36
Pressure : 180 lb. Cyls. 21" × 28"
Driving Wheels : 6' 9". T.E.: 23,325 lb.

32327 Trevithick
32328 Hackworth
32329 Stephenson
32330 Cudworth
32331 Beattie
32332 Stroudley
32333 Remembrance

Total 7

2-6-0 Class K

Introduced 1913
Weights : Loco. 63 tons 15 cwt.
Tender type : 24
Pressure : 180 lb. Cyls. 21" × 26"
Driving Wheels : 5' 6". T.E.: 26,580 lb.

32337	32342	32346	32350
32338	32343	32347	32351
32339	32344	32348	32352
32340	32345	32349	32353
32341			

Total 17

0-4-2T Class D1

(*Class continued from No. 32299*)

32358† 32359

(*Class continued No. 32605*)

0-4-4T Class D3

Introduced 1892
Weight 52 tons
Pressure : 170 lb. Cyls. $17\frac{1}{2}$" × 26"
Driving Wheels : 5' 6". T.E.: 17,435 lb.

32364†	32374†	32384†	32391†
32365†	32376†	32385†	32393†
32366†	32377†	32386†	32394†
32367†	32378†	32387†	32395†
32368†	32379†	32388†	32398†
32372†	32380†	32389†	
32373†	32383†	32390†	

Total 26

0-6-2T Classes E5 & E5X

	E5	E5X (Rebuilt from E5)
Introduced ...	1902	1911
	tons cwt.	*tons cwt.*
Weight ...	60 0	64 5
Pressure ...	{160 lb. / 175 lb.	170 lb.
Cyls.	17½"×26"	17½"×26"
Driving Wheels	5' 6"	5' 6"
T.E. ...	16,410 lb.	17,400 lb.

32399 E5	32404 E5
32400 E5	32405 E5
32401 E5X	32406 E5
32402 E5	

(*Classes continued No. 32567*)

0-6-2T Classes E6 & E6X

	E6	E6X (Rebuilt from E6)
Introduced ...	1904	1911
	tons cwt.	*tons cwt.*
Weight ...	61 0	63 0
Pressure {	160 lb. / 175 lb.	170 lb.
Cyls.	18"×26"	18"×26"
Driving Wheels	4' 6"	4' 6"
T.E. ... {	21,215 lb. / 23,205 lb.	22,540 lb.

32407 E6X	32413 E6
32408 E6	32414 E6
32409 E6	32415 E6
32410 E6	32416 E6
32411 E6X	32417 E6
32412 E6	32418 E6

Class E6 : Total 10

Class E6X : Total 2

4-4-2T Class H2

Introduced 1911
Weights : Loco. 68 tons 5 cwt.
Tender type : 15
Pressure : 200 lb. Cyls. 21" × 26"
Driving Wheels: 6' 7½". T.E.: 24,520 lb.

32421 South Foreland
32422 North Foreland
32423 The Needles
32424 Beachy Head
32425 Trevose Head
32426 St. Alban's Head

Total 6

0-6-0 Classes C2 & C2X

	C2	C2X (Rebuilt from C2)
Introduced ...	1893	1908
Weights :	*tons cwt.*	*tons cwt.*
Loco. ...	39 10	45 5
Tender type...	4	4
Pressure ...	160 lb.	170 lb.
Cyls.	17½"×26"	17½"×26"
Driving Wheels	5' 0"	5' 0"
T.E.	18,050 lb.	19,175 lb.

32434 C2X	32444 C2X
32436 C2	32445 C2X
32437 C2X	32446 C2X
32438 C2X	32447 C2X
32440 C2X	32448 C2X
32441 C2X	32449 C2X
32442 C2X	32450 C2X
32443 C2X	32451 C2X

(*Classes continued No. 32521*)

0-6-2T Class E3

(*Class continued from No. 32170*)

32453	32456	32459	32461
32454	32457	32460	32462
32455	32458		

Total 16

0-6-2T Classes E4 & E4X

		E4	E4X (Rebuilt from E4)
Introduced	...	1897–1903	1909–1911
		tons cwt.	tons cwt.
Weight		57 10 56 15	59 5
Pressure		160 lb. 170 lb.	170 lb.
Cyls.	...	17½"×26"	17½"×26"
Driving Wheels		5' 0"	5' 0"
T.E.	...	18,050 lb. 19,175 lb.	19,175 lb.

32463 E4
32464 E4
32465 E4
32466 E4X
32467 E4
32468 E4
32469 E4
32470 E4
32471 E4
32472 E4
32473 E4
32474 E4
32475 E4
32476 E4
32477 E4X
32478 E4X
32479 E4
32480 E4
32481 E4
32482 E4
32484 E4
32485 E4
32486 E4
32487 E4
32488 E4
32489 E4X
32490 E4
32491 E4
32492 E4
32493 E4
32494 E4
32495 E4
32496 E4
32497 E4
32498 E4
32499 E4
32500 E4
32501 E4
32502 E4
32503 E4
32504 E4
32505 E4
32506 E4
32507 E4
32508 E4
32509 E4
32510*E4
32511 E4
32512 E4
32513 E4
32514 E4
32515 E4
32516 E4
32517 E4
32518 E4
32519 E4
32520 E4

Class E4X : Total 4

(Class E4 Continued No. 32556)

* Working in I.O.W.

0-6-0 Classes C2 & C2X

(Classes continued from No. 32451)

32521 C2X
32522 C2X
32523 C2X
32524 C2X
32525 C2X
32526 C2X
32527 C2X
32528 C2X
32529 C2X
32532 C2X
32533 C2
32534 C2X
32535 C2X
32536 C2X
32537 C2X
32538 C2X
32539 C2X
32540 C2X
32541 C2X
32543 C2X
32544 C2X
32545 C2X
32546 C2X
32547 C2X
32548 C2X
32549 C2X
32550 C2X
32551 C2X
32552 C2X
32553 C2X
32554 C2X

Class C2 : Total 2
Class C2X : Total 45

0-6-2T Class E4

(Class continued from No. 32520)

32556 E4
32557 E4
32558 E4
32559 E4
32560 E4
32561 E4
32562 E4
32563 E4
32564 E4
32565 E4
32566 E4

(Class continued No. 32577)

0-6-2T Classes E5 & E5X

(Classes continued from No. 32406)

32567 E5
32568 E5
32570 E5X
32571 E5
32572 E5
32573 E5
32574 E5
32575 E5
32576 E5X

(Classes continued No. 32583)

0-6-2T Class E4

(Class continued from No. 32566)

32577
32578
32579
32580
32581
32582

Total 70

0-6-2T Classes E5 & E5X

(Classes continued from No. 32576)

32583 E5	32589 E5
32584 E5	32590 E5
32585 E5	32591 E5
32586 E5X	32592 E5
32587 E5	32593 E5
32588 E5	32594 E5

Class E5 : Total 24
Class E5X : Total 4

4-4-2T Class I1X

(Class continued from No. 32009)

32595 | 32596 | 32602 | 32603

Total 9

0-4-2T Class D1

(Class continued from No. 32359)

32605† 11
Service Locos 2

Total 13

0-6-2T Class E1/R

(Class continued from No. 32135)

32608 E1/R | 32610 E1/R

(Class continued No. 32695)

0-6-0T Class A1X

Rbt. from A class introduced 1872
Weight : 28 tons 5 cwt.
Pressure : 150 lb. Cyls. { 12" × 20" / 14 3/16" × 20"†
Driving Wheels : 4' 0".
T.E. : { 7,650 lb. / 10,695 lb.

32636†	32647	32661	32670*
32640	32655	32662	32678
32644	32659		

(Class continued I.O.W. Locos, p. 38)

* Formerly K. & E.S.R. No. 3.

0-6-0T Class E1

(Class continued from No. 32162)

0-6-2T Class E1/R

(Class continued from No. 32610)

32689 E1	32695 E1/R
32690 E1	32696 E1/R
32691 E1	32697 E1/R
32694 E1	

Class E1/R : Total 10

(Class E1 continued I.O.W. Locos, p. 38)

0-6-0 Class Q1

Introduced 1942
Weights : Loco. 51 tons 5 cwt.
Tender type : 23
Pressure : 230 lb. Cyls. 19" × 26"
Driving Wheels : 5' 1". T.E.: 30,080 lb.
(Former S.R. numbers C1-C40)

33001	33011	33021	33031
33002	33012	33022	33032
33003	33013	33023	33033
33004	33014	33024	33034
33005	33015	33025	33035
33006	33016	33026	33036
33007	33017	33027	33037
33008	33018	33028	33038
33009	33019	33029	33039
33010	33020	33030	33040

Total 40

4-6-2 Classes WC & BB

Introduced 1945
Weights : Loco. 86 tons 0 cwt.
Tender type : 30,39a
Pressure : 280 lb. Cyls. (3) 16 3/8" × 24"
Driving Wheels : 6' 2". T.E.: 31,050 lb.
(Former S.R. Nos. 21C101-70 (34001-70); remainder entered service numbered as shown)

"West Country" Class

34001 Exeter
34002 Salisbury
34003 Plymouth
34004 Yeovil
34005 Barnstaple
34006 Bude

34007 Wadebridge
34008 Padstow
34009 Lyme Regis
34010 Sidmouth
34011 Tavistock
34012 Launceston
34013 Okehampton
34014 Budleigh Salterton
34015 Exmouth
34016 Bodmin
34017 Ilfracombe
34018 Axminster
34019 Bideford
34020 Seaton
34021 Dartmoor
34022 Exmoor
34023 Blackmoor Vale
34024 Tamar Valley
34025 Rough Tor
34026 Yes Tor
34027 Taw Valley
34028 Eddystone
34029 Lundy
34030 Watersmeet
34031 Torrington
34032 Camelford
34033 Chard
34034 Honiton
34035 Shaftesbury
34036 Westward Ho !
34037 Clovelly
34038 Lynton
34039 Boscastle
34040 Crewkerne
34041 Wilton
34042 Dorchester
34043 Combe Martin
34044 Woolacombe
34045 Ottery St. Mary
34046 Braunton
34047 Callington
34048 Crediton

Total 48

"Battle of Britain" Class

34049 Anti-Aircraft Command
34050 Royal Observer Corps
34051 Winston Churchill
34052 Lord Dowding
34053 Sir Keith Park
34054 Lord Beaverbrook
34055 Fighter Pilot
34056 Croydon
34057 Biggin Hill
34058 Sir Frederick Pile
34059 Sir Archibald Sinclair
34060 25 Squadron
34061 73 Squadron
34062 17 Squadron
34063 229 Squadron
34064 Fighter Command
34065 Hurricane
34066 Spitfire
34067 Tangmere
34068 Kenley
34069 Hawkinge
34070 Manston
34071 601 Squadron
34072 257 Squadron
34073 249 Squadron
34074 46 Squadron
34075 264 Squadron
34076 41 Squadron
34077 603 Squadron
34078 222 Squadron
34079 141 Squadron
34080 74 Squadron
34081 92 Squadron
34082 615 Squadron
34083 605 Squadron
34084 253 Squadron
34085 501 Squadron
34086 219 Squadron
34087 145 Squadron
34088 213 Squadron
34089 602 Squadron
34090 66 Squadron

Total 42

NOTE : Not all the above nameplates have been fitted. The names selected and the locomotives to which they are allotted are therefore liable to alteration.

35001-35030 and I.o.W. 1-34

4-6-2 Class MN

Introduced 1941
Weights : Loco. 94 tons 15 cwt.
Tender types : 33, 34, 41
Pressure : 280 lb. Cyls. (3) 18" × 24"
Driving Wheels : 6' 2". T.E.: 37,515 lb.

(Former S.R. Nos. 21C1-20 (Nos. 35001-20) ; remainder entered service numbered as shown)

35001 Channel Packet
35002 Union Castle
35003 Royal Mail
35004 Cunard White Star
35005‡ Canadian Pacific
35006 Peninsular & Oriental S.N. Co.
35007 Aberdeen Commonwealth
35008 Orient Line
35009 Shaw Savill
35010 Blue Star
35011 General Steam Navigation
35012 United States Line
35013 Blue Funnel
35014 Nederland Line
35015 Rotterdam Lloyd
35016 Elders Fyffes
35017 Belgian Marine
35018 British India Line
35019 French Line CGT
35020 Bibby Line
35021 New Zealand Line
35022 Holland-America Line
35023 Holland-Afrika Line
35024 East Asiatic Company
35025 Brocklebank Line
35026* Lamport & Holt Line
35027* Port Line
35028* Clan Line
35029* Ellerman Lines
35030* Elder Dempster Lines

Total 30

‡ Fitted with mechanical stoker

* Not yet in service.

ISLE OF WIGHT ENGINES

0-6-0T Class E1

1 Medina
2 Yarmouth
3 Ryde
4 Wroxall

4
From p. 36 22

Total 26

0-6-0T Class A1X

8 Freshwater
13 Carisbrooke

2
From p. 36 10
Service Locos 2

Total 14

0-4-4T Class O2

14 Fishbourne
15 Cowes
16 Ventnor
17 Seaview
18 Ningwood
19 Osborne
20 Shanklin
21 Sandown
22 Brading
23 Totland
24 Calbourne
25 Godshill
26 Whitwell
27 Merstone
28 Ashey
29 Alverstone
30 Shorwell
31 Chale
32 Bonchurch
33 Bembridge
34 Newport

21
From p. 10 27

Total 48

SOUTHERN REGION SERVICE LOCOS.

No.	Old No.	Class	Station
‖ 49 S	—	Shunter	Broad Clyst Sleep. Depot
* 74 S	—	Bo-Bo	Durnsford Rd Power Stn.
* 75 S	—	Bo	Waterloo & City Rly.
77 S	0745	C14	Redbridge Sleep. Depot
‖ 343 S	—	Shunter	Eastleign Carr. Works
‖ 346 S	—	Inspection Car	Engin'r's Dept.
‡ 377 S	2635	AIX	Brighton Wks.
§ 400 S	—	0-4-0	S'hampton Dks.
500 S	1607	T	Meldon Quarry
515 S	L.B.S.C. 650 I.W. 9	AIX	Lancing Carr. Wks.
680 S	L.B.S.C. 654 SEC. 751,	A 1	"
700 S	2244	D I	Eastleigh**
701 S	2284	D I	Fratton**

* Electric § Fowler Diesel ‡ Repainted 1947 in Stroudley livery ‖ Petrol
** Oil Pumping Engines

POWER CLASSIFICATION

Some types of locomotive on the Western Section of the Southern Region are classified under letters A—K according to powers of haulage, "A" being the most powerful and " K " at the opposite end of the scale. The appropriate " haulage classification " letter has hitherto appeared on the side of the framing near the front buffer beam but is relegated to the cabside on engines recently repainted in " B.R." livery. The locomotives in each power classification are as follows :

A : G16, H15, H16, Lord Nelson, N15, Q1, S15, V.
B : Q, T14 **C :** 700 **D :** D15, L12
E : S11 **F :** K10, L11 **G :** 0395
H : T9 **I :** X6 **J :** A12
K : All tank locos (except G16, H16)

A similar system, except that "A" represents the lowest power, is in use in the Isle of Wight, as follows :

A : A1X **B :** O2 **C :** E1

The above classification is to be superseded by one based on the ex-L.M.S. system of power rating (*see inside back cover*).

DIMENSIONS OF BRITISH RAILWAYS DIESEL ELECTRIC LOCOMOTIVES

Region	Type	Date	Weight tons cwt.	Driving Wheels ft. ins.	H.P.	T.E.
L.M.	0-6-6-0	1947	121 10	3 6	1,600	41,400 lb.
L.M.	0-6-0	1936	{51 0 47 0}	4 0½	350	30,000 lb.
L.M.	0-6-0	1939	54 16	4 3	350	33,000 lb.
L.M.	0-6-0	1945	50 0	4 0½	350	33,000 lb.
L.M.	0-6-0	1934	40 10	3 6	250	24,000 lb.
E.	0-6-0	1944	51 0	4 0	350	32,000 lb.
W.	0-6-0	1936	{51 10 46 9}	4 0½	350	{30,000 lb. 33,500 lb.
S.	0-6-0	1937	55 5	4 6	350	30,000 lb.

DIMENSIONS OF BRITISH RAILWAYS ELECTRIC LOCOMOTIVES

Region	Class	Type	Date	Weight tons cwt.	Voltage	T.E.
S.	C.C.	Co + Co	1942-5	{99 14 104 14}	600 D.C.	40,000 lb.
E. & N.E.	E.M.I.	Bo + Bo	1941	87 18	1,500 D.C.	45,000 lb.
N.E.	E.B.I	Bo + Bo	1914	74 8	1,500 D.C.	28,000 lb.
N.E.	E.S.I	Bo + Bo	1905	56 0	600 D.C.	25,000 lb.
N.E.	E.E.I	2 - Co - 2	1922	110 1	1,500 D.C.	28,000 lb.

PRINCIPAL DIMENSIONS of SOUTHERN REGION STEAM LOCOMOTIVES

Entries in *italics* under the headings " Designers " and " Building Date " refer to engine classes officially listed as " Rebuilt."
Unless otherwise stated, two cylinders are understood. The number of cylinders above two is entered in brackets—e.g. (4)—in the " cylinders " column.
The building or rebuilding dates are those of the entire class and not necessarily those of the individual engines surviving.

Class	Wheels	Designer	Building Date	Weight of Loco. tons	cwt.	Boiler Pressure lb. per sq. in.	Cylinders in.	Driving Wheels	Tractive Effort at 85% B.P. lb.	No. of locos.	
A1(a)	0–6–0T	Stroudley	1872–80	27	10	150	12 × 20	4′ 0″	7,650	1	" Terriers "
A1X	0-6-0T	*Marsh* *	*1911–47*	28	5	150	12 × 20 / 14 3/16 × 20	4′ 0″	7,650 / 10,695	14	" Rooters "
A12	0-4-2	Adams	1887–95	42	7	160	18 × 26	6′ 0″	15,910	2	" Jubilees "
B1(b)	4-4-0	*Wainwright*	*1910–27*	45	2	170	18 × 26	7′ 0″	14,490	11	" Flying Bedsteads "
B4	0-4-0T	Adams / Drummond	1891–93 / 1908	33 / 32	9 / 18	140	16 × 22	3′ 9¾″	14,650	22	—
B4	4-4-0	R. Billinton	1899–02	51	10	180	19 × 26	6′ 9″	17,730	6	" Scotchmen "
B4X	4-4-0	*L. Billington* *	*1922–24*	58	1	180	20 × 26	6′ 9″	19,645	12	" Greybacks "
C	0-6-0	Wainwright	1900–08	43	16	160	18½ × 26	5′ 2″	19,520	106	—
C2	0-6-0	R. Billinton	1893–02	39	10	160	17½ × 26	5′ 0″	18,050	2	" Small Vulcans "
C2X	0-6-0	*Marsh* *	*1908–40*	45	5	170	17½ × 26	5′ 0″	19,175	45	' Large Vulcans "
C3	0-6-0	Marsh	1906	47	10	170	17½ × 26	5′ 0″	19,175	8	" Marsh Goods "
C14(c)	0-4-0T	*Urie*	*1913–23*	25	15	150	14 × 14	3′ 0″	9,720	3	" Potato Cans "
D	4-4-0	Wainwright	1901–07	50	0	175	19 × 26	6′ 8″	17,450	28	" Coppertops "
D1	4-4-0	*Maunsell**	*1921–27*	52	4	180	19 × 26	6′ 8″	17,950	20	—
D1	0-4-2T	Stroudley	1873–87	43	10	170	17 × 24	5′ 6″	15,185	13	" D Tanks "

* Rebuilt from preceding class.
(*a*) Service locomotive, see p. 39.
(*b*) Rebuilt from Stirling " B " Class, built 1898-99.
(c) Converted from Drummond 2-2-0T, built 1906-07.

ABBREVIATIONS—C.T., Crane Tank.
K.E.S.R., Kent & East Sussex Rly.
L.C.D.R., London, Chatham & Dover Rly.
P.D.S.W.J.R., Plymouth, Devonport & S.W. Junction Rly.
S.T., Saddle Tank.
W.T., Well Tank.

Principal Dimensions of Southern Region Locomotives—*continued*

Class	Wheels	Designer	Building Date	Weight of Loco. tons	cwt.	Boiler Pressure lb. per sq. in.	Cylinders in.	Driving Wheels	Tractive Effort at 85% B.P. lb.	No. of locos.	
D3	0-4-4T	R. Billinton	1892–96	52	17	170	17½ × 26	5′ 6″	17,435	26	"Bogie Tanks"
D15(a)	4-4-0	*Urie*	1915–16	61	11	180	20 × 26	6′ 7″	20,140	10	—
E	4-4-0	Wainwright	1905–09	52	5	180	19 × 26	6′ 6″	18,410	13	—
				53	10	160	20½ × 26		19,050	2	
E1	4-4-0	*Maunsell* *	1919–20	53	9	180	19 × 26	6′ 6″	18,410	11	—
E1	0-6-0T	Stroudley	1874–91	44	3	170	17 × 24	4′ 6″	18,560	26	"Black Tanks"
E1/R	0-6-2T	*Maunsell**	1927–29	50	5	170	17 × 24	4′ 6″	18,560	10	"E1 Radials"
E2	0-6-0T	L. Billinton	1913–16	52	15	170	17½ × 26	4′ 6″	21,305	10	—
				53	10						
E3	0-6-2T	R. Billinton	1894–95	56	10	160	17½ × 26	4′ 6″	20,055	16	"Small Radials"
						170			21,305		
E4	0-6-2T	R. Billinton	1897–03	57	10	160	17½ × 26	5′ 0″	18,050	70	"Radials"
				56	15	170			19,175		
E4X	0-6-2T	*Marsh* *	1909–11	59	5	170	17½ × 26	5′ 0″	19,175	4	—
E5	0-6-2T	R. Billinton	1902–04	60	0	160	17½ × 26	5′ 6″	16,410	24	"Large Radials"
						175			17,945		
E5X	0-6-2T	*Marsh* *	1911	64	5	170	17½ × 26	5′ 6″	17,435	4	—
E6	0-6-2T	R. Billinton	1904–05	61	0	160	18 × 26	4′ 6″	21,215	10	—
						175			23,205		
E6X	0-6-2T	*Marsh* *	1911	63	0	170	18 × 26	4′ 6″	22,540	2	—
F1(b)	4-4-0	*Wainwright*	1903–19	45	2	170	18 × 26	7′ 0″	14,490	4	"Jumbos"
G6	0-6-0T	Adams	1894–00	47	13	160	17½ × 24	4′ 10″	17,235	32	—
G16	4-8-0T	Urie	1921	95	2	180	22 × 28	5′ 1″	33,990	4	"Hump Engines"
H	0-4-4T	Wainwright	1904–15	54	8	160	18 × 26	5′ 6″	17,360	63	—
H1	4-4-2	Marsh	1905–06	68	5	200	19 × 26	6′ 7½″	20,070	3	"Atlantics"
H2	4-4-2	Marsh(e)	1911–12	68	5	200	21 × 26	6′ 7½″	24,520	6	"Atlantics"
H15	4-6-0	*Urie 330-334(c)*	1924–25	80	11	175	21 × 28	6′ 0″	25,510	6	—
		Urie 335(c)	1914	82	1						

H15		Urie 482–490	1914	81	5	180	21 × 28	6′ 0″	26,240	9	—
Contin-ued		Urie 491	1914								
		Maunsell 473–8, & 521–4	1924	79	19	180	21 × 28	6′ 0″	26,240	11	—
									Total	26	
H16	4-6-2T	Urie	1921–22	96	8	180	21 × 28	5′ 7″	28,200	5	" Green Tanks "
I1X	4-4-2T	*Maunsell* (*d*)	1925–32	71	18	180	17½ × 26	5′ 6″	18,460	9	" Wankers "
I3	4-4-2T	Marsh (32021)	1907	75	10	180	19 × 26	6′ 9″	17,730		
		32082–91 (e)	1912–13	76	0	180	21 × 26	6′ 7½″	22,065	26	" Marsh Tanks "
		(Others)	1908–10	76	0	180	20 × 26	6′ 7½″	20,015		
J	0-6-4T	Wainwright	1913	70	14	160	19½ × 26	5′ 6″	20,370	5	—
J1	4-6-2T	Marsh	1910	89	0	170	21 × 26	6′ 7½″	20,840	1	" Pacific Tanks "
J2	4-6-2T	Marsh(e)	1912	89	0	170	21 × 26	6′ 7½″	20,840	1	
K	2-6-0	L. Billinton	1913–21	63	15	180	21 × 26	5′ 6″	26,580	17	" Moguls "
K10	4-4-0	Drummond	1901–02	46	14	175	18½ × 26	5′ 7″	19,755	23	" Small Hoppers "
KES	0-8-0T	Hawthorn Leslie	1905	47	10	160	16 × 24	4′ 3″	16,385	1	(Ex-K.E.S.R.)
L	4-4-0	Wainwright	1914	57	9	180	19½ × 26	6′ 8″	18,910	22	" German Engines "
L1	4-4-0	Maunsell	1926	57	16	180	19½ × 26	6′ 8″	18,910	15	—
L11	4-4-0	Drummond	1903–07	50	11	175	18½ × 26	5′ 7″	19,755	40	" Large Hoppers "
L12(f)	4-4-0	*Urie*	1915–22	55	5	175	19 × 26	6′ 7″	17,675	20	" Bulldogs "
LN	4-6-0	Maunsell	1926–29	83	10	220	(4) 16½ × 26	6′ 7″	33,510	16	" Nelsons "
				84	16						
				60	3						
M7	0-4-4T	Drummond	1897–11	60	4	175	18½ × 26	5′ 7″	19,755	103	" Motor Tanks "
				62	0						
MN	4-6-2	Bulleid	1941–45	94	15	280	(3) 18 × 24	6′ 2″	37,515	30†	" Merchant Navy "
N	2-6-0	Maunsell	1917–34	61	4	200	19 × 28	5′ 6″	26,035	80	" Mongolipers "
N1	2-6-0	Maunsell	1922–30	64	5	200	(3) 16 × 28	5′ 6″	27,695	6	" Woolworths " —

NOTES

(*) Rebuilt from preceding Class.

(†) Includes 10 now being delivered (12/48).

(*a*) Rebuilt with Superheater from Drummond engines built 1912.

(*b*) Rebuilt with domed boilers from Stirling " F " Class built 1883-98.

(*c*) Nos. 330-335 rebuilt from Drummond 4-cyl. 4-6-0s built 1905-07.

(*d*) Rebuilt from Marsh I1 Class built 1906-07.

(*e*) Modified by L. Billinton.

(*f*) Rebuilt from Drummond engines built 1904-05.

Principal Dimensions of Southern Region Locomotives—*continued*

Class	Wheels	Designer	Building Date	Weight of Loco. tons	cwt.	Boiler Pressure lb. per sq. in.	Cylinders in.	Driving Wheels	Tractive Effort at 85% B.P. lb.	No. of locos.	
N15	4-6-0	Maunsell(448-52) (453–7)	1925	80 79	19 18	200	20½ × 28	6′ 7″	25,320	10	"Eastleigh Arthurs"
		Urie (736-54) (755)	1918–23	80	7	180	21 × 28 22 × 28	6′ 7″	23,915 26,245	19 1	"Urie Arthurs"
		Maunsell (763-92)	1925	80	19	200	20½ × 28	6′ 7″	25,320	30	"Scotch Arthurs"
		Maunsell (793-806)	1926–27	81	17	200	20½ × 28	6′ 7″	25,320	14	
									Total	74	
N15X	4-6-0	*Maunsell*(b)	1934–36	73	2	180	21 × 28	6′ 9″	23,325	7	"Remembrance"
O1	0-6-0	*Wainwright*(c)	1903–27 & 1945‡	41	1	150	18 × 26	5′ 1″ 5′ 2″	17,610 17,325	46	—
O2	0-4-4T	Adams	1889–95	46 48	18 8	160	17½ × 24	4′ 10″	17,235	48	—
P	0-6-0T	Wainwright	1909–10	28	10	160	12 × 18	3′ 9⅛″	7,810	8	—
Q	0-6-0	Maunsell	1938–39	49	10	200	19 × 26	5′ 1″	26,160	20	—
Q1	0-6-0	Bulleid	1942	51	5	230	19 × 26	5′ 1″	30,080	40	"Charlies
R	0-4-4T	Kirtley (L.C.D.R.)	1891–92	48	15	160	17½ × 24	5′ 6″	15,145	15	"Bob tails
R1	0-4-4T	Kirtley (d)	1900	52	3	160	17½ × 24	5′ 6″	15,145	13	—
R1	0-6-0T	*Wainwright* (e)	1910–22	46 46	8 15	160	18 × 26	5′ 1″ 5′ 2″ 5′ 1″	18,780 18,480 18,780	4 9	— —
S	0-6-0ST	*Maunsell* (f)	1917	53	10	160	18½ × 26	5′ 2″	19,520	1	—
S11	4-4-0	*Urie* (g)	1920–22	53	15	175	19 × 26	6′ 0″	19,390	10	—
S15	4-6-0	Urie (496-515)	1920–21	79	16	180	21 × 28	5′ 7″	28,200	45	—
		Maunsell (823-837) (m) (838-847)	1927–28 1927–36	80 79	14 5	200	20½ × 28	5′ 7″	29,855		
T	0-6-0T	Kirtley	1879–93	40	15	160	17½ × 24	4′ 6″	18,510	3	—

T1	0-4-4T	Adams	1888–96	57	2	160	18 × 26	5′ 7″	17,100	9	
T9	4-4-0	*Urie* (h)	1922–29	51 51 51	16 18 7	175	19 × 26	6′ 7″	17,675	66	"Greyhounds"
T14	4-6-0	*Urie* (j)	1915–18	76	10	175	(4) 15 × 26	6′ 7″	22,030	9	"Paddleboxes"
U	2-6-0	Maunsell (k)	1917 1928–31	62 63	6 0	200	19 × 28	6′ 0″	23,865	50	"U Boats"
U1	2-6-0	Maunsell (k)	1925–31	65	6	200	(3) 16 × 28	6′ 0″	25,385	21	"U Boats"
V	4-4-0	Maunsell	1930–35	67	2	220	(3) 16½ × 26	6′ 7″	25,135	40	"Schools"
W	2-6-4T	Maunsell	1931–36	90	14	200	(3) 16½ × 28	5′ 6″	29,450	15	—
W.C. & B.B.	4-6-2	Bulleid	1945	86	0	280	(3) 16⅝ × 24	6′ 2″	31,050	90	"West Country" "Battle of Britain"
Z	0-8-0T	Maunsell	1929	71	12	180	(3) 16 × 28	4′ 8″	29,375	8	—
700	0-6-0	*Urie* (m)	1920–29	46	14	180	19 × 26	5′ 1″	23,540	30	"Black Motors"
756	0-6-0T	Hawthorn Leslie	1907	35	15	170	14 × 22	3′ 10″	13,545	1	Ex-P.D.S.W.J.R.
757	0-6-2T	Hawthorn Leslie	1907	49	19	170	16 × 24	4′ 0″	18,495	2	Ex-P.D.S.W.J.R.
1302	0-4-0CT	Neilson	1881	17	17	120	11 × 20	3′ 3″	6,330	1	Crane
0298	2-4-0WT	Beattie	1874–75	37	16	160	16½ × 20	5′ 7″	11,050	3	"Beattie Tanks"
0395	0-6-0	Adams	1881–86	37 38	12 14	140 150	17½ × 26	5′ 1″	15,535 16,645	18	"Jumbos"
0458	0-4-0ST	Hawthorn Leslie	1890	21	2	120	12 × 20	3′ 2″	7,730	1	"Dock Engines"
0415	4-4-2T	Adams	1882–5	55	2	160	17½ × 24	5′ 7″	14,920	3	"Radial Tanks"
U.S.A.	0-6-0T	Vulcan Ironworks	1942–3	46	10	210	16½ × 24	4′ 6″	21,600	14	—
30948	0–6–0T	Kerr, Stuart	1917	40	0	160	17 × 24	5′ 7″	14,080	1	Ex-East Kent Rly.

NOTES

(†) Date of first 2-6-4T, subsequently rebuilt as Class U

(‡) O1 boiler fitted to East Kent Rly. No. 6 (Now 31372), which, however, retained the O-class Stirling cab.

(*a*) Incorporating parts of Drummond 4-cyl. 4-6-0s built 1908-11.

(*b*) Rebuilt from L. Billinton's "L" Class 4-6-4T built 1914-22

(*c*) Rebuilt from Stirling "O" Class built 1878-99.

(*d*) Modified by Wainwright. This Class and Class R have been rebuilt with H-Class boilers.

(*e*) Rebuilt from Stirling "R" Class built 1888-98.

(*f*) No. 1685 rebuilt from C Class.

(*g*) Rebuilt with Superheater from Drummond engines built 1903.

(*h*) Rebuilt with Superheater from Drummond engines built 1899-01.

(j) Rebuilt from Drummond 4-6-0 built 1911-12, modified by Maunsell 1930-31 with superheater.

(*k*) Class U includes 20 rebuilt "River" (K) Class 2-6-4T and Class U1 includes one rebuilt "River" (K1) Class (No. 31890). All rebuilt thus 1928.

(*m*) Rebuilt with Superheater from Drummond engines built 1897.

Service Locomotives are counted in the above totals.

SOUTHERN REGION LOCO TENDERS

The numbers in the extreme left-hand column refer to those shown against the entry "tender type" in the list of dimensions at the head of each class in the locomotive lists.

Ref. in Text	No. of wheels	Water (galls.)	Wheel-base ft.	in.	Weight full t.	c.	Engine Classes fitted
(1)	6	2,100	12	0	28	5	O1
(2)	6	2,500	13	0	28	13	O395, except as below.
(3)	6	2,650	12	0	30	10	F1
(4)	6	2,835	13	0	33	10	C2, C2x
(5)	6	2,985	13	0	35	15	C3 in part.
(6)	6	3,000	12	0	34	2	B1
(7)	6	3,000	13	0	35	5	B4
(8)	6	3,112	13	0	37	5	C3 in part
(9)	6	3,300	13	0	33	4	A12 and 0395 30567/72/80
(10)	6	3,300	13	0	38	5	C
(11)	6	3,300	13	0	39	0	D1
(12)	6	3,450	13	0	39	0	E1
(13)	6	3,450	13	0	39	2	D, E
(14)	6	3,450	13	0	40	6	L
(15)	6	3,500	13	0	39	5	H1, H2
(16)	6	3,500	13	0	39	5	N 31810-21/3-75 N1 31822
(17)	6	3,500	13	0	39	12	D15 T9 30300/1/4/7/10/1/2/3/36 S11 30395/7 "700" 30316/26/39/46/50, 30687/8/94, 30699-701
(18)	6	3,500	14	0	39	12	K10 30137/40/1 30345/84/93/4 L11 30440/1 L12 30416/7/9/21/2/4/5/30/1/3 T9 30281/2, 30704/26/9 "700" other than those listed under (17)
(19)	6	3,500	13	0	40	10	L1, Q, U31790—809, U1 31890
(20)	6	3,500	13	0	40	14	K10 30142/5/51/2/3, 30329/41/83/5/9/90

SOUTHERN REGION LOCO TENDERS— *Continued*

Ref. in Text	No. of wheels	Water (galls.)	Wheel-base ft.	in.	Weight full t.	c.	Engine Classes fitted
(21)	6	3,500	13	0	41	5	N15 30793-806
(22)	6	3,600	13	0	39	5	B4x
(23)	6	3,700	13	0	38	0	Q1
(24)	6	3,940	13	0	41	10	K
(25)	6	4,000	13	0	42	8	N (31400-14), N1 (other than 31822), U (other than 31790—809), U1 (other than 31890)
(26)	6	4,000	13	0	42	8	S15 30833-7
(27)	6	4,000	13	0	42	8	V
(28)	8	4,000	14	6	44	17	L11 (other than those listed above and below) S15 30504-10 ; K10, L12, S11, T9 (other than those listed above)
(29)	8	4,300	14	6	49	3	H15 30330-4 ; N15 30448-57
(30)	6	4,500	13	0	42	12	WC and BB (other than those listed below)
(31)	8	4,500	14	6	48	12	H15 30335
(32)	8	4,500	14	6	49	0	L11 30164/6, 30405/35/9
(33)	6	5,000	13	0	47	16	MN 35001-10
(34)	6	5,000	13	0	49	7	MN 35011-20
(35)	8	5,000	19	0	56	8	S15 30823-32, 30838-47
(36)	8	5,000	19	0	57	11	H15 30473-8, 30521/4 ; N15 30763-92 ; N15x
(37)	8	5,000	19	0	57	16	N15 30736-55 ; S15 30496-503, 30511-5
(38)	8	5,000	19	0	57	19	LN
(39)	8	5,200	19	0	57	14	H15 30482-90/1
(39a)	8	5,500	13	0	47	5	BB 34071-90
(40)	8	5,800	16	6	60	8	T14
(41)	6	6,000	13	0	52	7	MN 35021-30
(42)	8	Various	12	0	Various		O1‡

* Drummond

‡ Ex-LCDR " M " Class, water capacities average 2,510 gals. weights average 31 tons 0 cwt.

SOME S.R. LOCOMOTIVE HEAD SIGNALS

This list is not complete and gives only the principal one and two disc (or lamp) codes.

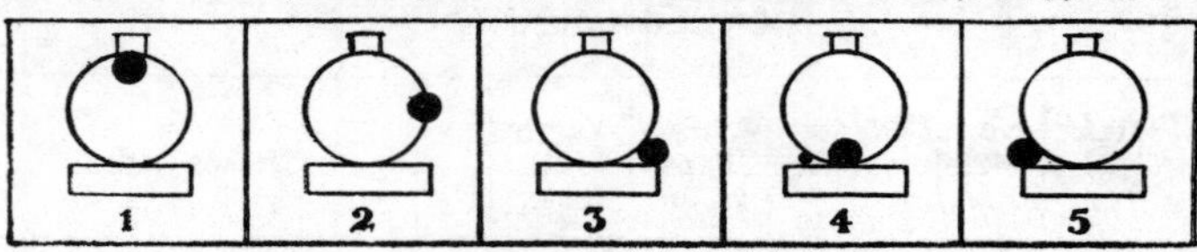

NO. 1

Victoria and Dover via Chatham
Victoria and Norwood Yard via Selhurst
Loughborough Sidings to Holborn
Ashford and Hastings
Reading and Margate via Redhill
Eastleigh and Bulford via Chandlers Ford and Andover
Southampton Terminus and Brockenhurst and Weymouth via Wimborne
Weymouth, Portland and Easton (Passenger Trains)
Plymouth Friary and Tavistock
Woking and Reading via Virginia Water West Curve
Exeter Central and Ilfracombe
Bodmin and Wadebridge
Petersfield and Midhurst
Exeter Central and Exmouth

NO. 2

Victoria or Clapham Junction and Holborn (L.L.)
London Bridge or Bricklayers' Arms and Portsmouth via Quarry line and Horsham
Via Mid Kent line and Beckenham Junction
Ashford and Eastbourne direct
Waterloo or Nine Elms and Southampton Terminus, direct (not boat trains)
Willesden and Feltham Yard via Gunnersbury
Waterloo or Nine Elms and Windsor via Twickenham
Southampton Central to Lymington
Yeovil Junction and Yeovil Town
Seaton Junction and Seaton
Barnstaple Junction and Torrington
Halwill and Bude

NO. 3

Victoria or Clapham Junction and Holborn
London Bridge or Bricklayers' Arms and Brighton via Quarry line
Tonbridge and Brighton via Eridge
Hastings via Mid Kent line, Oxted, Crowhurst Junction and Tonbridge
Dunton Green and Westerham
Ashford and Margate via Canterbury West
Lydd Branch
Canterbury West and Whitstable Harbour
Sandling Junction and Hythe
Folkestone Junction and Folkestone Harbour
Crowhurst and Bexhill
Swanley Junction and Gravesend West Street
Sittingbourne and Sheerness
Queenborough and Leysdown
Deal and Kearsney
Gravesend Central and Allhallows-on-Sea or Port Victoria
All stations to Feltham (except via Mortlake)
Weymouth and Portland and Easton (goods trains)
Bournemouth West and Brockenhurst via Wimborne

Right: Class "T" 0-6-0T No. 1602 (new No. 31602)

Below: Class "G6" 0-6-0T No. 351 (new No. 30351)

[*Photos: H. C. Casserley*

Right: Class "R1" 0-6-0T No. 1335 (new No. 31335)

[*Photo: A. F. Cook*

Above: Class "D3" 0-4-4T No. 2393 (new No. 32393)

[*Photo: H. C. Casserley*

Left: Class "M7" 0-4-4T No. 255 (new No. 30255)

[*Photo: B. V. Franey*

Below: Class "R" 0-4-4T No. 1665 (new No. 31665)

[*Photo: H. C. Casserley*

Above : Class "E1" 0-6-0T No. 2112 (new No. 32112)
[Photo : A. F. Cook

Right : Class "E5X" 0-6-2T No. 32586
[Photo: A. S. H.Taylor

Below: Class "E5" 0-6-2T No. 32584
[Photo : A. F. Cook

Left: Class "C14" 0-4-0T No. 3744 (new No. 30589)

[*Photo: H. C. Casserley*

Right: 0-4-0CT No. 1302 (new No. 31302)

[*Photo: H.C.Casserley*

Left: Diesel Shunter No. 400S (Docks Engineer's Dept., Southampton)

[*Photo: A. F. Cook*

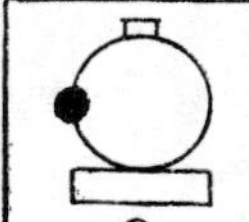

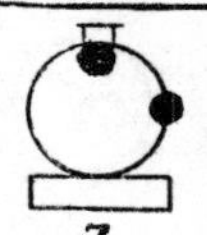

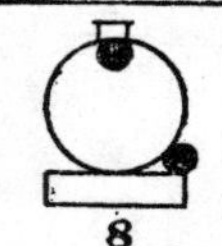

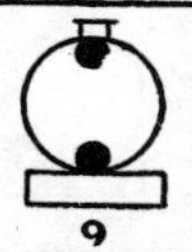

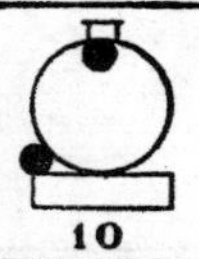

NO. 4

Victoria or Battersea Yard and Brighton via Redhill
Oxted and Eastbourne via Eridge
London Bridge and New Cross Gate via Bricklayers' Arms Junction
Horsham and Brighton
Brookwood and Bisley Camp
Alton and Fareham
Bentley and Bordon
Salisbury and Bulford
Axminster and Lyme Regis
Tipton St. John's and Exmouth
Wareham and Swanage
Brockenhurst and Lymington Pier
Bere Alston and Callington

NO. 5

Victoria or Stewarts Lane and Clapham Junction
Oxted and Tunbridge Wells West via East Grinstead (H.L.)
Pulborough, Midhurst and Chichester
Havant and Hayling Island
London Bridge and Bricklayers' Arms
Tonbridge and Maidstone West
Ashford (Kent) and Dover via Minster and Deal
Elham Valley line
Stewarts Lane to Victoria
Southampton Docks and Nine Elms via main line (market goods, fruit or potato train)
Light engines to Nine Elms

NO. 6

London Bridge or Bricklayers' Arms and Dover or Ramsgate via East Croydon Oxted and Tonbridge
Tonbridge and Hawkhurst
Battersea Yard and Kensington
Waterloo or Nine Elms and Reading via Twickenham
Willesden and Feltham Yard via Kew East Junction
Exeter Central and Sidmouth
Plymouth Friary and Turnchapel
Eastleigh or Southampton and Fawley
Bournemouth Central and Brockenhurst via Wimborne
Torrington and Halwill

NO. 7

Victoria or Battersea Yard and Portsmouth via Quarry line and Horsham
Via Maidstone East line to Victoria or Holborn
Waterloo or Nine Elms and Southampton Docks via Brentford, Chertsey and Woking

NO. 8

London Bridge or Bricklayers' Arms and Eastbourne or Hastings via Quarry line
Victoria or West London line and Ramsgate via Herne Hill or Catford Loop
London Bridge or Bricklayers' Arms and Hastings via Chislehurst and Tunbridge Wells Central

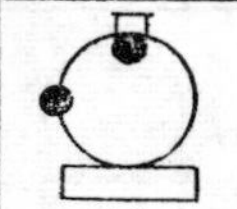

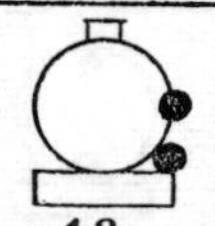

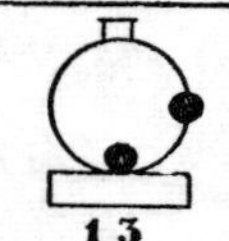

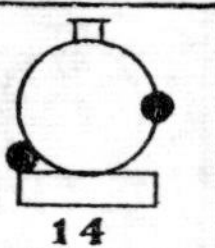

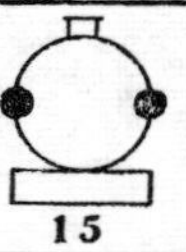

West London line to East Croydon via Crystal Palace (L.L.)
Special boat trains Waterloo and Southampton Docks via Northam
Special boat trains from Southampton Docks to Waterloo via Millbrook
Southampton and Andover via Redbridge

NO. 9

Victoria or Battersea Yard and Eastbourne or Hastings via Quarry line
London and Hither Green Sidings
Victoria and Folkestone Harbour or Dover Marine via Swanley, Otford and Tonbridge
Waterloo or Nine Elms and Plymouth
Bournemouth Central and Dorchester goods trains
Battersea Yard and Brent via New Kew Junction
Southampton Terminus and Portsmouth Harbour via Netley

NO. 10

London Bridge or Bricklayers' Arms and Portsmouth via Redhill and Horsham
Victoria or Battersea Yard and Norwood Yard via Crystal Palace (L.L.)
London Bridge and New Cross Gate to Eardley Sidings via Peckham Rye
Deptford Wharf and New Cross Gate
London Bridge or Bricklayers' Arms and Folkestone or Dover via Chislehurst, Tonbridge and Ashford
Dover and Margate via Deal and Minster Loop
Special boat trains Waterloo to Southampton Docks via Millbrook
Feltham to Wimbledon via Chertsey

NO. 11

Victoria or Battersea Yard and Portsmouth via Redhill and Horsham
Via Dartford Loop line
Victoria or Holborn and Hastings Branch via Orpington Loop and Tunbridge Wells Central
Bricklayers' Arms and Guildford via Leatherhead and Effingham Junction
Waterloo or Nine Elms and Southampton Terminus via Alton
Salisbury and Bournemouth West via Wimborne
Fareham and Gosport
Ballast trains to Meldon Quarry from Exeter Central and stations West thereof

NO. 12

Victoria or Battersea Yard and Portsmouth via Mitcham Junction
London Bridge or Bricklayers' Arms and Eastbourne or Hastings via Redhill
Victoria, Stewarts Lane or Holborn to North Kent line via Nunhead line
Nine Elms and Feltham Yard via Mortlake
Exeter Central to Nine Elms (market goods and fish)
Down main line goods trains terminating at Woking
Southampton Docks and Salisbury via Eastleigh

NO. 13

London Bridge or Bricklayers' Arms and Brighton via Redhill
Oxted and Brighton via East Grinstead (L.L.) and Lewes
Three Bridges and Tunbridge Wells West
West London line to Norwood Yard via Thornton Heath
Victoria or Holborn to Dover via Nunhead line and Maidstone East
Parcels and empty trains Waterloo to Clapham Junction (Kensington sidings)

Feltham Yard and Neasden via Kew East Junction
Portsmouth Harbour or Portsmouth and Southsea to Fratton Loco. Depot
Exeter Central and Exmouth Junction
Bournemouth West to Dorchester
Southampton and Salisbury via Redbridge

NO. 14

London Bridge and Portsmouth via Mitcham Junction
London Bridge, Oxted and Tunbridge Wells West via Hever
Oxted and Lewes or Seaford or Eastbourne via Haywards Heath and Keymer Junction (change to No. 5 or No. 21 code at Lewes)
London Bridge or Bricklayers' Arms and Dover via Chislehurst Loop and Maidstone East
Waterloo or Nine Elms and Brockenhurst and Bournemouth West via Sway

NO. 15

Via Bexley Heath line
Victoria, Stewarts Lane or Holborn via Nunhead line and Bexley Heath
Oxted and Brighton via Haywards Heath
Waterloo or Nine Elms and Reading via loop line
All trains terminating at Portsmouth and Southsea (trains from Salisbury to carry No. 17 to Eastleigh)
Exeter Central and Padstow
Light engines, Bournemouth Central or Bournemouth West to Bournemouth Central via triangle to turn
Light engines Eastleigh Loco. to Portsmouth and Southsea
Light engines to Guildford Loco. via Woking (except via Staines)

NO. 16

London Bridge or Bricklayers' Arms and Portsmouth via West Croydon
Victoria or Battersea Yard and Eastbourne or Hastings via Redhill
Oxted and Brighton via Eridge
London Bridge or Bricklayers' Arms and Ramsgate via Tonbridge and Canterbury West
Waterloo or Nine Elms and Woking via Richmond and Chertsey
Milk and empty trains to Clapham Junction via Byfleet curve and Richmond

NO. 17

London Bridge or Bricklayers' Arms and Tonbridge or Reading via East Croydon and Redhill (also Tonbridge and Reading)
Brighton and Hove via Preston Park Spur
Three Bridges and Eridge
Victoria or Holborn and Folkestone or Dover via Orpington Loop, Tonbridge and Ashford.
London Bridge or Bricklayers' Arms and Gillingham, Faversham, Ramsgate or Dover via Chislehurst Loop and Chatham
Waterloo or Nine Elms and Clapham Junction (empty trains and light engines)
Passenger trains Bournemouth Central and Weymouth

. 18

London Bridge or Bricklayers' Arms and Dover, Ramsgate or Hastings via Chislehurst, Swanley, Otford and Sevenoaks
Victoria, Oxted and Tunbridge Wells West via Hever
Holborn and Ramsgate via Herne Hill or Catford Loop
Light engines and trains requiring to run to up main loop, Clapham Junction, from stations westward
Southampton and Andover via Eastleigh
Light engines or engines with vehicles attached running round the triangle at Bournemouth West to turn

NO. 19

Victoria or Battersea Yard and Brighton via Quarry line
London Bridge or New Cross Gate and Norwood Yard
Tunbridge Wells West and Eastbourne
Victoria or Holborn and Ramsgate, Dover or Hastings via Nunhead line and Tonbridge
Horsham and Guildford
Waterloo or Nine Elms and Southampton Docks via East Putney
Salisbury and Portsmouth Harbour via Eastleigh
Portsmouth and Southsea to Salisbury via Eastleigh

NO. 20

Victoria, Stewarts Lane or Holborn to Ramsgate via Nunhead line, Chislehurst and Chatham
London Bridge or Bricklayers' Arms and North Kent line via Greenwich
Via Streatham Spur
Feltham Yard and Brent via Kew East Junction
Clapham Junction and Kensington
Portsmouth and Southsea to Salisbury via Redbridge
Salisbury and Portsmouth Harbour via Redbridge

NO. 21

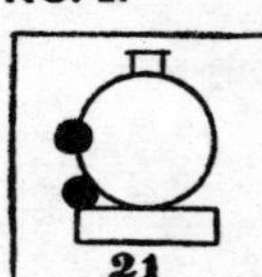

Victoria and Newhaven Harbour
Victoria or Holborn to Ramsgate via Nunhead line and Maidstone East
Waterloo or Nine Elms and Portsmouth via Woking and Guildford
Light engines from all stations to Feltham Loco.
Light engines from all stations West of Basingstoke to Eastleigh Loco.

There are several three disc codes in use though most of these are for race specials. The Plymouth-Brighton, Cardiff-Brighton and Bournemouth-Brighton through services are denoted by three disc codes and Royal Specials utilize the standard British four lamp head signal.

THE **ABC** OF BRITISH LOCOMOTIVES

PART 3

40000-59999

STEAM LOCOMOTIVES :
LONDON MIDLAND REGION
SCOTTISH (ex. L.M.S.) REGION

LONDON :

Ian Allan Ltd

1948

FOREWORD

This booklet lists all British Railways locomotives numbered between 40000 and 59999. This series of numbers includes all London Midland Region and Scottish (ex-L.M.S.) Region steam locos., i.e. steam locomotives of the former L.M.S.R. Under the general British Railways numbering scheme, the numbers of L.M.S.R. steam locomotives were increased by 40000, with certain exceptions which were to be completely renumbered. Renumbering is being carried out only as locomotives visit main works, and thus it will be some time before all locomotives bear the numbers shown in this book.

Former L.M.S.R. diesel and diesel-electric locomotives are to be renumbered, in common with all British Railways locomotives of similar propulsion, between 10000 and 29999, and details of them will be found in the ABC of British Raulways' Locomotives Nos. 10000-39999.

NOTES ON THE USE OF THIS BOOK

1. Where locomotives have been renumbered other than by the addition of 40000 to their former L.M.S.R. number the details of former L.M.S.R. numbers are given.
2. Where building of new locomotives is in progress, the numbers allocated to such engines have been included with a note to show that they are not yet in service.
3. All engines are fitted with two cylinders unless otherwise stated, e.g. (4) = four cylinders.
4. Tender weights have not been included in the lists of dimensions owing to the numerous variations in weight within individual classes.

The contents of this book are
correct to 31st August, 1948

2-6-2T 3P

Introduced : 1930.
Weight : { 70 tons 10 cwt. / 71 tons 16 cwt. †
Pressure : 200 lb.
Cyls. : 17½" × 26".
Driving Wheels : 5' 3".
Tractive Effort : 21,485 lb.
Walschaerts Valve Gear.
Superheated. Parallel Boiler.

40001	40019	40037†	40054
40002	40020	40038†	40055
40003	40021†	40039†	40056
40004	40022†	40040†	40057
40005	40023†	40041	40058
40006	40024†	40042	40059
40007	40025†	40043	40060
40008	40026†	40044	40061
40009	40027†	40045	40062
40010	40028†	40046	40063
40011	40029†	40047	40064
40012	40030†	40048	40065
40013	40031†	40049	40066
40014	40032†	40050	40067
40015	40033†	40051	40068
40016	40034†	40052	40069
40017	40035†	40053	40070
40018	40036†		Total 70

† Fitted with condensing apparatus.

2-6-2T 3P

Introduced 1935.
Weight : { 71 tons 5 cwt. / 72 tons 10 cwt. *
Pressure : 200 lb.
Cyls. : 17½" × 26".
Driving Wheels : 5' 3"
Tractive Effort : 21,485 lb.
Walschaerts Valve Gear.
Superheated. Taper boiler.

40071	40083	40095	40107
40072	40084	40096	40108
40073	40085	40097	40109
40074	40086	40098	40110
40075	40087	40099	40111
40076	40088	40100	40112
40077	40089	40101	40113
40078	40090	40102	40114
40079	40091	40103	40115
40080	40092	40104	40116
40081	40093	40105	40117
40082	40094	40106	40118

40119	40142	40165	40188
40120	40143	40166	40189
40121	40144	40167	40190
40122	40145	40168	40191
40123	40146	40169*	40192
40124	40147	40170	40193
40125	40148*	40171	40194
40126	40149	40172	40195
40127	40150	40173	40196
40128	40151	40174	40197
40129	40152	40175	40198
40130	40153	40176	40199
40131	40154	40177	40200
40132	40155	40178	40201
40133	40156	40179	40202
40134	40157	40180	40203*
40135	40158	40181	40204
40136	40159	40182	40205
40137	40160	40183	40206
40138	40161	40184	40207
40139	40162	40185	40208
40140	40163*	40186	40209
40141	40164	40187	Total 139

* Rebuilt with larger boiler, 1941.

4-4-0 2P

Introduced: 1914-21. S. & D.J.
Weight : Loco. 53 tons 7 cwt.
Pressure: 160 lb.
Cyls. : 20½" × 26"
Driving Wheels : 7' 0½".
Tractive Effort : 17,585 lb.
Superheated.

40322	40324	40325	40326
40323			Total 5

4-4-0 2P

Introduced : 1882-91. Midland. Rebuilt 1910 onwards.
Weight : Loco. 53 tons 7 cwt.
Pressure : 160 lb.
Cyls. : { 18" × 26". † / 20½" × 26".
Driving Wheels : { 6' 6½". † / 7' 0½".
Tractive Effort : { 15,960 lb. † / 17,585 lb.
† Non superheated engines. Remainde superheated.

40332	40353	40362	40377
40337	40356	40364	40383†
40351	40359	40370	40385†

40391†	40395	40396	40397
40394			

Total 17

4-4-0 2P

Introduced : 1891-1901. Midland Rebuilt 1912-23.
Weight : Loco. 53 tons 7 cwt.
Pressure : 160 lb.
Cyls. : 20½″ × 26″.
Driving Wheels : 7′ 0½″.
Tractive Effort : 17,585 lb.
Superheated.

40400	40443	40492	40528
40401	40444	40493	40529
40402	40446	40494	40530
40403	40447	40495	40531
40404	40448	40496	40532
40405	40450	40497	40533
40406	40452	40498	40534
40407	40453	40499	40535
40408	40454	40500	40536
40409	40455	40501	40537
40410	40456	40502	40538
40411	40458	40503	40539
40412	40459	40504	40540
40413	40461	40505	40541
40414	40462	40506	40542
40415	40463	40507	40543
40416	40464	40508	40544
40417	40466	40509	40545
40418	40468	40510	40546
40419	40470	40511	40547
40420	40471	40512	40548
40421	40472	40513	40549
40422	40477	40514	40550
40423	40478	40515	40551
40424	40479	40516	40552
40425	40480	40517	40553
40426	40482	40518	40554
40427	40483	40519	40555
40430	40484	40520	40556
40432	40485	40521	40557
40433	40486	40522	40558
40434	40487	40523	40559
40436	40488	40524	40560
40437	40489	40525	40561
40438	40490	40526	40562
40439	40491	40527	

Total 143

4-4-0 2P

Introduced : 1928-9. L.M.S.
Weight : Loco. 54 tons 1 cwt.
Pressure : 180 lb.
Cyls. : 19″ × 26″.
Driving Wheels : 6″ 9″.
Tractive Effort : 17,730 lb.
Superheated.

40563	40598	40632	40667
40564	40599	40633*	40668
40565	40600	40634*	40669
40566	40601	40635*	40670
40567	40602	40636	40671
40568	40603	40637	40672
40569	40604	40638	40673
40570	40605	40640	40674
40571	40606	40641	40675
40572	40607	40642	40676
40573	40608	40643	40677
40574	40609	40644	40678
40575	40610	40645	40679
40576	40611	40646	40680
40577	40612	40647	40681
40578	40613	40648	40682
40579	40614	40649	40683
40580	40615	40650	40684
40581	40616	40651	40685
40582	40617	40652	40686
40583	40618	40653	40687
40584	40619	40654	40688
40585	40620	40655	40689
40586	40621	40656	40690
40587	40622	40657	40691
40588	40623	40658	40692
40589	40624	40659	40693
40590	40625	40660	40694
40592	40626	40661	40695
40593	40627	40662	40696
40594	40628	40663	40697
40595	40629	40664	40698
40596	40630	40665	40699
40597	40631	40666	40700

Total 136

* Ex-S.D.J.R., Nos. 44, 45, and 46. (In same order).

4-4-0 3P

Introduced : 1901. Midland. Rebuilt and Superheated.
Weight : Loco. 55 tons 7 cwt.
Pressure : 175 lb.
Cyls. : 20½" × 26".
Driving Wheels : 6' 9".
Tractive Effort : 20,065 lb.

40711	40729	40740	40756
40720	40731	40741	40758
40726	40734	40743	40762
40727	40735	40745	
40728	40739	40747	

Total 18

4-4-0 (3-Cyl. Compd.) 4P

Introduced : 1924. L.M.S.
Weight : Loco. 61 tons 14 cwt.
Pressure 200 lb.
Cyls.: H.P. (2) 21"×26". L.P. (1) 19"×26"
Driving Wheels : 6' 9".
Tractive Effort : 22,650 lb. *
Superheated.

40900	40910	40920	40930
40901	40911	40921	40931
40902	40912	40922	40932
40903	40913	40923	40933
40904	40914	40924	40934
40905	40915	40925	40935
40906	40916	40926	40936
40907	40917	40927	40937
40908	40918	40928	40938
40909	40919	40929	40939

* T.E. of L.P. cylinders at 80 p.c. b.p.
(*Class continued Nos.* 41045-41199).

4-4-0 (3-Cyl. Compd.) 4P

Introduced : 1905. Midland.
Weight : Loco. 61 tons 14 cwt.
Pressure : 200 lb.
Cyls.: (2) 21"×26" L.P. (1) 19"×26" H.P.
Driving Wheels : 7' 0".
Tractive Effort : 21,840 lb. *
Superheated (Fowler).

41000†	41005‡	41009	41013
41001†	41006	41010	41014
41003†	41007	41011	41015
41004†	41008	41012	41016
41017	41025	41035	41042
41019	41027	41036	41043
41020	41028	41037	41044
41021	41030	41038	
41022	41031	41039	
41023	41032	41040	
41024	41034	41041	

Total 40

† Built Johnson, 1902-03, rebuilt, 1914-19.
‡ Built Deeley, 1905, rebuilt 1932.
* T.E. of L.P. cylinders at 80 p.c. b.p.

4-4-0 (3-Cyl. Compd.) 4P

(*Class continued from No.* 40939).

41045	41077	41109	41141
41046	41078	41110	41142
41047	41079	41111	41143
41048	41080	41112	41144
41049	41081	41113	41145
41050	41082	41114	41146
41051	41083	41115	41147
41052	41084	41116	41148
41053	41085	41117	41149
41054	41086	41118	41150
41055	41087	41119	41151
41056	41088	41120	41152
41057	41089	41121	41153
41058	41090	41122	41154
41059	41091	41123	41155
41060	41092	41124	41156
41061	41093	41125	41157
41062	41094	41126	41158
41063	41095	41127	41159
41064	41096	41128	41160
41065	41097	41129	41161
41066	41098	41130	41162
41067	41099	41131	41163
41068	41100	41132	41164
41069	41101	41133	41165
41070	41102	41134	41166
41071	41103	41135	41167
41072	41104	41136	41168
41073	41105	41137	41169
41074	41106	41138	41170
41075	41107	41139	41171
41076	41108	41140	41172

41173-41895

41173	41180	41187	41194
41174	41181	41188	41195
41175	41182	41189	41196
41176	41183	41190	41197
41177	41184	41191	41198
41178	41185	41192	41199
41179	41186	41193	

(from page 5) 40

155

Total 195

2-6-2T 2P

Introduced : 1946. L.M.S.
Weight : 63 tons 5 cwt.
Pressure : 200 lb.
Cyls. : 16″ × 24″.
Driving Wheels : 5′ 0″.
Tractive Effort : 17,410 lb.
Walschaerts Valve Gear.
Superheated. Taper Boiler.

41200	41208	41216	41224
41201	41209	41217	41225
41202	41210	41218	41226
41203	41211	41219	41227
41204	41212	41220	41228
41205	41213	41221	41229
41206	41214	41222	
41207	41215	41223	

N.B.—Still being delivered.

0-4-0ST 0F

Introduced : 1897. Midland.
Driving Wheels : 3′ 10″.

	Weight tons	Weight cwt.	Cyls.	T.E. lb.
41516*	23	3	20″ × 13″	8,745
41518*	32	3	20″ × 15″	11,640
41523†	32	3	20″ × 15″	12,475

Total 3

* Pressure : 140 lb.
† Pressure : 150 lb.

0-4-0T 0F

Introduced : 1907. Midland.
Weight : 32 tons 16 cwt.
Pressure : 160 lb.
Cyls. : 15″ × 22″.
Driving Wheels : 3′ 9¼.″
Tractive Effort : 14,635 lb.
Walschaerts Valve Gear.

41528	41531	41534	41536
41529	41532	41535	41537
41530	41533		

Total 10

0-6-0T 1F

Introduced : 1878. Midland.
Weight : 39 tons 11 cwt.
Cyls. : 17″ × 24″.
Driving Wheels : 4′ 7″.
Tractive Effort : 16,080 lb. (Pressure 150 lb).
15,005 lb. (Pressure 140 lb).

41660	41727	41793	41854
41661	41734	41794	41855
41664	41739	41795	41856
41666	41745	41797	41857
41671	41747	41803	41859
41672	41748	41804	41860
41676	41749	41805	41865
41682	41752	41811	41869
41686	41753	41813	41873
41690	41754	41814	41874
41695	41756	41820	41875
41699	41762	41824	41878
41702	41763	41826	41879
41706	41767	41829	41885
41708	41768	41833	41889
41710	41769	41835	41890
41711	41770	41838	41893
41712	41773	41839	41895
41713	41777	41844	
41720	41779	41846	
41724	41780	41847	
41725	41781	41852	
41726	41788	41853	

Total 87

0-4-4T 2P

Introduced : 1932. L.M.S.
Weight : 58 tons 1 cwt.
Pressure : 160 lb.
Cyls. : 18" × 26".
Driving Wheels : 5' 7".
Tractive Effort : 17,100 lb.

41900	41903	41906	41908
41901	41904	41907	41909
41902	41905		

Total 10

4-4-2T 2P

Introduced : 1900. L.T. & S.
Weight : 67 tons 15 cwt.
Pressure : 170 lb.
Cyls. : 19" × 26".
Driving Wheels : 6' 6".
Tractive Effort : 17,390 lb.

41910	41915	41919	41923
41911	41916	41920	41924
41912	41917	41921	41925
41913	41918	41922	41926
41914			

Total 17

4-4-2T 3P

Introduced: Nos. 41953-41964, L.T. & S. built 1897-8, rebuilt 1905-11. Nos. 41965-41968, L.T.& S., built 1909. Nos. 41928-41937, L.M.S., built 1923.

Weight : 41928-37 : 71 tons 10 cwt.; 41938-52 : 71 tons 10 cwt.; 41953-68 : 70 tons 15 cwt.
Pressure : 170 lb.
Cyls. : 19" × 26".
Driving Wheels : 6' 6".
Tractive Effort : 17,390 lb.

41928	41941	41954	41967
41929	41942	41955	41968
41930	41943	41956	41969
41931	41944	41957	41970
41932	41945	41958	41971
41933	41946	41959	41972
41934	41947	41960	41973
41935	41948	41961	41974
41936	41949	41962	41975
41937	41950	41963	41976
41938	41951	41964	41977
41939	41952	41965	41978
41940	41953	41966	

Total 51

0-6-2T 3F

Introduced : 1903. L.T. & S.
Weight : 64 tons 13 cwt.
Pressure : 170 lb.
Cyls. : 18" × 26".
Driving Wheels : 5' 3".
Tractive Effort : 19,320 lb.

41980	41984	41988	41991*
41981	41985	41989	41992*
41982	41986	41990*	41993*
41983	41987		

Total 14

* Built 1912, taken direct into M.R. stock.

2-6-4T 4P

Introduced : 1945. L.M.S.
Weight : 85 tons 5 cwt.
Pressure : 200 lb.
Cyls. : $19\frac{5}{8}$" × 26".
Driving Wheels : 5' 9".
Tractive Effort : 24,670 lb.
Walschaerts Valve Gear, Superheated, Taper boiler, Shorter coupled wheelbase.

42147	42173	42199	42225
42148	42174	42200	42226
42149	42175	42201	42227
42150	42176	42202	42228
42151	42177	42203	42229
42152	42178	42204	42230
42153	42179	42205	42231
42154	42180	42206	42232
42155	42181	42207	42233
42156	42182	42208	42234
42157	42183	42209	42235
42158	42184	42210	42236
42159	42185	42211	42237
42160	42186	42212	42238
42161	42187	42213	42239
42162	42188	42214	42240
42163	42189	42215	42241
42164	42190	42216	42242
42165	42191	42217	42243
42166	42192	42218	42244
42167	42193	42219	42245
42168	42194	42220	42246
42169	42195	42221	42247
42170	42196	42222	42248
42171	42197	42223	42249
42172	42198	42224	42250

42251	42264	42276	42288
42252	42265	42277	42289
42253	42266	42278	42290
42254	42267	42279	42291
42255	42268	42280	42292
42256	42269	42281	42293
42257	42270	42282	42294
42258	42271	42283	42295
42259	42272	42284	42296
42260	42273	42285	42297
42261	42274	42286	42298
42262	42275	42287	42299
42263			

(*Class continued No. 42673*).

N.B.—Still being delivered in 42147 series.

2-6-4T 4P

Introduced : 1927. L.M.S.
Weight : 86 tons 5 cwt.
Pressure : 200 lb.
Cyls. : 19" × 26".
Driving Wheels : 5' 9".
Tractive Effort : 23,125 lb.
Walschaerts Valve Gear.
Superheated. Parallel boiler.

42300	42323	42346	42369
42301	42324	42347	42370
42302	42325	42348	42371
42303	42326	42349	42372
42304	42327	42350	42373
42305	42328	42351	42374
42306	42329	42352	42375
42307	42330	42353	42376
42308	42331	42354	42377
42309	42332	42355	42378
42310	42333	42356	42379
42311	42334	42357	42380
42312	42335	42358	42381
42313	42336	42359	42382
42314	42337	42360	42383
42315	42338	42361	42384
42316	42339	42362	42385
42317	42340	42363	42386
42318	42341	42364	42387
42319	42342	42365	42388
42320	42343	42366	42389
42321	42344	42367	42390
42322	42345	42368	42391

42392	42401*	42409*	42417*
42393	42402*	42410*	42418*
42394	42403*	42411*	42419*
42395*	42404*	42412*	42420*
42396*	42405*	42413*	42421*
42397*	42406*	42414*	42422*
42398*	42407*	42415*	42423*
42399*	42408*	42416*	42424*
42400*			

Total 125

* Fitted with side-window cab.

2-6-4T 4P

Introduced : 1935. L.M.S.
Weight : 87 tons 17 cwt.
Pressure : 200 lb.
Cyls. : $19\frac{5}{8}'' \times 26''$.
Driving Wheels : 5' 9".
Tractive Effort : 24,670 lb.
Walschaerts Valve Gear.
Superheated. Taper boiler.

42425	42443	42461	42479
42426	42444	42462	42480
42427	42445	42463	42481
42428	42446	42464	42482
42429	42447	42465	42483
42430	42448	42466	42484
42431	42449	42467	42485
42432	42450	42468	42486
42433	42451	42469	42487
42434	42452	42470	42488
42435	42453	42471	42489
42436	42454	42472	42490
42437	42455	42473	42491
42438	42456	42474	42492
42439	42457	42475	42493
42440	42458	42476	42494
42441	42459	42477	
42442	42460	42478	

70

(*Class continued No. 42537*).

2-6-4T (3-Cyl.) 4P

Introduced : 1934. L.M.S.
Weight : 92 tons 5 cwt.
Pressure : 200 lb.
Cyls. : (3) 16" × 26".
Driving Wheels : 5' 9".
Tractive Effort : 24,600 lb.
Walschaerts Valve Gear.
Superheated. Taper boiler.

42500	42502	42504	42506
42501	42503	42505	42507

42508	42516	42524	42532
42509	42517	42525	42533
42510	42518	42526	42534
42511	42519	42527	42535
42512	42520	42528	42536
42513	42521	42529	
42514	42522	42530	
42515	42523	42531	

Total 37

2-6-4T 4P

(*Class continued from No.* 42494).

42537	42569	42601	42633
42538	42570	42602	42634
42539	42571	42603	42635
42540	42572	42604	42636
42541	42573	42605	42637
42542	42574	42606	42638
42543	42575	42607	42639
42544	42576	42608	42640
42545	42577	42609	42641
42546	42578	42610	42642
42547	42579	42611	42643
42548	42580	42612	42644
42549	42581	42613	42645
42550	42582	42614	42646
42551	42583	42615	42647
42552	42584	42616	42648
42553	42585	42617	42649
42554	42586	42618	42650
42555	42587	42619	42651
42556	42588	42620	42652
42557	42589	42621	42653
42558	42590	42622	42654
42559	42591	42623	42655
42560	42592	42624	42656
42561	42593	42625	42657
42562	42594	42626	42658
42563	42595	42627	42659
42564	42596	42628	42660
42565	42597	42629	42661
42566	42598	42630	42662
42567	42599	42631	42663
42568	42600	42632	42664

42665	42667	42669	42671
42666	42668	42670	42672

136

(From page 8) **70**

Total 206

2-6-4T 4P

(*Class continued from No.* 42299).

42673	42680	42687	42694
42674	42681	42688	42695
42675	42682	42689	42696
42676	42683	42690	42697
42677	42684	42691	42698
42678	42685	42692	42699
42679	42686	42693	

2-6-0 5F

Introduced : 1926. L.M.S.
Weight : Loco. 66 tons 0 cwt.
Pressure : 180 lb.
Cyls. : 21″ × 26″.
Driving Wheels : 5′ 6″.
Tractive Effort : 26,580 lb.
Walschaerts Valve Gear.
Superheated. Parallel boiler.

42700	42718	42736	42754
42701	42719	42737	42755
42702	42720	42738	42756
42703	42721	42739	42757
42704	42722	42740	42758
42705	42723	42741	42759
42706	42724	42742	42760
42707	42725	42743	42761
42708	42726	42744	42762
42709	42727	42745	42763
42710	42728	42746	42764
42711	42729	42747	42765
42712	42730	42748	42766
42713	42731	42749	42767
42714	42732	42750	42768
42715	42733	42751	42769
42716	42734	42752	42770
42717	42735	42753	42771

42772	42816	42860	42904
42773	42817	42861	42905
42774	42818*	42862	42906
42775	42819	42863	42907
42776	42820	42864	42908
42777	42821	42865	42909
42778	42822*	42866	42910
42779	42823	42867	42911
42780	42824*	42868	42912
42781	42825*	42869	42913
42782	42826	42870	42914
42783	42827	42871	42915
42784	42828	42872	42916
42785	42829*	42873	42917
42786	42830	42874	42918
42787	42831	42875	42919
42788	42832	42876	42920
42789	42833	42877	42921
42790	42834	42878	42922
42791	42835	42879	42923
42792	42836	42880	42924
42793	42837	42881	42925
42794	42838	42882	42926
42795	42839	42883	42927
42796	42840	42884	42928
42797	42841	42885	42929
42798	42842	42886	42930
42799	42843	42887	42931
42800	42844	42888	42932
42801	42845	42889	42933
42802	42846	42890	42934
42803	42847	42891	42935
42804	42848	42892	42936
42805	42849	42893	42937
42806	42850	42894	42938
42807	42851	42895	42939
42808	42852	42896	42940
42809	42853	42897	42941
42810	42854	42898	42942
42811	42855	42899	42943
42812	42856	42900	42944
42813	42857	42901	
42814	42858	42902	
42815	42859	42903	

Total 245

* Fitted 1931 with Rotary Cam Poppet Valve Gear.

2-6-0 5F

Introduced : 1933. L.M.S.
Weight : Loco. 69 tons 2 cwt.
Pressure : 225 lb.
Cyls. : 18″ × 28″.
Driving Wheels : 5′ 6″.
Tractive Effort : 26,290 lb.
Walschaerts Valve Gear.
Superheated. Taper boiler.

42945	42955	42965	42975
42946	42956	42966	42976
42947	42957	42967	42977
42948	42958	42968	42978
42949	42959	42969	42979
42950	42960	42970	42980
42951	42961	42971	42981
42952	42962	42972	42982
42953	42963	42973	42983
42954	42964	42974	42984

Total 40

2-6-0 4F

Introduced : 1947. L.M.S.
Weight : Loco. 59 tons 2 cwt.
Pressure : 225 lb.
Cyls. : 17½″ × 26″.
Driving Wheels : 5′ 3″.
Tractive Effort : 24,170 lb.
Walschaerts Valve Gear.
Superheated. Taper boiler.

43000	43010	43020	43030
43001	43011	43021	43031
43002	43012	43022	43032
43003	43013	43023	43033
43004	43014	43024	43034
43005	43015	43025	43035
43006	43016	43026	43036
43007	43017	43027	43037
43008	43018	43028	43038
43009	43019	43029	43039

N.B.—Still being delivered.

0-6-0 3F

Introduced : 1885. Midland.
Weight : Loco. 43 tons 17 cwt.
Pressure : 175 lb.
Cyls. : 18″ × 26″.
Driving Wheels : 4′ 11″.
Tractive Effort : 21,240 lb.
Rebuilt with non-superheated Belpaire boiler.

43137	43180	43185	43188
43174	43181	43186	43189
43178	43183	43187	

Total 11

Above : Class 4P 4-4-0 No. 41087

Right: Class 2P 4-4-0 No. 602 (New No. 40602)

[*Photos : H. C. Casserley*

Below : Class 3P 4-4-0 No. 739 (New No. 40739)

[*Photo: J. P. Wilson*

Class 4F 2-6-0 No. 3005 (New No. 43005) [*Photo : H. C. Casserley*

Class 5F 2-6-0 No. 2910 (New No. 42910) [*Photo : H. C. Casserley*

Class 2F 2-6-0 No. 6419 (New No. 46419) [*Photo : W. S. Garth*

Class 4P (3-cyl.) 2-6-4T No. 2524 (New No. 42524) [Photo . H. C. Casserley

Class 4P (2-cyl.) 2-6-4T No. 42199 [Photo : F. W. Regan

Class 4P 2-6-4T No. 2394 (New No. 42394) [Photo : B. V. Franey

Left : Class 7F 2-8-0 No. 13804 (New No. 53804)

[*Photo : W. S. Garth*

Below : Class 8F 2-8-0 No. 8602 (New No. 48602)

[*Photo : H. C. Casserley*

Left : The Lickey banker — 0-10-0 No. 22290 (New No. 58100)

[*Photo : H. C. Casserley*

0-6-0 3F

Introduced : 1896. S. & D.J.
Weight : Loco. 43 tons 17 cwt.
Pressure : 175 lb.
Cyls. : 18″ × 26″.
Driving Wheels : 5′ 3″.
Tractive Effort : 19,890 lb.
Rebuilt with superheated Belpaire boiler.

43194	43211	43218	43248
43201	43216	43228	43260
43204			

Total 9

0-6-0 3F

Introduced : 1885. Midland.
Weight : Loco. 43 ton 17 cwt.
Pressure : 175 lb.
Cyls. : 18″ × 26″.
Driving Wheels : 5′3″.
Tractive Effort : 19,890 lb.
All rebuilt with non-superheated Belpaire boilers.

43191	43242	43281	43317
43192	43243	43282	43318
43193	43244	43283	43319
43200	43245	43284	43321
43203	43246	43286	43323
43205	43247	43287	43324
43207	43249	43290	43325
43208	43250	43292	43326
43210	43251	43293	43327
43212	43252	43294	43329
43213	43253	43295	43330
43214	43254	43296	43331
43219	43256	43297	43332
43222	43257	43298	43333
43223	43258	43299	43334
43224	43259	43300	43335
43225	43261	43301	43336
43226	43263	43305	43337
43231	43266	43306	43339
43232	43267	43307	43340
43233	43268	43308	43341
43234	43271	43309	43342
43235	43273	43310	43344
43237	43274	43312	43351
43239	43275	43313	43355
43240	43277	43314	43356
43241	43278	43315	43357

43359	43456	43578	43658
43361	43457	43579	43660
43364	43458	43580	43661
43367	43459	43581	43662
43368	43462	43582	43664
43369	43463	43583	43665
43370	43464	43584	43667
43371	43468	43585	43668
43373	43469	43586	43669
43374	43474	43587	43673
43378	43476	43593	43674
43379	43482	43594	43675
43381	43484	43595	43676
43386	43490	43596	43678
43387	43491	43598	43679
43388	43494	43599	43680
43389	43496	43600	43681
43392	43497	43604	43682
43394	43499	43605	43683
43395	43502	43607	43684
43396	43506	43608	43686
43398	43507	43612	43687
43399	43509	43615	43690
43400	43510	43618	43693
43401	43514	43619	43698
43402	43515	43620	43705
43405	43520	43621	43709
43406	43521	43622	43710
43408	43522	43623	43711
43410	43523	43624	43712
43411	43524	43627	43714
43419	43529	43629	43715
43427	43531	43630	43717
43428	43538	43631	43721
43429	43540	43633	43723
43431	43544	43634	43724
43433	43546	43636	43727
43435	43548	43637	43728
43436	43550	43638	43729
43440	43553	43639	43731
43441	43558	43644	43734
43443	43562	43645	43735
43444	43565	43650	43737
43446	43568	43651	43742
43448	43570	43652	43745
43449	43572	43653	43747
43453	43574	43656	43748
43454	43575	43657	43749

43751	43757	43763	43770
43753	43759	43765	43771
43754	43760	43766	43772
43755	43762	43767	43773
43756			

Total 317

0-6-0 3F

Introduced : 1906. Midland.
Weight : Loco. 46 tons 3 cwt.
Pressure : 175 lb.
Cyls. : 18½″ × 26″.
Driving Wheels : 5′ 3″.
Tractive Effort : 21,010 lb.
Non-superheated Belpaire boiler.

43775	43791	43806	43821
43776	43792	43807	43822
43777	43793	43808	43823
43778	43795	43809	43824
43779	43796	43810	43825
43781	43797	43811	43826
43782	43798	43812	43827
43783	43799	43813	43828
43784	43800	43814	43829
43785	43801	43815	43830
43786	43802	43817	43832
43787	43803	43818	43833
43789	43804	43819	
43790	43805	43820	

Total 54

0-6-0 4F

Introduced : 1911. Midland.
Weight : 48 tons 15 cwt.
Pressure : 175 lb.
Cyls. : 20″ × 26″.
Driving Wheels : 5′ 3″.
Tractive Effort : 24,555 lb.
Superheated.

43835	43849	43863	43877
43836	43850	43864	43878
43837	43851	43865	43879
43838	43852	43866	43880
43839	43853	43867	43881
43840	43854	43868	43882
43841	43855	43869	43883
43842	43856	43870	43884
43843	43857	43871	43885
43844	43858	43872	43886
43845	43859	43873	43887
43846	43860	43874	43888
43847	43861	43875	43889
43848	43862	43876	43890

43891	43925	43959	43993
43892	43926	43960	43994
43893	43927	43961	43995
43894	43928	43962	43996
43895	43929	43963	43997
43896	43930	43964	43998
43897	43931	43965	43999
43898	43932	43966	44000
43899	43933	43967	44001
43900	43934	43968	44002
43901	43935	43969	44003
43902	43936	43970	44004
43903	43937	43971	44005
43904	43938	43972	44006
43905	43939	43973	44007
43906	43940	43974	44008
43907	43941	43975	44009
43908	43942	43976	44010
43909	43943	43977	44011
43910	43944	43978	44012
43911	43945	43979	44013
43912	43946	43980	44014
43913	43947	43981	44015
43914	43948	43982	44016
43915	43949	43983	44017
43916	43950	43984	44018
43917	43951	43985	44019
43918	43952	43986	44020
43919	43953	43987	44021
43920	43954	43988	44022
43921	43955	43989	44023
43922	43956	43990	44024
43923	43957	43991	44025
43924	43958	43992	44026

Total 192

0-6-0 4F

Introduced : 1924. L.M.S.
Weight : Loco. 48 tons 15 cwt.
Pressure : 175 lb.
Cyls. : 20″ × 26″.
Driving Wheels : 5′ 3″.
Tractive Effort : 24,555 lb.
Superheated.

44027	44032	44037	44042
44028	44033	44038	44043
44029	44034	44039	44044
44030	44035	44040	44045
44031	44036	44041	44046

44047	44095	44143	44191	44239	44287	44335	44383
44048	44096	44144	44192	44240	44288	44336	44384
44049	44097	44145	44193	44241	44289	44337	44385
44050	44098	44146	44194	44242	44290	44338	44386
44051	44099	44147	44195	44243	44291	44339	44387
44052	44100	44148	44196	44244	44292	44340	44388
44053	44101	44149	44197	44245	44293	44341	44389
44054	44102	44150	44198	44246	44294	44342	44390
44055	44103	44151	44199	44247	44295	44343	44391
44056	44104	44152	44200	44248	44296	44344	44392
44057	44105	44153	44201	44249	44297	44345	44393
44058	44106	44154	44202	44250	44298	44346	44394
44059	44107	44155	44203	44251	44299	44347	44395
44060	44108	44156	44204	44252	44300	44348	44396
44061	44109	44157	44205	44253	44301	44349	44397
44062	44110	44158	44206	44254	44302	44350	44398
44063	44111	44159	44207	44255	44303	44351	44399
44064	44112	44160	44208	44256	44304	44352	44400
44065	44113	44161	44209	44257	44305	44353	44401
44066	44114	44162	44210	44258	44306	44354	44402
44067	44115	44163	44211	44259	44307	44355	44403
44068	44116	44164	44212	44260	44308	44356	44404
44069	44117	44165	44213	44261	44309	44357	44405
44070	44118	44166	44214	44262	44310	44358	44406
44071	44119	44167	44215	44263	44311	44359	44407
44072	44120	44168	44216	44264	44312	44360	44408
44073	44121	44169	44217	44265	44313	44361	44409
44074	44122	44170	44218	44266	44314	44362	44410
44075	44123	44171	44219	44267	44315	44363	44411
44076	44124	44172	44220	44268	44316	44364	44412
44077	44125	44173	44221	44269	44317	44365	44413
44078	44126	44174	44222	44270	44318	44366	44414
44079	44127	44175	44223	44271	44319	44367	44415
44080	44128	44176	44224	44272	44320	44368	44416
44081	44129	44177	44225	44273	44321	44369	44417
44082	44130	44178	44226	44274	44322	44370	44418
44083	44131	44179	44227	44275	44323	44371	44419
44084	44132	44180	44228	44276	44324	44372	44420
44085	44133	44181	44229	44277	44325	44373	44421
44086	44134	44182	44230	44278	44326	44374	44422
44087	44135	44183	44231	44279	44327	44375	44423
44088	44136	44184	44232	44280	44328	44376	44424
44089	44137	44185	44233	44281	44329	44377	44425
44090	44138	44186	44234	44282	44330	44378	44426
44091	44139	44187	44235	44283	44331	44379	44427
44092	44140	44188	44236	44284	44332	44380	44428
44093	44141	44189	44237	44285	44333	44381	44429
44094	44142	44190	44238	44286	44334	44382	44430

44431	44475	44519	44563
44432	44476	44520	44564
44433	44477	44521	44565
44434	44478	44522	44566
44435	44479	44523	44567
44436	44480	44524	44568
44437	44481	44525	44569
44438	44482	44526	44570
44439	44483	44527	44571
44440	44484	44528	44572
44441	44485	44529	44573
44442	44486	44530	44574
44443	44487	44531	44575
44444	44488	44532	44576
44445	44489	44533	44577
44446	44490	44534	44578
44447	44491	44535	44579
44448	44492	44536	44580
44449	44493	44537	44581
44450	44494	44538	44582
44451	44495	44539	44583
44452	44496	44540	44584
44453	44497	44541	44585¶
44454	44498	44542	44586
44455	44499	44543	44587
44456	44500	44544	44588
44457	44501	44545	44589
44458	44502	44546	44590
44459	44503	44547	44591
44460	44504	44548	44592
44461	44505	44549	44593
44462	44506	44550	44594
44463	44507	44551	44595
44464	44508	44552¶	44596
44465	44509	44553	44597
44466¶	44510	44554	44598¶
44467	44511	44555	44599
44468	44512	44556	44600
44469	44513	44557*	44601
44470	44514	44558*	44602
44471	44515	44559*	44603
44472	44516	44560*	44604
44473	44517	44561*	44605
44474	44518	44562	44606

Total 580

¶ Fitted for Oil-burning.

* Ex-S. & D.J.R., Nos. 57-61 (in same order) built 1922.

4-6-0 **5**

Introduced : 1934. L.M.S.
Weight : Loco. 72 tons 2 cwt.
Pressure : 225 lb.
Cyls. : 18½″ × 28″.
Driving Wheels : 6′ 0″.
Tractive Effort : 25,455 lb.
Walschaerts Valve Gear, unless otherwise shown.
Superheated. Taper boiler.

44698	44730	44762†	44794
44699	44731	44763†	44795
44700	44732	44764†	44796
44701	44733	44765†	44797
44702	44734	44766†	44798
44703	44735	44767§	44799
44704	44736	44768	44800
44705	44737	44769	44801
44706	44738ø	44770	44802
44707	44739ø	44771	44803
44708	44740ø	44772	44804
44709	44741ø	44773	44805
44710	44742	44774	44806
44711	44743	44775	44807
44712	44744	44776	44808
44713	44745	44777	44809
44714	44746	44778	44810
44715	44747‡	44779	44811
44716	44748‡	44780	44812
44717	44749‡	44781	44813
44718	44750‡	44782	44814
44719	44751‡	44783	44815
44720	44752‡	44784	44816
44721	44753‡	44785	44817
44722	44754‡	44786	44818
44723	44755‡	44787	44819
44724	44756‡	44788	44820
44725	44757‡	44789	44821
44726	44758†	44790	44822
44727	44759†	44791	44823
44728	44760†	44792	44824
44729	44761†	44793	44825

†Fitted with roller bearings and Walschaerts Valve Gear.

‡ Fitted with roller bearings and Caprotti Valve Gear.

§ Fitted with roller bearings and Stephenson Valve Gear.

ø Fitted with Caprotti Valve Gear.

44826
44827¶
44828
44829¶
44830¶
44831
44832
44833
44834
44835
44836
44837
44838
44839
44840
44841
44842
44843
44844¶
44845
44846
44847
44848
44849
44850
44851
44852
44853
44854
44855
44856
44857
44858
44859
44860
44861
44862
44863
44864
44865
44866
44867
44868
44869
44870
44871
44872
44873
44874
44875
44876
44877
44878
44879
44880
44881
44882
44883
44884
44885
44886
44887
44888
44889
44890
44891
44892
44893
44894
44895
44896
44897
44898
44899
44900
44901
44902
44903
44904
44905
44906
44907
44908
44909
44910
44911
44912
44913
44914
44915
44916
44917
44918
44919
44920
44921
44922
44923
44924
44925
44926
44927
44928
44929
44930
44931
44932
44933
44934
44935
44936
44937
44938
44939
44940
44941
44942
44943
44944
44945
44946
44947
44948
44949
44950
44951
44952
44953
44954
44955
44956
44957
44958
44959
44960
44961
44962
44963
44964
44965
44966
44967
44968
44969
44970
44971
44972
44973
44974
44975
44976
44977
44978
44979
44980
44981
44982
44983
44984
44985
44986
44987
44988
44989
44990
44991
44992
44993
44994
44995
44996
44997
44998
44999
45000
45001
45002
45003
45004
45005
45006
45007
45008
45009
45010
45011
45012
45013
45014
45015
45016
45017
45018
45019
45020
45021
45022
45023
45024
45025
45026
45027
45028
45029
45030
45031
45032
45033
45034
45035
45036
45037
45038
45039
45040
45041
45042
45043
45044
45045
45046
45047
45048
45049
45050
45051
45052
45053
45054
45055
45056
45057
45058
45059
45060
45061
45062
45063
45064
45065
45066
45067
45068
45069
45070
45071
45072
45073
45074
45075
45076
45077
45078
45079
45080
45081
45082
45083
45084
45085
45086
45087
45088
45089
45090
45091
45092
45093
45094
45095
45096
45097
45098
45099
45100
45101
45102
45103
45104
45105
45106
45107
45108
45109
45110
45111
45112
45113
45114
45115
45116
45117
45118
45119
45120
45121
45122
45123
45124
45125
45126
45127
45128
45129
45130
45131
45132
45133
45134
45135
45136
45137
45138
45139
45140
45141
45142
45143
45144
45145
45146
45147
45148
45149
45150
45151
45152
45153
45154*
45155
45156*
45157*
45158*
45159
45160
45161
45162
45163
45164
45165
45166
45167
45168
45169
45170
45171
45172
45173
45174
45175
45176
45177
45178
45179
45180
45181
45182
45183
45184
45185
45186
45187
45188
45189
45190
45191
45192
45193

¶ Fitted for Oil-burning.
* 45154 Lanarkshire Yeomanry.
45156 Ayrshire Yeomanry.
45157 The Glasgow Highlander
45158 Glasgow Yeomanry.

45194	45242	45290	45338
45195	45243	45291	45339
45196	45244	45292	45340
45197	45245	45293	45341
45198	45246	45294	45342
45199	45247	45295	45343
45200	45248	45296	45344
45201	45249	45297	45345
45202	45250	45298	45346
45203	45251	45299	45347
45204	45252	45300	45348
45205	45253	45301	45349
45206	45254	45302	45350
45207	45255	45303	45351
45208	45256	45304	45352
45209	45257	45305	45353
45210	45258	45306	45354
45211	45259	45307	45355
45212	45260	45308	45356
45213	45261	45309	45357
45214	45262	45310	45258
45215	45263	45311	45359
45216	45264	45312	45360
45217	45265	45313	45361
45218	45266	45314	45362
45219	45267	45315	45363
45220	45268	45316	45364
45221	45269	45317	45365
45222	45270	45318	45366
45223	45271	45319	45367
45224	45272	45320	45368
45225	45273	45321	45369
45226	45274	45322	45370
45227	45275	45323	45371
45228	45276	45324	45372
45229	45277	45325	45373
45230	45278	45326	45374
45231	45279	45327	45375
45232	45280	45328	45376
45233	45281	45329	45377
45234	45282	45330	45378
45235	45283	45331	45379
45236	45284	45332	45380
45237	45285	45333	45381
45238	45286	45334	45382
45239	45287	45335	45383
45240	45288	45336	45384
45241	45289	45337	45385

45386	45415	45444	45473
45387	45416	45445	45474
45388	45417	45446	45475
45389	45418	45447	45476
45390	45419	45448	45477
45391	45420	45449	45478
45392	45421	45450	45479
45393	45422	45451	45480
45394	45423	45452	45481
45395	45424	45453	45482
45396	45425	45454	45483
45397	45426	45455	45484
45398	45427	45456	45485
45399	45428	45457	45486
45400	45429	45458	45487
45401	45430	45459	45488
45402	45431	45460	45489
45403	45432	45461	45490
45404	45433	45462	45491
45405	45434	45463	45492
45406	45435	45464	45493
45407	45436	45465	45494
45408	45437	45466	45495
45409	45438	45467	45496
45410	45439	45468	45497
45411	45440	45469	45498
45412	45441	45470	45499
45413	45442	45471	
45414	45443	45472	

(Still being delivered in 44698 series).

"Patriot" Class

4-6-0 5XP & 6P*

Introduced . 1930-34, Superheated. Parallel boiler. L.M.S.
Rebuilt from 1946 with Taper boiler and classified 6P.

Weight : Loco. { 80 tons 15 cwt. (5XP). 82 tons 15 cwt. (6P).

Pressure : { 200 lb. (5XP). 250 lb. (6P).

Cyls. : { (3) 18″ × 26″ (5XP). (3) 17″ × 26″ (6P)

Driving Wheels : 6′ 9″.

Tractive Effort : { 26,520 lb. (5XP). 29,570 lb. (6P).

Walschaerts Valve Gear.

Class 6P indicated thus* : Remainder 5XP.

45500 Patriot

45501 St. Dunstan's
45502 Royal Naval Division
45503 The Leicestershire Regt.
45504 Royal Signals
45505 The Royal Army
45506 [Ordnance Corps
45507 Royal Tank Corps
45508
45509
45510
45511 Isle of Man
45512*Bunsen
45513
45514*Holyhead
45515 Caernarvon
45516 The Bedfordshire and
45517 [Hertfordshire Regt.
45518 Bradshaw
45519 Lady Godiva
45520 Llandudno
45521*Rhyl
45522 Prestatyn
45523 Bangor
45524 Blackpool
45525 Colwyn Bay
45526*Morecambe and Heysham
45527 Southport
45528*
45529*
45530*Sir Frank Ree
45531*Sir Frederick Harrison
45532*Illustrious
45533 Lord Rathmore
45534 E. Tootal Broadhurst
45535 Sir Herbert Walker, K.C.B.
45536 Private W. Wood, V.C.
45537 Private E. Sykes, V.C.
45538 Giggleswick
45539 E. C. Trench
45540*Sir Robert Turnbull
45541 Duke of Sutherland
45542
45543 Home Guard
45544
45545
45546 Fleetwood
45547
45548 Lytham St. Annes
45549
45550
45551

Total 52

"Jubilee" Class
4-6-0 5XP & 6P

Introduced : 1934. L.M.S.
Weight : Loco. 79 tons 11 cwt.
Pressure : { 225 lb. (5XP). 250 lb. (6P).
Cyls. : 17" × 26".
Driving Wheels : 6' 9".
Tractive Effort : { 26,610 lb. (5XP). 29,570 lb. (6P).
Walschaerts Valve Gear.
Superheated. Taper boiler.
Class 6P : Nos. 45735/6.
Class 5XP : Remainder.

45552 Silver Jubilee
45553 Canada
45554 Ontario
45555 Quebec
45556 Nova Scotia
45557 New Brunswick
45558 Manitoba
45559 British Columbia
45560 Prince Edward Island
45561 Saskatchewan
45562 Alberta
45563 Australia
45564 New South Wales
45565 Victoria
45566 Queensland
45567 South Australia
45568 Western Australia
45569 Tasmania
45570 New Zealand
45571 South Africa
45572 Eire
45573 Newfoundland
45574 India
45575 Madras
45576 Bombay
45577 Bengal
45578 United Provinces
45579 Punjab
45580 Burma
45581 Bihar and Orissa

"Jubilee" Class—*continued*

45582 Central Provinces
45583 Assam
45584 North West Frontier
45585 Hyderabad
45586 Mysore
45587 Baroda
45588 Kashmir
45589 Gwalior
45590 Travancore
45591 Udaipur
45592 Indore
45593 Kolhapur
45594 Bhopal
45595 Southern Rhodesia
45596 Bahamas
45597 Barbados
45598 Basutoland
45599 Bechuanaland
45600 Bermuda
45601 British Guiana
45602 British Honduras
45603 Solomon Islands
45604 Ceylon
45605 Cyprus
45606 Falkland Islands
45607 Fiji
45608 Gibraltar
45609 Gilbert and Ellice Islands
45610 Gold Coast
45611 Hong Kong
45612 Jamaica
45613 Kenya
45614 Leeward Islands
45615 Malay States
45616 Malta G.C.
45617 Mauritius
45618 New Hebrides
45619 Nigeria
45620 North Borneo
45621 Northern Rhodesia
45622 Nyasaland
45623 Palestine
45624 St. Helena
45625 Sarawak
45626 Seychelles
45627 Sierra Leone
45628 Somaliland
45629 Straits Settlements
45630 Swaziland
45631 Tanganyika
45632 Tonga
45633 Aden
45634 Trinidad
45635 Tobago
45636 Uganda
45637 Windward Islands
45638 Zanzibar
45639 Raleigh
45640 Frobisher
45641 Sandwich
45642 Boscawen
45643 Rodney
45644 Howe
45645 Collingwood
45646 Napier
45647 Sturdee
45648 Wemyss
45649 Hawkins
45650 Blake
45651 Shovell
45652 Hawke
45653 Barham
45654 Hood
45655 Keith
45656 Cochrane
45657 Tyrwhitt
45658 Keyes
45659 Drake
45660 Rooke
45661 Vernon
45662 Kempenfelt
45663 Jervis
45664 Nelson
45665 Lord Rutherford of [Nelson
45666 Cornwallis
45667 Jellicoe
45668 Madden
45669 Fisher
45670 Howard of Effingham
45671 Prince Rupert
45672 Anson
45673 Keppel
45674 Duncan
45675 Hardy
45676 Codrington

45677 Beatty
45678 De Robeck
45679 Armada
45680 Camperdown
45681 Aboukir
45682 Trafalgar
45683 Hogue
45684 Jutland
45685 Barfleur
45686 St. Vincent
45687 Neptune
45688 Polyphemus
45689 Ajax
45690 Leander
45691 Orion
45692 Cyclops
45693 Agamemnon
45694 Bellerophon
45695 Minotaur
45696 Arethusa
45697 Achilles
45698 Mars
45699 Galatea
45700 Britannia
45701 Conqueror
45702 Colossus
45703 Thunderer
45704 Leviathan
45705 Seahorse
45706 Express
45707 Valiant
45708 Resolution
45709 Implacable
45710 Irresistible
45711 Courageous
45712 Victory
45713 Renown
45714 Revenge
45715 Invincible
45716 Swiftsure
45717 Dauntless
45718 Dreadnought
45719 Glorious
45720 Indomitable
45721 Impregnable
45722 Defence
45723 Fearless
45724 Warspite
45725 Repulse
45726 Vindictive
45727 Inflexible
45728 Defiance
45729 Furious
45730 Ocean
45731 Perseverance
45732 Sanspareil
45733 Novelty
45734 Meteor
45735*Comet
45736*Phoenix
45737 Atlas
45738 Samson
45739 Ulster
45740 Munster
45741 Leinster
45742 Connaught **Total 191**

* Rebuilt with larger, superheated, higher pressure taper boilers in 1942, and reclassified 6P in 1943.

"Claughton" Class

4-6-0 5XP

Introduced : 1921. L.N.W.
Weight : Loco. 79 tons 9 cwt.
Pressure : 200 lb.
Cyls. : (4) 15¾" × 26".
Driving Wheels : 6' 9".
Tractive Effort : 27,070 lb.
Walschaerts Valve Gear.
Superheated.
Rebuilt 1928 with large Belpaira boiler.

46004 **Total 1**

"Royal Scot" Class

4-6-0 6P

Introduced : 1927. Superheated, with Parallel boiler. Rebuilt from 1943 with superheated Taper boiler, double blast pipe, and new cylinders as shown †.
Weight : Loco. 83 tons (Rebuilt). 84 tons 1 cwt (No. 46170). 84 tons 18 cwt. (Un-rebulit).
Pressure : 250 lb.
Cyls. : (3) 18" × 26".
Driving Wheels : 6' 9".
Tractive Effort : 33,150 lb.
Walschaerts Valve Gear.

46100 Royal Scot

46101†Royal Scots Grey
46102 Black Watch
46103†Royal Scots Fusilier
46104†Scottish Borderer
46105†Cameron Highlander
46106 Gordon Highlander
46107 Argyll and Sutherland Highlander
46108†Seaforth Highlander
46109†Royal Engineer
46110 Grenadier Guardsman
46111†Royal Fusilier
46112†Sherwood Forester
46113 Cameronian
46114†Coldstream Guardsman
46115†Scots Guardsman
46116†Irish Guardsman
46117†Welsh Guardsman
46118†Royal Welch Fusilier
46119†Lancashire Fusilier
46120†Royal Inniskilling Fusilier
46121†H.L.I.
46122†Royal Ulster Rifleman
46123 Royal Irish Fusilier
46124†London Scottish
46125†3rd Carabinier
46126†Royal Army Service Corps
46127†Old Contemptibles
46128†The Lovat Scouts
46129†The Scottish Horse
46130 The West Yorkshire Regiment
46131†The Royal Warwickshire Regiment
46132†The King's Regiment Liverpool
46133†The Green Howards
46134 The Cheshire Regiment
46135†The East Lancashire Regiment
46136 The Border Regiment
46137 The Prince of Wales's Volunteers (South Lancashire)
46138†The London Irish Rifleman
46139†The Welch Regiment
46140 The King's Royal Rifle Corps
46141 The North Staffordshire Regiment
46142 The York and Lancaster Regiment
46143 The South Staffordshire Regiment
46144†Honourable Artillery Company
46145†The Duke of Wellington's Regt. (West Riding)
46146†The Rifle Brigade
46147†The Northamptonshire Regiment
46148 The Manchester Regiment
46149†The Middlesex Regiment
46150†The Life Guardsman
46151 The Royal Horse Guardsman
46152†The King's Dragoon Guardsman
46153 The Royal Dragoon
46154†The Hussar
46155 The Lancer
46156 The South Wales Borderer
46157†The Royal Artilleryman
46158 The Loyal Regiment
46159†The Royal Air Force
46160†Queen Victoria's Rifleman
46161†King's Own
46162†Queen's Westminster Rifleman
46163 Civil Service Rifleman
46164 The Artists' Rifleman
46165 The Ranger (12th London Regt.)
46166†London Rifle Brigade
46167 The Hertfordshire Regiment
46168†The Girl Guide
46169†The Boy Scout
46170‡British Legion

Total 71

‡ Rebuilt from 6399 "Fury" in 1935.

"Princess Royal" Class

4-6-2 **7P**

Introduced : 1933. L.M.S.
Weight : Loco. 104 tons 10 cwt.
Pressure : 250 lb.
Cyls : (4) 16¼" × 28".
Driving Wheels : 6' 6".
Tractive Effort : 40,285 lb.
Walschaerts Valve Gear.
Superheated Taper Boiler.

46200 The Princess Royal
46201 Princess Elizabeth
46202‡
46203 Princess Margaret Rose
46204 Princess Louise
46205 Princess Victoria
46206 Princess Marie Louise
46207 Princess Arthur of Connaught
46208 Princess Helena Victoria
46209 Princess Beatrice
46210 Lady Patricia
46211 Queen Maud
46212 Duchess of Kent

Total 13

‡ Turbine driven locomotive.

"Princess Coronation" Class

4-6-2 **7P**

Introduced : 1937. L.M.S.
Weight: 105 tons 5 cwt. (108 tons 2 cwt. Streamlined).
Pressure : 250 lb.
Cyls. : (4) 16½" × 28".
Driving Wheels : 6' 9".
Tractive Effort : 40,000 lb.
Walschaerts Valve Gear.
Superheated. Taper Boiler.

46220 Coronation
46221 Queen Elizabeth
46222 Queen Mary
46223 Princess Alice
46224 Princess Alexandra
46225 Duchess of Gloucester
46226*Duchess of Norfolk
46227 Duchess of Devonshire
46228 Duchess of Rutland
46229 Duchess of Hamilton
46230 Duchess of Buccleuch
46231 Duchess of Atholl
46232 Duchess of Montrose
46233 Duchess of Sutherland
46234 Duchess of Abercorn
46235 City of Birmingham
46236 City of Bradford
46237 City of Bristol
46238 City of Carlisle
46239 City of Chester
46240 City of Coventry
46241 City of Edinburgh
46242 City of Glasgow
46243*City of Lancaster
46244 King George VI
46245 City of London
46246 City of Manchester
46247 City of Liverpool
46248 City of Leeds
46249 City of Sheffield
46250 City of Lichfield
46251 City of Nottingham
46252 City of Leicester
46253 City of St. Albans
46254 City of Stoke-on-Trent
46255 City of Hereford
46256†Sir William A. Stanier, F.R.S.
46257†City of Salford

Total 38

*Streamlined Locomotives.
†With Roller bearings and other detail alterations.

2-6-0 **2F**

Introduced : 1946. L.M.S.
Weight : Loco 47 tons 2 cwt.
Pressure : 200 lb.
Cyls. : 16" × 24".
Driving Wheels : 5' 0".
Tractive Effort : 17,410 lb.
Walschaerts Valve Gear.
Superheated. Taper boiler.

46400	46409	46418	46427
46401	46410	46419	46428
46402	46411	46420	46429
46403	46412	46421	46430
46404	46413	46422	46431
46405	46414	46423	46432
46406	46415	46424	46433
46407	46416	46425	46434
46408	46417	46426	

(Still being delivered).

2-4-2T 1P

Introduced : 1890. L.N.W.
Weight : 50 tons 10 cwt.
Pressure : 150 lb.
Cyls. : 17″ × 24″.
Driving Wheels : 5′ 8½″.
Tractive Effort : 12,910 lb.

46601	46637	46669	46711
46603	46639	46676	46712
46604	46643	46680	46727
46616	46654	46683	46742
46620	46656	46687	46749
46628	46658	46688	46757
46632	46663	46701	
46635	46666	46710	

Total 30

2-4-2T 2P

Introduced : 1890. L. & Y.
Weight : 55 tons 19 cwt.
Pressure : 180 lb.
Cyls. : 17½″ × 26″.
Driving Wheels : 5′ 8″.
Tractive Effort : 18,360 lb.
(Sold by L. & Y. to Wirral Rly. and absorbed into L.M.S. stock 1923).

46762 **Total 1**

0-6-2T 2P

Introduced : 1898. L.N.W.
Weight : 52 tons 6 cwt.
Pressure : 150 lb.
Cyls. : 18″ × 24″.
Driving Wheels : 5′ 2½″.
Tractive Effort · 15,865 lb.

46876	46906	46917	46924
46899	46912	46922	46931
46900			

Total 9

0-4-0ST 0F

(Saddle Tanks built by Kitsons).
Introduced : 1932. L.M.S.
Weight : 33 tons 0 cwt.
Pressure : 160 lb.
Cyls. : 15½″ × 30″.
Driving Wheels : 3′ 10″.
Tractive Effort : 14,205 lb.

47000	47002	47003	47004
47001			

Total 5

0-6-0T 2F

Introduced 1928. L.M.S.
Weight : 43 tons 12 cwt.
Pressure : 160 lb.
Cyls. : 17″ × 22″.
Driving Wheels : 3′ 11″.
Tractive Effort : 18,400lb.
Walschaerts Valve Gear.
For use in dockyards.

47160	47163	47166	47168
47161	47164	47167	47169
47162	47165		

Total 10

0-4-0T Sentinel

Introduced : 1929-30. L.M.S.
Geared Drive.

47180	47182	47184	47191†
47181	47183	47190†	

†Ex-S. & D.J. Nos. 101 and 102.
(For dimensions see table)

Total 7

0-6-0T 3F

Introduced : 1899. Midland.
Weight : 43 tons 17 cwt.
Pressure : 160 lb.
Cyls. : 18″ × 26″.
Driving :Wheels : 4′ 7″.
Tractive Effort : 20,835 lb.

47200	47215	47230	47245
47201	47216	47231	47246
47202	47217	47232	47247
47203	47218	47233	47248
47204	47219	47234	47249
47205	47220	47235	47250
47206	47221	47236	47251
47207	47222	47237	47252
47208	47223	47238	47253
47209	47224	47239	47254
47210	47225	47240	47255
47211	47226	47241	47256
47212	47227	47242	47257
47213	47228	47243	47258
47214	47229	47244	47259

Total 60

0-6-0T 3F

Introduced : 1924. L.M.S.
Weight : 49 tons 10 cwt.
Pressure : 160 lb.
Cyls. : 18″ × 26″.
Driving Wheels : 4′ 7″.
Tractive Effort : 20,835 lb.

47260	47301	47342	47383
47261	47302	47343	47384
47262	47303	47344	47385
47263	47304	47345	47386
47264	47305	47346	47387
47265	47306	47347	47388
47266	47307	47348	47389
47267	47308	47349	47390
47268	47309	47350	47391
47269	47310*	47351	47392
47270	47311*	47352	47393
47271	47312*	47353	47394
47272	47313*	47354	47395
47273	47314*	47355	47396
47274	47315*	47356	47397
47275	47316*	47357	47398
47276	47317	47358	47399
47277	47318	47359	47400
47278	47319	47360	47401
47279	47320	47361	47402
47280	47321	47362	47403
47281	47322	47363	47404
47282	47323	47364	47405
47283	47324	47365	47406
47284	47325	47366	47407
47285	47326	47367	47408
47286	47327	47368	47409
47287	47328	47369	47410
47288	47329	47370	47411
47289	47330	47371	47412
47290	47331	47372	47413
47291	47332	47373	47414
47292	47333	47374	47415
47293	47334	47375	47416
47294	47335	47376	47417
47295	47336	47377	47418
47296	47337	47378	47419
47297	47338	47379	47420
47298	47339	47380	47421
47299	47340	47381	47422
47300	47341	47382	47423

47424	47473	47521	47570
47425	47474	47522	47571
47426	47475	47523	47572
47427	47476	47524	47573
47428	47477	47525	47574
47429	47478	47526	47575
47430	47479	47527	47576
47431	47480	47528	47577
47432	47481	47529	47578
47433	47482	47530	47579
47434	47483	47531	47580
47435	47484	47532	47581
47436	47485	47533	47582
47437	47486	47534	47583
47438	47487	47535	47584
47439	47488	47536	47585
47440	47489	47537	47586
47441	47490	47538	47587
47442	47491	47539	47588
47443	47492	47540	47590
47444	47493	47541	47591
47445	47494	47542	47592
47446	47495	47543	47593
47447	47496	47544	47594
47448	47497	47545	47595
47449	47498	47546	47596
47450	47499	47547	47597
47451	47500	47548	47598
47452	47501	47549	47599
47453	47502	47550	47600
47454	47503	47551	47601
47455	47504	47552	47602
47457	47505	47554	47603
47458	47506	47555	47604
47459	47507	47556	47605
47460	47508	47557	47606
47461	47509	47558	47608
47462	47510	47559	47609
47463	47511	47560	47610
47464	47512	47561	47612
47465	47513	47562	47614
47466	47514	47563	47615
47467	47515	47564	47616
47468	47516	47565	47618
47469	47517	47566	47619
47470	47518	47567	47620
47471	47519	47568	47621
47472	47520	47569	47622

47623	47637	47651	47668
47624	47638	47652	47669
47625	47639	47653	47670
47626	47640	47654	47671
47627	47641	47655	47672
47628	47642	47656	47673
47629	47643	47657	47674
47630	47644	47658	47675
47631	47645	47661	47676
47632	47646	47662	47677
47633	47647	47664	47678
47634	47648	47665	47679
47635	47649	47666	47680
47636	47650	47667	47681

Total 412

* Ex-S. & D.J.R., Nos. 19-25, built 1929.

0-4-2ST 1F

Introduced : 1901. L.N.W.
Weight : 34 tons 17 cwt.
Pressure : 150 lb.
Cyls. : 17″ × 24″.
Driving Wheels : 4′ 5½″.
Tractive Effort : 16,530 lb.
Square saddle tank. Bissel truck.

47862	47865

Total 2

0-8-2T 6F

Introduced : 1911. L.N.W.
Weight : 72 tons 10 cwt.
Pressure : 170 lb.
Cyls. : 20½″ × 24″.
Driving Wheels : 4′ 5½″.
Tractive Effort : 27,240 lb.

47875	47881	47885	47888
47877	47884	47887	47896

Total 8

0-8-4T 7F

Introduced : 1923. L.M.S.
Weight : 88 tons 0 cwt.
Pressure : 185 lb.
Cyls. : 20½″ × 24″.
Driving Wheels : 4′ 5½″.
Tractive Effort : 29,815 lb.

47931	47936	47951	47956
47932	47937	47954	47958
47933	47939		

Total 10

2-6-6-2T Beyer-Garratt

Introduced : { 3 in 1927 / 30 in 1930 } L.M.S.
Weight : 155 tons 10 cwt.
Pressure : 190 lb.
Cyls. : (4) 18½″ × 26″.
Driving Wheels : 5′ 3″.
Tractive Effort : 45,620 lb.
Walschaerts Valve Gear.
Superheated.

47967	47976	47985	47994
47968	47977	47986	47995
47969	47978	47987	47996
47970	47979	47988	47997
47971	47980	47989	47998
47972	47981	47990	47999
47973	47982	47991	
47974	47983	47992	
47975	47984	47993	

Total 33

2-8-0 8F

Introduced : 1935. L.M.S.
Weight : Loco. 72 tons 2 cwt.
Pressure : 225 lb.
Cyls. : 18½″ × 28″.
Driving Wheels : 4′ 8½″.
Tractive Effort : 32,440 lb.
Walschaerts Valve Gear.
Superheated. Taper Boiler.

48000	48050	48081	48106
48001	48053	48082	48107
48002	48054	48083	48108
48003	48055	48084	48109
48004	48056	48085	48110
48005	48057	48088	48111
48006	48060	48089	48112
48007	48062	48090	48113
48008	48063	48092	48114
48009	48064¶	48093	48115
48010	48065	48095	48116
48011	48067	48096	48117
48017	48069	48097	48118
48024	48070	48098	48119
48026	48073	48099	48120
48027	48074	48100	48121
48029	48075	48101	48122
48033	48076	48102	48123
48035	48078	48103	48124
48036	48079	48104	48125
48037	48080	48105	48126

48127	48175	48223	48323	48371	48419†	48467†	48529‡
48128	48176	48224	48324	48372	48420†	48468†	48530‡
48129	48177	48225	48325	48373	48421†	48469†	48531‡
48130	48178	48264§	48326	48374	48422†	48470†	48532‡
48131	48179	48265§	48327	48375	48423†	48471†	48533‡
48132	48180	48266§	48328	48376	48424†	48472†	48534‡
48133	48181	48267§	48329	48377	48425†	48473†	48535‡
48134	48182	48268§	48330	48378	48426†	48474†	48536‡
48135	48183	48269§¶	48331	48379	48427†	48475†	48537‡
48136	48184	48270§	48332	48380	48428†	48476†	48538‡
48137	48185	48271§	48333	48381	48429†	48477†	48539‡
48138	48186	48272§	48334	48382	48430†	48478†	48540‡
48139	48187	48273§¶	48335	48383	48431†	48479†	48541‡
48140	48188	48274§	48336	48384	48432†	48490	48542‡
48141	48189	48275§	48337	48385¶	48433†	48491	48543‡
48142	48190	48276§	48338	48386¶	48434†	48492	48544‡
48143	48191¶	48277§	48339	48387	48435†	48493	48545‡
48144	48192	48278§	48340	48388	48436†	48494	48546‡
48145	48193	48279§	48341	48389	48437†	48495	48547‡
48146	48194	48280§	48342	48390	48438†	48500‡	48548‡
48147	48195	48281§	48343	48391	48439†	48501‡	48549‡
48148	48196	48282§	48344	48392	48440†	48502‡	48550‡
48149	48197	48283§	48345	48393	48441†	48503‡	48551‡
48150	48198	48284§	48346	48394	48442†	48504‡	48552‡
48151	48199	48285§	48347	48395	48443†	48505‡	48553‡
48152	48200	48293††	48348	48396	48444†	48506‡	48554‡
48153	48201	48301	48349	48397	48445†	48507‡	48555‡
48154	48202	48302	48350	49398	48446†	48508‡	48556‡
48155	48203	48303	48351	48399	48447†	48509‡	48557‡
48156	48204	48304	48352	48400†	48448†	48510‡	48558‡
48157	48205	48305	48353	48401†	48449†	48511‡	48559‡
48158	48206	48306	48354	48402†	48450†	48512‡	48600*
48159	48207	48307	48355	48403†	48451†	48513‡	48601*
48160	48208	48308	48356	48404†	48452†	48514‡	48602*
48161	48209	48309	48357	48405†	48453†	48515‡	48603*
48162	48210	48310	48358	48406†	48454†	48516‡	48604*
48163	48211	48311	48359	48407†	48455†	48517‡	48605*
48164	48212	48312	48360	48408†	48456†	48518‡	48606*¶
48165	48213	48313	48361	48409†	48457†	48519‡	48607*
48166	48214	48314	48362	48410†	48458†	48520‡	48608*
48167	48215	48315	48363	48411†	48459†	48521‡	48609*
48168	48216	48316	48364	48412†	48460†	48522‡	48610*
48169	48217	48317	48365	48413†	48461†	48523‡	48611*
48170	48218	48318	48366	48414†	48462†	48524‡	48612*
48171	48219	48319	48367	48415†	48463†	48525‡	48613*
48172	48220	48320	48368	48416†	48464†	48526‡	48614*
48173	48221	48321	48369	48417†	48465†	48527‡	48615*
48174	48222	48322	48370¶	48418†	48466†	48528‡	48616*

48617*	48648*	48679*	48710**
48618*	48649*	48680*	48711**
48619*	48650*	48681*	48712**
48620*	48651*	48682*	48713**
48621*	48652*	48683*	48714**
48622*	48653¶*	48684*	48715**
48623*	48654*	48685*	48716**
48624*	48655*	48686*	48717**
48625*	48656*	48687*	48718**
48626*	48657*	48688*	48719**
48627*	48658*	48689*	48720**
48628*	48659*	48690*	48721**
48629*	48660*	48691*	48722**
48630*	48661*	48692*	48723**
48631*	48662*	48693*	48724**
48632*	48663*	48694*	48725**
48633*	48664*	48695*	48726**
48634*	48665*	48696*	48727**
48635*	48666*	48697*	48728**
48636*	48667*	48698*	48729**
48637*	48668*	48699*	48730**
48638*	48669*	48700*	48731**
48639*	48670*	48701*	48732**
48640*	48671*	48702*	48733**
48641*	48672*	48703*	48734**
48642*	48673*	48704*	48735**
48643*	48674*	48705**	48736**
48644*	48675*	48706**	48737**
48645*	48676*	48707**	48738**
48646*	48677*	48708**	48739**
48647*	48678*	48709**	48740**

48741**	48749**	48757**	48765**
48742**	48750**	48758**	48766**
48743**	48751**	48759**	48767**
48744**	48752**	48760**	48768**
48745**	48753**	48761**	48769**
48746**	48754**	48762**	48770**
48747**	48755**	48763**	48771**
48748**	48756**	48764**	48772**

Total 624

*S.R.-built, 1942-4.
†G.W.-built, 1943-5.
‡L.N.E.-built, 1943-5.
§Ex-War Dept., built by North British Loco. Co., 1942.
**Ex-L.N.E.R. Class "O6" (3500-67 in same sequence) on loan to and renumbered by L.M.S.R., 1947. Nos. 48705-29 built by S.R., Brighton 1944, for L.N.E.R. use.
††Ex-War Dept., built by Beyer Peacock & Co., 1940.
¶Fitted for oil burning.

4-6-0 — 4F

Introduced : 1908. L.N.W.
Weight : Loco. 63 tons 0 cwt.
Pressure : 175 lb.
Cyls. : 19″ × 26″.
Driving Wheels. : 5′ 2½″
Tractive Effort : 22,340 lb.
Some rebuilt with Belpaire Boilers.

48801 | 48824 | 48834

Total 3

0-8-0 — 6F & 7F

Prototype design, Webb 1892, L.N.W.R. No. 2524, now No. 49011. All other Webb locos. of this type were compound and have been converted to simple expansion. Chronology of existing Nos. between 48892 and 49454 excepting No. 49011 above, is as follows.

Webb 3-cyl. compound, built 1893-1900, converted to simple by Whale, 1904-9 : Nos. between 48953-49010 and 49012-49064.

***Webb 4-cyl. compound, built 1901-4, converted to simple by Whale, Bowen, Cooke, Beames, and Hughes at dates bracketed :** 48901-52 (1923-7), 48892-9 (1923-5), 49065-76/85/90/9, 49100/20/2/32/3/42 (1906-10) 49145-53 (1910-17), 49265-7/72-3/92, 49304/19/24/31 (1917-8), 49335-46 (1918-20), 49347/8 (1908/7 respectively), 49349-94 (1921-23), 49425 (1922).

Whale-Bowen Cooke 2-cyl. simple, non-superheated, 160 lb. pressure, new engines 1910, L.N.W.R. Class "G" : Nos. 490/7-84/86-9/91-8, 49101-19/21/3-31/4-41/3/4, 49154. (49154 was the first engine of this type to be superheated in 1912 and classed "G1.").

Bowen Cooke 2-cyl. simple superheated, 160 lb. pressure, new engines L.N.W.R. Class G1, built as bracketed dates : 49155-49200 (1912), 49201-24 (1913), 49225-54 (1914), 49255-64 (1916), 49268-71/4-9 (1917), 49280-91/3-9, 49300-3/5-18/20-3/5-30/2-4 (1918).

(*continued on page* 39)

Class 3P 4-4-0 No. 54445 [Photo : P. Ransome-Wallis

Class 4P 4-6-0 No. 14630 (New No. 54360) [Photo : H. C. Casserley

"Ben" Class 2P 4-4-0 No. 14398 *Ben Alder* (New No. 54398)
[Photo : P. Ransome-Wallis

Class 5 4-6-0 No. 5005 (New No. 45005) with domeless boiler

Class 5 4-6-0 No. 44998

Class 5 4-6-0 No. 4751 (New No. 44751) with Caprotti valve gear

[Photos : P. Ransome-Wallis

Class 7P 4-6-2 No. 46236 *City of Bradford* [*Photo; C. C. B. Herbert*

Class 7P 4-6-2 No. 6209 *Princess Beatrice* (New No. 46209)
[*Photo : P. Ransome-Wallis*

LONDON

4–

Above: Unrebuilt "Royal Scot" Class 6P 4-6-0's Nos. 46137 *The Prince of Wales's Volunteers (South Lancashire)* and 6110 *Grenadier Guardsman* (New No. 46110) double-heading a down Liverpool express near Berkhamsted.

[*Photo: H. C. Casserley*

Below: Rebuilt "Royal Scot" Class 6P 4-6-0 No. 6122 *Royal Ulster Rifleman* (New No. 46122) climbs Camden bank with the 6 p.m. Manchester express.

[*Photo: F. R. Hebron*

MIDLAND
0's

Above : "Patriot" Class 4-6-0 No. 5503 *The Leicestershire Regiment* (New No. 45503), nears Watford with an up Birmingham express.

[*Photo : F. R. Hebron*

Left centre : Class 6P 4-6-0 No. 6170 *British Legion* (New No. 46170), rebuilt from high pressure loco No. 6399 *Fury*.

[*Photo · J. C. Flemons*

Below : "Jubilee" Class 5XP 4-6-0 No. 5576 *Bombay* (New No. 45576) makes the ascent of Shap with a Glasgow-Liverpool express.

[*Photo : Canon E. Treacy*

Above : Class 2F 0-6-0 No. 58249
[Photo : *H. C. Casserley*

Left : Class 3F 0-6-0 No. 3265 (New No. 43265)
[Photo : E. D. Bruton

Below : Class 4F 0-6-0 No. 43929
[Photo : *H. C. Casserley*

Above : Class 2F 0-6-0 No. 28128 (New No. 58330)
[Photo: H. C. Casserley

Right : Class 3F 0-6-0 No. 17651 (New No. 57651)
[P. Ransome-Wallis

Below : Class 3F 0-6-0 No. 17695 (New No. 57695)
[Photo: A. B. Crompton

Class 7F 0-8-0 No. 9615 (New No. 49615) [*Photo : H. C. Casserley*

Class 6F 0-8-0 [*Photo : P. Ransome-Wallis*

Class 7F 0-8-0 No. 12906 (New No. 52906) [*Photo : H. C. Casserley*

Bowen Cooke 2-cyl. simple, superheated, 175 lb. pressure, new engines L.N.W.R. Class G2, built 1921-2 : Nos. 49395-49424, 49426-54.

*The following numbers listed were converted by Whale from 0-8-0 to 2-8-0 type (compound as before) at dates bracketed—48892, 49266, 49319/90 (1904); 49267, 49349 (1905) ; 48894/5/8, 49340/3/5/51/3/67/74/93 (1906) ; 48896/7/9, 49359/65/72 (1907) ; 48893, 49363/73/86 (1908). They were reconverted to 0-8-0 type 2-cyl. simple propulsion 1917-25.

The L.N.W.R. classifications (above) have since been somewhat modified. Class G1. 6F comprises 160 lb. boilers, Class G2a, 7F comprises 175 lb. boilers, and is restricted to engines originally built, or rebuilt with 160 lb. boilers and since re-boilered at the higher pressure. Class G2, 7F comprises the 1921-2 lot, built new with 175 lb. boilers.

All three classes carry superheater boilers, many of them with Belpaire fireboxes, and the modernisation now in progress aims at converting the G1 class engines into G2a, by substituting 175 lb. boilers, and so increasing the available tractive effort, and placing the engines so done in the 7F power class.

Dimensions common to all three classes—Cyls. 20½″ × 24″. Wheels 4′ 5½″.
Tractive Effort : Class G1 25,640 lb., Classes G2a and G2 28,045 lb.

0-8-0 G1 Class 6F

Engines of this class are now being rebuilt to G2a Class (7F).

48892	49054	49159	49279
48894	49058	49162	49283
48902	49059	49165	49285
48904	49060	49166	49297
48906	49067	49171	49303
48908	49071	49179	49305
48911	49075	49183	49320
48912	49076	49184	49324
48913	49083	49187	49326
48918	49085	49190	49332
48924	49089	49193	49334
48929	49091	49194	49338
48931	49092	49195	49346
48935	49098	49204	49349
48939	49100	49208	49353
48962	49102	49213	49359
49011	49107	49221	49364
49012	49124	49222	49370
49015	49128	49232	49371
49017	49133	49241	49384
49030	49135	49248	
49032	49136	49255	
49040	49140	49259	
49043	49151	49261	
49052	49152	49263	
49053	49156	49269	

0-8-0 G2a Class 7F

48893	48896	48898	48901
48895	48897	48899	48903

48905	49005	49049	49104
48907	49006	49050	49105
48909	49007	49051	49106
48914	49008	49055	49108
48915	49009	49057	49109
48917	49010	49061	49110
48920	49014	49062	49111
48921	49016	49063	49112
48922	49018	49064	49113
48925	49019	49065	49114
48926	49020	49066	49115
48927	49021	49068	49116
48930	49022	49069	49117
48932	49023	49070	49119
48933	49024	49072	49120
48934	49025	49073	49121
48936	49026	49074	49122
48940	49027	49077	49123
48941	49028	49078	49125
48942	49029	49079	49126
48943	49031	49080	49127
48944	49033	49081	49129
48945	49034	49082	49130
48948	49035	49084	49132
48950	49036	49086	49134
48951	49037	49087	49137
48952	49039	49088	49138
48953	49041	49090	49139
48954	49042	49093	49141
48964	49044	49094	49142
48966	49045	49096	49143
49002	49046	49097	49144
49003	49047	49099	49145
49004	49048	49101	49146

49147	49216	49280	49339
49148	49217	49281	49340
49149	49218	49282	49341
49150	49219	49284	49342
49153	49220	49287	49343
49154	49223	49288	49344
49155	49224	49289	49345
49157	49226	49290	49347
49158	49227	49291	49348
49160	49228	49292	49350
49161	49229	49293	49351
49163	49230	49294	49352
49164	49234	49296	49354
49167	49235	49298	49355
49168	49237	49299	49356
49169	49238	49300	49357
49170	49239	49301	49358
49172	49240	49302	49360
49173	49242	49304	49361
49174	49243	49306	49363
49176	49244	49307	49365
49177	49245	49308	49366
49178	49246	49310	49367
49180	49247	49311	49368
49181	49249	49312	49369
49185	49252	49313	49372
49186	49253	49314	49373
49188	49254	49315	49375
49189	49256	49316	49376
49191	49257	49317	49377
49192	49258	49318	49378
49196	49260	49319	49379
49198	49262	49321	49381
49199	49264	49322	49382
49200	49265	49323	49385
49202	49266	49325	49386
49203	49267	49327	49387
49205	49268	49328	49388
49207	49270	49329	49389
49209	49271	49330	49390
49210	49275	49331	49391
49211	49276	49333	49392
49212	49277	49335	49393
49214	49278	49337	49394

NOTE
For purposes of classification the locomotives on pages 39 and 40 are not in numerical order.

0-8-0 7F

G2 Class

49395	49410	49425	49440
49396	49411	49426	49441
49397	49412	49427	49442
49398	49413	49428	49443
49399	49414	49429	49444
49400	49415	49430	49445
49401	49416	49431	49446
49402	49417	49432	49447
49403	49418	49433	49448
49404	49419	49434	49449
49405	49420	49435	49450
49406	49421	49436	49451
49407	49422	49437	49452
49408	49423	49438	49453
49409	49424	94439	49454

	60
G1	98
G2a	320
Total	478

0-8-0 7F

Introduced : 1929. L.M.S.
Weight : Loco. 60 tons 15 cwt.
Pressure : 200 lb.
Cyls. : 19½″ × 26″
Driving Wheels : 4′ 8½″.
Tractive Effort : 29,745 lb.
Superheated.

49500	49514	49528	49542
49501	49515	49529	49543
49502	49516	49530	49544
49503	49517	49531	49545
49504	49518	49532	49546
49505	49519	49533¶	49547
49506	49520	49534	49548
49507	49521	49535	49549
49508	49522	49536	49550
49509	49523	49537	49551
49510	49524	49538	49552
49511¶	49525	49539	49553
49512	49526	49540	49554
49513	49527	49541	49555

49556	49586	49616	49646
49557	49587	49617	49647
49558	49588	49618	49648
49559	49589	49619	49649
49560	49590	49620	49650
49561	49591	49621	49651
49562	49592	49622	49652
49563	49593	49623	49653
49564	49594	49624	49654
49565	49595	49625	49655
49566	49596	49626	49656
49567	49597	49627	49657
49568	49598	49628	49658
49569	49599	49629	49659
49570	49600	49630	49660
49571	49601	49631	49661
49572	49602	49632	49662
49573	49603	49633	49663
49574	49604	49634	49664
49575	49605	49635	49665
49576	49606	49636	49666
49577	49607	49637	49667
49578	49608	49638	49668
49579	49609	49639	49669
45980	49610	49640	49670¶
49581	49611	49641	49671
49582	49612	49642¶	49672
49583	49613¶	49643	49673
49584	49614	49644	49674
49585	49615	49645	

¶ Fitted for Oil-burning. **Total 175**

4-6-0 5P

Introduced : 1908. L.&Y. Rebuilt 1921.

Weight : Loco { 79 tons 1 cwt. (Nos. 50412/23/55). 77 tons 18 cwt. (Nos. (50432/42/8).

Pressure : 180 lb.

Cyls. : { (4) 16½" × 26". (Nos. 50412/55). (4) 15¾" × 26". (Nos. 50432/42/8).

Driving Wheels : 6' 3".

Tractive Effort : { 28,880 lb. (Nos. 50412/23/55). 26,315 lb. (Nos. 50432/42/8).

Walschaerts Valve Gear.
Superheated.

50412	50442	50455
50432	50448	

Total 5

2-4-2T 2P

Introduced : 1889. L. & Y.

Weight : 55 tons 19 cwt.

Pressure : 180 lb.

Cyls : { 18" × 26". 17½" × 26"†.

Driving Wheels: 5' 8".

Tractive Effort : { 18,955 lb. 18,360 lb.†

50621	50675†	50748	50823*
50622	50676	50749	50829*
50623	50678†	50750	50831*
50625	50681	50752†	50840*
50630	50686	50755	50842*
50631	50687	50757	50844*
50633	50689	50762	50849*
50634†	50692	50764	50850*
50636	50695	50765	50852*
50639	50696	50766†	50855*†
50640	50697	50777	50859*
50642	50703	50778	50865*†
50643†	50705	50781	50869*
50644	50711	50788	50872
50646	50712	50793	50873
50647	50714†	50795†	50880
50648	50715†	50798	50886
50650	50720	50799†	50887
50651	50721	50801	50889
50652†	50725	50802	50892
50653†	50731	50804†	50896
50655	50732	50806	50898
50656†	50735	50807†	50899
50660	50736	50812	
50665†	50738	50813	
50670	50743	50815†	
50671	50746	50818	

Total 104

* These locos are rebuilt with larger bunkers holding 4 tons of coal instead of 2 tons, but are otherwise similar to the rest. No. 50823 (L.Y.R. No. 34) first repuild, 1898.

† Cyls. : 17½" × 26". T.E.: 18,360 lb.

2-4-2T 3P

Introduced : 1898. L. & Y.
Weight : Various 66 tons 9 cwt. to 60 tons 5 cwt.
Pressure : 180 lb.
Cyls. : { 19½" × 26". (Nos. 50925/43/50). 20½" × 26" (remainder)
Tractive Effort: { 22,445 lb. (Nos. 50925/43/50). 24,585 lb. (remainder)
Driving Wheels : 5' 8".
Built with 4-ton bunkers.
Rebuilt with Belpaire Boilers, 1912.
Some superheated 1914-22.

50891	50909	50943	50951
50893	50925	50945	50953

Total 8

0-4-0ST 0F

Introduced : 1891. L. & Y.
Weight : 21 tons 5 cwt.
Pressure : 160 lb.
Cyls. : 13" × 18".
Driving Wheels : 3' 0⅜".
Tractive Effort : 11,335 lb.

51202	51217	51230	51240
51204	51218	51231	51241
51206	51221	51232	51244
51207	51222	51234	51246
51212	51227	51235	51253
51216	51229	51237	

Total 23

0-6-0ST 2F

Designed as 0-6-0 tender engines Barton Wright, 1877, L.Y.R. (Cl. 23). Rebuilt as 0-6-0ST by Aspinall, 1891-1900.
Weight : 43 tons 17 cwt.
Pressure : 140 lb.
Cyls. : 17½" × 26".
Driving Wheels : 4' 6".
Tractive Effort : 17,545 lb.

51307	51338	51375	51405
51313	51342	51376	51408
51316	51343	51379	51410
51318	51345	51381	51412
51319	51348	51390	51413
51321	51353	51396	51415
51323	51358	51397	51419
51325	51361	51400	51423
51336	51371	51404	51424
51425	51458	51482	51503
51427	51460	51484	51504
51429	51462	51486	51506
51432	51464	51487	51510
51436	51467	51488	51511
51438	51468	51489	51512
51439	51469	51490	51513
51441	51470	51491	51514
51443	51471	51492	51516
51444	51472	51495	51519
51445	51474	51496	51521
51446	51475	51497	51524
51447	51477	51498	51526
51453	51479	51499	51530
51457	51481	51500	

Total 95

0-6-0T 1F

Introduced : 1897. L. & Y. (Cl. 24).
Weight : 43 tons 17 cwt.
Pressure : 140 lb.
Cyls. : 17" × 24".
Driving Wheels : 4' 0".
Tractive Effort : 15,285 lb.

51535	51537	51544	51546
51536			

Total 5

0-6-0 2F

Introduced : 1887. L. & Y.
Weight : Loco. 39 tons 1 cwt.
Pressure : 140 lb.
Cyls. 17½" × 26".
Driving Wheels : 4' 6".
Tractive Effort : 17,545 lb.

52016	52030	52043	52053
52019	52031	52044	52056
52021	52034	52045	52059
52022	52036	52047	52063
52023	52037	52049	52064
52024	52041	52051	

Total 23

0-6-0 3F

Introduced : 1889. L. & Y.
Weight : Loco. 42 tons 3 cwt.
Pressure : 180 lb.
Cyl. : 18" × 26".
Driving Wheels : 5' 1".
Tractive Effort : 21,130 lb.

52088	52091	52093	52095
52089	52092	52094	52098

52099	52175	52260	52355
52100	52176	52262	52356
52102	52177	52266	52357
52103	52179	52268	52358
52104	52181	52269	52360
52105	52182	52270	52362
52107	52183	52271	52363
52108	52184	52272	52365
52110	52186	52273	52366
52111	52189	52275	52368
52112	52191	52278	52369
52118	52192	52279	52374
52119	52194	52280	52376
52120	52196	52284	52378
52121	52197	52285	52379
52123	52201	52288	52381
52124	52203	52289	52382
52125	52207	52290	52386
52126	52208	52293	52387
52129	52212	52294	52388
52132	52215	52296	52389
52133	52216	52299	52390
52135	52217	52300	52393
52136	52218	52304	52397
52137	52219	52305	52399
52138	52220	52309	52400
52139	52225	52311	52403
52140	52229	52312	52404
52141	52230	52317	52405
52143	52231	52319	52407
52150	52232	52321	52408
52154	52233	52322	52410
52156	52235	52326	52411
52157	52236	52328	52412
52159	52237	52330	52413
52160	52238	52331	52414
52161	52239	53333	52415
52162	52240	52334	52416
52163	52243	52336	52418
52164	52244	52338	52427
52165	52245	52341	52428
52166	52246	52343	52429
52167	52248	52345	52430
52169	52250	52348	52431
52170	52252	52349	52432
52171	52253	52350	52433
52172	52255	52351	52435
52174	52258	52353	52437

52438	52448	52460	52523
52439	52449	52461	52524
52440	52450	52464	52525
52441	52452	52465	52526
52442	52453	52466	52527
52443	52454	52515	52529
52444	52455	52517	
52445	52456	52518	
52446	52458	52521	
52447	52459	52522	

Total 235

NOTE :
For purposes of classification, the locomotives listed on pages 41-3 are not in numerical order

0-6-0 3F

Introduced : 1913. Furness.
Weight : Loco. 42 tons 13 cwt.
Pressure : 170 lb.
Cyls. : 18″ × 26″.
Driving Wheels : 4′ 7½″
Tractive Effort : 21,935 lb.

52494	52501	52509	52510
52499	52508		

Total 6

0-6-0 3F

Introduced : 1909. L. & Y.
Weight : Loco. 46 tons 10 cwt.
Pressure : 180 lb.
Cyls. : 20½″ × 26″.
Driving Wheels : 5′ 1″.
Tractive Effort : 27,405 lb.
Superheated.

52528	52559	52580	52598
52541	52561	52581	52602
52542	52569	52582	52607
52545	52572	52583	52608
52549	52574	52586	52609
52551	52575	52587	52615
52554	52576	52588	52616
52557	52578	52590	52619
52558	52579	52592	

Total 35

0-8-0 6F

Introduced : 1901. L. & Y.
Weight : Loco. 53 tons 16 cwt.
Pressure : 180 lb.
Cyls. : 20″ × 26″.
Driving Wheels : 4′ 6″.
Tractive Effort : 29,465 lb.

52727	52821	52827	52834
52782	52822	52828	52839
52806	52825	52831	

Total 11

0-8-0 7F

Introduced : 1912. L. & Y. (Cl. 31).
Weight : Loco. 66 tons 4 cwt.
Pressure : 180 lb.
Cyls. : 21½″ × 26″.
Driving Wheels : 4′ 6″.
Tractive Effort : 34,055 lb.
Superheated.

52856	52886	52916	52956
52857	52906	52945	52962
52870	52910	52952	52971
52877	52913		

Total 14

2-8-0 7F

Introduced : 1914. S. & D. J.
Weight: Loco (53800-5) 64 tons 15 cwt.
(53806-10) 68 tons 11 cwt.
Pressure : 190 lb.
Cyls. : 21″ × 28″
Driving Wheels : 4′ 8½″.
Tractive Effort : 35,295 lb.
Walschaerts Valve Gear.
Superheated.

53800	53803	53806	53809
53801	53804	53807	53810
53802	53805	53808	

Total 11

(S. & D.J. Nos. 80-90.)
N.B.—53806-10 : built 1925, with larger boilers.

4-4-0 2P

Introduced 1898. Caledonian.
Weight : Loco. 56 tons 10 cwt.
Pressure : 180 lb.
Cyls. : 19″ × 26″.
Driving Wheels : 6′ 6″.
Tractive Effort : 18,410 lb.

54363 (Dunalastair IV Cl. 1910)

Total 1

4-4-0 "Loch" Class 2P

Introduced : 1896. Highland.
Weight : Loco. 54 tons 10 cwt.
Pressure : 180 lb.
Cyls. 19″ × 24″.
Driving Wheels : 6′ 3½″.
Tractive Effort : 17,560 lb.
(Rebuilt with C. Rly. non-superheater boiler).

54385 Loch Tay

Total 1

4-4-0 "Ben" Class 2P

Introduced 1898. Highland.
Weight : Loco. 46 tons 17 cwt.
Pressure : 180 lb.
Cyls. : 18¼″ × 26″.
Driving Wheels : 6′ 0″.
Tractive Effort : 18,400 lb.

54397 Ben-y-Gloe
54398 Ben Alder
54399 Ben Wyvis
54401 Ben Vrackie
54403 Ben Attow
54404 Ben Clebrig
54409 Ben Alisky
54410 Ben Dearg

Total 8

4-4-0 3P

Introduced : 1907. Caledonian.
Weight : Loco. 59 tons 0 cwt.
Pressure : 180 lb.
Cyls.: 20¼″ × 26″.
Driving Wheels : 6′ 6″.
Tractive Effort : 20,915 lb.
Dunalastair IV Class, rebuilt, Superheated.

54438 Rebuilt 1917
54439 ,, 1915

Total 2

4-4-0 3P

Introduced : 1910. Caledonian.
Weight : Loco. 59 tons 0 cwt.
Pressure : 180 lb.
Cyls. 20¼″ × 26″.
Driving Wheels : 6′ 6″.
Tractive Effort : 20,915 lb.
Dunalastair IV Class. Superheated.

54440	54444	54447	54450
54441	54445	54448	54451
54443	54446	54449	54452

54453	54455	54457	54459
54454	54456	54458	54460

Total 20

4-4-0 3P

Introduced : 1916. Caledonian.
"713" and "918" classes.
Weight : Loco. 61 tons 5 cwt.
Pressure : 180 lb.
Cyls. 20″ × 26″.
Driving Wheels : 6′ 6″.
Tractive Effort : 20,400 lb.
Superheated.

54461	54465	54469	54473
54462	54466	54470	54474
54463	54467	54471	54475
54464	54468	54472	54476

Total 16

4-4-0 3P

Introduced : 1920. Caledonian.
(Nos. 66-97).
Weight : Loco. 61 tons 5 cwt.
Pressure : 180 lb.
Cyls. : 20½″ × 26″.
Driving Wheels : 6′ 6″.
Tractive Effort : 21,435 lb.
Superheated.

54477	54485	54493	54501
54478	54486	54494	54502
54479	54487	54495	54503
54480	54488	54496	54504
54481	54489	54497	54505
54482	54490	54498	54506
54483	54491	54499	54507
54484	54492	54500	54508

Total 32

4-6-0 4P

Introduced : 1925-6. L.M.S.
(Modified Caledonian "60" Class).
Weight : Loco. 74 tons 15 cwt.
Pressure : 180 lb.
Cyls. : 20½″ × 26″.
Driving Wheels : 6′ 1″.
Tractive Effort : 22,900 lb.
Superheated.

54630	54638	54642	54647
54634	54639	54645	54648
54635	54640	54646	54649
54636	54641		

Total 14

4-6-0 4P

Introduced : 1916. Caledonian.
Weight : Loco. 75 tons 0 cwt.
Pressure : 180 lb.
Cyls. : 20″ × 26″.
Driving Wheels : 6′ 1″.
Tractive Effort : 21,795 lb.
Superheated.

54650	54652	54653	54654
54651			

Total 5

4-6-0 "Clan" Class 4P

Introduced : 1919. Highland.
Weight : Loco. 62 Tons 5 cwt.
Pressure : 175 lb.
Cyls. : 21″ × 26″.
Driving Wheels : 6′ 0″.
Tractive Effort : 23,688 lb.
Walschaerts Valve Gear.
Superheated.

54767 Clan Mackinnon

Total 1

0-4-4T 0P

Introduced : 1905. Highland.
Weight : 35 tons 15 cwt.
Pressure : 150 lb.
Cyls. : 14″ × 20″.
Driving heels : 4′ 6″.
Tractive Effort : 9,255 lb.

55051	55053

Total 2

0-4-4T 2P

Introduced : 1895. Caledonian.
Weight : 53 tons 16 cwt.
Pressure : 180 lb.
Cyls. : 18″ ×26″.
Driving Wheels : 5′ 9″.
Tractive Effort : 18,680 lb.
(Originally fitted with condensing apparatus).

55119	55126	55134	55141
55121	55127	55135	55142
55122	55129	55136	55143
55123	55130	55138	55144
55124	55132	55139	55145
55125	55133	55140	55146

Total 24

0-4-4T 2P

Introduced: 1900. Caledonian.
Weight: 53 tons 19 cwt.
Pressure: 180 lbs.
Cyls.: 18" × 26".
Driving Wheels: 5' 9".
Tractive Effort: 18,680 lb.

55159	55179	55200	55220
55160	55181	55201	55221
55161	55182	55202	55222
55162	55183	55203	55223
55164	55184	55204	55224
55165	55185	55206	55225
55166	55186	55207	55226
55167	55187	55208	55227
55168	55188	55209	55228
55169	55189	55210	55229
55170	55191	55211	55230
55171	55192	55212	55231
55172	55193	55213	55232
55173	55194	55214	55233
55174	55195	55215	55234
55175	55196	55216	55235
55176	55197	55217	55236
55177	55198	55218	
55178	55199	55219	

Total 74

0-4-4T 2P

Introduced: 1922. Caledonian. (Nos. 431-4
Weight: 57 tons 17 cwt.
Pressure: 180 lb.
Cyls.: 18¼" × 26".
Driving Wheels: 5' 9".
Tractive Effort: 19,200 lb.
Fitted with cast-iron front buffer beam for banking purposes.

55237	55238	55239	55240

Total 4

0-4-4T 2P

Introduced: 1925. Caledonian type enlarged L.M.S.
Weight: 59 tons 12 cwt.
Pressure: 180 lb.
Cyls.: 18¼" × 26".
Driving Wheels: 5' 9".
Tractive Effort: 19,200 lb.

55260	55263	55266	55268
55261	55264	55267	55269
55262	55265		

Total 10

4-6-2T 4P

Introduced: 1917. Caledonian.
Weight: 91 tons 13 cwt.
Pressure: 180 lb.
Cyls.: 19½" × 26".
Driving Wheels: 5' 9".
Tractive Effort: 21,920 lb.
Superheated.

55350	55353	55356	55360
55351	55354	55359	55361
55352			

Total 9

0-4-0ST 0F

Introduced: 1885. Caledonian.
Weight: 27 tons 7 cwt.
Pressure: 160 lb.
Cyls.: 14" × 20".
Driving Wheels: 3' 8".
Tractive Effort: 12,115 lb.

56010	56026	56030	56035
56011	56027	56031	56038
56020	56028	56032	56039
56025	56029		

Total 14

0-6-0T 2F

Introduced: 1912. Caledonian. ("Dock" Class).
Weight: 47 tons 15 cwt.
Pressure: 160 lb.
Cyls.: 17" × 22".
Driving Wheels: 4' 0".
Tractive Effort: 18,015 lb.

56151	56157	56163	56169
56152	56158	56164	56170
56153	56159	56165	56171
56154	56160	56166	56172
56155	56161	56167	56173
56156	56162	56168	

Total 23

0-6-0T 3F

Introduced: 1896. Caledonian.
Weight: 49 tons 15 cwt.
Pressure: 160 lb.
Cyls.: 18" × 26".
Driving Wheels: 4' 6".
Tractive Effort: 21,215 lb.

56230	56233	56236	56239
56231	56234	56237	56240
56232	56235	56238	56241

56242	56277	56312	56347
56243	56278	56313	56348
56244	56279	56314	56349
56245	56280	56315	56350
56246	56281	56316	56351
56247	56282	56317	56352
56248	56283	56318	56353
56249	56284	56319	56354
56250	56285	56320	56355
56251	56286	56321	56356
56252	56287	56322	56357
56253	56288	56323	56358
56254	56289	56324	56359
56255	56290	56325	56360
56256	56291	56326	56361
56257	56292	56327	56362
56258	56293	56328	56363
56259	56294	56329	56364
56260	56295	56330	56365
56261	56296	56331	56366
56262	56297	56332	56367
56263	56298	56333	56368
56264	56299	56334	56369
56265	56300	56335	56370
56266	56301	56336	56371
56267	56302	56337	56372
56268	56303	56338	56373
56269	56304	56339	56374
56270	56305	56340	56375
56271	56306	56341	56376
56272	56307	56342	
56273	56308	56343	
56274	56309	56344	
56275	56310	56345	
56276	56311	56346	

Total 147

0-6-0 2F

Introduced : 1883. Caledonian.
Weight : Loco. 42 tons 4 cwt.
Pressure : 180 lb.
Cyls. : 18″ × 26″.
Driving Wheels : 5′ 0″.
Tractive Effort : 21,480 lb.
(102 engines fitted with Westinghouse brake for working passenger trains)

57230	57233	57236	57239
57231	57234	57237	57240
57232	57235	57238	57241

57242	57294	57351	57403
57243	57295	57352	57404
57244	57296	57353	57405
57245	57298	57354	57407
57246	57299	57355	57409
57247	57300	57356	57410
57249	57302	57357	57411
57250	57303	57358	57412
57251	57305	57359	57413
57252	57306	57360	57414
57253	57307	57361	57415
57254	57309	57362	57416
57255	57310	57363	57417
57256	57311	57364	57418
57257	57312	57365	57419
57258	57314	57366	57420
57259	57315	57367	57421
57260	57316	57368	57423
57261	57317	57369	57424
57262	57318	57370	57425
57263	57319	57372	57426
57264	57320	57373	57427
57265	57321	57375	57429
57266	57322	57377	57430
57267	57323	57378	57431
57268	57324	57379	57432
57269	57325	57381	57433
57270	57326	57382	57434
57271	57328	57383	57435
57272	57329	57384	57436
57273	57331	57385	57437
57274	57332	57386	57438
57275	57334	57387	57439
57276	57335	57388	57440
57277	57336	57389	57441
57278	57337	57390	57443
57279	57338	57391	57444
57280	57339	57392	57445
57282	57340	57393	57446
57283	57341	57394	57447
57284	57342	57395	57448
57285	57344	57396	57449
57286	57345	57397	57450
57287	57346	57398	57451
57288	57347	57399	57452
57289	57348	57400	57453
57291	57349	57401	57454
57292	57350	57402	57455

57456	57461	57466	57470
57457	57462	57467	57471
57458	57463	57468	57472
57459	57464	57469	57473
57460	57465		

Total 222

N.B.—57325-57473 built by Lambie and McIntosh.

0-6-0 3F

Introduced : 1899. Caledonian..
Weight : Loco. 45 tons 14 cwt.
Pressure : 180 lb.
Cyls. : 18½" × 26".
Driving Wheels : 5' 0".
Tractive Effort : 22,690 lb.
(20 engines fitted with Westinghouse brake for working passenger trains)

57550	57576	57600	57625
57552	57577	57601	57626
57553	57578	57602	57627
57554	57579	57603	57628
57555	57580	57604	57629
57556	57581	57605	57630
57557	57582	57606	57631
57558	57583	57607	57632
57559	57584	57608	57633
57560	57585	57609	57634
57561	57586	57611	57635
57562	57587	57612	57636
57563	57588	57613	57637
57564	57589	57614	57638
57565	57590	57615	57639
57566	57591	57617	57640
57568	57592	57618	57642
57569	57593	57619	57643
57570	57594	57620	57644
57571	57595	57621	57645
57572	57596	57622	
57573	57597	57623	
57575	57599	57624	

Total 89

0-6-0 3F

Introduced : 1918. Caledonian. ("294" Class).
Weight : Loco. 50 tons 13 cwt.
Pressure : 180 lb.
Cyls. : 18½" × 26".
Driving Wheels: 5' 0".
Tractive Effort : 22,690 lb.
Superheated.

57650	57658	57667	57673
57651	57659	57668	57674
57652	57661	57669	57679
57653	57663	57670	57681
57654	57665	57671	57682
57655	57666	57672	

Total 23

0-6-0 3F

Introduced : 1919. Caledonian ("670" Class).
Weight : Loco. 50 tons 13 cwt.
Pressure : 180 lb.
Cyls.: 18½" × 26".
Driving Wheels : 5' 0".
Tractive Effort : 22,690 lb.
Superheated.

57684	57688	57690	57691
57686	57689		

Total 6

0-6-0 3F

Introduced : 1900. Highland.
Weight : Loco. 43 tons 10 cwt.
Pressure : 175 lb.
Cyls.: 18½" × 26".
Driving Wheels : 5' 0".
Tractive Effort : 21,470 lb.

57693	57695	57698	57702
57694	57697	57699	

Total 7

4-6-0 4F

Introduced : 1918. Highland ("Clan Goods" Class).
Weight : Loco. 56 tons 9 cwt.
Pressure : 175 lb.
Cyls.: 20½" × 26".
Driving Wheels : 5' 3".
Tractive Effort : 25,800.
Walschaerts Valve Gear. Superheated.

57950	57953	57955	57956
57951	57954		

Total 6

"Prince of Wales" Class

4-6-0 4P

Introduced : 1911. L.N.W.
Weight : Loco. 66 tons 5 cwt.
Pressure : 180 lb.
Cyls.: 20½" × 26".
Driving Wheels : 6' 3".
Tractive Effort : 22,290 lb.
Superheated.
(Former L.M.S. numbers in brackets)

58000 (25648) Queen of the Belgians
58001 (25673) Lusitania
58002 (25752)

Total 3

"Precursor" Class

4-4-0 3P

Introduced : 1904. L.N.W.
Weight : Loco. 59 tons 17 cwt.
Pressure : 180 lb.
Cyls.: 20½" × 26".
Driving Wheels : 6' 9".
Tractive Effort : 20,640.
Rebuilt with superheated Belpaire boiler.
(Former L.M.S. number in brackets)

58010 (25297) Sirocco

2-4-0 1P

Introduced : 1876. Midland.
(Former L.M.S. numbers in brackets)

58020 (20155)

Built : 1876
Weight : 40 tons 10 cwt
Pressure : 140 lb.
Cyls.: 18" × 24".
Driving Wheels : 6' 3".
Tractive Effort : 12,340 lb.

58022 (20216)

Built : 1879.
Weight : 40 tons 16 cwt.
Pressure : 140 lb.
Cyls.: 18" × 26".
Driving Wheels : 6' 9".
Tractive Effort : 12,375 lb.

0-4-4T 1P

Introduced : 1875. Midland.
Weight : 53 tons 4 cwt.
Pressure : 140 lb.
Cyls.: 18" × 24".
Driving Wheels : 5' 7".
Tractive Effort : 13,810 lb.

(Former L.M.S. number in brackets)

58030	(1239)	58034	(1251)
58031	(1246)	58035	(1252)
58032	(1247)	58036	(1255)
58033	(1249)	58038	(1261)

Total 8

0-4-4T 1P

Introduced : 1881. Midland.
Weight : 53 tons 4 cwt.
Pressure : 58039-58 140 lb.
58059-91 150 lb.
Cyls.: 18" × 24".
Driving Wheels : 5' 4".
Tractive Effort : 58039-58 14,460 lb.
58059-91 15,490 lb.
Some rebuilt with Belpaire boilers
(Former L.M.S. numbers in brackets)

58039	(1272)	58067	(1370)
58040	(1273)	58068	(1371)
58041	(1275)	58069	(1373)
58042	(1278)	58070	(1375)
58043	(1287)	58071	(1377)
58045	(1295)	58072	(1379)
58046	(1298)	58073	(1382)
58047	(1303)	58074	(1389)
58048	(1315)	58075	(1390)
58049	(1322)	58076	(1396)
58050	(1324)	58077	(1397)
58051	(1330)	58078	(1402)
58052	(1337)	58079	(1406)
58053	(1340)	58080	(1411)
58054	(1341)	58081	(1413)
58056	(1344)	58082	(1416)
58057	(1348)	58083	(1420)
58058	(1350)	58084	(1421)
58059	(1353)	58085	(1422)
58060	(1357)	58086	(1423)
58061	(1358)	58087	(1424)
58062	(1360)	58088	(1425)
58063	(1365)	58089	(1426)
58064	(1366)	58090	(1429)
58065	(1367)	58091	(1430)
58066	(1368)		

Total 51

2-4-0T 1P

Introduced : 1877. L.N.W.
Weight : 38 tons 4 cwt.
Pressure : 150 lb.
Cyls.: 17″ × 20″.
Driving Wheels : 4′ 8½″.
Tractive Effort : 13,045 lb.
(Former L.M.S. number in brackets)

58092 (26428) **Total 1**

0-10-0

Introduced : 1919. Midland.
Weight : Loco. 73 tons 13 cwt.
Pressure : 180 lb.
Cyls. (4) : 16¾″ × 28″.
Driving Wheels : 4′ 7½″.
Tractive Effort : 43,315 lb.
Walschaerts Valve Gear.
(Former L.M.S. number in brackets)

58100 (22290) **Total 1**

Used for banking heavy trains on the Lickey incline.

0-6-0 2F

Introduced : 1868. Midland.
Weight : Loco. 37 tons 12 cwt.
Pressure : 160 lb.
Cyls.: 18″ × 24″.
Driving Wheels : 5′ 3″.
Tractive Effort : 16,785 lb.
Double Frames. Reboilered.
(Former L.M.S. numbers in brackets)

58110	(22630)*	58112	(22853)
58111	(22846)	58113	(22863)

Total 4

* Round top firebox ; the remainder Belpaire boilers.

0-6-0 2F

Introduced : 1875. Midland.
Weight: Loco. Various. 40 tons 3 cwt. to 37 tons 12 cwt.
Pressure : 160 lb.
Cyls.: 18″ × 26″.
Driving Wheels : 4′ 11″.
Tractive Effort : 19,420 lb.
Several rebuilt with small non-superheated Belpaire boilers.
(Former L.M.S. numbers in brackets)

58114	(22900)	58120	(22912)
58115	(22901)	58121	(22913)
58116	(22902)	58122	(22915)
58117	(22904)	58123	(22918)
58118	(22907)	58124	(22920)
58119	(22911)	58125	(22921)

58126	(22924)	58168	(2995)
58127	(22926)	58169	(2996)
58128	(22929)	58170	(2997)
58129	(22931)	58171	(2998)
58130	(22932)	58172	(2999)
58131	(22933)	58173	(23000)
58132	(22934)	58174	(23001)
58133	(22935)	58175	(23002)
58134	(22940)	58176	(23003)
58135	(22944)	58177	(23005)
58136	(22945)	58178	(23006)
58137	(22946)	58179	(23007)
58138	(22947)	58180	(23008)
58139	(22950)	58181	(23009)
58140	(22951)	58182	(23010)
58141	(22953)	58183	(23011)
58142	(22954)	58184	(23012)
58143	(22955)	58185	(23013)
58144	(22958)	58186	(23014)
58145	(22959)	58187	(23018)
58146	(22963)	58229	(3130)
58147	(22965)	58230	(3134)
58148	(22967)	58231	(3138)
58149	(22968)	58232	(3140)
58151	(22970)	58233	(3144)
58152	(22971)	58234	(3149)
58153	(22974)	58235	(3150)
58154	(22975)	58236	(3151)
58155	(22976)	58237	(3154)
58156	(22977)	58238	(3156)
58157	(22978)	58239	(3157)
58158	(22982)	58240	(3161)
58159	(22983)	58241	(3164)
58160	(22984)	58242	(3166)
58161	(2987)	58243	(3168)
58162	(2988)	58244	(3171)
58163	(2989)	58245	(3173)
58164	(2990)	58246	(3175)
58165	(2992)	58247	(3176)
58166	(2993)	58248	(3177)
58167	(2994)		

Total 93

N.B.—Nos. 58161-58172 and 58173-58187 were originally built with Cyls. 17½″ × 26″, and driving wheels 4′ 10″.

0-6-0 2F

Introduced : 1878. Midland.
Weight : Loco. Various. 40 tons 3 cwt. to 37 tons 12 cwt.
Pressure : 160 lb.
Cyls.: 18″ × 26″.
Driving Wheels : 5′ 3″.
Tractive Effort : 18,185 lb.
Several rebuilt with small non-superheated Belpaire boilers.

(Former L.M.S. numbers in brackets)

58188	(3023)	58249	(3190)
58189	(3027)	58251	(3229)
58190	(3031)	58252	(3262)
58191	(3035)	58253	(3264)
58192	(3037)	58254	(3270)
58193	(3038)	58255	(3311)
58194	(3039)	58256	(3360)
58195	(3042)	58257	(3372)
58196	(3044)	58258	(3377)
58197	(3045)	58259	(3385)
58198	(3047)	58260	(3420)
58199	(3048)	58261	(3423)
58200	(3049)	58262	(3425)
58201	(3051)	58264	(3445)
58202	(3052)	58265	(3451)
58203	(3054)	58267	(3477)
58204	(3058)	58368	(3479)
58206	(3062)	58269	(3485)
58207	(3064)	58270	(3489)
58208	(3066)	58271	(3492)
58209	(3071)	58272	(3493)
58211	(3074)	58273	(3503)
58212	(3078)	58274	(3508)
58213	(3084)	58275	(3511)
58214	(3090)	58276	(3512)
58215	(3094)	58277	(3516)
58216	(3095)	58278	(3517)
58217	(3096)	58279	(3525)
58218	(3098)	58280	(3526)
58219	(3099)	58281	(3527)
58220	(3101)	58282	(3533)
58221	(3103)	58283	(3536)
58222	(3108)	58284	(3537)
58223	(3109)	58285	(3539)
58224	(3113)	58286	(3543)
58225	(3118)	58287	(3545)
58226	(3119)	58288	(3551)
58228	(3127)	58289	(3559)

58290	(3561)	58302	(3691)
58291	(3564)	58303	(3696)
58293	(3571)	58304	(3703)
58294	(3592)	58305	(3707)
58295	(3603)	58306	(3725)
58296	(3617)	58307	(3726)
58297	(3632)	58308	(3738)
58298	(3648)	58309	(3739)
58299	(3655)	58310	(3764)
58300	(3688)		

Total 95

N.B.—Nos. 58188-58228 originally built with Cyls. $17\frac{1}{2}$″ × 26″ and driving wheels 5′ $2\frac{1}{2}$″

For the purposes of classification, engines on pages 50 and 51 are not in numerical order.

0-6-0 2F

Introduced : 1873. L.N.W.
Weight : Loco. 32 ton 0 cwt.
Pressure : 150 lb.
Cyls.: 17″ × 24″.
Driving Wheels : 4′ $5\frac{1}{2}$″.
Tractive Effort : 16,530 lb.

(For Coal Traffic.)

(Former L.M.S. numbers in brackets)

58321	(28091)	58342	(28221)
58322	(28093)	58343	(28227)
58323	(28100)	58344	(28233)
58324	(28104)	58346	(28239)
58326	(28106)	58347	(28245)
58327	(28107)	58348	(28246)
58328	(28115)	58349	(28247)
58329	(28116)	58350	(28251)
58330	(28128)	58351	(28253)
58331	(28133)	58352	(28256)
58332	(28141)	58353	(28262)
58333	(28152)	58354	(28263)
58334	(28158)	58355	(28271)
58335	(28166)	58356	(28295)
58336	(28172)	58359	(28309)
58338	(28199)	58360	(28312)
58340	(28205)	58361	(28313)
58341	(28216)		

Total 35

0-6-0 2F

Introduced: 1887. L.N.W. ("Cauliflowers").
Weight: Loco. 36 tons 10 cwt.
Pressure: 150 lb.
Cyls.: 18" × 24".
Driving Wheels: 5' 2½".
Tractive Effort: 15,865 lb.
(Former L.M.S. numbers in brackets)

58362	(28318)	58398	(28515)
58363	(28333)	58399	(28521)
58364	(28335)	58400	(28525)
58365	(28337)	58401	(28526)
58367	(28339)	58402	(28527)
58368	(28345)	58403	(28529)
58369	(28370)	58404	(28531)
58371	(28385)	58406	(28543)
58372	(28392)	58407	(28544)
58373	(28403)	58409	(28548)
58375	(28408)	58410	(28549)
58376	(28417)	58411	(28551)
58377	(28428)	58412	(28553)
58378	(28430)	58413	(28555)
58379	(28442)	58414	(28556)
58380	(28443)	58415	(28559)
58381	(28450)	58416	(28561)
58382	(28451)	58417	(28575)
58383	(28457)	58418	(28580)
58384	(28458)	58419	(28583)
58385	(28460)	58420	(28585)
58386	(28464)	58421	(28589)
58388	(28487)	58422	(28592)
58389	(28492)	58424	(28598)
58391	(28499)	58425	(28608)
58392	(28505)	58426	(28611)
58393	(28507)	58427	(28616)
58394	(28509)	58429	(28619)
58396	(28512)	58430	(28622)
58397	(28513)		

Total 58

0-6-0T 2F

Introduced: 1879. North London.
Weight: 45 tons 10 cwt.
Pressure: 160 lb.
Cyls.: 17" × 24".
Driving Wheels: 4' 4".
Tractive Effort: 18,140 lb.
(Former L.M.S. numbers in brackets)

58850	(27505)	58851	(27509)
58852	(27510)	58858	(27520)
58853	(27512)	58859	(27522)
58854	(27513)	58860	(27527)
58855	(27514)	58861	(27528)
58856	(27515)	58862	(27530)
58857	(27517)	58863	(27532)

Total 14

0-4-2ST Crane Engine

(Square saddle)
Designed: Sharp-Stewart, 1858, as 0-4-0T. (North London.)
Weight: 32 tons 6 cwt.
Pressure: 120 lb.
Cyls.: 13" × 17".
Driving Wheels: 3' 10".
Tractive Effort: 6,370 lb.
(Former L.M.S. number in brackets)

58865 (27217) **Total 1**

0-6-0ST 2F

Designed: Webb, 1891. L.N.W.
Rebuilt, Whale, 1906, from 0-6-0 tender engines.
Weight: 34 tons 10 cwt.
Pressure: 150 lb.
Cyls.: 17" × 24".
Driving Wheels: 4' 5½".
Tractive Effort: 16,530 lb.
(Former L.M.S. number in brackets)

58870 (27480) **Total 1**

0-6-2T 2F

Introduced: 1882. L.N.W.
Weight: 43 tons 15 cwt.
Pressure: 150 lb.
Cyls.: 17" × 24".
Driving Wheels: 4' 5½".
Tractive Effort: 16,530 lb.
For coal traffic.
(Former L.M.S. numbers in brackets)

58880	(27553)	58890	(27619)
58881	(27561)	58891	(27621)
58882	(27562)	58892	(27625)
58883	(27580)	58893	(27627)
58884	(27585)	58894	(27635)
58885	(27586)	58895	(27654)
58886	(27591)	58896	(27669)
58887	(27596)	58897	(27674)
58888	(27602)	58898	(27681)
58889	(27603)	58899	(7692)

58900	(7699)	58919	(7773)
58902	(7710)	58921	(7782)
58903	(7711)	58923	(7789)
58904	(7720)	58924	(7791)
58905	(7721)	58925	(7794)
58906	(7730)	58926	(7799)
58907	(7733)	58927	(7802)
58908	(7737)	58928	(7803)
58910	(7741)	58929	(7808)
58911	(7746)	58930	(7816)
58912	(7751)	58932	(7822)
58913	(7752)	58933	(7829)
58914	(7756)	58934	(7830)
58915	(7757)	58935	(7833)
58916	(7759)		
58917	(7765)		

Total 50

Steam Rail Motor

0-4-0T locomotive combined with coach on unit underframe.

Designed : Whale, 1905. L.N.W.R.

Weight : 43 tons 8 cwt.

Pressure : 175 lb.

Cyls.: 9½″ × 15″.

Driving Wheels : 3′ 9″.

Tractive Effort : 4,475 lb.

Coach No. 29988

Total 1

CHIEF MECHANICAL ENGINEERS

BRITISH RAILWAYS (L.M. Region)

H. G. Ivatt ... 1948—

L.M.S.

George Hughes ... 1923—1925
Sir Henry Fowler ... 1925—1931
E. H. J. Lemon (Sir Ernest Lemon) 1931—1932
Sir William Stanier ... 1932—1944
Charles E. Fairburn ... 1944—1945
H. G. Ivatt ... ... 1945—1947

LOCOMOTIVE SUPERINTENDENTS AND C.M.E.'S—L.M.S. CONSTITUENT COMPANIES*

CALEDONIAN RAILWAY

Robert Sinclair (First loco engineer)† ... 1847—1856
Benjamin Connor ... 1856—1876
George Brittain ... ... 1876—1882
Dugald Drummond ... 1882—1890
Hugh Smellie 1890
J. Lambie ... ... 1890—1895
J. F. McIntosh ... 1895—1914
William Pickersgill ... 1914—1923

† Exclusive of previous service with amalgamated company.

FURNESS RAILWAY

R. Mason ... ... 1890—1897
W. F. Pettigrew ... ... 1897—1918
D. J. Rutherford ... ... 1918—1923

Previous to Mason, F.R. locomotives were designed by contract with "outside" builders.

GLASGOW AND SOUTH WESTERN RLY.

Patrick Stirling ... ... 1853—1866
James Stirling ... ... 1866—1877
Hugh Smellie ... ... 1877—1890
James Manson ... ... 1890—1912
Peter Drummond ... 1912—1918
R. H. Whitelegg ... ... 1918—1923

HIGHLAND RAILWAY

William Stroudley (First loco engineer) ... 1866—1869
David Jones ... ... 1869—1896
Peter Drummond ... 1896—1911
F. G. Smith ... ... 1912—1915
C. Cumming ... ... 1915—1923

*The status and title of Chief Mechanical Engineer were created by the L.Y.R. for J. A. F. Aspinall in 1886.

LOCOMOTIVE SUPERINTENDENTS AND C.M.E'S. (*continued*)

L. & Y.R.

Sir John Hawkshaw (Consultant),* Hurst and Jenkins successively to 1868

W. Hurst	1868—1876
W. Barton Wright ...	1876—1886
John A. F. Aspinall ...	1886—1899
H. A. Hoy	1899—1904
George Hughes	1904—1922

L.N.W.R.

Francis Trevithick and J. E. McConnell, first loco engineers, 1846, with Alexander Allan largely responsible for design at Crewe.*

John Ramsbottom ...	1857—1871
Francis William Webb ...	1871—1903
George Whale	1903—1909
Charles John Bowen-Cooke	1909—1920
Capt. Hewitt Pearson Montague Beames ...	1920—1921
George Hughes	1922

The L. & Y. amalgamated with L.N.W.R. in 1921.

L.T. & S.R.

Thomas Whitelegg ...	1880—1910
Robert Harben Whitelegg	1910—1912

(LTSR absorbed by M.R., control of locos. transferred to Derby as from Aug., 1912.)

MARYPORT & CARLISLE

Hugh Smellie	1870—1878
J. Campbell	1878—
William Coulthard ...	* —1904
J. B. Adamson	1904—1923

MIDLAND RAILWAY

Matthew Kirtley (First loco engineer) ...	1844—1873
Samuel Waite Johnson ...	1873—1903
Richard Mountford Deeley	1903—1909
Henry Fowler	1909—1923

*Date of actual entry into office not known.

NORTH LONDON RAILWAY

(Worked by L. & N.W. by agreement dated Dec., 1908.)

William Adams	1853—1873
J. C. Park	1873—1893
Henry J. Pryce	1893—1908

NORTH STAFFORDSHIRE RAILWAY

L. Clare	1876—1882
L. Longbottom	1882—1902
J. H. Adams	1902—1915
J. A. Hookham	1915—1923

W. Angus was Loco. Supt. at Stoke prior to 1876. No earlier records can be traced.

NORTHERN COUNTIES COMMITTEE

Bowman Malcolm ...	1876—1922
W. K. Wallace	1922—1930
H. P. Stewart	1930—1933
M. Patrick	1933—

SOMERSET AND DORSET JOINT RAILWAY

Until leased by Mid. and L. & S.W. (as from 1st Nov., 1875) locomotives were bought from outside builders, principally George England of Hatcham Iron Works, S.E. After the above date, Derby and its various Loco. Supts. and CMEs have acted for S. & D.J., aided by a resident Loco. Supt. stationed at Highbridge works.

WIRRAL

Eric G. Barker	1892—1902
T. B. Hunter	1903—1923

Barker of the Wirral Railway is noteworthy for originating the 4-4-4 tank type in this country (1896).

Above: Ex-L.N.W Class 1F 2-4-2T No. 6711 (New No. 46711)
[*Photo: H. C. Casserley*

Right : Class 7F 0-8-4T No. 7956 (New No. 47956)
[*Photo · C. R. L. Coles*

Below : Class 6F 0-8-2T No. 7887 (New No. 47887)
[*Photo: H. C. Casserley*

Above : Class 1F 0-6-0T No. 1686 (New No. 41686)
[*Photo : A. B. Crompton*

Left : Class 2P 0-4-4T No. 15225 (New No. 55225)
[*Photo : P. Ransome-Wallis*

Below : Service loco. (Crewe) 0-6-0ST No. 3323
[*Photo : R. Tourret*

Class 3P 4-4-2T No. 2148 (New No. 41966) [*Photo : H. C. Casserley*

Class 2P 2-4-2T No. 6762 (New No. 46762) [*Photo : J. A. Wood*

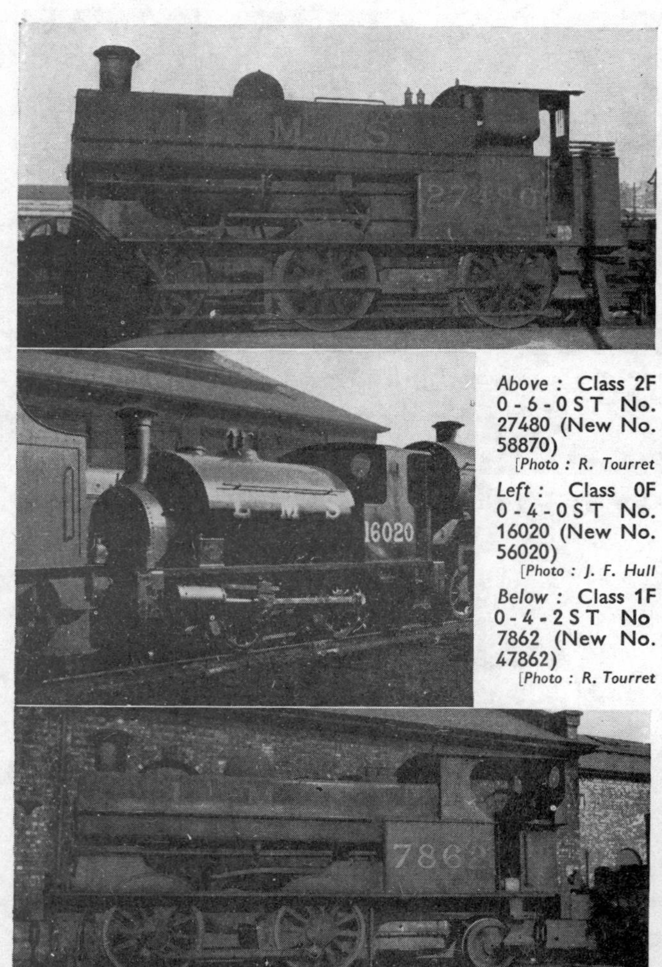

Above : Class 2F 0-6-0ST No. 27480 (New No. 58870)
[*Photo : R. Tourret*

Left : Class 0F 0-4-0ST No. 16020 (New No. 56020)
[*Photo : J. F. Hull*

Below : Class 1F 0-4-2ST No 7862 (New No. 47862)
[*Photo : R. Tourret*

FORMER L.M.S. SERVICE LOCOMOTIVES

Type	Description	L.M.S. No.	Former Coy.	Depot
0—4—0S.T.		41509	M.R.	Derby
Diesel		2	—	Beeston
0—6—0S.T.	Special	3323	L.N.W.R.	Crewe
0—6—0S.T.	"	C.D.3.	"	Wolverton
0—6—0S.T.	"	C.D.6.	"	"
0—6—0S.T.	"	C.D.7.	"	"
0—6—0S.T.	"	C.D.8.	"	"
0—6—0S.T.		51304	L.Y.R. (558)	Horwich
0—6—0S.T.		51305	" (553)	"
0—6—0S.T.		51324	" (552)	"
0—6—0S.T.		51368	" (131)	"
0—6—0S.T.		51394	" (173)	"
0—4—0	Battery Shunter	41550	M.R.	West India Docks
0—4—0	Battery Shunter	—	— N.S.R.	Elec. Engr's. Dept.

NOTE.—The L.N.W.R. locomotives still retain their original numbers.

HISTORIC LOCOMOTIVES PRESERVED IN STORE

Type	Name	Late Owning Company	Former L.M.S. No.
2—4—0	—	M.R.	20002
2—2—2	" Columbine "	L.N.W.R.	—
2—2—2	" Cornwall "	"	3020
2—4—0	" Hardwicke "	"	790*
0—4—0T	" Pet "**	"	—
4—2—2	—	M.R.	118†
0—4—0	" Coppernob "	F.R.	3
4—2—2	—	C.R.	123§
4—6—0	—	H.R.	103‡
0—4—2	" Lion "	Liverpool and Manchester Rly.	—

*L.M.S., No. 5031.
†L.M.S., No.673.
**18" gauge Works Tramway.
§L.M.S. No. 14010.
‡L.M.S. No. 17916.

LONDON MIDLAND REGION
SCOTTISH (ex.L.M.S.) REGION

MOTIVE POWER DEPOTS WITH CODES

Heavy type thus, **Rugby**, indicates a main district depot. In addition to depots shown, there are several sub-depots, the engines attached to which bear the code of the main district depot.

Depot	*Code*
Willesden	1A
Camden	1B
Watford	1C
Rugby	2A
Nuneaton	2D
Warwick	2E
Coventry	2F
Bletchley	2B
Northampton	2C
Bescot	3A
Bushbury	3B
Walsall	3C
Aston	3D
Monument Lane	3E
Shrewsbury	4A
Swansea	4B
Upper Bank	4C
Abergavenny	4D
Tredegar	4E
Crewe North	5A
Crewe South	5B
Stafford	5C
Stoke	5D
Alsager	5E
Uttoxeter	5F
Chester	6A
Mold Junction	6B
Birkenhead	6C
Llandudno Junc.	7A
Bangor	7B
Holyhead	7C
Rhyl	7D
Edge Hill	8A
Warrington	8B
Speke Junction	8C
Widnes	8D
Longsight	9A
Stockport	9B
Macclesfield	9C
Buxton	9D
Springs Branch	10A
Preston	10B
Patricroft	10C
Plodder Lane	10D
Sutton Oak	10E
Carnforth	11A
Barrow	11B
Oxenholme	11D
Tebay	11E
Carlisle (Kingmoor)	12A
Carlisle (Upperby)	12B
Penrith	12C
Workington	12D
Moor Row	12E
Beattock	12F
Dumfries	12G
Stranraer	12H
Plaistow	13A
Devons Road	13B
Tilbury	13C
Shoeburyness	13D
Upminster	13E
Cricklewood	14A
Kentish Town	14B
St. Albans	14C
Wellingboro'	15A
Kettering	15B
Leicester	15C
Bedford	15D
Nottingham	16A
Peterborough	16B
Kirkby	16C
Mansfield	16D
Derby	17A
Burton	17B
Coalville	17C
Rowsley	17D
Toton	18A
Westhouses	18B
Hasland	18C
Staveley	18D
Sheffield	19A
Millhouses	19B
Canklow	19C
Heaton Mersey	19D
Belle Vue	19E
Trafford Park	19F
Leeds	20A
Stourton	20B
Royston	20C
Normanton	20D
Manningham	20E
Skipton	20F
Hellifield	20G
Lancaster	20H
Saltley	21A
Bournville	21B
Bromsgrove	21C
Stratford-on-Avon	21D
Bristol	22A
Gloucester	22B
Bath	22C
Templecombe	22D
Highbridge	22E
Bank Hall	23A
Aintree	23B
Southport	23C
Wigan (C)	23D
Accrington	24A
Rose Grove	24B
Lostock Hall	24C
Lower Darwen	24D
Blackpool	24E
Fleetwood	24F
Wakefield	25A
Huddersfield	25B
Goole	25C
Mirfield	25D
Sowerby Bridge	25E
Low Moor	25F
Farnley Junction	25G
Newton Heath	26A
Agecroft	26B
Bolton	26C
Bury	26D
Bacup	26E
Lees	26F
Polmadie	27A
Greenock	27B
Hamilton	27C
Motherwell	28A
Edinburgh	28B
Carstairs	28C
Perth	29A
Aberdeen	29B
Dundee	29C
Forfar	29D
Corkerhill	30A
Hurlford	30B
Ardrossan	30C
Ayr	30D
St. Rollox	31A
Stirling	31B
Oban	31C
Grangemouth	31D
Dawsholm	31E
Inverness	32A
Aviemore	32B
Forres	32C

PRINCIPAL DIMENSIONS

TENDER ENGINES

Page	Power Classification	Class	Designer	Original Owning Co.	Building or Rebuilding Date	Boiler Pressure	Cylinders	Driving Wheels	Weight Engine in Working Order	Tractive Effort at 85% B.P.
						lb. per sq. in.			T. Cwt.	lb.
4-6-2										
25	7P	"Princess Coronation" ...	Stanier	L.M.S.	1937	250	(4) 16½×28	6′ 9″	105·5‡	40,000
25	7P	"Princess Royal" ...	Stanier	L.M.S.	1933	250	(4) 16¼×28	6′ 6″	104·10‖	40,285
4-6-0										
23	6P	Rebuilt "Scot"	Fowler (1927) ... Reb. Stanier	L.M.S.	1943	250	(3) 18×26	6′ 9″	84·1	33,150
23	6P	"Royal Scot"	Fowler	L.M.S.	1927	250	(3) 18×26	6′ 9″	84·18	33,150
21	6P	Rebuilt "Jubilee" ...	Stanier	L.M.S.	1942	250	(3) 17×26	6′ 9″	82·0	29,570
20	6P	Rebuilt "Patriot" ...	Fowler (1930) ... Reb. Ivatt	L.M.S.	1946	250	(3) 17×26	6′ 9″	82·0	29,570
21	5XP	"Jubilee"	Stanier	L.M.S.	1934	225	(3) 17×26	6′ 9″	79·11	26,610
20	5XP	"Patriot"	Fowler	L.M.S.	1930	200	(3) 18×26	6′ 9″	80·15	26,520
23	5XP	Rebuilt "Claughton" ...	Bowen Cooke (1921) Reb. Fowler	L.N.W.	1928	200	(4) 15¾×26	6′ 9″	79·9	27,070
18	5	....	Stanier	L.M.S.	1934	225	O 18½×28	6′ 0″	72·2	25,455
41	5P	....	Hughes (1908) ... Rebuilt	L. & Y.	1921	180	(4) 16½×26	6′ 3″	79·1	28,880
41	5P	....	Hughes	L. & Y.	1921	180	(4) 16½×26	6′ 3″	79·1	28,880
41	5P	....	Hughes	L. & Y.	1922	180	(4) 15¾×26	6′ 3″	77·18	26,315
49	4P	"Prince of Wales" ...	Bowen Cooke	L.N.W.	1911	180	20½×26	6′ 3″	66·5	22,290
30	4F	"19-inch Goods" ...	Whale	L.N.W.	1908	175	19×26	5′ 2½″	63·0	22,340
45	4P	....	Pickersgill	L.M.S.	1925	180	O 20½×26	6′ 1″	74·15	21,900
45	4P	....	Pickersgill	Cal.	1916	180	O 20×26	6′ 1″	75·0	21,795
45	4P	"Clan"	Cumming	High.	1919	175	O 21×26	6′ 0″	62·5	23,690
48	4F	"Clan Goods"	Cumming	High.	1918	175	O 20½×26	5′ 3″	56·9	25,800

Page	Power Classi-fication	Class	Designer	Original Owning Co.	Building or Re-building Date	Boiler Press-ure	Cylinders	Driving Wheels	Weight Engine in Working Order	Tractive Effort at 85% B.P.
						lb. per sq. in.			T. Cwt.	lb.
4-4-0										
5	4P	Compound	Fowler	L.M.S.	1924	200	(1) 19×26 (2) 21×26	6′ 9″	61·14	22,650
5	4P	Compound	Deeley	Mid.	1905	200	(1) 19×26 (2) 21×26	7′ 0″	61·14	21,840
49	3P	" Precursor "	Whale	L.N.W.	1904	180	20½×26	6′ 9″	59·17	20,640
5	3P	....	Johnson	Mid.	1901	175	20½×26	6′ 9″	55·7	20,065
45	3P	....	Pickersgill	Cal.	1920	180	20½×26	6′ 6″	61·5	21,435
45	3P	....	Pickersgill	Cal.	1916	180	20×26	6′ 6″	61·5	20,400
44	3P	" Dunalastair IV " ... Suphtr.	McIntosh	Cal.	1910	180	20¼×26	6′ 6″	59·0	20,915
44	3P	" Dunalastair IV " ... Suphtr. Rebt.	McIntosh	Cal.	1907	180	20¼×26	6′ 6″	59·0	20,915
4	2P	....	Fowler	L.M.S.	1928	180	19×26	6′ 9″	54·1	17,730
4	2P	....	Fowler	S. & D.J.	1930	180	19×26	6′ 9″	54·1	17,730
3	2P	....	Fowler	S. & D.J.	1914+	160	20½×26	7′ 0½″	53·7	17,585
4	2P	....	Johnson (1891+) ... Reb. Fowler	Mid.	1912+	160	20½×26	7′ 0½″	53·7	17,585
3	2P	....	Johnson (1882+) ... Reb. Fowler	Mid.	1910+	160	20½×26	7′ 0½″	53·7	17,585
44	2P	....	McIntosh	Cal.	1898	180	19×26	6′ 6″	56·10	18,410
44	2P	" Ben "	P. Drummond ...	High.	1898	180	18¼×26	6′ 0″	46·17	18,400
44	2P	" Loch "	Jones	High.	1896	180	O 19×24	6′ 3½″	54·10	17,560
2-6-6-2T										
28		" Garratt "	Fowler and Beyer Peacock	L.M.S.	1927	190	(4) 18½×26	5′ 3″	155·10ø	45,620

2-8-0										
28	8F	....	Stanier	L.M.S.	1935	225	O 18½ × 28	4′ 8½″	72·2	32,440
44	7F	....	Fowler	S. & D.J.	1914	190	O 21 × 28	4′ 8½″	{68·11 / 64·15}	35,295
2-6-0										
10	5F	....	Stanier ...	L.M.S.	1933	225	O 18 × 28	5′ 6″	69·2	26,290
9	5F	....	Hughes/Fowler ...	L.M.S.	1926	180	O 21 × 26	5′ 6″	66·0	26,580
10	4F	....	Ivatt	L.M.S.	1947	225	O 17½ × 26	5′ 3″	59·2	24,170
25	2F	....	Ivatt	L.M.S.	1946	200	O 16 × 24	5′ 0″	47·2	17,410
2-4-0										
49	1P	....	Johnson	Mid.	1879	140	18 × 26	6′ 9″	40·16	12,375
49	1P	....	Johnson	Mid.	1876	140	18 × 24	6′ 3″	40·10	12,340
0-10-0										
50		....	Fowler	Mid.	1919	180	(4) 16½ × 28	4′ 7½″	73·13	43,315
0-8-0										
40	7F	....	Fowler	L.M.S.	1929	200	19½ × 26	4′ 8½″	60·15	29,745
39	7F	G2a	See notes on page 00			175	20½ × 24	4′ 5½″	62·0	28,045
40	7F	G2				175	20½ × 24	4′ 5½″	62·0	28,045
39	6F	G1				160	20½ × 24	4′ 5½″	60·5	25,640
44	7F	....	Hughes	L. & Y.	1912	180	21½ × 26	4′ 6″	66·4	34,055
44	6F	....	Aspinall	L. & Y.	1901	180	20 × 26	4′ 6″	53·16	29,465
0-6-0										
16	4F	....	Fowler	L.M.S.	1924	175	20 × 26	5′ 3″	48·15	24,555
16	4F	....	Fowler	S. & D.J.	1922	175	20 × 26	5′ 3″	48·15	24,555
16	4F	....	Fowler	Mid.	1911	175	20 × 26	5′ 3″	48·15	24,555

Page	Power Classification	Class	Designer	Original Owning Co.	Building or Re-building Date	Boiler Pressure	Cylinders	Driving Wheels	Weight Engine in Working Order	Tractive Effort at 85% B.P.
						lb. per sq. in.			T. Cwt.	lb.
0-6-0—*continued*										
43	3F	....	Hughes	L. & Y.	1909	180	20½×26	5′ 1″	46·10	27,405
42	3F	....	Aspinall	L. & Y.	1889	180	18×26	5′ 1″	42·3	21,130
16	3F	....	Deeley	Mid.	1906	175	18½×26	5′ 3″	46·3	21,010
15	3F	....	Johnson/Deeley ...	Mid.	1885	175	18×26	5′ 3″	43·17	19,890
10	3F	....	Johnson	Mid.	1885	175	18×26	4′ 11″	43·17	21,240
15	3F	....	Johnson	S. & D.J.	1896	175	18×26	5′ 3″	43·17	19,890
42	3F	....	Pettigrew	Fur.	1913	170	18×26	4′ 7½″	42.13	21,935
48	3F	....	Pickersgill	Cal.	1919	180	18½×26	5′ 0″	50·13	22,690
48	3F	....	Pickersgill	Cal.	1918	180	18½×26	5′ 0″	50·13	22,690
48	3F	....	McIntosh	Cal.	1899	180	18½×26	5′ 0″	45·14	22,690
48	3F	....	P. Drummond ...	High.	1900	175	18¼×26	5′ 0″	43·10	21,470
52	2F	" Cauliflower "	Webb	L.N.W.	1887	150	18×24	5′ 2½″	36·10	15,865
51	2F	....	Webb	L.N.W.	1873	150	17×24	4′ 5½″	32·0	16,530
42	2F	....	Barton Wright ...	L. & Y.	1887	140	17½×26	4′ 6″	39·1	17,545
51	2F	....	Johnson	Mid.	1878	160	18×26	5′ 3″	Various from 40t. 3c. to 37t. 12c.	18,185
50	2F	....	Johnson	Mid.	1875	160	18×26	4′ 11″		19,420
50	2F	....	Kirtley	Mid.	1868	160	18×24	5′ 3″		16,785
47	2F	....	D. Drummond ...	Cal.	1883	180	18×26	5′ 0″	42·4	21,480

TANK ENGINES

Page	Power Classification	Class	Designer	Original Owning Co.	Building or Re-building Date	Boiler Pressure	Cylinders	Driving Wheels	Weight Engine in Working Order	Tractive Effort at 85% B.P.
4-6-2T										
46	4P	....	Pickersgill	Cal.	1917	180	O 19½×26	5′ 9″	91·13	21,920
4-4-2T										
7	3P	....	Whitelegg	L.M.S.	1923	170	O 19×26	6′ 6″	71·10	17,390
7	3P	....	Whitelegg	L.T. & S.	1897	170	O 19×26	6′ 6″	70·15	17,390
7	2P	....	Whitelegg	L.T. & S.	1900	170	O 19×26	6′ 6″	67·15	17,390

2-6-4T										
7	4P	....	Fairburn	L.M.S.	1945	200	O $19\frac{5}{8} \times 26$	5′ 9″	85·5	24,670
8	4P	....	Stanier	L.M.S.	1935	200	O $19\frac{5}{8} \times 26$	5′ 9″	87·17	24,670
8	4P	....	Stanier	L.M.S.	1934	200	(3) 16×26	5′ 9″	92·5	24,600
8	4P	....	Fowler	L.M.S.	1927	200	O 19×26	5′ 9″	86·5	23,125
2-6-2T										
3	3P	....	Stanier (Reb.) ...	L.M.S.	1941	200	O $17\frac{1}{2} \times 26$	5′ 3″	72·10	21,485
3	3P	....	Stanier	L.M.S.	1935	200	O $17\frac{1}{2} \times 26$	5′ 3″	71·5	21,485
3	3P	....	Fowler	L.M.S.	1930	200	O $17\frac{1}{2} \times 26$	5′ 3″	70·10††	21,485
6	2P	....	Ivatt	L.M.S.	1946	200	O 16×24	5′ 0″	63·5	17,410
2-4-2T										
42	3P	....	Aspinall/Hughes ...	L. & Y.	1898+	180	{ $20\frac{1}{2} \times 26$ / $19\frac{1}{2} \times 26$ }	5′ 8″ / 5′ 8″	Various from 66t. 9c. to 60t. 5c.	{ 24,585 / 22,245 }
41	2P	....	Aspinall	L. & Y.	1889	180	18×26	5′ 8″	57·0	18,955
41	2P	....	Aspinall	L. & Y.	1889	180	$17\frac{1}{2} \times 26$	5′ 8″	55·19	18,360
26	2P	....	Aspinall	Wirral	1890	180	$17\frac{1}{2} \times 26$	5′ 8″	55·19	18,360
26	1P	....	Webb	L.N.W.	1890	150	17×24	5′ 8½″	50·10	12,910
2-4-0T										
50	1P	....	Webb	L.N.W.	1877	150	17×20	4′ 8½″	38·4	13,045
0-8-4T										
28	7F	....	Beames	L.N.W.	1923	185	$20\frac{1}{2} \times 24$	4′ 5½″	88·0	29,815
0-8-2T										
28	6F	....	Bowen Cooke ...	L.N.W.	1911	170	$20\frac{1}{2} \times 24$	4′ 5½″	72·10	27,240

Page	Power Classification	Class	Designer	Original Owning Co.	Building or Re-building Date	Boiler Pressure	Cylinders	Driving Wheels	Weight Engine in Working Order	Tractive Effort at 85% B.P.
						lb. per sq. in.			T. Cwt.	lb.
0-6-2T										
7	3F		Whitelegg	Mid.*	1912*	170	18×26	5′ 3″	64·13	19,320
26	2P		Webb	L.N.W.	1898	150	18×24	5′ 2½″	52·6	15,865
52	2F		Webb	L.N.W.	1882	150	17×24	4′ 5½″	43·15	16,530
0-6-0T										
27	3F		Fowler	L.M.S.	1924	160	18×26	4′ 7″	49·10	20,835
27	3F		Fowler	S. & D.J.	1929	160	18×26	4′ 7″	46·3	20,835
26	3F		Johnson	Mid.	1899	160	18×26	4′ 7″	43·17	20,835
46	3F		McIntosh	Cal.	1896	160	18×26	4′ 6″	49·15	21,235
26	2F		Fowler	L.M.S.	1928	160	O 17×22	3′ 11″	43·12	18,400
52	2F		Park	N.L.	1879	160	O 17×24	4′ 4″	45·10	18,140
46	2F		McIntosh	Cal.	1912	160	O 17×22	4′ 0″	47·15	18,015
42	1F		Aspinall	L. & Y.	1897	140	O 17×24	4′ 0″	43·17	15,285
6	1F		Johnson	Mid.	1878	{150	17×24	4′ 7″	39·11	16,080
						{140	17×24	4′ 7″	39·11	15,005
0-6-0ST										
52	2F		Webb (1891)† Reb. Whale	L.N.W.	1906†	150	17×24	4′ 5½″	34·10	16,530
42	2F		Barton Wright (1877)§§ Reb. Aspinall	L. & Y.	1891+§§	140	17½×26	4′ 6″	43·17	17,545
0-4-4T										
7	2P		Stanier	L.M.S.	1932	160	18×26	5′ 7″	58·1	17,100
46	2P		McIntosh	L.M.S.	1925	180	18¼×26	5′ 9″	59·12	19,200
46	2P		Pickersgill	Cal.	1922	180	18¼×26	5′ 9″	57·17	19,200
46	2P		McIntosh	Cal.	1900	180	18×26	5′ 9″	53·19	18,680
45	2P		McIntosh	Cal.	1895	180	18×26	5′ 9″	53·16	18,680

49	1P	....	Johnson	Mid.	1881	{150	18 × 24	5′ 4″	53·4	15,490
						{140	18 × 24	5′ 4″	53·4	14,460
49	1P	....	Johnson	Mid.	1875	140	18 × 24	5′ 7″	53·4	13,810
45	0P	....	P. Drummond ...	High.	1905	150	14 × 20	4′ 6″	35·15	9,255

0-4-2ST

26	1F	....	Webb	L.N.W.	1901	150	17 × 24	4′ 5½″	34·17	16,530
52	Engine Crane	....	Sharp-Stewart ...	N.L.	1858§	120	13 × 17	3′ 10″	32·6	6,370

0-4-0T

6	0F	....	Deeley	Mid.	1907	160	O 15 × 22	3′ 9¾″	32.16	14,635
26		Sentinel (47190-1)... ...	....	S. & D.J.	1929	275	(4) 6¾ × 9	—	27.15	15,500
26		Sentinel (47180/1/2/3) ...	....	L.M.S.	1930	275	6¾ × 9	—	20.17	11,800
26		Sentinel (47184) ...	....	L.M.S.	1932	275	6¾ × 9	—	18.18	11,800
53		Rail Motor¶	Whale	L.N.W.	1905	175	9½ × 15	3′ 9″	43.8	4,475

0-4-0ST

26	0F	....	Stanier	L.M.S.	1932	160	O 15½ × 20	3′ 10″	33·0	14,205
23	0F	"Pugs"	Aspinall ...	L. & Y.	1891	160	O 13 × 18	3′ 0⅝″	21·5	11,335
6	0F	....	Johnson	Mid.	1897	150	O 15 × 20	3′ 10″	32·3	12,475
6	0F	....	Johnson	Mid.	1897	140	O 15 × 20	3′ 10″	32·3	11,640
6	0F	....	Johnson	Mid.	1897	140	O 13 × 20	3′ 10″	23·3	8,745
46	0F	....	D. Drummond ...	Cal.	1885	160	O 14 × 20	3′ 8″	27·7	12,115

NOTES

Tractive effort calculated to nearest 5 lb.
O —(in Cylinders column). Outside cylinders.
+ —(after date) Building or rebuilding continued subsequently
† —Designed in 1903 for L.T. & S. but taken direct into Midland stock when built.
‖ —Turbomotive 110t. 11c.
‡ —Streamlined engines 108t. 2c.

ø —Complete weight of unit in working order.
† —Rebuilt from 1891 0-6-0 tender engine.
§ —Originally 0-4-0T.
¶ —Combined with coach on unit underframe.
†† —Engines fitted with condensing apparatus 71t. 16c.
§§ —Rebuilt from 1877 0-6-0 tender engines.

THE ABC OF BRITISH LOCOMOTIVES

Edited by A. F. Cook

PART 4 60000-79999

STEAM LOCOMOTIVES :
EASTERN, NORTH-EASTERN
SCOTTISH (ex-L.N.E.) REGION
and M.O.S. 2-8-0

LONDON :

Ian Allan Ltd

1948

FOREWORD

THIS booklet lists all British Railways locomotives numbered between 60000 and 69999, and Ministry of Supply 2-8-0 locos numbered between 70000 and 79999 on loan to British Railways. This series of numbers includes all Eastern, North-Eastern and Scottish (ex-L.N.E.R.) steam locomotives, i.e. steam locomotives of the former L.N.E.R. Under the general British Railways renumbering scheme, the numbers of L.N.E.R. steam locomotives were increased by 60000, with the exception of Classes W1 and L1. Renumbering is being carried out only as locomotives visit main works for repairs, and thus it will be some time before all locomotives bear the numbers shown in this book.

Former L.N.E.R. electric and diesel electric locomotives have been renumbered in the 20000 and 15000 series, and details of them will be found in "ABC of British Railways Locomotives" Part 2 (Nos. 10000-39999).

ROUTE AVAILABILITY OF LOCOMOTIVES

Restrictions on the working of locomotives over the routes of the former L.N.E.R. are denoted by Route Availability numbers. In general a locomotive is not permitted to work over a line of lower R.A. number than itself. The scheme is as follows :

R.A.1 : F7, J15, J62, J63, J65, J71, Y1, Y3, Y6, Y7, Y8, Y10, Y11, Z4.

R.A.2 : E4, J24, J67/1, J70, J72, J77, J93, Y9, Z5.

R.A.3 : B12/1, D3, D41, F2 (modified for Eastern Section), F3, F4, F5, J3, J4, J10, J21, J25, J36, J66, J67/2, J68, J69, J88, J92, N9, N10.

R.A.4 : A6, B9, B12/3, D2, D31, D40, F1, F6, G5, J1, J5, J17, J26, J55, J83, N4, N5/2, N8, N13, N14, Q5, V4.

R.A.5 : A5, A8, B1, B2, B3, B4, B5, B6, B17/1, B17/4, C12, C13, C14, D1, D9, D15, D16, F2, J2, J6, J11, J19, J20, J27, J52, J73, J75, J94, K2, L2, M2, N1, N5/3, N7.

R.A.6 : C15, C16, D10, D11, D20, D29, D30, D32, D33, D34, J35, J39, J50, K1, K4, N2, N15, O1, O2, O3, O4, O7, Q6, V1, Y4.

R.A.7: A7, A10, B7, B8, B16/1, B17/5, C1, C4, L1, L3, Q7, U1, V3.

R.A.8 : B16/2, B16/3, C7, D49, J37, J38, K3, K5, Q1, S1, T1.

R.A.9 : A1, A2, A3, A4, V2, W1.

LOAD CLASSIFICATION

Freight locomotives of the Eastern Region are divided into the following " Load Classes," in ascending order of power. Certain N.E. Region classes which have been used on the Eastern Region are also included :

Load 1 : J10.
Load 2 : B4, B5, J1, J2, J3, J4, J21, J24, J66, J67, N1, N2, N4, N5.
Load 3 : B9, B12, B13, J5, J6, J11, J15, J52, J55, J68, J69, J77, J94.
Load 4 : B8, J17, J25, J50.
Load 5 : B1, J19, J26, J27, J39, K2.
Load 6 : B7, B16, J20, K3. K5, L3, Q1, Q4, Q5, Q6.
Load 7 : A2, O4, V2.
Load 8 : O1, O2, O3, O7, Q7, " Austerity."

NOTES ON THE USE OF THIS BOOK

In the lists of locomotives which follow :

1. Many of the classes listed are sub-divided, the sub-divisions being denoted in some cases by " Parts " shown thus : D16/3. At the head of each class will be found a list of such sub-divisions, if any, usually arranged in order of introduction. Each part is given there a reference mark by which its relevant dimensions, if differing from other parts, and the locos it comprises, in the list may be identified. Any other differences between locomotives are also indicated, with reference marks, below the details of the class's introduction. For further remarks on the classification of ex-L.N.E.R. locos, see the note on p. 72.

2. The lists of dimensions at the head of each class show locomotives fitted with two inside cylinders unless otherwise stated, e.g. (O) = two outside cylinders.

3. The following method is used to denote superheated locomotives, the letters being inserted, where applicable, after the boiler pressure details : Su = All engines superheated.
SS = Some engines superheated.

4. The date on which the first locomotive of a class was built is denoted by " Introduced." If the oldest locomotive still running was built at a later date, that also is indicated.

5. Where locomotives have been renumbered other than in the general British Railways scheme (see Foreword, p. 2), former L.N.E.R. numbers are shown in brackets.

6. The numbers of locomotives in service have been checked to **September 6th, 1948.**

7. **S denotes Service (Departmental) locomotive. This reference letter is introduced only for the reader's guidance and is not borne by the locomotive concerned.**

NUMERICAL LIST OF ENGINES AND CLASSES

4-6-2 Class A4

Introduced 1935. Streamlined.
* Inside cylinder reduced to 17".
† Non-corridor tender (remainder corridor).
Weights : Loco. 102 tons 19 cwt.
Tender { 64 tons 19 cwt. / 60 tons 7 cwt.†
Pressure : 250 lb. Su.
Cyls. { (3) 18½"×26". / (2) 18½"×26". (1) 17"×26"*
Driving Wheels : 6' 8"
T.E. { 35455 lb. / 33616 lb.*

60001† Sir Ronald Matthews
60002† Sir Murrough Wilson
60003* Andrew K. McCosh
60004† William Whitelaw
60005† Sir Charles Newton
60006 Sir Ralph Wedgwood
60007 Sir Nigel Gresley
60008 Dwight D. Eisenhower
60009 Union of South Africa
60010 Dominion of Canada
60011 Dominion of India
60012* Commonwealth of Australia
60013 Dominion of New Zealand
60014* Silver Link
60015 Quicksilver
60016 Silver King
60017 Silver Fox
60018† Sparrow Hawk
60019† Bittern
60020†*Dominion of Pakistan
60021† Wild Swan
60022 Mallard
60023† Golden Eagle
60024 Kingfisher
60025 Falcon
60026 Miles Beevor
60027 Merlin
60028 Walter K. Whigham
60029 Woodcock
60030† Golden Fleece
60031* Golden Plover
60032† Gannet
60033 Seagull
60034 Lord Faringdon

Total 34

4-6-2 Classes A10 & A3

A10* Introduced 1922; original Gresley Pacific.
Weights : Loco. 92 tons 9 cwt.
Tender 56 tons 6 cwt.
Pressure : 180 lb. Su. Cyls.: 20"×26"
Driving Wheels : 6' 8"
T.E.: 29,835 lb. Su.

A3 Introduced 1927 ; development of A10 with 220 lb. pressure (prototype and others rebuilt from A10). Some have G.N.-type tender† with coal rails, remainder L.N.E.R. pattern.
Weights : Loco. 96 tons 5 cwt.
Tender { 56 tons 6 cwt.† / 57 tons 18 cwt.
Pressure : 220 lb. Su. Cyls.: 19"×26"
Driving Wheels : 6' 8" T.E.: 32,910 lb.

60035 Windsor Lad
60036 Colombo
60037 Hyperion
60038 Firdaussi
60039 Sandwich
60040 Cameronian
60041 Salmon Trout
60042 Singapore
60043 Brown Jack
60044 Melton
60045 Lemberg
60046 Diamond Jubilee
60047 Donovan
60048 Doncaster
60049 Galtee More
60050 Persimmon
60051 Blink Bonny
60052 Prince Palatine
60053 Sansovino
60054 Prince of Wales
60055 Woolwinder
60056 Centenary
60057 Ormonde
60058 Blair Athol
60059 Tracery
60060 The Tetrarch

60061 Pretty Polly
60062 Minoru
60063 Isinglass
60064 Tagalie
60065 Knight of Thistle
60066 Merry Hampton
60067 Ladas
60068* Sir Visto
60069 Sceptre
60070 Gladiateur
60071 Tranquil
60072 Sunstar
60073 St. Gatien
60074 Harvester
60075 St. Frusquin
60076 Galopin
60077 The White Knight
60078 Night Hawk
60079 Bayardo
60080 Dick Turpin
60081 Shotover
60082 Neil Gow
60083 Sir Hugo
60084 Trigo
60085 Manna
60086 Gainsborough
60087 Blenheim
60088 Book Law
60089 Felstead
60090 Grand Parade
60091 Captain Cuttle
60092 Fairway
60093 Coronach
60094 Colorado
60095 Flamingo
60096 Papyrus
60097 Humorist
60098 Spion Kop
60099 Call Boy
60100 Spearmint
60101 Cicero
60102 Sir Frederick Banbury
60103 Flying Scotsman
60104 Solario
60105 Victor Wild
60106 Flying Fox
60107 Royal Lancer
60108 Gay Crusader
60109 Hermit
60110 Robert the Devil
60111 Enterprise
60112 St. Simon

Totals : Class A10 1
Class A3 77

4-6-2 Class A1

A1/1* Introduced 1945. Thompson rebuild of A10.
A1 Development of A1/1 for new construction (under construction).
Weights : Loco. { 101 tons.* / 104 tons 2 cwt.
Tender 60 tons 7 cwt.
Pressure : 250 lb. Su.
Cyls.: (3) 19″×26″
Driving Wheels : 6′ 8″ T.E.: 37,400 lb.

60113* Great Northern
60114 | 60115 | 60116

4-6-2 Class A2

A2/2* Introduced 1943. Original Thompson Pacific, rebuilt from Gresley Class P2 2-8-2 (introduced 1934).
Weight : Loco. 101 tons 10 cwt.
Pressure : 225 lb. Su.
Cyls.: (3) 20″×26″
Driving Wheels : 6′ 2″ T.E.: 40,320 lb.
A2/1† Introduced 1944. Development of Class A2/2, incorporating Class V2 2-6-2 type boiler.
Weight : Loco. 98 tons.
Pressure : 225 lb. Su.
Cyls.: (3) 19″×26″
Driving Wheels : 6′ 2″ T.E.: 36,385 lb.
A2/3‡ Introduced 1946. Development of Class A2/2 for new construction.
Weight : Loco. 101 tons 10 cwt.
Pressure : 250 lb. Su.
Cyls.: (3) 19″×26″
Driving Wheels : 6′ 2″ T.E.: 40,430 lb.
A2§ Introduced 1947. Peppercorn development of Class A2/3 with shorter wheelbase.
Weight : Loco. 101 tons.
Pressure : 250 lb. Su.
Cyls.: (3) 19″×26″
Driving Wheels : 6′ 2″ T.E.: 40,430 lb.
Tender weight (all parts): 60 tons 7 cwt. (except Nos. 60508-10, 52 tons).

60500‡ Edward Thompson
60501* Cock o' the North
60502* Earl Marischal
60503* Lord President
60504* Mons Meg
60505* Thane of Fife

60506* Wolf of Badenoch
60507† Highland Chieftain
60508† Duke of Rothesay
60509† Waverley
60510† Robert the Bruce
60511‡ Airborne
60512‡ Steady Aim
60513‡ Dante
60514‡ Chamossaire
60515‡ Sun Stream
60516‡ Hycilla
60517‡ Ocean Swell
60518‡ Tehran
60519‡ Honeyway
60520‡ Owen Tudor
60521‡ Watling Street
60522‡ Straight Deal
60523‡ Sun Castle
60524‡ Herringbone
60525§ A. H. Peppercorn
60526§ Sugar Palm
60527§ Sun Chariot
60528§ Tudor Minstrel
60529§ Pearl Diver
60530§ Sayajirao
60531§ Bahram
60532§ Blue Peter
60533§ Happy Knight
60534§ Irish Elegance
60535§ Hornet's Beauty
60536§ Trimbush
60537§ Bachelor's Button
60538§ Velocity
60539§ Bronzino

Totals :
Class A2 15 Class A2/2 6
Class A2/1 4 Class A2/3 15

4-6-4 Class W1

Introduced 1937. Rebuilt from experimental high-pressure 4-cyl. compound with water-tube boiler, introduced 1929.
Weights : Loco. 107 tons 17 cwt.
Tender 60 tons 7 cwt.
Pressure : 250 lb. Su.
Cyls.: (3) 20"×26"
Driving Wheels : 6' 8" T.E.: 41,435 lb.
(Former L.N.E.R. number in brackets)

60700 (10000) **Total 1**

2-6-2 Class V2

Introduced 1936.
Weights : Loco. 93 tons 2 cwt.
Tender 52 tons.
Pressure : 220 lb. Su.
Cyls.: (3) 18½"×26"
Driving Wheels : 6' 2" T.E.: 33,730 lb

60800 Green Arrow
60801
60802
60803
60804
60805
60806
60807
60808
60809 The Snapper, The East Yorkshire Regiment, The Duke of York's Own
60810
60811
60812
60813
60814
60815
60816
60817
60818
60819
60820
60821
60822
60823
60824
60825
60826
60827
60828
60829
60830
60831
60832
60833
60834
60835 The Green Howard, Alexandra, Princess of Wales's Own Yorkshire Regiment

60836
60837
60838
60839
60840
60841
60842
60843
60844
60845
60846
60847 St. Peter's School, York, A.D. 627
60848
60849
60850
60851
60852
60853
60854
60855
60856
60857
60858
60859
60860 Durham School
60861
60862
60863
60864
60865
60866
60867
60868
60869
60870
60871
60872 King's Own Yorkshire Light Infantry
60873 Coldstreamer

60874	60882	60890	60898
60875	60883	60891	60899
60876	60884	60892	60900
60877	60885	60893	60901
60878	60886	60894	60902
60879	60887	60895	60903
60880	60888	60896	60904
60881	60889	60897	60905

60906	60926	60946	60966
60907	60927	60947	60967
60908	60928	60948	60968
60909	60929	60949	60969
60910	60930	60950	60970
60911	60931	60951	60971
60912	60932	60952	60972
60913	60933	60953	60973
60914	60934	60954	60974
60915	60935	60955	60975
60916	60936	60956	60976
60917	60937	60957	60977
60918	60938	60958	60978
60919	60939	60959	60979
60920	60940	60960	60980
60921	60941	60961	60981
60922	60942	60962	60982
60923	60943	60963	60983
60924	60944	60964	
60925	60945	60965	

Total 184

4-6-0 Class B1

Introduced 1942.
Weights : Loco. 71 tons 3 cwt.
Tender 52 tons.
Pressure : 225 lb. Su.
Cyls.: (O) 20″ × 26″
Driving Wheels : 6′ 2″ T.E.: 26,880 lb.

61000 Springbok
61001 Eland
61002 Impala
61003 Gazelle
61004 Oryx
61005 Bongo
61006 Blackbuck
61007 Klipspringer
61008 Kudu
61009 Hartebeeste
61010 Wildebeeste
61011 Waterbuck
61012 Puku
61013 Topi
61014 Oribi
61015 Duiker
61016 Inyala
61017 Bushbuck
61018 Gnu

61019	Nilghai
61020	Gemsbok
61021	Reitbok
61022	Sassaby
61023	Hirola
61024	Addax
61025	Pallah
61026	Ourebi
61027	Madoqua
61028	Umseke
61029	Chamois
61030	Nyala
61031	Reedbuck
61032	Stembok
61033	Dibatag
61034	Chiru
61035	Pronghorn
61036	Ralph Assheton
61037	Jairou
61038	Blacktail
61039	Steinbok
61040	Roedeer

61041	61067	61093	61119
61042	61068	61094	61120
61043	61069	61095	61121
61044	61070	61096	61122
61045	61071	61097	61123
61046	61072	61098	61124
61047	61073	61099	61125
61048	61074	61100	61126
61049	61075	61101	61127
61050	61076	61102	61128
61051	61077	61103	61129
61052	61078	61104	61130
61053	61079	61105	61131
61054	61080	61106	61132
61055	61081	61107	61133
61056	61082	61108	61134
61057	61083	61109	61135
61058	61084	61110	61136
61059	61085	61111	61137
61060	61086	61112	61138
61061	61087	61113	61139
61062	61088	61114	61140
61063	61089	61115	61141
61064	61090	61116	61142
61065	61091	61117	61143
61066	61092	61118	61144

61145	61156	61167	61178
61146	61157	61168	61179
61147	61158	61169	61180
61148	61159	61170	61181
61149	61160	61171	61182
61150	61161	61172	61183
61151	61162	61173	61184
61152	61163	61174	61185
61153	61164	61175	61186
61154	61165	61176	61187
61155	61166	61177	61188

61189	Sir William Gray
61190	
61191	
61192	
61193	
61194	
61195	
61196	
61197	
61198	
61199	
61200	
61201	
61202	
61203	
61204	
61205	
61206	
61207	
61208	
61209	
61210	
61211	
61212	
61213	
61214	
61215	William Henton Carver
61216	
61217	
61218	
61219	
61220	
61221	Sir Alexander Erskine-Hill
61222	
61223	

61224
61225
61226
61227
61228
61229
61230
61231
61232
61233
61234
61235
61236
61237 Geoffrey H. Kitson
61238 Leslie Runciman
61239
61240 Harry Hinchliffe
61241 Viscount Ridley
61242 Alexander Reith Gray
61243 Sir Harold Mitchell
61244 Strang Steel
61245 Murray of Elibank
61246 Lord Balfour of Burleigh
61247 Lord Burghley
61248 Geoffrey Gibbs
61249 FitzHerbert Wright
61250 A. Harold Bibby
61251 Oliver Bury

61252	61272	61292	61312
61253	61273	61293	61313
61254	61274	61294	61314
61255	61275	61295	61315
61256	61276	61296	61316
61257	61277	61297	61317
61258	61278	61298	61318
61259	61279	61299	61319
61260	61280	61300	61320
61261	61281	61301	61321
61262	61282	61302	61322
61263	61283	61303	61323
61264	61284	61304	61324
61265	61285	61305	61325
61266	61286	61306	61326
61267	61287	61307	61327
61268	61288	61308	61328
61269	61289	61309	61329
61270	61290	61310	61330
61271	61291	61311	61331
61332	61334	61336	61338
61333	61335	61337	61339

Total 340

4-6-0 Class B8

Introduced 1913.
Weights : Loco. 74 tons 7 cwt.
Tender 48 tons 6 cwt.
Pressure : 180 lb. Su. Cyls.: 21½″ × 26″
Driving Wheels : 5′ 7″ T.E.: 27,445 lb.

61353
61357 Earl Roberts of Kandahar

Total 2

4-6-0 Class B7

B7/1 Introduced 1921. Original G.C. locos.
B7/2* Introduced 1923. Post-grouping locos. with smaller chimney and cab.
Weights : Loco. 79 tons 10 cwt.
Tender 48 tons 6 cwt.
Pressure : 180 lb. Su.
Cyls.: (4) 16″ × 26″
Driving Wheels : 5′ 8″ T.E.: 29,950 lb.

61361	61371	61382	61391*
61362	61374	61385	61392*
61365	61375	61386	61395*
61366	61376	61387	61396*
61367	61377	61388*	
61368	61379	61389*	
61370	61381	61390*	

Totals : Class B7/1 18
Class B7/2 7

4-6-0 Class B16

B16/1 Introduced 1920. N.E. design with inside Stephenson gear.
B16/2* Introduced 1937. Gresley rebuild of B16/1 with outside Walschaerts' gear and conjugate gear for inside cylinder.
B16/3† Introduced 1944. Thompson rebuild of B16/1 with three Walschaerts' gears.

Weights : Loco. { 77 tons 14 cwt. / 79 tons 4 cwt.* / 78 tons 19 cwt.†
Tender 46 tons 12 cwt.
Pressure : 180 lb. Su.
Cyls.: (3) 18½″ × 26″
Driving Wheels : 5′ 8″ T.E.: 30,030 lb.

61400	61418†	61436	61454†
61401	61419	61437*	61455*
61402	61420†	61438*	61456
61403†	61421*	61439†	61457*
61404	61422	61440	61458
61405	61423	61441	61459
61406*	61424	61442	61460
61407†	61425	61443	61461
61408	61426	61444†	61462
61409	61427	61445	61463
61410	61428	61446	61464†
61411	61429	61447	61465
61412	61430	61448†	61466
61413	61431	61449†	61467†
61414	61432	61450	61468†
61415	61433	61451	
61416	61434	61452	
61417†	61435*	61453†	

Totals : Class B16/1 48
Class B16/2 7
Class B16/3 14

4-6-0 Class B9

Introduced 1906. Later superheated.
Weights : Loco. 65 tons.
Tender 48 tons 6 cwt.
Pressure : 180 lb. Su.
Cyls.: (O) 19″ × 26″
Driving Wheels : 5′ 4″ T.E.: 22,440 lb.

61469 | 61470 | 61475

Total 3

4-6-0 Class B4

B4/4* Introduced 1906. Original design with slide valves, later superheated.
B4/3 Introduced 1925. B4/3 rebuilt with piston valves and larger cyls. (B4/1 and B4/2 corresponded to B4/3 and B4/4 before cutting down to L.N.E.R. loading gauge.)

Weights : Loco. { 70 tons 14 cwt.* / 71 tons 15 cwt.
Tender 40 tons 6 cwt.
Pressure : 180 lb. Su.
Cyls.:(O) { 19″ × 26″* / 21″ × 26″
Driving Wheels : 6′ 7″
T.E. { 18, 180 lb.* / 22,205 lb.

61482* Immingham
61483 | 61485 | 61488

Totals : Class B4/3 3
Class B4/4 1

4-6-0 Class B3

B3/3 Introduced 1943. 2-cyl. rebuild of B3/2, with 100A(B1) boiler. (B3/1, introduced 1918, were 4-cyl. locos with Belpaire boilers ; B3/2, introduced 1928, were rebuilds of B3/1 with Caprotti valves.)

Weights : Loco. 71 tons 7 cwt.
Tender 48 tons 6 cwt.
Pressure : 225 lb. Su.
Cyls.: (O) 20″ × 26″
Driving Wheels : 6′ 9″ T.E.: 24,555 lb.

61497 **Total 1**

4-6-0 Class B12

B12/1* Introduced 1911. G.E. design with small Belpaire boiler.
B12/3 Introduced 1932. Gresley rebuild of B12/1 with large round-topped boiler and long-travel valves.
B12/1† Introduced 1943. Rebuild of B12/1 with small round-topped boiler, retaining original valves.
(B12/2 was a development of B12/1 with Lentz valves, since rebuilt to B12/3.)

Weights : Loco. { 63 tons.*† / 69 tons 10 cwt.
Tender 39 tons 6 cwt.
Pressure : 180 lb. Su. Cyls.: 20″ × 28″
Driving Wheels : 6′ 6″ T.E.: 21,970 lb.

61501*	61505†	61510	61514
61502*	61507†	61511†	61515
61503*	61508†	61512	61516
61504†	61509	61513*	61517

61519	61537	61554	61568
61520	61538	61555	61569
61521*	61539*	61556	61570
61523	61540	61557	61571
61524†	61541	61558	61572
61525	61542	61559	61573
61526†	61543*	61560*	61574
61528*	61545	61561	61575
61529*	61546	61562	61576
61530	61547	61563*	61577
61532†	61549	61564	61578
61533	61550	61565	61579
61535	61552*	61566	61580
61536*	61553	61567	

Totals : Class B12/1 21
Class B12/3 50

4-6-0 Classes B2 & B17

B17/1* Introduced 1928. Locos with G.E.-type tenders.
B17/4† Introduced 1936. Locos with L.N.E.R. 4200-gallon tenders.
B17/5‡ Introduced 1937. Rebuild of B17/4 with streamlined casing.
§ Fitted with 100A (B1 type) boiler. (B17/2 and B17/3 were variants of B17/1 now included in that part.)

Weights : Loco. { 77 tons 5 cwt */†/§ ; 80 tons 10 cwt.‡ }
Tender { 39 tons 6 cwt.* ; 52 tons † ; 52 tons 13 cwt.‡ }
Pressure : { 180 lb. Su. ; 225 lb. Su.§ }
Cyls.: (3) 17½″×26″
Driving Wheels : 6′ 8″
T.E.: { 22,485 lb. ; 28,555 lb.§ }

B2** Introduced 1945. 2-cyl. rebuild of B17, with 100A boiler and ex-N.E. tender.
B2†† Introduced 1945, with L.N.E.R. tender.

Weights : Loco. 73 tons 10 cwt.
Tender { 46 tons 12 cwt.** ; 52 tons †† }
Pressure : 225 lb. Su.
Cyls.: (O) 20″×26″
Driving Wheels : 6′ 8″ T.E.: 24,865 lb.

61600* Sandringham
61601* Holkham
61602* Walsingham
61603**Framlingham
61604* Elveden
61605*§Lincolnshire Regiment
61606* Audley End
61607**Blickling
61608* Gunton
61609* Quidenham
61610* Honingham Hall
61611* Raynham Hall
61612* Houghton Hall
61613* Woodbastwick Hall
61614**Castle Hedingham
61615††Culford Hall
61616**Fallodon
61617**Ford Castle
61618* Wynyard Park
61619* Welbeck Abbey
61620* Clumber
61621* Hatfield House
61622*§Alnwick Castle
61623*§Lambton Castle
61624* Lumley Castle
61625* Raby Castle
61626* Brancepeth Castle
61627* Aske Hall
61628* Harewood House
61629* Naworth Castle
61630* Tottenham Hotspur
61631* Serlby Hall
61632††Belvoir Castle
61633*§Kimbolton Castle
61634* Hinchingbrooke
61635* Milton
61636* Harlaxton Manor
61637* Thorpe Hall
61638* Melton Hall
61639**Norwich City
61640* Somerleyton Hall
61641* Gayton Hall
61642* Kilverstone Hall
61643* Champion Lodge
61644* Earlham Hall
61645* The Suffolk Regiment
61646* Gilwell Park
61647† Helmingham Hall
61648† Arsenal
61649† Sheffield United
61650† Grimsby Town
61651† Derby County

61652†§Darlington
61653† Huddersfield Town
61654†§Sunderland
61655† Middlesbrough
61656† Leeds United
61657† Doncaster Rovers
61658* The Essex Regiment
61659‡ East Anglian
61660† Hull City
61661† Sheffield Wednesday
61662† Manchester United
61663† Everton
61664†§Liverpool
61665† Leicester City
61666†§Nottingham Forest
61667† Bradford
61668† Bradford City
61669† Barnsley
61670‡ City of London
61671††Royal Sovereign
61672† West Ham United

Totals : Class B2 9
Class B17/1 40
Class B17/4 22
Class B17/5 2

4-6-0 Class B5

Introduced 1902.
* As built with slide valves.
† Rebuilt with piston valves. (All later superheated.)
Weights : Loco. {64 tons 3 cwt.* / 65 tons 4 cwt.†}
Tender 48 tons 6 cwt.
Pressure : 180 lb. Su.
Cyls. (O) {19″×26″* / 21″×26″†}
Driving Wheels : 5′ 8″
T.E.: {24,030 lb.* / 25,800 lb.†}

61680* 61686† 61688† 61689*

Total 4

4-6-0 Class B13

Introduced 1899 (Survivor built 1906). Later rebuilt to counter-pressure loco for loco testing purposes.
Pressure: 160 lb. Cyls.: (O) 20″×26″
Driving Wheels : 6′ 1½″ T.E.: 19,310 lb.

61699S

Total 1

2-6-2 Class V4

Introduced 1941.
Weights : Loco. 70 tons 8 cwt.
Tender 42 tons 15 cwt.
Pressure : 250 lb. Su.
Cyls.: (3) 15″×26″
Driving Wheels : 5′ 8″ T.E.: 27,420 lb.

61700 Bantam Cock
61701

Total 2

2-6-0 Class K2

K2/2 Introduced 1914.
K2/1* Introduced 1931. Rebuilt from small-boilered K1 (introduced 1912).
† K2/2 fitted with side-window cab in Scottish Region.
Weights : Loco. 64 tons 8 cwt.
Tender 43 tons 2 cwt.
Pressure : 180 lb. Su.
Cyls.: (O) 20″×26″
Driving Wheels : 5′ 8″ T.E.: 23,400 lb.

61720*	61731	61742	61753
61721*	61732	61743	61754
61722*	61733	61744	61755
61723*	61734	61745	61756
61724*	61735	61746	61757
61725*	61736	61747	61758
61726*	61737	61748	61759
61727*	61738	61749	61760
61728*	61739	61750	61761
61729*	61740	61751	61762
61730	61741	61752	61763

61764† Loch Arkaig
61765
61766
61767
61768
61769
61770
61771
61772† Loch Lochy
61773
61774† Loch Garry
61775† Loch Treig
61776†
61777
61778
61779†
61780
61781† Loch Morar

Class V2 2-6-2 No. 60956 [*Photo : E. V. Fry*

Class V4 2-6-2 No. 1701 (New No. 61701) [*Photo : B. V. Franey*

Class K4 2-6-0 No. 61998 *MacLeod of MacLeod* [*Photo : P. Ransome-Wallis*

Top : Class B17/5 4-6-0 No. 61659 *East Anglian* [A. F. Cook

Centre: Class B3/3 4-6-0 No. 1497 (New No. 61497) [H. C. Casserley

Bottom: Class B17/4 4-6-0 No. 61661 *Sheffield Wednesday* [B.V.Franey

Top: Class B12/1 4-6-0 No. 1507 (New No. 61507) [*Photo : H. C. Casserley*
Centre : Class B12/3 4-6-0 No. 61570 [*Photo : E. V. Fry*
Bottom : Class D49/1 4-4-0 No. 2708 *Argyllshire* (New No. 62708) [*Photo : E. V. Fry*

Above: Class O2/3 2-8-0 No. 3978 (New No. 63978) [*Photo : H. C. Casserley*

Left : Class O4/8 2-8-0 No. 3613 (New No. 63613) [*Photo : B. V. Franey*

Below: Class O3 2-8-0 No. 3479 (New No. 63479) [*Photo : B. V. Franey*

61782† Loch Eil
61783† Loch Sheil
61784†
61785†
61786†
61787† Loch Quoich
61788† Loch Rannoch
61789† Loch Laidon
61790† Loch Lomond
61791† Loch Laggan
61792†
61793†
61794† Loch Oich

Totals : Class K2/1 10
Class K2/2 65

2-6-0 Classes K3 & K5

K3/2 Introduced 1924. Development of G.N. design, built to L.N.E.R. loading gauge.
K3/3* Introduced 1929. Differ in details only, such as springs, from K3/2.
‡ K3/2 fitted with ex-G.N. tender.
(K3/1 were ex-G.N. locos (introduced 1920), with G.N. cabs, and K3/4, K3/5 and K3/6 were variations of K3/2, differing in weight and details. These locos have now been modified to K3/2.)
Weights : Loco. 72 tons 12 cwt.
Tender { 52 tons.
43 tons 2 cwt.‡
Pressure : 180 lb. Su.
Cyls.: (3) 18½"×26"
Driving Wheels : 5' 8" T.E.: 30,030 lb.
K5† Introduced 1945. 2-cyl. rebuild of K3.
Weights : Loco. 71 tons 5 cwt.
Tender 52 tons.
Pressure : 225 lb. Su.
Cyls.: (O) 20"×26"
Driving Wheels : 5' 8" T.E.: 29,250 lb.

61800	61811	61822	61833
61801	61812‡	61823	61834
61802	61813	61824	61835
61803	61814	61825	61836
61804	61815	61826	61837
61805	61816	61827	61838
61806	61817	61828	61839
61807	61818	61829	61840
61808	61819	61830	61841‡
61809	61820	61831	61842
61810	61821	61832	61843

61844	61882*	61920	61958
61845	61883*	61921	61959
61846	61884*	61922	61960
61847	61885*	61923	61961
61848	61886*	61924	61962
61849	61887*	61925	61963
61850	61888*	61926	61964
61851	61889*	61927	61965
61852	61890	61928	61966
61853	61891	61929	61967
61854‡	61892	61930	61968
61855‡	61893	61931	61969
61856‡	61894	61932	61970
61857‡	61895	61933	61971
61858‡	61896	61934	61972
61859‡	61897	61935	61973
61860	61898	61936	61974
61861	61899	61937	61975
61862	61900	61938	61976
61863†	61901	61939	61977
61864	61902	61940	61978
61865	61903	61941	61979
61866	61904	61942	61980
61867	61905	61943	61981
61868	61906	61944	61982
61869	61907	61945	61983
61870*	61908	61946	61984
61871*	61909	61947	61985
61872*	61910	61948	61986
61873*	61911	61949	61987
61874*	61912	61950	61988
61875*	61913	61951	61989
61876*	61914	61952	61990
61877*	61915	61953	61991
61878*	61916	61954	61992
61879*	61917	61955	
61880*	61918	61956	
61881*	61919	61957	

Totals : Class K3/2 172
Class K3/3 20
Class K5 1

2-6-0 KI & K4

K4 Introduced 1937. Gresley loco for West Highland line.
Weights : Loco. 68 tons 8 cwt.
Tender 44 tons 4 cwt.
Pressure : 200 lb. Su.
Cyls.: (3) 18½″×26″
Driving Wheels : 5′ 2″ T.E.: 36,600 lb.

KI* Introduced 1945. Thompson 2-cyl. loco. (Prototype rebuilt from K4.)
Weights : Loco. 66 tons 17 cwt.
Tender 44 tons 4 cwt.
Pressure : 225 lb. Su.
Cyls.: (O) 20″×26″
Driving Wheels : 5′ 8″ T.E.: 32,080 lb.

61993 Loch Long
61994 The Great Marquess
61995 Cameron of Locheil
61996 Lord of the Isles
61997* MacCailin Mor
61998 MacLeod of MacLeod

Totals : Class KI 1
Class K4 5

4-4-0 Class D31

Introduced 1890. (Rebuilt from 1918.)
Weights : Loco. 46 tons 8 cwt.
Tender 33 tons 9 cwt.
Pressure : 175 lb. Cyls.: 18½″×26″
Driving Wheels : 6′ 6″ T.E.: 16,515 lb.

62059	62060	62065	62072

Total 4

4-4-0 Class D3

Introduced 1896. (Rebuilt from 1912 with larger boiler.) *Vide p. 72.*
* Rebuilt with side-window cab for working officers' saloons.
Weights : Loco. 45 tons 14 cwt.
Tender 38 tons 10 cwt.
Pressure : 175 lb. Cyls.: 17½″×26″
Driving Wheels : 6′ 8″ T.E.: 14,805 lb.

62000*	62125	62133	62140
62116	62128	62135	62145
62123	62131	62137	62148
62124	62132	62139	

Total 15

4-4-0 Class D2

Introduced 1897 (**see note p. 72**).
* Rebuilt with superheater.
Weights : Loco. 47 tons 10 cwt.
Tender 40 tons 18 cwt.
Pressure : { 175 lb.
170 lb. Su.*
Cyls.: 17½″×26″
Driving Wheels : 6′ 8″
T.E.: { 14,805 lb.
14,380 lb.*

62150	62161	62177*	62190
62151	62163*	62179	62193
62152	62165*	62180*	62194
62153	62167*	62181	62197
62154	62172	62187*	62199*
62156*	62173	62188	
62160*	62175	62189*	

Total 26

4-4-0 Class DI

Introduced 1911 (**see note p. 72**).
Weights : Loco. 53 tons 6 cwt.
Tender 43 tons 2 cwt.
Pressure : 170 lb. Su. Cyls.: 18½″×26″
Driving Wheels : 6′ 8″ T.E.: 16,075 lb.

62203	62207	62209	62215
62205	62208	62214	

Total 7

4-4-0 Class D41

Introduced 1893.
Weights : Loco. 45 tons.
Tender 37 tons 8 cwt.
Pressure : 165 lb. Cyls.: 18″×26″
Driving Wheels : 6′ 1″ T.E.: 16,185 lb.

62225	62232	62243	62252
62227	62234	62246	62255
62228	62235	62247	62256
62229	62240	62248	
62230	62241	62249	
62231	62242	62251	

Total 21

4-4-0 Class D40

Introduced 1899.
* Introduced 1920. Superheated locos.
Weights : Loco. { 46 tons 7 cwt. / 48 tons 13 cwt.*
Tender 37 tons 8 cwt.
Pressure : 165 lb. SS. Cyls.: 18" × 26"
Driving Wheels : 6' 1" T.E.: 16,185 lb.

62260	62264	62268	62271
62261	62265	62269	62272
62262	62267	62270	

62273* George Davidson
62274* Benachie
62275* Sir David Stewart
62276* Andrew Bain
62277* Gordon Highlander
62278* Hatton Castle
62279* Glen Grant

Total 18

4-4-0 Class D9

Introduced 1901. Since rebuilt with superheater.
Pressure : 180 lb. Su. Cyls.: 19" × 26"
Driving Wheels : 6' 9" T.E.: 17,730 lb.

62300	62307 Queen Mary		
62301	62308	62315	62324
62302	62309	62317	62325
62303	62311	62318	62329
62304	62312	62319	62330
62305	62313	62321	62332
62306	62314	62322	62333

Total 26

4-4-0 Class D20

D20/1 Introduced 1899. Since superheated.
D20/2* Introduced 1936. D20/1 rebuilt with long-travel valves.
Weights : Loco. { 54 tons 2 cwt. / 55 tons 9 cwt.*
Tender { 41 tons 4 cwt. / 43 tons.*
Pressure : 175 lb. Su. Cyls.: 19" × 26"
Driving Wheels : 6' 10" T.E.: 17,025 lb.

62340	62344	62349*	62354
62341	62345	62351	62355
62342	62347	62352	62357
62343	62348	62353	62358
62359	62371*	62380	62390
62360*	62372	62381	62391
62361	62373	62382	62392
62362	62374	62383	62395
62363	62375	62384	62396
62365	62376	62386	62397
62366	62377	62387	
62369	62378	62388	
62370	62379	62389	

Totals : Class D20/1 46
Class D20/2 3

4-4-0 Class D29

Introduced 1909.
Weights : Loco. 54 tons 4 cwt.
Tender 46 tons.
Pressure : 190 lb. Su. Cyls.: 19" × 26"
Driving Wheels : 6' 6" T.E.: 19,435 lb.

62401 Dandie Dinmont
62402 Redgauntlet
62404 Jeanie Deans
62405 The Fair Maid
62406 Meg Merrilies
62409 Helen MacGregor
62410 Ivanhoe
62411 Lady of Avenel
62412 Dirk Hatteraick
62413 Guy Mannering

Total 10

4-4-0 Class D30

D30/1* Introduced 1912.
D30/2 Introduced 1914. Development of D30/1 with detail differences.
Weights : Loco. { 57 tons 6 cwt.* / 57 tons 16 cwt.
Tender { 46 tons.* / 46 tons 13 cwt.
Pressure : 165 lb. Su. Cyls.: 20" × 26"
Driving Wheels : 6' 6" T.E.: 18,700 lb.

62417* Hal o' the Wynd
62418 The Pirate
62419 Meg Dods
62420 Dominie Sampson
62421 Laird o' Monkbarns
62422 Caleb Balderstone
62423 Dugald Dalgetty
62424 Claverhouse
62425 Ellangowan

62426 Cuddie Headrigg
62427 Dumbiedykes
62428 The Talisman
62429 The Abbot
62430 Jingling Geordie
62431 Kenilworth
62432 Quentin Durward
62434 Kettledrummle
62435 Norna
62436 Lord Glenvarloch
62437 Adam Woodcock
62438 Peter Poundtext
62439 Father Ambrose
62440 Wandering Willie
62441 Black Duncan
62442 Simon Glover

Totals : Class D30/1 1
Class D30/2 24

4-4-0 Class D32

Introduced 1906. Since superheated.
Weights : Loco. 53 tons 14 cwt.
Tender 40 tons.
Pressure : 180 lb. Su. Cyls.: 19"×26"
Driving Wheels : 6' 0" T.E.: 19,945 lb

62445	62449	62451	62454
62446			

Total 5

4-4-0 Class D33

Introduced 1909. Since superheated.
Weights : Loco. 54 tons 3 cwt.
Tender 44 tons 11 cwt.
Pressure : 180 lb. Su. Cyls.: 19"×26"
Driving Wheels : 6' 0" T.E.: 19,945 lb.

62455	62459	62461	62464
62457	62460	62462	62466
62458			

Total 9

4-4-0 Class D34

Introduced 1913.
Weighis : Loco. 57 tons 4 cwt.
Tender 46 tons 13 cwt.
Pressure : 165 lb. Su. Cyls.: 20"×26"
Driving Wheels : 6' 0" T.E.: 20,260 lb.

62467 Glenfinnan
62468 Glen Orchy
62469 Glen Douglas
62470 Glen Roy
62471 Glen Falloch
62472 Glen Nevis
62473 Glen Spean
62474 Glen Croe
62475 Glen Beasdale
62476 Glen Sloy
62477 Glen Dochart
62478 Glen Quoich
62479 Glen Sheil
62480 Glen Fruin
62481 Glen Ogle
62482 Glen Mamie
62483 Glen Garry
62484 Glen Lyon
62485 Glen Murran
62487 Glen Arklet
62488 Glen Aladale
62489 Glen Dessary
62490 Glen Fintaig
62492 Glen Garvin
62493 Glen Gloy
62494 Glen Gour
62495 Glen Luss
62496 Glen Loy
62497 Glen Mallie
62498 Glen Moidart

Total 30

4-4-0 Classes D15 & D16

D15* Introduced 1904. Belpaire boiler development of original "Claud Hamilton" class, some rebuilt from D14.

D16/2† Introduced 1923. "Super Claud"—D15 with larger boiler, some rebuilt from D15.

D16/3‡ Introduced 1933. Rebuild of D15 with larger round-topped boiler and modified footplating.

D16/3§ Introduced 1933. Rebuild of D15 with larger round-topped boiler, modified footplating and 8" piston valves.

D16/3** Introduced 1936. Rebuild of D15 with larger round-topped boiler, modified footplating and 9½" piston valves.

D16/3†† Introduced 1938. Rebuild of D16/2 with round-topped boiler, but retaining original footplating and slide valves.

D16/3‡‡ Introduced 1939. Rebuild of D16/2 with round-topped boiler and modified footplating, retaining slide valves.

(At grouping the remaining locos of the "Claud Hamilton" class retaining small round-topped boilers were classified D14. Saturated locos of D15 were originally classified D15, superheated locos with short smokeboxes D15/1 and superheated locos with extended smokeboxes D15/2. All the remaining locos were converted to D15/2 and then known simply as D15. D16/1 were the original D16 locos with short smokeboxes.)

Weights : Loco. { 52 tons 4 cwt.* / 54 tons 18 cwt.† / 55 tons 18 cwt. }
(All D16/3)
Tender 39 tons 5 cwt.
Pressure : 180 lb. Su. Cyls.: 19" × 26"
Driving Wheels : 7' 0" T.E.: 17,095 lb.

62501*	62531‡	62562††	62592††
62502*	62532**	62564††	62593‡
62503*	62533‡	62565††	62594**
62505*	62534‡	62566‡	62596††
62506*	62535**	62567‡	62597‡
62507*	62536**	62568§	62598‡
62508*	62538*	62569††	62599**
62509*	62539‡	62570†	62601††
62510‡	62540‡	62571‡	62602**
62511‡	62541‡	62572‡	62603†
62512*	62542††	62573††	62604‡
62513‡	62543†	62574‡	62605††
62514‡	62544††	62575‡	62606††
62515‡	62545‡	62576**	62607††
62516‡	62546§¶	62577†	62608‡
62517‡	62547†	62578††	62609§
62518‡	62548‡	62579‡	62610‡
62519‡	62549‡	62580††	62611††
62520*	62551‡	62581**	62612†
62521‡	62552†	62582‡	62613†
62522‡	62553†	62583**	62614‡‡
62523‡	62554††	62584††	62615††
62524‡	62555‡	62585‡	62616††
62525‡	62556††	62586‡	62617††
62526‡	62557††	62587§	62618††
62527‡	62558†	62588§	62619††
62528*	62559‡	62589††	62620††
62529‡	62560§	62590†	
62530‡	62561‡	62591†	

Totals : Class D15 12
Class D16/2 12
Class D16/3 90

¶ Named *Claud Hamilton*

4-4-0 Class D10

Introduced 1913. Robinson "Director" class.
Weights : Loco. 61 tons.
Tender 48 tons 6 cwt.
Pressure : 180 lb. Su. Cyls.: 20" × 26'
Driving Wheels : 6' 9" T.E.: 19,645 lb.

62650 Prince Henry
62651 Purdon Viccars
62652 Edwin A. Beazley
62653 Sir Edward Fraser
62654 Walter Burgh Gair
62655 The Earl of Kerry
62656 Sir Clement Royds
62657 Sir Berkeley Sheffield
62658 Prince George
62659 Worsley-Taylor

Total 10

4-4-0 Class D11

D11/1* Introduced 1920. Robinson "Large Director," development of D10.

D11/2 Introduced 1924. Post-grouping locos built to Scottish loading gauge. From 1938 the class has been rebuilt with long-travel valves.

Weights : Loco. 61 tons 3 cwt.
Tender 48 tons 6 cwt.
Pressure : 180 lb. Su. Cyls.: 20" × 26"
Driving Wheels : 6' 9" T.E.: 19,645 lb.

62660* Butler-Henderson
62661* Gerard Powys Dewhurst
62662* Prince of Wales
62663* Prince Albert
62664* Princess Mary
62665* Mons
62666* Zeebrugge
62667* Somme
62668* Jutland
62669* Ypres
62670* Marne
62671 Bailie MacWheeble
62672 Baron of Bradwardine
62673 Evan Dhu
62674 Flora MacIvor
62675 Colonel Gardiner
62676 Jonathan Oldbuck
62677 Edie Ochiltree
62678 Luckie Mucklebackit

62679 Lord Glenallan
62680 Lucy Ashton
62681 Captain Craigengelt
62682 Haystoun of Bucklaw
62683 Hobbie Elliott
62684 Wizard of the Moor
62685 Malcolm Graeme
62686 The Fiery Cross
62687 Lord James of Douglas
62688 Ellen Douglas
62689 Maid of Lorn
62690 The Lady of the Lake
62691 Laird of Balmawhapple
62692 Allan-Bane
62693 Roderick Dhu
62694 James Fitzjames

Totals : Class D11/1 11
Class D11/2 24

4-4-0 Class D49

D49/1* Introduced 1927. Piston valve locos.

D49/2† Introduced 1928. Development of D49/1 with Lentz Rotary Cam poppet valves.

D49/4‡ Introduced 1942. Rebuild of D49/2 with two inside cyls. of D11 pattern.
(D49/3 comprised locos 62720-4 as built with Lentz Oscillating Cam poppet valves. From 1938 these locos were converted to D49/1. 62751-75 have larger valves than the earlier D49/2, and were at first classified D49/4.)

§ Fitted with ex-G.C. tender.
|| Fitted with ex-N.E. tender.
The remainder have L.N.E.R. tenders.

Weights : Loco. { 66 tons.* / 64 tons 10 cwt.† / 62 tons.‡
Tender { 52 tons. / 48 tons 6 cwt.§ / 44 tons 2 cwt.||

Pressure : 180 lb. Su.
Cyls. { (3) 17" × 26"*† / 20" × 26"‡
Driving Wheels : 6' 8"
T.E.: { 21,555 lb.*† / 19,890 lb.‡

62700*§ Yorkshire
62701*§ Derbyshire
62702*§ Oxfordshire
62703*|| Hertfordshire
62704*§ Stirlingshire
62705*§ Lanarkshire
62706*§ Forfarshire
62707*§ Lancashire
62708*§ Argyllshire
62709*§ Berwickshire
62710*§ Lincolnshire
62711*§ Dumbartonshire
62712*§ Morayshire
62713*§ Aberdeenshire
62714*§ Perthshire
62715*§ Roxburghshire
62716*§ Kincardineshire
62717*§ Banffshire
62718*§ Kinross-shire
62719*§ Peebles-shire
62720*|| Cambridgeshire
62721*|| Warwickshire
62722*|| Huntingdonshire
62723*|| Nottinghamshire
62724*|| Bedfordshire
62725*§ Inverness-shire
62726† The Meynell
62727†|| The Quorn
62728*§ Cheshire
62729*§ Rutlandshire
62730*§ Berkshire
62731*§ Selkirkshire
62732*§ Dumfries-shire
62733*§ Northumberland
62734*§ Cumberland
62735*§ Westmorland
62736† The Bramham Moor
62737† The York and Ainsty
62738† The Zetland
62739† The Badsworth
62740† The Bedale
62741† The Blankney
62742† The Braes of Derwent
62743† The Cleveland
62744† The Holderness
62745† The Hurworth
62746† The Middleton
62747† The Percy
62748† The Southwold

62749†	The Cottesmore
62750†	The Pytchley
62751†	The Albrighton
62752†	The Atherstone
62753†	The Belvoir
62754†	The Berkeley
62755†	The Bilsdale
62756†	The Brocklesby
62757†	The Burton
62758†	The Cattistock
62759†	The Craven
62760†	The Cotswold
62761†	The Derwent
62762†	The Fernie
62763†	The Fitzwilliam
62764†	The Garth
62765†	The Goathland
62766†	The Grafton
62767†	The Grove
62768‡	The Morpeth
62769†	The Oakley
62770†	The Puckeridge
62771†	The Rufford
62772†	The Sinnington
62773†	The South Durham
62774†	The Staintondale
62775†	The Tynedale

Totals : Class D49/1 34
Class D49/2 41
Class D49/4 1

2-4-0 Class E4

Introduced 1891.
* Fitted with side-window cab.
Weights : Loco. 40 tons 6 cwt.
Tender 30 tons 13 cwt.
Pressure : 160 lb. Cyls.: $17\frac{1}{2}'' \times 24''$
Driving Wheels : 5' 8" T.E.: 14,700 lb.

62780	62785	62790	62795*
62781*	62786	62791	62796
62782	62787	62792	62797*
62783	62788*	62793*	
62784*	62789	62794	

Total 18

4-4-2 Class C1

Introduced 1902. (Oldest survivor built 1904.)
* Retaining slide valves (others built or rebuilt with piston valves).
Weights : Loco. 69 tons 12 cwt.
Tender 43 tons 2 cwt.
Pressure : 170 lb. Su.
Cyls.:(O) $\begin{cases} 19'' \times 24''* \\ 20'' \times 24'' \end{cases}$
Driving Wheels : 6' 8"
T.E.: $\begin{cases} 15,650 \text{ lb.}* \\ 17,340 \text{ lb.} \end{cases}$

62810	62828	62875*	62881
62817	62839	62877	62885
62822	62854		

Total 10

4-4-2 Class C4

C4/2* Introduced 1902. Slide valves, originally saturated.
C4/4† Introduced 1911. Rebuilt with superheater and piston valves.
(C4/1 and C4/3 were locos of C4/2 and C4/4 before cutting down to L.N.E.R. loading gauge.)
Weights : Loco. $\begin{cases} \text{70 tons 17 cwt.}* \\ \text{71 tons 18 cwt.}† \end{cases}$
Tender 48 tons 6 cwt.
Pressure : 180 lb. Su.
Cyls.:(O) $\begin{cases} 19'' \times 26''* \\ 21'' \times 26''† \end{cases}$
Driving Wheels : 6' 9"
T.E.: $\begin{cases} 17,730 \text{ lb.}* \\ 21,660 \text{ lb.}† \end{cases}$

62900†	62908*	62915†	62919†
62901†	62909†	62916†	62923†
62902*	62910†	62917*	62925†
62903†	62912*	62918*	

Totals : Class C4/2 5
Class C4/4 10

4-4-2 Class C7

Introduced 1911.
Weights : Loco. 79 tons 5 cwt.
Tender 46 tons 12 cwt.
Pressure : 175 lb. Su.
Cyls.: (3) $16\frac{1}{2}'' \times 26''$
Driving Wheels : 6' 10" T.E.: 19,300 lb.

62970	62992

Total 2

2-8-0 Class O7

Introduced 1943. ex-W.D. locos taken into L.N.E.R. stock 1946.
Weights : Loco. 70 tons 5 cwt.
Tender 55 tons 10 cwt.
Pressure : 225 lb. Su.
Cyls.: (O) 19" × 28"
Driving Wheels : 4' 8½" T.E.: 34,215 lb.

63000	63041	63082	63123
63001	63042	63083	63124
63002	64043	63084	63125
63003	63044	63085	63126
63004	63045	63086	63127
63005	63046	63087	63128
63006	63047	63088	63129
63007	63048	63089	63130
63008	63049	63090	63131
63009	63050	63091	63132
63010	63051	63092	63133
63011	63052	63093	63134
63012	63053	63094	63135
63013	63054	63095	63136
63014	63055	63096	63137
63015	63056	63097	63138
63016	63057	63098	63139
63017	63058	63099	63140
63018	63059	63100	63141
63019	63060	63101	63142
63020	63061	63102	63143
63021	63062	63103	63144
63022	63063	63104	63145
63023	63064	63105	63146
63024	63065	63106	63147
63025	63066	63107	63148
63026	63067	63108	63149
63027	63068	63109	63150
63028	63069	63110	63151
63029	63070	63111	63152
63030	63071	63112	63153
63031	63072	63113	63154
63032	63073	63114	63155
63033	63074	63115	63156
63034	63075	63116	63157
63035	63076	63117	63158
63036	63077	63118	63159
63037	63078	63119	63160
63038	63079	63120	63161
63039	63080	63121	63162
63040	63081	63122	63163

63164	63173	63182	63191
63165	63174	63183	63192
63166	63175	63184	63193
63167	63176	63185	63194
63168	63177	63186	63195
63169	63178	63187	63196
63170	63179	63188	63197
63171	63180	63189	63198
63172	63181	63190	63199

Total 200

0-8-0 Class Q4

Q4/1* Introduced 1902. Saturated locos.
Q4/2† Introduced 1914. Superheated rebuild, retaining slide valves.
Q4/2‡ Introduced 1914. Rebuilt with superheater and piston valves.
Weights : Loco. { 62 tons 8 cwt.* / 63 tons.† / 64 tons 1 cwt.‡
Tender 48 tons 6 cwt.
Pressure : 180 lb. SS.
Cyls.: (O) { 19" × 26"*† / 21" × 26"‡
Driving Wheels : 4' 8"
T.E.: { 25,645 lb.*† / 31,325 lb.‡

63200†	63212†	63224*	63234*
63201†	63213‡	63225‡	63235†
63202*	63214‡	63226*	63236†
63203*	63216†	63227*	63238†
63204*	63217†	63228†	63240†
63205*	63219†	63229†	63241*
63206†	63220‡	63231†	63243†
63207†	63221‡	63232‡	
63210†	63223†	63233†	

Totals : Class Q4/1 9
Class Q4/2 25

0-8-0 Class Q5

Q5/1 (Slide valve) Introduced 1901.
Q5/1* (Piston valve) Introduced 1903.
Q5/2† Introduced 1933. Rebuild of Q5/1 with larger boiler from withdrawn Q10 locos.
Weights : Loco. { 58 tons 8 cwt. Q5/1 / 60 tons 4 cwt.†
Tender 40 tons 8 cwt.
Pressure: 175 lb. Cyls.: (O) 20" × 26"
Driving Wheels : 4' 7¼" T.E.: 28,000 lb.

63251	63255	63257	63260
63253†	63256	63259	63261

63262	63283*	63300	63322†
63263†	63284*	63301†	63323
63267	63285*	63303	63326
63270*	63286*	63305†	63327
63271*	63287*	63306†	63328
63272*	63289*	63307	63330
63273*	63290*	63308	63331
63274*	63291*	63311	63332
63275*	63292*	63312	63333
63276*	63293*	63313	63334
63277*	63294*	63314	63335
63278*	63295*	63316†	63336
63280*	63296*	63317	63338
63281*	63297*	63318	
63282*	63299*	63319	

Totals : Class Q5/1 59
Class Q5/2 7

0-8-0 Class Q6

Introduced 1913.
* Some locos are fitted with tenders from withdrawn B15 locos.
Weights : Loco. 65 tons 18 cwt.
Tender { 44 tons 2 cwt. / 44 tons.*
Pressure : 180 lb. Su.
Cyls.: (O) 20″×26″
Driving Wheels : 4′ 7½″ T.E.: 28,800 lb.

63340	63361	63382	63403
63341	63362	63383	63404
63342	63363	63384	63405
63343	63364	63385	63406
63344	63365	63386	63407
63345	63366	63387	63408
63346	63367	63388	63409
63347	63368	63389	63410
63348	63369	63390	63411
63349	63370	63391	63412
63350	63371	63392	63413
63351	63372	63393	63414
63352	63373	63394	63415
63353	63374	63395	63416
63354	63375	63396	63417
63355	63376	63397	63418
63356	63377	63398	63419
63357	63378	63399	63420
63358	63379	63400	63421
63359	63380	63401	63422
63360	63381	63402	63423

63424	63433	63442	63451
63425	63434	63443	63452
63426	63435	63444	63453
63427	63436	63445	63454
63428	63437	63446	63455
63429	63438	63447	63456
63430	63439	63448	63457
63431	63440	63449	63458
63432	63441	63450	63459

Total 120

0-8-0 Class Q7

Introduced 1919.
Weights : Loco. 71 tons 12 cwt.
Tender 44 tons 2 cwt.
Pressure : 180 lb. Su.
Cyls.: (3) 18½″×26″
Driving Wheels : 4′ 7¼″ T.E.: 36,965 lb.

63460	63464	63468	63472
63461	63465	63469	63473
63462	63466	63470	63474
63463	63467	63471	

Total 15

2-8-0 Class O3

Introduced 1913.
Weights : Loco. 76 tons 4 cwt.
Tender 43 tons 2 cwt.
Pressure : 180 lb. Su.
Cyls.: (O) 21″×28″
Driving Wheels : 4′ 8″ T.E.: 33,735 lb.

63475	63479	63483	63488
63476	63480	63484	63491
63477	63481	63485	63493
63478	63482	63486	

Total 15

2-8-0 Classes O1 & O4

O4/1* Introduced 1911. Original G.C. design with small Belpaire boiler, steam and vacuum brakes and water scoop.
O4/3† Introduced 1917. Ex-R.O.D. locos with steam brake only and no scoop. Taken into L.N.E.R. stock from 1924.
O4/2‡ Introduced 1925. O4/3 with cab and boiler mountings reduced to Scottish loading gauge.
O4/5§ Introduced 1932. Rebuilt with shortened O2-type boiler and separate smokebox saddle.

O4/6** Introduced 1924. Rebuilt from O5, retaining higher cab (63912-20 with side-windows).

O4/7†† Introduced 1939. Rebuilt with shortened O2-type boiler, retaining G.C. smokebox.

O4/8‡‡ Introduced 1944. Rebuilt with 100A(B1) boiler, retaining original cylinders.

(O4/4 were rebuilds with O2 boilers, since rebuilt again ; O5 was a G.C. development of O4 with larger Belpaire boiler.)

Weights: Loco. { 73 tons 4 cwt.*/†/‡/** ; 74 tons 13 cwt.§ ; 73 tons 17 cwt.†† ; 72 tons 10 cwt.‡‡ }

Tender { 48 tons 6 cwt. (with scoop) ; 47 tons 6 cwt. (without scoop) }

Pressure : 180 lb. Su.

Cyls.: (O) 21" × 26"

Driving Wheels : 4' 8" T.E.: 31,325 lb.

O1§§ Introduced 1944. Rebuilt with 100A boiler, Walschaerts' valve gear and new cylinders.

Weights : Loco. 73 tons 6 cwt.
Tender as O4.

Pressure : 225 lb. Su.

Cyls.: (O) 20" × 26"

Driving Wheels : 4' 8" T.E.: 35,520 lb.

63570††
63571*
63572*
63573*
63574*
63575‡‡
63576*
63577*
63578§§
63579§§
63580*
63581*
63582††
63583*
63584*
63585*
63586*
63587*
63588††
63589§
63590§§
63591§§
63592§§
63593*
63594§§
63595††
63596††
63597*
63598*
63599*
63600††
63601*
63602*
63603††
63604*
63605*
63606*
63607*
63608*
63609*
63610§§
63611*
63612*
63613‡‡
63614*
63615††
63616††
63617*
63618*
63619§§
63620*
63621*
63622*
63623*
63624*
63625*
63626*
63627*
63628§
63629†
63630§§
63631*
63632*
63633‡‡
63634††
63635*
63636†
63637†
63638†
63639†
63640*
63641†
63642†
63643††
63644‡
63645†
63646§§
63647‡
63648‡
63649†
63650§§
63651‡‡
63652§§
63653‡‡
63654*
63655††
63656†
63657†
63658*
63659†
63660*
63661††
63662††
63663§§
63664*
63665†
63666†
63667†
63668†
63669††
63670§§
63671*
63672†
63673††
63674‡
63675††
63676§§
63677*
63678§§
63679†
63680‡
63681†
63682‡
63683*
63684*
63685†
63686†
63687§§
63688†
63689§§
63690‡
63691†
63692*
63693*
63694†
63695†
63696†
63697†
63698*
63699††
63700*
63701†
63702†
63703†
63704‡
63705††
63706††
63707*
63708††
63709‡
63710*
63711§§
63712§§
63713†
63714†
63715†
63716†
63717†
63718†
63719*
63720†
63721†
63722*
63723*
63724†
63725§§
63726§
63727*
63728†
63729†
63730‡
63731†
63732†
63733†
63734†
63735†
63736*
63737†
63738‡‡
63739†
63740§§
63741†
63742†
63743*
63744†
63745§
63746†
63747††
63748††
63749††
63750†
63751†
63752§§
63753†
63754†
63755§§
63756†
63757*
63758††
63759†
63760§§
63761††
63762*
63763†
63764†
63765†
63766†
63767†
63768§§
63769†
63770††
63771†
63772††
63773§§
63774†
63775††
63776†
63777§§
63778*
63779†
63780§§
63781†
63782†
63783†
63784§§
63785‡‡
63786§§
63787†
63788§

63789§§	63836‡‡	63877†
63790†	63837†	63878†
63791†	63838†	63879§§
63792§§	63839††	63880††
63793†	63840†	63881†
63794††	63841†	63882‡‡
63795§§	63842†	63883†
63796§§	63843††	63884††
63797*	63845†	63885†
63798†	63846†	63886§§
63799*	63847‡	63887§§
63800†	63848††	63888†
63801†	63849†	63889†
63802‡‡	63850†	63890§§
63803§§	63851§	63891††
63804†	63852†	63893‡‡
63805*	63853‡‡	63894††
63806§§	63854§§	63895†
63807†	63855†	63897†
63808§§	63856†	63898†
63809*	63857††	63899†
63812†	63858†	63900†
63813†	63859†	63901§§
63816§	63860††	63902**
63817§§	63861†	63904**
63818‡‡	63862†	63905**
63819‡‡	63863§§	63906**
63821†	63864†	63907**
63822†	63865§§	63908**
63823†	63867§§	63911**
63824††	63868§§	63912**
63827‡‡	63869§§	63913**
63828‡‡	63870†	63914**
63829†	63872§§	63915**
63832†	63873†	63917**
63833†	63874§§	63920**
63835†	63876††	

Totals :

Class O1	52
Class O4/1	70
Class O4/2	11
Class O4/3	119
Class O4/5	7
Class O4/6	13
Class O4/7	41
Class O4/8	16

2-8-0 Class O2

O2/1* Introduced 1921. Development of experimental Gresley 3-cyl. loco (L.N.E.R. 3921).

O2/2† Introduced 1924. Development of O2/1 with detail differences, subsequently rebuilt with side-window cab, and reduced boiler mountings.

O2/3 Introduced 1932. Development of O2/2 with side-window cab and reduced boiler mountings.

O2 (100A)‡ Introduced 1943. Rebuilt with 100A (B1 type) boiler and smokebox extended backwards (3924 retaining G.N. cab).

Weights : Loco. { 75 tons 16 cwt.*† / 78 tons 13 cwt. / 74 tons 2 cwt.‡ }
Tender { 43 tons 2 cwt. (63922-46) / 52 tons (63947-87) }

Pressure : 180 lb. Su.

Cyls.: (3) $18\frac{1}{2}'' \times 26''$

Driving Wheels : 4′ 8″ T.E.: 36,470 lb.

63922*	63939†	63956	63973
63923*	63940†	63957	63974
63924‡	63941†	63958	63975
63925*	63942†	63959	63976
63926*	63943†	63960	63977
63927*	63944†	63961	63978
63928*	63945†	63962‡	63979
63929*	63946†	63963	63980
63930*	63947‡	63964	63981
63931*	63948	63965	63982
63932‡	63949	63966	63983
63933†	63950‡	63967	63984
63934†	63951	63968	63985
63935†	63952	63969	63986
63936†	63953	63970	63987
63937†	63954	63971	
63938†	63955	63972	

Totals :

Class O2 (100A)	5
Class O2/1	9
Class O2/2	14
Class O2/3	38

0-6-0 Classes J3 & J4

J4* Introduced 1896. Ivatt development of standard Stirling 0-6-0.
J3 Introduced 1912. Larger boilered rebuild of J4 (some rebuilt from Stirling domeless locos, oldest survivor built 1892) **(see note p. 72)**.

Weights : Loco. { 41 tons 5 cwt.* / 42 tons 12 cwt.
Tender { 34 tons 18 cwt.* / 38 tons 10 cwt.
Pressure : 175 lb. Cyls.: 17½″ × 26″
Driving Wheels : 5′ 2″ T.E.: 19,105 lb.

64105	64118	64129	64150
64106	64119	64131	64151
64107	64120*	64132	64153
64109*	64121*	64133	64158
64110*	64122	64135	64160*
64112*	64123	64137	64162*
64114	64124	64140	64163
64115	64125	64141	
64116	64127	64142	
64117	64128	64148	

Totals : Class J3 30
Class J4 7

0-6-0 Class J6

Introduced 1911 (see note p. 72).
Weights : Loco. 50 tons 10 cwt.
Tender 43 tons 2 cwt.
Pressure : 170 lb. Su. Cyls.: 19″ × 26″
Driving Wheels : 5′ 2″ T.E.: 21,875 lb.

64170	64188	64206	64224
64171	64189	64207	64225
64172	64190	64208	64226
64173	64191	64209	64227
64174	64192	64210	64228
64175	64193	64211	64229
64176	64194	64212	64230
64177	64195	64213	64231
64178	64196	64214	64232
64179	64197	64215	64233
64180	64198	64216	64234
64181	64199	64217	64235
64182	64200	64218	64236
64183	64201	64219	64237
64184	64202	64220	64238
64185	64203	64221	64239
64186	64204	64222	64240
64187	64205	64223	64241

64242	64252	64262	64272
64243	64253	64263	64273
64244	64254	64264	64274
64245	64255	64265	64275
64246	64256	64266	64276
64247	64257	64267	64277
64248	64258	64268	64278
64249	64259	64269	64279
64250	64260	64270	
64251	64261	64271	

Total 110

0-6-0 Class J11

Introduced 1901. Parts 1 and 4 have 3,250 gallon tenders ; Parts 2 and 5 4,000 gallon. Parts 1 and 2 have high boiler mountings ; Parts 4 and 5 low. All Parts 4 and 5 are superheated, and some of Parts 1 and 2. There are frequent changes between these parts
J11/3* Introduced 1942. Rebuilt with long-travel piston valves and boiler higher pitched.

Weights: Loco. { 51 tons 19 cwt. (Sat.) / 52 tons 2 cwt. (Su.) / 53 tons 6 cwt.*
Tender { 44 tons 3 cwt. (3,250 gall.) / 48 tons 6 cwt. (4,000 gall.)
Pressure : 180 lb. SS. Cyls.: 18½″ × 26″
Driving Wheels : 5′ 2″ T.E.: 21,960 lb.

64280	64300	64320	64340
64281	64301	64321	64341
64282	64302	64322	64342
64283*	64303	64323	64343
64284*	64304*	64324	64344
64285	64305	64325	64345
64286	64306	64326	64346*
64287	64307	64327	64347
64288	64308	64328	64348
64289	64309	64329	64349
64290	64310	64330	64350
64291	64311	64331	64351
64292	64312	64332	64352*
64293	64313	64333	64353
64294	64314*	64334	64354*
64295	64315	64335	64355
64296	64316*	64336	64356
64297	64317	64337	64357
64298	64318*	64338	64358
64299	64319	64339	64359*

64360	64384	64408	64432
64361	64385	64409	64433
64362*	64386*	64410	64434
64363	64387	64411	64435
64364*	64388	64412	64436
64365	64389	64413	64437
64366	64390	64414	64438
64367	64391	64415	64439*
64368	64392	64416	64440
64369	64393	64417*	64441*
64370	64394	64418	64442*
64371	64395	64419	64443
64372	64396	64420	64444
64373*	64397	64421	64445
64374	64398	64422	64446
64375*	64399	64423	64447
64376	64400	64424	64448
64377	64401	64425	64449
64378	64402*	64426	64450*
64379*	64403	64427*	64451
64380	64404	64428	64452
64381	64405	64429	64453
64382	64406*	64430	
64383	64407	64431	

Totals : Class J11/3 24
Class J11 150
(other parts)

0-6-0 Class J35

J35/5* Introduced 1906. Piston valves.
J35/4 Introduced 1908. Slide valves.
(Parts 1, 2 and 3 were variations of Parts 4 and 5 before superheating.)
Weights : Loco. { 51 tons.* / 50 tons 15 cwt.
Tender { 38 tons 1 cwt.* / 37 tons 15 cwt.
Pressure : 180 lb. Su. Cyls.: 18½" × 26"
Driving Wheels : 5' 0" T.E.: 22,080 lb.

64460*	64473*	64484	64494
64461*	64474*	64485	64495
64462*	64475*	64486	64496
64463*	64476*	64487	64497
64464*	64477*	64488	64498
64466*	64478	64489	64499
64468*	64479	64490	64500
64470*	64480	64491	64501
64471*	64482	64492	64502
64472*	64483	64493	64504

64505	64514	64522	64530
64506	64515	64523	64531
64507	64516	64524	64532
64509	64517	64525	64533
64510	64518	64526	64534
64511	64519	64527	64535
64512	64520	64528	
64513	64521	64529	

Totals : Class J35/4 55
Class J35/5 15

0-6-0 Class J37

Introduced 1914.
Weights : Loco. 54 tons 14 cwt.
Tender 40 tons 19 cwt.
Pressure : 180 lb. Su. Cyls.: 19½" × 26"
Driving Wheels : 5' 0" T.E.: 25,210 lb.

64536	64562	64588	64614
64537	64563	64589	64615
64538	64564	64590	64616
64539	64565	64591	64617
64540	64566	64592	64618
64541	64567	64593	64619
64542	64568	64594	64620
64543	64569	64595	64621
64544	64570	64596	64622
64545	64571	64597	64623
64546	64572	64598	64624
64547	64573	64599	64625
64548	64574	64600	64626
64549	64575	64601	64627
64550	64576	64602	64628
64551	64577	64603	64629
64552	64578	64604	64630
64553	64579	64605	64631
64554	64580	64606	64632
64555	64581	64607	64633
64556	64582	64608	64634
64557	64583	64609	64635
64558	64584	64610	64636
64559	64585	64611	64637
64560	64586	64612	64638
64561	64587	64613	64639

Total 104

0-6-0 Class J19

Introduced 1912. Rebuilt with round-topped boiler from 1934.

* Rebuilt with 19" cyls. and 180 lb. pressure.

† Rebuilt with 19" cyls. and 160 lb. pressure.

Weights : Loco. 50 tons 7 cwt.
Tender 38 tons 5 cwt.

Pressure : { 170 lb. Su. / 180 lb. Su.* / 160 lb. Su.† }

Cyls.: { 20" × 26" / 19" × 26"*† }

Driving Wheels : 4' 11"

T.E.: { 27,430 lb. / 26, 215 lb.* / 23,300 lb.† }

64640	64649	64658	64667
64641	64650	64659	64668
64642	64651	64660	64669
64643	64652	64661	64670
64644	64653	64662	64671*
64645	64654	64663	64672†
64646	64655	64664*	64673
64647	64656	64665	64674
64648	64657	64666	

Total 35

0-6-0 Class J20

J20* Introduced 1920. Belpaire boiler

J20/1 Introduced 1943. Rebuilt with B12/1 type round-topped boiler.

Weights : Loco. 54 tons 15 cwt.
Tender 38 tons 5 cwt.

Pressure : 180 lb. Su. Cyls.: 20" × 28"

Driving Wheels : 4' 11" T.E.: 29,045 lb.

64675*	64682	64689*	64696*
64676*	64683*	64690*	64697
64677	64684	64691	64698*
64678	64685	64692*	64699
64679	64686	64693	
64680	46687*	64694	
64681	64688	64695	

Totals : Class J20 9
Class J20/1 16

0-6-0 Class J39

Introduced 1926.

J39/1 Standard 3,500 gallon tender.

J39/2* Standard 4,200 gallon tender

J39/3† Various ex-N.E. tenders (3,940 gallon on 64843-5, 4,125 gallon on 64855-9)

Weights : Loco. 57 tons 17 cwt.
Tender { 44 tons 4 cwt. / 52 tons 13 cwt.* } and others

Pressure : 180 lb. Su. Cyls.: 20" × 26"

Driving Wheels : 5' 2" T.E.: 25,665 lb.

64700	64738	64776	64814
64701	64739	64777	64815
64702	64740	64778	64816
64703	64741	64779	64817
64704	64742	64780	64818
64705	64743	64781	64819
64706	64744	64782	64820*
64707	64745	64783	64821*
64708	64746	64784*	64822*
64709	64747	64785*	64823
64710	64748	64786*	64824
64711	64749	64787*	64825
64712	64750	64788*	64826
64713	64751	64789*	64827
64714	64752	64790*	64828
64715	64753	64791*	64829
64716	64754	64792*	64830
64717	64755	64793*	64831
64718	64756	64794*	64832
64719	64757	64795*	64833
64720	64758	64796	64834
64721	64759	64797	64835
64722	64760	64798	64836
64723	64761	64799	64837
64724	64762	64800	64838*
64725	64763	64801	64839*
64726	64764	64802	64840*
64727	64765	64803	64841*
64728	64766	64804	64842†
64729	64767	64805	64843†
64730	64768	64806	64844†
64731	64769	64807	64845†
64732	64770	64808	64846
64733	64771	64809	64847
64734	64772	64810	64848
64735	64773	64811	64849
64736	64774	64812	64850
64737	64775	64813	64851

64852	64887*	64922*	64957*
64853	64888*	64923*	64958*
64854	64889*	64924*	64959*
64855†	64890*	64925*	64960*
64856†	64891*	64926*	64961*
64857†	64892*	64927*	64962*
64858†	64893*	64928*	64963*
64859†	64894*	64929*	64964*
64860	64895*	64930*	64965*
64861	64896*	64931*	64966*
64862	64897*	64932*	64967*
64863	64898*	64933	64968*
64864	64899*	64934	64969*
64865	64900*	64935	64970*
64866	64901*	64936	64971†
64867	64902*	64937	64972†
64868	64903*	64938	64973†
64869	64904*	64939	64974†
64870	64905*	64940	64975†
64871	64906*	64941	64976†
64872*	64907*	64942	64977†
64873*	64908*	64943	64978†
64874*	64909*	64944	64979†
64875*	64910*	64945*	64980†
64876*	64911*	64946*	64981†
64877*	64912*	64947*	64982†
64878*	64913*	64948*	64983†
64879*	64914*	64949*	64984†
64880*	64915*	64950*	64985†
64881*	64916*	64951*	64986†
64882*	64917*	64952*	64987†
64883*	64918*	64953*	64988†
64884*	64919*	64954*	
64885*	64920*	64955*	
64886*	64921*	64956*	

Totals : Class J39/1 156
Class J39/2 106
Class J39/3 27

0-6-0 Class J1

Introduced 1908 (**see note p. 72**).
Weights : Loco. 46 tons 14 cwt.
Tender 43 tons 2 cwt.
Pressure : 175 lb. Cyls.: 18″×26″
Driving Wheels : 5′ 8″ T.E.: 18,430 lb.

65002	65005	65008	65013
65003	65006	65009	65014
65004	65007	65010	

Total 11

0-6-0 Class J2

Introduced 1912 (**see note p. 72**).
Weights : Loco. 50 tons 10 cwt.
Tender 43 tons 2 cwt.
Pressure : 170 lb. Su. Cyls.: 19″×26″
Driving Wheels : 5′ 8″ T.E.: 19,945 lb.

65015	65018	65020	65022
65016	65019	65021	65023
65017			

Total 9

0-6-0 Class J21

Introduced 1886. Majority built as 2-cyl. compounds and later rebuilt as simple locos. (**see note p. 71**).

* Saturated with Joy's gear and slide valves.
† Rebuilt with superheater and piston valves.
‡ Rebuilt with piston valves, superheater removed, 24″ piston stroke.
§ Rebuilt with piston valves, superheater removed, 26″ piston stroke.

Weights : Loco. { 42 tons 1 cwt.* / 43 tons 15 cwt.† / 42 tons 9 cwt.‡§ }
Tender 36 tons 19 cwt.
Pressure : 160 lb. SS.
Cyls.: { 18″×24″* / 19″×24″†‡ / 19″×26″§ }
T.E.: { 17,265 lb.* / 19,240 lb.†‡ / 20,840 lb.§ }
Driving Wheels : 5′ 1¼″

65025‡	65056*	65081‡	65103†
65026‡	65057†	65082†	65104‡
65027‡	65058‡	65083‡	65105‡
65028†	65059‡	65084†	65107‡
65029*	65060‡	65086*	65108‡
65030‡	65061†	65088†	65109†
65033†	65062†	65089†	65110†
65035‡	65064†	65090†	65111‡
65036‡	65066‡	65091†	65112*
65037†	65067‡	65092†	65114*
65038†	65068†	65093‡	65116*
65039‡	65070‡	65094‡	65117‡
65040†	65072‡	65095†	65118‡
65041*	65073*	65097†	65119†
65042‡	65075†	65098†	65120*
65043§	65076‡	65099‡	65121†
65044*	65077†	65100‡	65122*
65047†	65078†	65101‡	65123†
65051*	65079‡	65102‡	
65052†	65080‡		

Total 77

0-6-0 Class J10

J10/2* Introduced 1892. Original locos with small tenders.
J10/4† Introduced 1896. Development of J10/2 with larger bearings and larger tenders.
J10/6 Introduced 1901. Locos with larger bearings and small tenders.
Weights : Loco. 41 tons 6 cwt.
Tender { 37 tons 6 cwt. / 43 tons.†
Pressure : 160 lb. Cyls.: 18″×26″
Driving Wheels : 5′ 1″ T.E.: 18,780 lb.

65126*	65147†	65169†	65190
65127*	65148†	65170†	65191
65128*	65149†	65171†	65192
65130*	65151†	65172	65193
65131	65153†	65173	65194
65132†	65154†	65175	65196
65133†	65155†	65176	65197
65134†	65156†	65177	65198
65135†	65157†	65178†	65199
65136†	65158†	65179	65200
65137†	65159†	65180	65201
65138†	65160†	65181	65202
65139	65161†	65182	65203
65140†	65162	65183	65204
65141†	65163	65184	65205
65142†	65164†	65185	65208
65143†	65165†	65186	65209
65144†	65166†	65187	
65145†	65167†	65188	
65146†	65168	65189	

Totals : Class J10/2 4
Class J10/4 35
Class J10/6 38

0-6-0 Class J36

Introduced 1888.
Weights : Loco. 41 tons 19 cwt.
Tender 33 tons 9 cwt.
Pressure : 165 lb. Cyls.: $18\frac{1}{4}$″×26″
Driving Wheels : 5′ 0″ T.E.: 19,690 lb.

65210	65221	65229	65237
65211	65222	65230	65238
65213	65224	65231	65239
65214	65225	65232	65240
65215	65226	65233 Plumer	
65216	Haig	65234	65241
65217	65227	65235	65242
65218	65228	65236 Horne	
65243 Maude		65294	65320
65244	65270	65295	65321
65245	65271	65296	65322
65246	65273	65297	65323
65247	65274	65298	65324
65248	65275	65300	65325
65249	65276	65303	65327
65250	65277	65304	65329
65251	65278	65305	65330
65252	65279	65306	65331
65253	65280	65307	65333
65254	65281	65308	65334
65255	65282	65309	65335
65257	65283	65310	65338
65258	65285	65311	65339
65259	65286	65312	65340
65260	65287	65313	65341
65261	65288	65314	65342
65264	65290	65315	65343
65265	65291	65316	65344
65266	65292	65317	65345
65267	65293	65318	65346
65268 Allenby		65319	

Total 118

0-6-0 Class J15

Intro. 1883. (Oldest survivor built 1886.)
* Fitted with side-windows and tender cab for Colne Valley line.
Weights : Loco. 37 tons 2 cwt.
Tender 30 tons 13 cwt.
Pressure : 160 lb. Cyls.: $17\frac{1}{2}$″×24″
Driving Wheels : 4′ 11″ T.E.: 16,940 lb.

65350	65370	65388	65408
65351	65371	65389	65409
65353	65372	65390	65412
65354	65373	65391*	65413
65355	65374	65392	65414
65356	65375	65393	65415
65357	65376	65395	65416
65359	65377	65396	65417
65361	65378	65397	65419
65362	65379	65398	65420
65363	65381	65401	65422
65364	65382	65402	65423
65365	65384	65404	65424*
65366	65385	65405*	65425
65367	65386	65406	65426
65369	65387	65407	65427

Right : Class D20/1 4-4-0 No. 2383 (New No. 62383)

[*Photo* : *B. V. Franey*

Below : Class D1 4-4-0 No. 62203

[*Photo* : *E. V. Fry*

Above : Class D3 4-4-0 No. 62131

Right : Class D9 4-4-0 No. 2325 (New No. 62325)

[*Photos* : *E. V. Fry*

Top : Class D40 4-4-0 No. 2260 (New No. 62260) [*Photo : H. C. Casserley*
Centre : Class D29/2 4-4-0 No. 2411 *Lady of Avenel* (New No. 62411)
[*Photo : P. Ransome-Wallis*
Bottom : Class D41 4-4-0 No. 2228 (New No. 62228) [*Photo : H. C. Casserley*

Top : Class D16/3 4-4-0 No. 62578 [*Photo : E. V. Fry*
Centre : Class D15 4-4-0 No. 2520 (New No. 62520) [*Photo : P. Ransome-Wallis*
Bottom: Class E4 2-4-0 No. 2786 (New No. 62786) [*Photo : B. V. Franey*

EASTERN & NORTH

Above : Class A3 No. 103 *Flying Scotsman* (New No. 60103) at the head of a down semi-fast near Retford.

[*Photo : Eric Oldham*

Below : Class A2/3 No. 523 *Sun Castle* (New No. 60523) with the 3.30 p.m. King's Cross-Newcastle express near New Southgate.

[*Photo : E. R. Wethersett*

EASTERN PACIFICS

Above : Class A4 No. 60034 *Lord Faringdon* pulls out of King's Cross with the 1.10 p.m. Leeds express.

[*Photo : Roy E. Vincent*

Left : Class A1/1 No. 113 *Great Northern* (New No. 60113) south of Potters Bar with the up "Yorkshire Pullman."

Below : Class A2 No. 60533 *Happy Knight* breasts Potters Bar summit with the 1 p.m. King's Cross-Edinburgh express.

[*Photos : P. Ransome-Wallis*

Top : Class J6 0-6-0 No. 4264 (New No. 64264)
Centre : Class J19/2 0-6-0 No. 4648 (New No. 64648)
Bottom : Class J25 0-6-0 No. 5664 (New No. 65664)

[*Photos : B. V. Franey*

Top: Class J11/3 0-6-0 No. 4379 (New No. 64379) [*Photo : H. C. Casserley*

Centre: Class J39/1 0-6-0 No. 4761 (New No. 64761) [*Photo : B. Y. Franey*

Bottom : Class J36 0-6-0 No. 5255 (New No. 65255) [*Photo : H. C. Casserley*

Top : Class Q4/2 0-8-0 No. 3235 (New No. 63235) [*Photo : E. V. Fry*
Centre : Class Q5/2 0-8-0 No. 3301 (New No. 63301) [*Photo : P. Ransome-Wallis*
Bottom : Class U1 2-8-8-2 No. 9999 (New No. 69999) [*Photo : H. C. Casserley*

65428	65441	65454	65467
65429	65442	65455	65468
65430	65443	65456	65469
65431	65444	65457	65470
65432*	65445	65458	65471
65433	65446	65459	65472
65434	65447	65460	65473
65435	65448	65461	65474
65436	65449	65462	65475
65437	65450	65463	65476
65438*	65451	65464	65477
65439	65452	65465	65478
65440	65453	65466	65479

Total 116

0-6-0 Class J5

Introduced 1909 (**see note p. 72**).
* Rebuilt with superheater.
Weights : Loco. 47 tons 6 cwt.
Tender 43 tons 2 cwt.
Pressure : { 175 lb. / 170 lb. Su.* Cyls.: 18" × 26"
Driving Wheels : 5' 2"
T.E.: { 20,210 lb. / 19,630 lb.*

65480*	65485	65490	65495
65481	65486	65491	65496
65482	65487	65492	65497
65483	65488	65493	65498
65484	65489*	65494	65499

Total 20

0-6-0 Class J17

Introduced 1901. Many rebuilt from round-top boiler J16, introduced 1900.
*Fitted with small tender.
Weights : Loco. 45 tons 8 cwt.
Tender { 30 tons 12 cwt.* / 38 tons 5 cwt.
Pressure : 180 lb. Su. Cyls.: 19" × 26"
Driving Wheels : 4' 11" T.E.: 24,340 lb.

65500*	65510*	65520	65530
65501*	65511*	65521	65531
65502*	65512*	65522	65532
65503*	65513*	65523	65533
65504*	65514*	65524	65534
65505*	65515*	65525	65535
65506*	65516*	65526	65536
65507*	65517*	65527	65537
65508*	65518*	65528*	65538
65509	65519*	65529	65539

65540	65554	65567	65580
65541	65555	65568	65581
65542	65556	65569	65582
65543	65557	65570	65583
65544	65558	65571	65584
65545	65559	65572	65585
65546	65560	65573	65586
65547	65561	65574	65587
65548	65562	65575	65588
65549	65563	65576	65589
65551	65564	65577	
65552	65565	65578	
65553	65566	65579	

Total 89

0-6-0 Class J24

Introduced 1894 (**see note p. 71**).
* Original design, saturated with slide valves.
† Rebuilt with superheater and piston valves.
‡ Rebuilt with piston valves, super heater removed.
Weights : Loco. { 38 tons 10 cwt.* / 39 tons 11 cwt.†‡
Tender 36 tons 19 cwt.
Pressure : 160 lb. SS.
Cyls.: { 18" × 24"* / 18½" × 24"†‡
Driving Wheels : 4' 7¼"
T.E.: { 19,140 lb.* / 20,220 lb. †‡

65600*	65609*	65623*	65633†
65601*	65611†	65624†	65634*
65602*	65614*	65626*	65636†
65603†	65615*	65627‡	65640*
65604*	65617†	65628‡	65641*
65606†	65619*	65629‡	65642*
65607*	65621‡	65631†	65644‡
65608*	65622*	65632*	

Total 31

0-6-0 Class J25

Introduced 1898 (see note p. 71).
*Original design, saturated with slide valves.
† Rebuilt with superheater and piston valves.
‡ Rebuilt with piston valves, superheater removed.

Weights: Loco. { 39 tons 11 cwt.* / 41 tons 14 cwt.† / 40 tons 17 cwt.‡
Tender 36 tons 19 cwt.
Pressure: 160 lb. SS. Cyls.: 18½"×26"
Driving Wheels: 4'7¼" T.E.: 21,905 lb.

65645†	65665†	65687*	65708*
65646†	65666*	65688*	65710*
65647*	65667*	65689*	65712*
65648*	65668*	65690*	65713*
65649*	65669†	65691*	65714*
65650*	65670*	65692‡	65715*
65651*	65671*	65693*	65716*
65653*	65672*	65694*	65717†
65654‡	65673‡	65695*	65718*
65655*	65675*	65696*	65720*
65656*	65676*	65697*	65721*
65657*	65677‡	65698*	65723*
65658*	65679*	65699*	65724*
65659†	65680*	65700*	65725*
65660*	65681‡	65702‡	65726*
65661*	65683‡	65703*	65727*
65662†	65684‡	65705*	65728*
65663*	65685*	65706†	
65664*	65686*	65707*	

Total 74

0-6-0 Class J26

Introduced 1904 (see note p. 71).
Weights: Loco. 46 tons 16 cwt.
Tender 36 tons 19 cwt.
Pressure: 180 lb. Cyls.: 18½"×26"
Driving Wheels: 4'7¼" T.E.: 24,640 lb.

65730	65740	65750	65760
65731	65741	65751	65761
65732	65742	65752	65762
65733	65743	65753	65763
65734	65744	65754	65764
65735	65745	65755	65765
65736	65746	65756	65766
65737	65747	65757	65767
65738	65748	65758	65768
65739	65749	65759	65769
65770	65773	65776	65778
65771	65774	65777	65779
65772	65775		

Total 50

0-6-0 Class J27

Introduced 1906 (see note p. 71).
* Introduced 1921. Superheated with piston valves.
† Introduced 1943. Piston valves, superheater removed.

Weights: Loco. { 47 tons Sat. / 49 tons 10 cwt. Su.
Tender 36 tons 19 cwt.
Pressure: 180 lb. SS. Cyls.: 18½"×26"
Driving Wheels: 4'7¼" T.E.: 24,640 lb.

65780	65809	65838	65867
65781	65810	65839	65868
65782	65811	65840	65869
65783	65812	65841	65870
65784	65813	65842	65871
65785	65814	65843	65872
65786	65815	65844	65873
65787	65816	65845	65874
65788	65817	65846	65875
65789	65818	65847	65876
65790	65819	65848	65877
65791	65820	65849	65878
65792	65821	65850	65879
65793	65822	65851	65880
65794	65823	65852	65881
65795	65824	65853	65882
65796	65825	65854	65883
65797	65826	65855	65884
65798	65827	65856	65885
65799	65828	65857	65886
65800	65829	65858	65887
65801	65830	65859	65888
65802	65831	65860	65889
65803	65832	65861	65890
65804	65833	65862	65891
65805	65834	65863	65892
65806	65835	65864	65893
65807	65836	65865	65894
65808	65837	65866	

Total 115

0-6-0 Class J38

Introduced 1926. Boiler 6″ longer than J39 and smokebox 6″ shorter.
* Rebuilt with J39 boiler.
Weights : Loco. 58 tons 19 cwt.
Tender 44 tons 4 cwt.
Pressure : 180 lb. Su. Cyls.: 20″×26″
Driving Wheels : 4′ 8″ T.E.: 28,415 lb.

65900	65909	65918*	65927*
65901	65910	65919	65928
65902	65911	65920	65929
65903*	65912	65921	65930
65904	65913	65922	65931
65905	65914	65923	65932
65906*	65915	65924	65933
65907	65916	65925	65934
65908*	65917*	65926*	

Total 35

2-4-2T Class F7

Introduced 1909.
Weight : 45 tons 14 cwt.
Pressure : 160 lb. Cyls.: 15″×22″
Driving Wheels : 4′ 10″ T.E.: 11,605 lb.

67093	67094

Total 2

2-4-2T Class F1

Introduced 1889. (Oldest survivor built 1891.)
Weight : 60 tons 12 cwt.
Pressure : 160 lb. Cyls.: 18″×24″
Driving Wheels : 5′ 7″ T.E.: 15,785 lb.

67099	67100

Total 2

2-4-2T Class F2

Introduced 1898.
* Push-and-pull fitted.
Weight : 62 tons 6 cwt.
Pressure : 160 lb. Cyls.: 18″×26″
Driving Wheels : 5′ 7″ T.E.: 17,100 lb.

67104*	67107	67109*	67112*
67106*	67108	67111*	67113

Total 8

2-4-2T Class F3

Introduced 1893. (Oldest survivor built 1895) (see note p. 72).
Weight : 58 tons 12 cwt.
Pressure : 160 lb. Cyls.: 17½″×24″
Driving Wheels : 5′ 8″ T.E.: 14,710 lb.

67124	67127	67139	67149
67126	67128	67140	67150

Total 8

2-4-2T Class F4

Introduced 1884. (Oldest survivor built 1906) (see note p. 72).
* Push-and-pull fitted.
Weight : 53 tons 19 cwt.
Pressure : 160 lb. Cyls.: 17½″×24″
Driving Wheels : 5′ 4″ T.E.: 15,620 lb.

67151*	67158	67167	67182
67152	67160	67171	67183
67153	67162	67174	67184
67154	67163	67175	67186
67155	67164	67176	67187
67156	67165	67177	
67157	67166	67178	

Total 26

2-4-2T Class F5

Introduced 1911. (Rebuilt from F4, oldest survivor originally built 1903.) (see note page 72).
Weight : 53 tons 19 cwt.
Pressure : 180 lb. Cyls.: 17½″×24″
Driving Wheels : 5′ 4″ T.E.: 17,570 lb.

67188	67196	67204	67212
67189	67197	67205	67213
67190	67198	67206	67214
67191	67199	67207	67215
67192	67200	67208	67216
67193	67201	67209	67217
67194	67202	67210	
67195	67203	67211	

Total 30

2-4-2T Class F6

Introduced 1911 (67218/9 rebuilt from F4, originally built 1904) (see note p. 72).
Weight : 56 tons 9 cwt.
Pressure : 180 lb. Cyls.: 17½″×24″
Driving Wheels : 5′ 4″ T.E.: 17,570 lb.

67218	67220	67222	67224
67219	67221	67223	67225

67226	67230	67234	67237
67227	67231	67235	67238
67228	67232	67236	67239
67229	67233		

Total 22

0-4-4T Class G5

Introduced 1894.
* Push-and-pull fitted.
† Rebuilt with larger tanks.
Weight : 54 tons 4 cwt.
Pressure : 160 lb. Cyls.: 18"×24"
Driving Wheels : 5' 1½" T.E.: 17,265 lb.

67240	67268	67296	67325
67241	67269	67297*	67326
67242	67270	67298	67327
67243	67271	67299	67328
67244	67272	67300	67329
67245	67273*	67301	67330
67246	67274	67302	67331
67247	67275	67303	67332
67248	67276	67304	67333
67249	67277	67305*	67334
67250*	67278	67307	67335
67251	67279*	67308	67336
67252	67280*	67309	67337*
67253*	67281*	67310	67338
67254	67282*	67311*	67339*
67255	67283	67312	67340*†
67256	67284	67313	67341
67257	67285	67314	67342
67258	67286*	67315	67343
67259	67287	67316	67344
67260	67288	67317	67345
67261*	67289	67318	67346
67262	67290	67319	67347
67263	67291	67320	67348
67264	67292	67321	67349
67265	67293	67322*	
67266	67294	67323*	
67267	67295	67324	

Total 109

4-4-2T Class C12

Introduced 1898.
* Boiler pressure reduced to 170 lb.
Weight : 62 tons 6 cwt.
Pressure : { 175 lb. / 170 lb.* } Cyls.: 18"×26"
Driving Wheels : 5' 8"
T.E.: { 18,425 lb. / 17,900 lb.* }

67350	67363*	67375	67387
67351	67364	67376	67389
67352	67365	67377	67390
67353	67366	67379	67391
67354*	67367	67380	67392
67356	67368	67381	67393
67357	67369	67382	67394
67359	67371	67383	67395
67360	67372	67384	67397
67361	67373	67385	67398*
67362	67374*	67386	67399*

Total 44

4-4-2T Class C13

Introduced 1903.
* Push-and-pull fitted.
Weight : 66 tons 13 cwt.
Pressure : 160 lb. Su. Cyls.: 18"×26"
Driving Wheels : 5' 7" T.E.: 17,100 lb.

67400	67410	67420*	67430
67401	67411	67421*	67431
67402	67412	67422	67432
67403	67413	67423	67433*
67404	67414	67424	67434
67405	67415	67425	67435
67406	67416*	67426	67436*
67407	67417*	67427	67437
67408	67418*	67428	67438*
67409	67419	67429	67439

Total 40

4-4-2T Class C14

Introduced 1907. Development of C13 with detail differences.
Weight : 71 tons.
Pressure : 160 lb. Su. Cyls.: 18"×26"
Driving Wheels : 5' 7" T.E.: 17,100 lb.

67440	67443	67446	67449
67441	67444	67447	67450
67442	67445	67448	67451

Total 12

4-4-2T Class C15

Introduced 1911.
* Push-and-pull fitted.
Weight : 68 tons 15 cwt.
Pressure : 175 lb. Cyls.: 18" × 26"
Driving Wheels : 5' 9" T.E.: 18,160 lb.

67452	67460*	67468	67476
67453	67461	67469	67477
67454	67462	67470	67478
67455	67463	67471	67479
67456	67464	67472	67480
67457	67465	67473	67481
67458	67466	67474	
67459	67467	67475	

Total 30

4-4-2T Class C16

Introduced 1915.
* Superheater removed.
Weight : 72 tons 10 cwt.
Pressure : 165 lb. SS. Cyls.: 19" × 26"
Driving Wheels : 5' 9" T.E.: 19,080 lb.

67482	67488	67494	67500
67483*	67489	67495	67501
67484	67490	67496	67502
67485	67491	67497	
67486	67492	67498	
67487	67493	67499	

Total 21

2-6-2T Classes V1 & V3

V1 Introduced 1930.
V3* Introduced 1939. Development of V1 with higher pressure (locos below 67682 rebuilt from V1).
Weights : 84 tons.
86 tons 16 cwt.*
Pressure : { 180 lb. Su. / 200 lb. Su.* }
Cyls.: (3) 16" × 26"
Driving Wheels : 5' 8"
T.E.: { 22,465 lb. / 24,960 lb.* }

67600	67609	67618	67627	67636	67650	67664	67678
67601	67610	67619	67628	67637	67651	67665	67679
67602	67611	67620	67629	67638	67652	67666	67680
67603	67612	67621	67630	67639	67653	67667	67681
67604	67613	67622	67631	67640	67654	67668	67682*
67605	67614	67623	67632	67641	67655	67669*	67683*
67606	67615	67624	67633	67642	67656	67670	67684*
67607	67616	67625	67634*	67643	67657	67671	67685*
67608	67617	67626	67635	67644	67658	67672*	67686*
				67645	67659	67673	67687*
				67646	67660	67674	67688*
				67647	67661	67675*	67689*
				67648	67662	67676	67690*
				67649	67663	67677	67691*

Totals : Class V1 78
Class V3 14

2-6-4T Class L1

Introduced 1945.
Weight : 89 tons 9 cwt.
Pressure : 225 lb. Cyls.: (O) 20" × 26"
Driving Wheels : 5' 2" T.E.: 32,080 lb.
(*Former L.N.E.R. numbers in brackets*)

67701 (9000)	67716 (9015)
67702 (9001)	67717
67703 (9002)	67718
67704 (9003)	67719
67705 (9004)	67720
67706 (9005)	67721
67707 (9006)	67722
67708 (9007)	67723
67709 (9008)	67724
67710 (9009)	67725
67711 (9010)	67726
67712 (9011)	67727
67713 (9012)	67728
67714 (9013)	67729
67715 (9014)	67730

Total 30

0-6-0ST Class J94

Introduced 1943. (Bought from M.O.S. 1946.)
Weight : 48 tons 5 cwt.
Pressure : 170 lb. Cyls.: 18" × 26"
Driving Wheels : 4' 3" T.E.: 23,870 lb.

68006	68008	68010	68012
68007	68009	68011	68013

68014	68031	68048	68065
68015	68032	68049	68066
68016	68033	68050	68067
68017	68034	68051	68068
68018	68035	68052	68069
68019	68036	68053	68070
68020	68037	68054	68071
68021	68038	68055	68072
68022	68039	68056	68073
68023	68040	68057	68074
68024	68041	68058	68075
68025	68042	68059	68076
68026	68043	68060	68077
68027	68044	68061	68078
68028	68045	68062	68079
68029	68046	68063	68080
68030	68047	68064	

Total 75

0-4-0T (Tram Locos) Class Y6

Introduced 1883. (Oldest survivor built 1897.)
Weight : 21 tons 5 cwt.
Pressure : 140 lb. Cyls.: 11″ × 15″
Driving Wheels : 3′ 1″ T.E.: 5,835 lb.

68082	68083

Total 2

0-4-0T Class Y7

Introduced 1888. (Survivors built 1923)
Weight : 22 tons 14 cwt.
Pressure : 140 lb. Cyls.: 14″ × 20″
Driving Wheels : 3′ 6½″ T.E.: 11,040 lb.

68088S	68089

Total 2

0-4-0T Class Y8

Introduced 1890.
Weight : 15 tons 10 cwt.
Pressure : 140 lb. Cyls.: 11″ × 15″
Driving Wheels : 3′ 0″ T.E.: 6,000 lb.

68090	68091

Total 2

0-4-0ST Class Y9

Introduced 1882.
* Many of these locos run permanently attached to wooden tenders, some by loose couplings and others by central drawgear.

Weights : Loco. 27 tons 16 cwt.
Tender 6 tons.*
Pressure : 130 lb. Cyls. : (O) 14″ × 20″
Driving Wheels : 3′ 8″ T.E.: 9,845 lb.

68092	68101	68110	68119
68093	68102	68111	68120
68094	68103	68112	68121
68095	68104	68113	68122
68096	68105	68114	68123
68097	68106	68115	68124
68098	68107	68116	
68099	68108	68117	
68100	68109	68118	

Total 33

0-4-0T Class Y4

Introduced 1913.
Weight : 38 tons 1 cwt.
Pressure : 180 lb. Cyls.: (O) 17″ × 20″
Driving Wheels : 3′ 10″ T.E.: 19,225 lb.

68125	68127	68128	68129S
68126			

Total 5

0-4-0T Class Y1

Single-speed Geared Sentinel Locomotives. The four parts of this class differ in details, including size of boiler and fuel capacity.

Y1/1* Introduced 1925.
Y1/2† Introduced 1927.
Y1/3** Introduced 1926.
Y1/4‡ Introduced 1927.
§ Sprocket gear ratio 9 : 25 (remainder 11 : 25).

Weights : 20 tons 17 cwt.*, 19 tons 16 cwt.†, 14 tons.**, 19 tons 7 cwt.‡
Pressure : 275 lb. Su. Cyls.: 6¾″ × 9″
Driving Wheels : 2′ 6″
T.E.: 7,260 lb., 8,870 lb.§

68130S*	68133S*	68137†
68131S*	68135S*	68138†
68132S*	68136S‡	68139**

68140†	68145† §	68150† §
68141†	68146† §	68151† §
68142†	68147† §	68152S*
68143† §	68148† §	68153S†
68144† §	68149† §	

Totals : Class Y1/1 5
Class Y1/2 15
Class Y1/3 2
Class Y1/4 1

0-4-0T Class Y3

Two-speed Geared Sentinel Locos.
Introduced 1927.
* Sprocket gear ratio 15 : 19 (remainder 19 : 19).
Weight : 20 tons 16 cwt.
Pressure : 275 lb. Su. Cyls.: 6¾″ × 9″
Driving Wheels : 2′ 6″
T.E.: Low Gear : 12,600 lb.
High Gear : 4,705 lb.
Low Gear : 15,960 lb.*
High Gear : 5,960 lb.*

68154	68162	68171	68179
68155	68163	68172	68180*
68156	68164	68173S	68181*
68157	68165	68174	68182*
68158	68166S	68175	68183*
68159	68167	68176	68184
68160	68168	68177S	68185
68161	68169	68178S	

Total 31

0-4-0T Class Y10

Double - ended Two - speed Geared Sentinel Loco.
Introduced 1930.
Weight : 23 tons 19 cwt.
Pressure : 275 lb. Su. Cyls.: 6¾″ × 9″
Driving Wheels : 3′ 2″
T.E.: Low Gear : 11,435 lb.
High Gear : 7,965 lb.

68186

Total 1

0-4-0T (Petrol) Class Y11

Introduced 1921.
Weight : 8 tons. H.P.: 40.

68188 | 68189

Total 2

0-4-2T Class Z4

Introduced 1915.
Weight : 25 tons 17 cwt.
Pressure : 160 lb. Cyls.: (O) 13″ × 20″
Driving Wheels : 3′ 6″ T.E.: 10,945 lb.

68190 | 68191

Total 2

0-4-2T Class Z5

Introduced 1915.
Weight : 30 tons 18 cwt.
Pressure : 160 lb. Cyls.: (O) 14″ × 20″
Driving Wheels : 4′ 0″ T.E.: 11,105 lb.

68192 | 68193

Total 2

0-6-0ST Class J62

Introduced 1897.
Weight : 30 tons 17 cwt.
Pressure : 150 lb. Cyls.: (O) 13″ × 20″
Driving Wheels : 3′ 6″ T.E.: 10,260 lb.

68200 | 68201 | 68203

Total 3

0-6-0T Class J63

Introduced 1906.
Weight : 37 tons 9 cwt.
Pressure : 150 lb. Cyls.: (O) 13″ × 20″
Driving Wheels : 3′ 6″ T.E.: 10,260 lb

68204	68206	68208	68210
68205	68207	68209	

Total 7

0-6-0T Class J65

Introduced 1889 (see note p. 72).
Weight : 36 tons 11 cwt.
Pressure : 160 lb. Cyls.: 14″ × 20″
Driving Wheels : 4′ 0″ T.E.: 11,105 lb.

68211 | 68214 | 68215

Total 3

0-6-0T (Tram Locos) Class J70

Introduced 1903.
Weight : 27 tons 1 cwt.
Pressure : 180 lb. Cyls.: (O) 12″ × 15″
Driving Wheels : 3′ 1″ T.E.: 8,930 lb.

68216	68219	68222	68225
68217	68220	68223	68226
68218	68221	68224	

Total 11

0-6-0T Class J71

Introduced 1886.
* † Altered cylinder dimensions.
Weight : 37 tons 12 cwt.
Pressure : 140 lb. Dr. Wheels : 4′ 7¼″
Cyls.: 16″ × 22″; 16¾″ × 22″*; 18″ × 22″† T.E.: 12,130 lb.; 13,300 lb.*; 15,355 lb.†

68230*	68253*	68277	68298
68231	68254	68278	68299
68232	68255	68279	68300
68233	68256	68280*	68301
68234*	68258*	68281	68302*
68235	68259*	68282	68303*
68236	68260	68283	68304*
68238	68262	68284	68305*
68239	68263	68285	68306*
68240	68264	68286*	68307*
68242	68265	68287*	68308*
68243	68266	68288	68309*
68244	68267	68289*	68310*
68245	68268	68290	68311*
68246*	68269	68291	68312†
68247	68270	68292	68313*
68248	68271	68293*	68314
68249	68272	68294	68316*
68250*	68273	68295	
68251	68275	68296	
68252*	68276	68297	

Total 81

0-6-0ST Class J55

Introduced 1912. (Rebuilt from domeless locos, introduced 1891.)
* Pressure reduced to 160 lb.
Weight : 45 tons 16 cwt.
Pressure : 175 lb.; 160 lb.* Cyls.: 17½″ × 26″
Driving Wheels : 4′ 8″ T.E.: 21,150 lb.; 19,340 lb.*

68317	68319S*

Total 2

0-6-0T Class J88

Introduced 1904.
Weight : 38 tons 14 cwt.
Pressure : 130 lb. Cyls.: (O) 15″ × 22″
Driving Wheels : 3′ 9″ T.E.: 12,155 lb.

68320	68323	68326	68329
68321	68324	68327	68330
68322	68325	68328	68331
68332	68338	68344	68350
68333	68339	68345	68351
68334	68340	68346	68352
68335	68341	68347	68353
68336	68342	68348	68354
68337	68343	68349	

Total 35

0-6-0T Class J73

Introduced 1891.
Weight : 46 tons 15 cwt.
Pressure : 160 lb. Cyls.: 19″ × 24″
Driving Wheels : 4′ 7¼″ T.E.: 21,320 lb.

68355	68358	68361	68363
68356	68359	68362	68364
68357	68360		

Total 10

0-6-0T Class J75

Introduced 1901. (Survivor built 1908.)
Weight : 47 tons 7 cwt.
Pressure : 175 lb. Cyls.: 18″ × 26″
Driving Wheels : 4′ 6″ T.E.: 23,205 lb.

68365 **Total 1**

0-6-0T Class J66

Introduced 1886.
Weight : 40 tons 6 cwt.
Pressure : 160 lb. Cyls.: 16½″ × 22″
Driving Wheels : 4′ 0″ T.E.: 16,970 lb.

68370S	68375	68380	68385
68371	68376	68381	68386
68372	68377	68382	68387
68373	68378	68383	68388
68374	68379	68384	

Total 19

0-6-0T Class J77

Introduced 1899. (Rebuilt from 0-4-4T originally built 1874-84.)
* Darlington rebuilds with square-cornered cab roof (remainder York rebuilds with rounded cab).

Weight : 43 tons.
Pressure : 160 lb. Cyls.: 17"×22"
Driving Wheels : 4' 1¼" T.E.: 17,560 lb.

68390	68404*	68417	68431
68391	68405*	68420*	68432*
68392*	68406	68421	68433
68393*	68407	68422	68434
68395*	68408	68423	68435
68396	68409	68424	68436
68397*	68410	68425	68437
68398	68412*	68426	68438
68399	68413	68427	68440*
68400	68414	68428	
68401	68415	68429	
68402	68416	68430	

Total 45

0-6-0T Class J83

Introduced 1900.
Weight : 45 tons 5 cwt.
Pressure : 150 lb. Cyls.: 17"×26"
Driving Wheels : 4' 6" T.E.: 17,745 lb.

68442	68452	68463	68473
68443	68453	68464	68474
68444	68454	68465	68475
68445	68455	68466	68476
68446	68456	68467	68477
68447	68457	68468	68478
68448	68458	68469	68479
68449	68459	68470	68480
68450	68460	68471	68481
68451	68461	68472	

Total 39

0-6-0T Class J93

Introduced 1897.
Weight : 37 tons 14 cwt.
Pressure : 150 lb. Cyls.: (O) 16"×20"
Driving Wheels : 3' 7" T.E.: 15,180 lb.

68489 **Total 1**

0-6-0T Classes J67 & J69

(See note p. 72)

J67/1* Introduced 1890. Original design with 160 lb. pressure.

J69 Introduced 1902. Development of J67 with 180 lb. pressure and larger tanks (some rebuiltf rom J67).

J67/2† Introduced 1937. Rebuild of J69 with 160 lb. boiler.

Weights : 40 tons.* / 42 tons 9 cwt. / 41 tons 8 cwt.†

Pressure : 160 lb.*† / 180 lb. Cyls.: 16½"×22"

Driving Wheels : 4' 0"

T.E.: 16,970 lb.*† / 19,090 lb.

68490*	68522*	68554	68588*
68491	68523*	68555	68589*
68492*	68524	68556	68590*
68493*	68525	68557	68591*
68494	68526	68558	68592*
68495	68527	68559	68593*
68496*	68528	68560	68594*
68497	68529†	68561	68595*
68498*	68530	68562	68596
68499	68531†	68563	68597†
68500	68532	68565	68598
68501	68533	68566	68599
68502	68534	68567	68600
68503	68535	68568	68601
68504	68536†	68569	68602
68505	68537	68570	68603
68507	68538	68571	68605
68508	68540†	68572†	68606*
68509*	68541	68573	68607
68510*	68542	68574	68608*
68511*	68543	68575	68609†
68512*	68544	68576	68610†
68513*	68545	68577	68611*
68514*	68546	68578	68612
68515*	68547†	68579	68613
68516*	68548	68581	68616*
68517*	68549	68583*	68617
68518*	68550	68584*	68618
68519*	68551	68585	68619
68520*	68552	68586*	68621
68521*	68553	68587	68623

68625	68629	68632	68635
68626	68630	68633	68636
68628†	68631		

Totals : Class J67/1 35
Class J67/2 10
Class J69 89

0-6-0T Class J68

Introduced 1912. Development of J69 with side-window cab (see note p. 72)
Weight : 42 tons 9 cwt.
Pressure : 180 lb. Cyls.: 16½" × 22"
Driving Wheels : 4' 0" T.E.: 19,090 lb.

68638	68646	68654	68662
68639	68647	68655	68663
68640	68648	68656	68664
68641	68649	68657	68665
68642	68650	68658	68666
68643	68651	68659	
68644	68652	68660	
68645	68653	68661	

Total 29

0-6-0 Crane Tank Class J92

Introduced 1891. (Rebuilt from 0-6-0T originally built 1868.)
Weight : 40 tons 8 cwt.
Pressure : 140 lb. Cyls.: 16" × 22"
Driving Wheels : 4' 0" T.E.: 13,960 lb.

68667S | 68668S | 68669S

Total 3

0-6-0T Class J72

Introduced 1898.
* Altered cylinder dimensions.
Weight : 38 tons 12 cwt.
Pressure : 140 lb. Cyls.: { 17" × 24" / 18" × 24"* }
Driving Wheels : 4' 1¼"
T.E.: { 16,760 lb. / 18,790 lb.* }

68670	68678	68686	68694
68671	68679	68687	68695
68672	68680	68688	68696
68673	68681	68689	68697
68674	68682	68690	68698
68675	68683	68691	68699
68676	68684	68692	68700
68677	68685*	68693	68701
68702	68716	68730	68744
68703	68717	68731	68745
68704	68718	68732	68746
68705	68719	68733	68747
68706	68720	68734	68748
68707	68721	68735	68749
68708	68722	68736	68750
68709	68723	68737	68751
68710	68724	68738	68752
68711	68725	68739	68753
68712	68726	68740	68754
68713	68727	68741	
68714	68728	68742	
68715	68729	68743	

Total 81

0-6-0ST Class J52

J52/2 Introduced 1897. Ivatt standard saddletank with domed boiler.
J52/1* Introduced 1922. Rebuild of Stirling domeless saddletank (introduced 1892)—non-condensing.
J52/1† Introduced 1922. Condensing rebuild of Stirling locos.
‡ J52/2 with boiler pressure raised to 175 lb. Weight : 51 tons 14 cwt.
Pressure : { 170 lb. / 175 lb.* } Cyls.: 18" × 26"
Driving Wheels: 4' 8" T.E. { 21,735 lb. / 22,370 lb.‡ }

68757†	68778†	68799*	68820
68758†	68779*	68800*	68821
68759†	68780*	68801*	68822
68760†	68781†	68802*	68823
68761†	68782S*	68803*	68824
68762*	68783†	68804*	68825
68763*	68784†	68805	68826
68764*	68785†	68806	68827
68765*	68786*	68807	68828
68766*	68787†	68808	68829
68767*	68788†	68809	68830
68768*	68789*	68810	68831
68769*	68790*	68811	68832
68770*	68791†	68812	68833
68771*	68792*	68813	68834
68772*	68793†	68814	68835
68773†	68794†	68815	68836
68774†	68795†	68816	68837
68775*	68796†	68817	68838
68776†	68797*	68818	68839
68777†	68798*	68819	68840‡

68841	68854	68867	68880
68842	68855	68868	68881
68843	68856	68869	68882
68844	68857	68870	68883
68845	68858	68871	68884
68846	68859	68872	68885
68847	68860‡	68873	68886
68848	68861	68874	68887
68849	68862	68875	68888
68850	68863	68876‡	68889
68851	68864	68877	
68852	68865	68878	
68853	68866	68879	

Totals : Class J52/1 48
Class J52/2 85

0-6-0T Class J50

J50/2* Introduced 1922. 68900-19 rebuilt from smaller J51, built 1915-22.
J50/3† Introduced 1926. Post-grouping development with detail differences.
J50/1‡ Introduced 1929. Rebuilt from smaller J51, built 1913-4.
J50/4§ Introduced 1937. Development of J50/3 with larger bunker.

Weights : 56 tons 6 cwt.‡ / 58 tons 3 cwt.†§ / 57 tons.
Pressure : 175 lb. Cyls.: 18½″×26″
Driving Wheels : 4′ 8″ T.E.: 23,635 lb.

68890‡	68908*	68926*	68944†
68891‡	68909*	68927*	68945†
68892‡	68910*	68928*	68946†
68893‡	68911*	68929*	68947†
68894‡	68912*	68930*	68948†
68895‡	68913*	68931*	68949†
68896‡	68914*	68932*	68950†
68897‡	68915*	68933*	68951†
68898‡	68916*	68934*	68952†
68899‡	68917*	68935*	68953†
68900*	68918*	68936*	68954†
68901*	68919*	68937*	68955†
68902*	68920*	68938*	68956†
68903*	68921*	68939*	68957†
68904*	68922*	68940†	68958†
68905*	68923*	68941†	68959†
68906*	68924*	68942†	68960†
68907*	68925*	68943†	68961†

68962†	68970†	68978§	68986§
68963†	68971†	68979§	68987§
68964†	68972†	68980§	68988§
68965†	68973†	68981§	68989§
68966†	68974†	68982§	68990§
68967†	68975†	68983§	68991§
68968†	68976†	68984§	
68969†	68977†	68985§	

Totals : Class J50/1 10
Class J50/2 40
Class J50/3 38
Class J50/4 14

2-6-4T Class L3

Introduced 1914.
* Altered cylinder dimensions.
Weight : 97 tons 9 cwt.
Pressure : 180 lb. Su. Cyls. 21″×26″ / 20″×26″*
Driving Wheels: 5′ 1″ T.E. 28,760 lb. / 26,085 lb.*

69050	69055	69060	69066
69051	69056	69061*	69067
69052	69057	69062	69068
69053	69058	69064	69069
69054	69059	69065	

Total 19

2-6-4T Class L2

Introduced 1925.
Weight : 87 tons 7 cwt.
Pressure: 200 lb. Su. Cyls.:(O) 19″×26″
Driving Wheels : 5′ 6″ T.E.: 26.035 lb.

69070 | 69071 **Total 2**

0-6-4T Class M2

Introduced 1915.
Weight : 71 tons 1 cwt.
Pressure : 160 lb. Su. Cyls.: 20″×26″
Driving Wheels : 5′ 9″ T.E.: 20,500 lb.

69076 Robert H. Selbie
69077 Charles Jones

Total 2

0-6-2T Class N10

Introduced 1902.
Weight : 57 tons 14 cwt.
Pressure : 160 lb. Cyls.: $18\frac{1}{2}'' \times 26''$
Driving Wheels : 4′ $7\frac{1}{2}''$ T.E.: 21,905 lb.

69090	69095	69100	69105
69091	69096	69101	69106
69092	69097	69102	69107
69093	69098	69103	69108
69094	69099	69104	69109

Total 20

0-6-2T Class N13

Introduced 1913.
Pressure : 175 lb. Cyls.: 18″×26″
Driving Wheels : 4′ 6″ T.E.: 23,205 lb.

69111	69114	69116	69118
69112	69115	69117	69119
69113			

Total 9

0-6-2T Class N14

Introduced 1909.
Pressure : 175 lb. Cyls.: 18″×26″
Driving Wheels : 4′ 6″ T.E.: 23,205 lb.

69120 | 69124 | 69125

Total 3

0-6-2T Class N15

N15/2* Introduced 1910. Cowlairs incline banking locos.
N15/1 Introduced 1910. Development of N15/2 with smaller bunker for normal duties.
Weight : { 62 tons 1 cwt.* / 60 tons 18 cwt.
Pressure : 175 lb. Cyls.: 18″×26″
Driving Wheels : 4′ 6″ T.E.: 23,205 lb.

69126*	69138	69150	69162
69127*	69139	69151	69163
69128*	69140	69152	69164
69129*	69141	69153	69165
69130*	69142	69154	69166
69131*	69143	69155	69167
69132	69144	69156	69168
69133	69145	69157	69169
69134	69146	69158	69170
69135	69147	69159	69171
69136	69148	69160	69172
69137	69149	69161	69173

69174	69187	69200	69213
69175	69188	69201	69214
69176	69189	69202	69215
69177	69190	69203	69216
69178	69191	69204	69217
69179	69192	69205	69218
69180	69193	69206	69219
69181	69194	69207	69220
69182	69195	69208	69221
69183	69196	69209	69222
69184	69197	69210	69223
69185	69198	69211	69224
69186	69199	69212	

Totals : Class N15/1 93
Class N15/2 6

0-6-2T Class N4

N4/2 Introduced 1889.
N4/4* Introduced 1892. Development of N4/2 with larger bunker.
N4/1 and N4/3 were N4/2 and N4/4 with longer chimney.
Weights : { 61 tons 10 cwt. / 61 tons 19 cwt.*
Pressure : 160 lb. Cyls.: 18″×26″
Driving Wheels : 5′ 1″ T.E.: 18,780 lb.

69225	69231	69237	69244*
69226	69232	69239	69245*
69227	69233	69240	69246*
69228	69234	69241	69247*
69229	69235	69242*	
69230	69236	69243*	

Totals : Class N4/2 16
Class N4/4 6

0-6-2T Class N5

N5/2 Introduced 1891.
N5/3* Introduced 1915. N5/2 rebuilt with larger tanks, bunker and cyls. (N5/1 was N5/2 with longer chimney).
Weights : { 62 tons 7 cwt. / 64 tons 13 cwt.*
Pressure : 160 lb. Cyls.: { 18″×26″ / $18\frac{1}{2}'' \times 26''$*
Driving Wheels: 5′ 1″ T.E. { 18,780 lb. / 19,840 lb.*

69250	69255	69260	69265
69251	69256	69261	69266
69252	69257	69262	69267
69253	69258	69263	69268
69254	69259	69264	69269

69270	69296	69322	69348
69271	69297	69323	69349
69272	69298	69324	69350
69273	69299	69325	69351
69274	69300	69326	69352
69275	69301	69327	69353
69276	69302	69328	69354
69277	69303	69329	69355
69278	69304	69330	69356
69279	69305	69331	69357
69280	69306	69332	69358
69281	69307	69333	69359
69282	69308	69334	69360
69283	69309	69335	69361
69284	69310	69336	69362
69285	69311*	69337	69363
69286	69312	69338	69364
69287	69313	69339	69365
69288	69314	69340	69366
69289	69315	69341	69367
69290	69316	69342	69368
69291	69317	69343	69369
69292	69318	69344	69370
69293	69319	69345	
69294	69320	69346	
69295	69321	69347	

Totals : Class N5/2 120
Class N5/3 1

0-6-2T Class N8

* Introduced 1886. Saturated with Joy's gear and slide valves (majority rebuilt from compounds).

† Rebuilt with superheater, Stephenson gear and piston valves, 24″ piston stroke.

‡ As † but with 26″ stroke.

§ Rebuilt with Stephenson gear and piston valves, superheater removed, 24″ stroke.

**As § but with 26″ piston stroke.

Weights : { 56 tons 5 cwt.* § **
58 tons 14 cwt.† ‡

Pressure : 160 lb. SS.

Cyls.: { 18″ × 24″*
19″ × 24″† §
19″ × 26″‡ **

Driving Wheels : 5′ 1¼″

T.E.: { 17,265 lb.*
19,235 lb.† §
20,840 lb.‡ **

69371†	69372§	69373†	69374§
69375**	69382**	69390†	69397§
69376†	69383§	69391†	69398†
69377†	69384†	69392*	69399§
69378§	69385†	69393†	69400**
69379†	69386‡	69394†	69401‡
69380†	69387§	69395†	
69381**	69389*	69396*	

Total 30

0-6-2T Class N9

Introduced 1893.
Weight : 56 tons 10 cwt.
Pressure : 160 lb. Cyls.: 19″ × 26″
Driving Wheels : 5′ 1¼″ T.E.: 20,840 lb.

69410	69415	69422	69426
69411	69418	69423	69427
69413	69420	69424	69428
69414	69421	69425	69429

Total 16

0-6-2T Class N1

* Introduced 1907. Prototype of class.
Introduced 1907. Standard design with shorter tanks and detail differences (**see note p. 72**).

† Rebuilt with superheater and reduced pressure.

‡ Fitted with condensing gear.

Weights : { 64 tons 14 cwt.*
65 tons 17 cwt.

Pressure : { 175 lb. Cyls.: 18″ × 26″
170 lb. Su.†

Driving Wheels: 5′ 8″ T.E. { 18,430 lb.
17,900 lb.†

69430*	69445‡	69459	69473
69431‡	69446	69460‡	69474
69432‡	69447	69461‡	69475‡
69433‡	69448	69462‡	69476‡
69434‡	69449	69463‡	69477‡
69435†‡	69450‡	69464†‡	69478†‡
69436†	69451‡	69465‡	69479†‡
69437†‡	69452†	69466‡	69480‡
69439†‡	69453‡	69467‡	69481‡
69440	69454	69468‡	69482†‡
69441‡	69455‡	69469‡	69483†
69442‡	69456‡	69470‡	69484‡
69443	69457‡	69471‡	69485‡
69444	69458‡	69472†	

Total 55

0-6-2T Class N2

(see note p. 72).

N2/2* Introduced 1925. Post-grouping development of ex-G.N. N2/1, introduced 1920, which class is now included in N2/2. Condensing gear and small chimney.

N2/2† Condensing gear removed, retaining small chimney.

N2/3‡ Introduced 1925. Locos built non-condensing with large chimney.

N2/4§ Introduced 1928. Development of N2/2, slightly heavier. Condensing gear and small chimney.
(The small chimneys are to suit the Metropolitan loading gauge, for working to Moorgate St. Condensing gear has been removed from or added to certain locos transferred from or to the London area.)

Weights: 70 tons 5 cwt.* †
70 tons 8 cwt.‡
71 tons 9 cwt.§

Pressure: 170 lb. Su. Cyls.: 19″×26″

Driving Wheels: 5′ 8″ T.E.: 19,945 lb.

69490*	69515†	69540*	69565‡
69491*	69516†	69541*	69566‡
69492*	69517*	69542*	69567‡
69493*	69518†	69543*	69568§
69494*	69519†	69544*	69569§
69495*	69520*	69545*	69570§
69496*	69521*	69546*	69571§
69497*	69522*	69547*	69572§
69498*	69523*	69548*	69573§
69499*	69524*	69549*	69574§
69500†	69525*	69550†	69575§
69501†	69526*	69551†	69576§
69502†	69527*	69552†	69577§
69503†	69528*	69553†	69578§
69504*	69529*	69554†	69579§
69505†	69530*	69555§	69580§
69506*	69531*	69556§	69581§
69507†	69532*	69557†	69582§
69508†	69533*	69558†	69583§
69509†	69534*	69559†	69584§
69510†	69535*	69560†	69585§
69511†	69536*	69561†	69586§
69512*	69537*	69562‡	69587§
69513†	69538*	69563‡	69588§
69514†	69359*	69564‡	69589§
69590§	69592§	69594‡	69596‡
69591§	69593§	69595‡	

Totals: Class N2/2 70
Class N2/3 9
Class N2/4 28

0-6-2T Class N7

N7 (G.E.)* Introduced 1914. Original G.E. design.

N7/1† Introduced 1925. Post-grouping development of N7 (G.E.) with detail differences.

N7/2‡ Introduced 1926. Development of N7/1 with long-travel valves.

N7/3§ Introduced 1927. Doncaster-built version of N7/2 with round-topped boiler.

N7/4** Introduced 1940. N7 (G.E.) rebuilt with round-topped boiler, retaining short-travel valves.

N7/3†† Introduced 1943. N7/1 rebuilt with round-topped boiler, retaining short-travel valves.

N7/3‡‡ Introduced 1943. N7/2 rebuilt with round-topped boiler.

Weights: 62 tons 5 cwt.*
63 tons 13 cwt.†
64 tons 17 cwt.‡
61 tons 16 cwt.**
64 tons.§ †† ‡‡

Pressure: 180 lb. Su. Cyls.: 18″×24″
Driving Wheels: 4′ 10″ T.E.: 20,515 lb.

69600**	69620**	69640†
69601**	69621**	69641†
69602*	69622††	69642†
69603**	69623†	69643†
69604**	69624†	69644†
69605**	69625†	69645†
69606**	69626†	69646†
69607**	69627†	69647††
69608**	69628†	69648††
69609*	69629†	69649††
69610**	69630†	69650††
69611**	69631†	69651††
69612**	69632††	69652††
69613**	69633††	69653†
69614**	69634†	69654†
69615**	69635††	69655†
69616**	69636††	69656††
69617**	69637†	69657†
69618**	69638†	69658†
69619**	69639††	69659†

69660††	69685‡‡	69710§
69661†	69686‡‡	69711§
69662†	69687‡‡	69712§
69663††	69688‡	69713§
69664††	69689‡	69714§
69665†	69690‡	69715§
69666††	69691‡‡	69716§
69667†	69692‡‡	69717§
69668†	69693‡‡	69718§
69669††	69694‡	69719§
69670†	69695‡	69720§
69671†	69696‡‡	69721§
69672‡	69697‡‡	69722§
69673‡	69698‡	69723§
69674‡	69699‡‡	69724§
69675‡‡	69700‡	69725§
69676‡‡	69701‡‡	69726§
69677‡‡	69702§	69727§
69678‡‡	69703§	69728§
69679‡‡	69704§	69729§
69680‡	69705§	69730§
69681‡	69706§	69731§
69682‡‡	69707§	69732§
69683‡	69708§	69733§
69684‡	69709§	

Totals : Class N7 3
Class N7/1 32
Class N7/2 14
Class N7/3 66
Class N7/4 19

4-6-2T Class A7

Introduced 1910. Later rebuilt with superheater and reduced pressure.
* Saturated.
Weight : 87 tons 10 cwt.
Pressure : {160 lb. Su. / 180 lb.*}
Cyls.: (3) 16½" × 26"
Driving Wheels : 4' 7¼"
T.E.: {26,140 lb. / 29,405 lb.*}

69770	69775*	69780	69785
69771	69776	69781	69786
69772	69777	69782	69787*
69773	69778*	69783	69788
69774	69779	69784	69789

Total 20

4-6-2T Class A6

Introduced 1915. (Rebuilt from Worsdell Class "W" 4-6-0T, introduced 1907.) Later superheated.
* Saturated.
Weights : {79 tons. / 78 tons.*}
Pressure : 175 lb. SS. Cyls.: 19" × 26"
Driving Wheels : 5' 1½" T.E.: 23,830 lb.

69791	69794*	69796	69798*
69792	69795*	69797	69799*
69793			

Total 9

4-6-2T Class A5

A5/1 Introduced 1911.
A5/2* Introduced 1925. Post-grouping development of A5/1 with reduced boiler mountings and detail differences.
Weights : {85 tons 18 cwt. / 90 tons 11 cwt.*}
Pressure : 180 lb. Su. Cyls.: 20" × 26"
Driving Wheels : 5' 7" T.E.: 23,750 lb.

69800	69811	69822	69833*
69801	69812	69823	69834*
69802	69813	69824	69835*
69803	69814	69825	69836*
69804	69815	69826	69837*
69805	69816	69827	69838*
69806	69817	69828	69839*
69807	69818	69829	69840*
69808	69819	69830*	69841*
69809	69820	69831*	69842*
69810	69821	69832*	

Totals : Class A5/1 30
Class A5/2 13

4-6-2T Class A8

Introduced 1931. (Rebuilt from Raven Class "D" 4-4-4T, introduced 1913.)
Weight : 86 tons 18 cwt.
Pressure : 175 lb. Su.
Cyls.: (3) 16½" × 26"
Driving Wheels : 5' 9" T.E.: 22,940 lb.

69850	69856	69862	69868
69851	69857	69863	69869
69852	69858	69864	69870
69853	69859	69865	69871
69854	69860	69866	69872
69855	69861	69867	69873

69874	69880	69886	69891
69875	69881	69887	69892
69876	69882	69888	69893
69877	69883	69889	69894
69878	69884	69890	
69879	69885		Total 45

0-8-4T Class S1

S1/1* Introduced 1907. Since rebuilt with superheater.
S1/2† Introduced 1932. S1/1 rebuilt with booster and superheater, booster since removed.
S1/3‡ Introduced 1932. New locos built with booster, booster later removed.

Weights : 99 tons 6 cwt.* / 99 tons 2 cwt.† / 99 tons 1 cwt.‡
Pressure : 180 lb. Su.
Cyls.: (3) 18"×26"
Driving Wheels : 4' 8" T.E.: 34,525 lb.

69900*	69902*	69904‡	69905‡
69901†	69903*		

Totals : Class S1/1 3
Class S1/2 1
Class S1/3 2

4-8-0T Class T1

Introduced 1909.
* Rebuilt with superheater.
Weight : 85 tons 8 cwt.
Pressure : 175 lb. SS.
Cyls.: (3) 18"×26"
Driving Wheels: 4' 7½" T.E.: 34,080 lb.

69910	69914*	69917	69920
69911	69915	69918	69921
69912	69916	69919	69922
69913			Total 13

0-8-0T Class Q1

Rebuilt from Q4 0-8-0, introduced 1902.
*Introduced 1942. 1,500 gallon tanks.
Introduced 1943. 2,000 gallon tanks.
Weights : 69 tons 18 cwt.* / 73 tons 13 cwt.
Pressure: 180 lb. Cyls.: (O) 19"×26"
Driving Wheels : 4' 8" T.E.: 25,645 lb.

69925*	69929	69932	69935
69926*	69930	69933	69936
69927*	69931	69934	69937
69928*			Total 13

2-8-8-2T Class U1 (Beyer-Garratt Loco)

Introduced 1925.
Weight : 178 tons 1 cwt.
Pressure : 180 lb. Su.
Cyls.: (6) 18½"×26"
Driving Wheels : 4' 8" T.E.: 72,940 lb.

69999 Total 1

Ministry of Supply "Austerity" 2-8-0s

On Loan to British Railways as at September 8th, 1948.

Introduced 1943.
Weights : Loco. 70 tons 5 cwt.
Tender 55 tons 10 cwt.
Pressure : 225 lb. Cyls.: (O) 19"×28"
Driving Wheels : 4' 8½" T.E.: 34,215 lb.

Key: E — On loan to Eastern, North-Eastern, or Scottish Regions (no differentiation is made, as such engines are liable to be seen in any of the three Regions).
S — On loan to Southern Region.
W— On loan to Western Region

70801W	70877 E	77026W
70802 E	70878 S	77027W
70807 E	77000W	77028W
70808W	77001W	77029W
70809W	77003 E	77030 S
70811 S	77004 E	77031 E
70814W	77005W	77032 E
70817 E	77006 E	77034 E
70825W	77007 S	77035 E
70829W	77008 E	77036 E
70833W	77010 E	77037 E
70834 E	77012W	77039 E
70836W	77013 E	77040W
70838W	77014W	77041 E
70839 E	77015W	77042 E
70843W	77016 E	77044 E
70850 E	77017 E	77047 E
70853 S	77018 E	77048W
70864W	77019 E	77049W
70865W	77020 E	77050 E
70866W	77022 E	77051 E
70871 E	77023 E	77052 S
70875W	77024 E	77053W
70876W	77025W	77054W

Above : Class F5 2-4-2T No. 67203
[Photo : Roy E. Vincent

Right: Class J67/1 0-6-0T No. 8519 (New No. 68519)
[Photo : C. C. B. Herbert

Below : Class F3 2-4-2T No. 7126 (New No. 67126)
[Photo : P. Ransome-Wallis

Class J52/2 0-6-0T No. 68840

[*Photo : E. V. Fry*

Class J77 0-6-0T No. 8397 (New No. 68397)

[*Photo : B. V. Franey*

Class Y9 0-4-0ST No. 8123 (New No. 68123)

[*Photo : H. C. Casserley*

Class Z4 0-4-2T No. 8191 (New No. 68191)

[*Photo . H. C. Casserley*

Class N5/2 0-6-2T No. 9343 (New No. 69343)

[*Photo : E. V. Fry*

Class N9 0-6-2T No. 9410 (New No. 69410)

[*Photo : E. V. Fry*

Class N14 0-6-2T No. 9120 (New No. 69120)

[*Photo : P. Ransome-Wallis*

Class N7/3 0-6-2T No. 69703

[*Photo : A. F. Cook*

Class V3 2-6-2T
No. 67684

[*Photo* :
P. Ransome-Wallis

Class L1 2-6-4T
No. 67711

[*Photo* :
P. Ransome-Wallis

Class A6 4-6-2T
No. 9794 (New
No. 69794)

[*Photo* : *A. F. Cook*

Class T1 4-8-0T
No. 69917

[*Photo* :
P. Ransome-Wallis

77055 E	77118 E	77186 E	77261 E	77351 E	77432 E
77056 S	77119 E	77187 E	77263 E	77352 E	77433 E
77057 E	77120 E	77192W	77270 S	77353 E	77434 E
77058W	77121 E	77195 E	77271 E	77355 S	77436 E
77059 S	77122 S	77196W	77274 E	77356 E	77439 E
77060W	77123W	77198 E	77278 E	77358 E	77440 E
77061 E	77124 E	77199 E	77280W	77359 S	77441 E
77062 S	77126W	77200W	77283 E	77362 E	77442 E
77063 E	77127 E	77201 E	77286 S	77364 E	77443W
77064W	77128 E	77202W	77288W	77365 E	77444 S
77066 E	77129 E	77203W	77289W	77368W	77445 E
77067 E	77130W	77204 E	77291W	77371 E	77449 E
77068 E	77135 E	77205 S	77292 E	77372 E	77451W
77070 E	77138 E	77206 E	77294W	77374 E	77452 E
77071 E	77141W	77207 E	77296 S	77375 E	77453 E
77072W	77142W	77208 E	77297W	77378W	77454 E
77073 E	77144 E	77209 E	77302 E	77379 S	77455 E
77074 S	77145W	77210W	77303 E	77380W	77456 E
77075 E	77147 E	77212W	77305 E	77381 E	77457 E
77076 E	77148W	77214W	77306 E	77386 E	77458 E
77077W	77149 E	77215 E	77307 E	77388W	77459 E
77078 E	77150 S	77218 E	77309 E	77390 E	77460 S
77079W	77151W	77221 E	77310W	77392 E	77461 E
77080 E	77152 E	77222 E	77311 S	77393W	77462 E
77081 E	77155 E	77225 E	77312 E	77394 E	77463W
77085 E	77157 E	77226 S	77313 E	77395 E	77464 E
77086 S	77160W	77227 E	77314 E	77398W	77465 E
77087 E	77161W	77228 E	77315 E	77399 E	77466W
77088 E	77162 E	77229W	77317 E	77401 E	77467 E
77089 E	77163 E	77230 E	77319 E	77402 E	77468 E
77090 S	77164 E	77231 E	77320 E	77404 E	77469 E
77092W	77165W	77232 E	77321 S	77406 E	77470 E
77094 S	77166 E	77234W	77323 E	77407W	77471W
77095 E	77167 E	77235 E	77324 E	77408W	77476 E
77096 E	77169 E	77237 E	77325W	77411 E	77479W
77097W	77170 E	77241W	77326W	77413 E	77480 E
77098 S	77171W	77242W	77327 E	77414 E	77481 S
77099W	77173 E	77247W	77328 E	77415 E	77484 E
77101 S	77174 E	77248 E	77329 E	77416 E	77485 S
77102W	77175 E	77249 E	77330W	77418 E	77488 E
77103 S	77176 E	77252 E	77332W	77419 E	77489W
77104 E	77178 E	77253 E	77334 E	77421W	77492 E
77106W	77179W	77255W	77335W	77424 E	77494 E
77107 E	77180 S	77256 S	77338 E	77425 E	77497 E
77108 S	77181 E	77257W	77340 S	77426 E	77499 E
77111 E	77182 E	77258 E	77342 E	77428 E	77503 E
77115W	77184W	77259 S	77348W	77429W	77508W
77116W	77185 E	77260 E	77350 E	77431 E	78510W

78512W	78569 S	78616 E	79184 E	79228W	79276 E
78514 E	78572 E	78621W	79186 E	79229 E	79278W
78521W	78575 E	78624W	79190W	79232W	79279W
78522 E	78578 E	78632W	79194 E	79234W	79280 E
78525 E	78585 E	78637 E	79195W	79235W	79281 S
78526 E	78587 E	78643 E	79198 E	79239 E	79282W
78531 S	78588 E	78650 E	79199 S	79242 E	79283W
78532 E	78590W	78666 S	79202 E	79243 E	79294W
78537 E	78592 E	78671W	79203 S	79244W	79298W
78538 E	78594 E	78681W	79204 E	79254W	79301W
78541W	78595W	78682 E	79206 E	79259 E	79302W
78542W	78596 S	78683 E	79207 S	79261W	79303W
78543W	78597 S	78684 E	79208 E	79262 S	72304W
78544W	78598 E	78685W	79209 E	79263 E	79306 E
78546W	78599 E	78688 S	79210 S	79264 E	79307W
78551W	78600 E	78695W	79214W	79265 E	79309W
78553 E	78601 E	78700 E	79215W	79266W	79310 E
78554W	78602W	78705 S	79219W	79268W	79311W
78556W	78604W	78714W	79220 E	79269W	79312 E
78559 E	78607W	78715 E	79221W	79271 E	
78561 E	78609 E	78717W	79224W	79272W	
78563W	78610 E	79178 E	79225W	79273W	
78564 E	78614 E	79181 E	79226W	79274W	
78568 E	78615W	79182 E	79227 E	79275W	

LOCOMOTIVE SUPERINTENDENTS
AND CHIEF MECHANICAL ENGINEERS OF THE L.N.E.R.

Great Northern Railway

A. Sturrock	1850—1866
P. Stirling	1866—1895
H. A. Ivatt	1896—1911
H. N. Gresley	1911—1922

North Eastern Railway

E. Fletcher	1854—1883
A. McDonnell*	1883—1884
T. W. Worsdell	1885—1890
W. Worsdell	1890—1910
Sir Vincent Raven ...	1910—1922

Great Eastern Railway

R. Sinclair	1862—1866
S. W. Johnson	1866—1873
W. Adams	1873—1878
M. Bromley	1878—1881
T. W. Worsdell	1881—1885
J. Holden	1885—1907
S. D. Holden	1908—1912
A. J. Hill	1912—1922

Lancashire, Derbyshire and East Coast Railway

R. A. Thom	1902—1907

Manchester, Sheffield and Lincolnshire Railway

Richard Peacock	—1854
W. G. Craig	1854—1859
Charles Sacre	1859—1886
T. Parker	1886—1893
H. Pollitt	1893—1897

Great Central Railway

H. Pollitt	1897—1900
J. G. Robinson	1900—1922

Hull and Barnsley Railway

M. Stirling	1885—1922

Midland and Great Northern Joint Railway

W. Marriott	1884—1924

North British Railway

T. Wheatley†	1867—1874
D. Drummond	1875—1882
M. Holmes	1882—1903
W. P. Reid	1903—1919
W. Chalmers	1919—1922

* Between McDonnell and T. W. Worsdell there was an interval during which office was covered by a locomotive committee.

† Previous to whom, the records are indeterminate.

PRINCIPAL DIMENSIONS OF EX-L.N.E.R. LOCOMOTIVES AND INDEX TO CLASSES

Tractive effort calculated to nearest 5lb. S—Superheated. SS—Some Superheated.

Class	Type	Designer	Originating Pre-Grouping Owner (if any)	Building or Re-building Date	Weight of Loco.	Boiler Pressure	Cylinders	Driving Wheels	Tractive Effort at 85% B.P.	Page
					T. Cwt.	Lb. per sq. in.	Ins.		Lb.	
A–1	4–6–2	Peppercorn	—	1948	104 2	250S	(3) 19 ×26	6′ 8″	37,400	5
A–1/1	4–6–2	Gresley (1922) ... Reb. Thompson	G.N.R.	1945	101 0	250S	(3) 19 ×26	6′ 8″	37,400	5
A–2	4–6–2	Peppercorn	—	1947–48	101 0	250S	(3) 19 ×26	6′ 2″	40,430	5
A–2/1	4–6–2	Thompson	—	1944–45	98 0	225S	(3) 19 ×26	6′ 2″	36,385	5
A–2/2	4–6–2	Gresley (Cl.P2. 1934-36) Reb. Thompson	—	1943–44	101 10	225S	(3) 20 ×26	6′ 2″	40,320	5
A–2/3	4–6–2	Thompson	—	1946–47	101 10	250S	(3) 19 ×26	6′ 2″	40,430	5
A–3	4–6–2	Gresley	—	1927–34	96 5	250S	(3) 19 ×26	6′ 8″	32,910	4
A–4	4–6–2	Gresley	—	1935–38	102 19	250S	(3) 18½ ×26	6′ 8″	{35,455 / 33,616‡	4
A–5/1	4–6–2T	Robinson ...	G.C.R.	1911–23	85 18	180S	20 ×26	5′ 7″	23,750	55
A–5/2	4–6–2T	Robinson-Gresley ...	—	1925–26	90 11	180S	20 ×26	5′ 7″	23,750	55
A–6*	4–6–2T	W. Worsdell (1907-08) Reb. Raven	N.E.R.	1915–16	{78 0 / 79 0S}	175SS	19 ×26	5′ 1¼″	23,830	55
A–7	4–6–2T	Raven	N.E.R.	1910–11	87 10	{180 / 160S}	(3) 16½ ×26	4′ 7¼″	{29,405 / 26,140	55
A–8†	4–6–2T	Raven (1913-22) ... Reb. Gresley	N.E.R.	1931–6	86 18	175	(3) 16½ ×26	5′ 9″	22,940	55
A–10	4–6–2	Gresley ...	G.N.R.	1924	92 9	180S	(3) 20 ×26	6′ 8″	29,835	4
B–1	4–6–0	Thompson	—	1942–48	71 3	225S	O 20 ×26	6′ 2″	26,880	7
B–2	4–6–0	Gresley (1928-37) ... Reb. Thompson	—	1945–47	73 10	225S	O 20 ×26	6′ 8″	24,865	11
B–3	4–6–0	Robinson (1920) ... Reb. Thompson	G.C.R.	1943	71 7	225S	O 20 ×26	6′ 9″	24,555	10

*Class A6 rebuilt from Worsdell 4-6-0T, N.E.R., Class W. †Class A8 rebuilt from N.E.R. 4-4-4T, Class D. (L.N.E.R. H1)
‡ With 17″ ×26″ inside cylinder.

Class	Type	Designer	Originating Pre-Grouping Owner (if any)	Building or Re-building Date	Weight of Loco.	Boiler Pressure	Cylinders	Driving Wheels	Tractive Effort at 85% B.P.	Page
					T. Cwt.	Lb. per sq. in.	Ins.		Lb.	
B–4/3 B–4/4	4–6–0	Robinson	G.C.R.	1906	71 15 70 14	180S	O 21 ×26 O 19 ×26	6′ 7″	22,205 18,180	10 10
B–5	4–6–0	Robinson	G.C.R.	1902–04	64 3 65 4	180S	O 19 ×26 O 21 ×26	6′ 1″	19,670 24,030	12
B–7	4–6–0	Robinson	G.C.R.	1921–24	79 10	180S	(4) 16 ×26	5′ 8″	29,950	9
B–8	4–6–0	Robinson	G.C.R.	1913–15	74 7	180S	21½×26	5′ 7″	27,445	9
B–9	4–6–0	Robinson	G.C.R.	1906	65 0	180S	O 19 ×26	5′ 4″	22,440	10
B–12/1	4–6–0	S. D. Holden	G.E.R.	1911–20	63 0	180S	20 ×28	6′ 6″	21,970	10
B–12/3	4–6–0	B–12, Reb. Gresley ...	—	1932–44	69 10	180S	20 ×28	6′ 6″	21,970	10
B–13*	4–6–0	W. Worsdell ...	N.E.R.	1906	62 10	160S	O 20 ×26	6′ 1½″	19,310	12
B–16	4–6–0	Raven	N.E.R.	1919–24	77 14	180S	(3) 18½×26	5′ 8″	30,030	10
B–16/2	4–6–0	B–16, Reb. Gresley ...	—	1937–40	79 4	180S	(3) 18½×26	5′ 8″	30,030	10
B–16/3	4–6–0	B–16, Reb. Thompson	—	1944–47	78 19	180S	(3) 18½×26	5′ 8″	30,030	10
B–17	4–6–0	Gresley	—	1928–37	77 5	180S 225S	(3) 17½×26	6′ 8″	22,480 28,555	11
B–17/5	4–6–0	Gresley	—	1937	80 10	180S	(3) 17½×26	6′ 8″	22,480	11
C–1	4–4–2	Ivatt	G.N.R.	1904–10	69 12	170S	O 19 ×24 O 20 ×24	6′ 8″ 6′ 8″	15,650 17,340	23
C–4/2 C–4/4	4–4–2	Robinson	G.C.R.	1903–06	70 17 71 18	180S	O 19 ×26 O 21 ×26	6′ 9″	17,730 21,660	23 23
C–7	4–4–2	Raven	N.E.R.	1911–18	79 5	175S	(3) 16½×26	6′ 10″	19,300	23
C–12	4–4–2T	Ivatt	G.N.R.	1898–07	62 6	170 175	18 ×26	5′ 8″	17,900 18,425	44
C–13	4–4–2T	Robinson	G.C.R.	1903–05	66 13	160S	18 ×26	5′ 7″	17,100	44
C–14	4–4–2T	Robinson	G.C.R.	1907	71 0	160S	18 ×26	5′ 7″	17,100	44
C–15	4–4–2T	Reid	N.B.R.	1911–13	68 15	175	18 ×26	5′ 9″	18,160	45
C–16	4–4–2T	Reid	N.B.R.	1915–21	72 10	165SS	19 ×26	5′ 9″	19,080	45
D–1	4–4–0	Ivatt	G.N.R.	1911	53 6	170S	18½×26	6′ 8″	16,075	18
D–2	4–4–0	Ivatt	G.N.R.	1897–09	47 10	170S 175	17½×26	6′ 8″	14,380 14,805	18
D–3	4–4–0	Ivatt (1896-9) ... Reb. Gresley	G.N.R.	1912–28	45 14	175	17½×26	6′ 8″	14,805	18

D–9	4–4–0	Robinson	G.C.R.	1901–04	55 14	180S	19 × 26	6′ 9″	17,730	19
D–10	4–4–0	Robinson	G.C.R.	1913	61 0	180S	20 × 26	6′ 9″	19,645	21
D–11	4–4–0	Robinson	G.C.R.	1920–24	61 3	180S	20 × 26	6′ 9″	19,645	21
D–15	4–4–0	J. Holden	G.E.R.	1900–03	52 4	180S	19 × 26	7′ 0″	17,095	20
D–16/2	4–4–0	Reb. Holden J. Holden	G.E.R.	1923–30	54 18	180S	19 × 26	7′ 0″	17,095	20
D–16/3	4–4–0	Reb. Hill & Hill D–15 & D–16/2 Reb. Gresley	—	1933–48	55 18	180S	19 × 26	7′ 0″	17,095	20
D–20	4–4–0	W. Wordsell ...	N.E.R.	1899–07	54 2	175S	19 × 26	6′ 10″	17,025	19
D–20/2	4–4–0	D–20 Reb. Gresley ...	—	1936–42	55 9	175S	19 × 26	6′ 10″	17,025	19
D–29	4–4–0	Reid	N.B.R.	1909–11	54 4	190S	19 × 26	6′ 6″	19,435	19
D30/1 }	4–4–0	Reid	N.B.R.	{ 1912	57 6 }	165S	20 × 26	6′ 6″	18,700	19
D30/2 }				{ 1914–20	57 16 }					19
D–31	4–4–0	Holmes (1890-9) ... Reb. Reid & Chalmers	N.B.R.	1918–24	46 8	175S	18½ × 26	6′ 6″	16,515	18
D–32	4–4–0	Reid	N.B.R.	1906	53 14	180S	19 × 26	6′ 0″	19,945	20
D–33	4–4–0	Reid	N.B.R.	1909–10	54 3	180S	19 × 26	6′ 0″	19,945	20
D–34	4–4–0	Reid	N.B.R.	1913–20	57 4	165S	20 × 26	6′ 0″	20,260	20
D–40	4–4–0	{ Pickersgill	G.N. of S.R.	1899–15	46 7	165	18 × 26	6′ 1″	16,185	19
		{ Heywood	—	1920–21	48 13	165S	18 × 26	6′ 1″	16,185	
D–41	4–4–0	Pickersgill and J. Johnson	G.N. of S.R.	1893–98	45 0	165	18 × 26	6′ 1″	16,185	18
D–49/1	4–4–0	Gresley	—	1927–29	66 0	180S	(3) 17 × 26	6′ 8″	21,555	22
D–49/2	4–4–0	Gresley	—	1928–35	64 10	180S	(3) 17 × 26	6′ 8″	21,555	22
D–49/4	4–4–0	Reb. Thompson ...	—	1942	62 0	180S	20 × 26	6′ 8″	19,890	22
E–4	2–4–0	J. Holden	G.E.R.	1891–02	40 6	160	17½ × 24	5′ 8″	14,700	23
F–1	2–4–2T	Parker	M.S. & L.R.	1889–92	60 12	160	18 × 24	5′ 7″	15,785	43
F–2	2–4–2T	Pollitt	G.C.R.	1898	62 6	160	18 × 26	5′ 7″	17,100	43
F–3	2–4–2T	J. Holden	G.E.R.	1895–02	58 12	160	17½ × 24	5′ 8″	14,710	43
F–4	2–4–2T	J. Holden	G.E.R.	1906–09	53 19	160	17½ × 24	5′ 4″	15,620	43
F–5	2–4–2T	J. Holden	G.E.R.	1903–09	53 19	180	17½ × 24	5′ 4″	17,570	43
F–6	2–4–2T	J. and S. D. Holden ...	G.E.R.	1904–11	56 9	180	17½ × 24	5′ 4″	17,570	43
F–7	2–4–2T	S. D. Holden	G.E.R.	1909	45 14	160	15 × 22	4′ 10″	11,605	43
G–5	0–4–4T	W. Worsdell ...	N.E.R.	1894–01	54 4	160	18 × 24	5′ 1½″	17,265	44
J–1	0–6–0	Ivatt	G.N.R.	1908	46 14	175	18 × 26	5′ 8″	18,430	31
J–2	0–6–0	Ivatt	G.N.R.	1912	50 10	170S	19 × 26	5′ 8″	19 945	31

* Counter pressure locomotive for testing purposes.

Class	Type	Designer	Originating Pre-Grouping Owner (if any)	Building or Re-building Date	Weight of Loco.	Boiler Pressure	Cylinders	Driving Wheels	Tractive Effort at 85% B.P	Page
					T. Cwt.	Lb. per sq. in.	Ins.		Lb.	
J-3	0-6-0	P. Stirling and Ivatt Reb. Gresley (1892-01)	G.N.R.	1912–28	42 12	175	17½ × 26	5′ 2″	19,105	28
J-4	0-6-0	P. Stirling and Ivatt ...	G.N.R.	1896–01	41 5	175	17½ × 26	5′ 2″	19,105	28
J-5	0-6-0	Ivatt	G.N.R.	1909–10	47 6	175 170S	18 × 26	5′ 2″	20,210 19,630	41
J-6	0-6-0	Ivatt and Gresley ...	G.N.R.	1911–22	50 10	170S	19 × 26	5′ 2″	21,875	28
J-10	0-6-0	Parker and Pollitt ...	M.S. & L.R.	1892–02	41 6	160	18 × 26	5′ 1″	18,780	32
J-11	0-6-0	Robinson ...	G.C.R.	1901–10	51 19 52 2	180SS	18½ × 26	5′ 2″	21,960	28
J-11/3	0-6-0	Reb. Thompson	—	1942–7	53 6	180S	18½ × 26			28
J-15	0-6-0	J. Holden	G.E.R.	1886–13	37 2	160	17½ × 24	4′ 11″	16,940	32
J-17	0-6-0	J. Holden	G.E.R.	1900–10	45 8	180S	19 × 26	4′ 11″	24,340	41
J-19	0-6-0	Hill (1912-20) ... Reb. Gresley	G.E.R.	1934–9	50 7	170S 180S 160S	20 × 28 19 × 28	4′ 11″ 4′ 11″	27,430 26,215 23,300	30
J-20	0-6-0	Hill	G.E.R.	1920–22	54 15	180	20 × 28	4′ 11″	29,045	30
J-21	0-6-0	T. W. Worsdell ... Reb. W. Worsdell T. W. Worsdell ... Reb. Raven	N.E.R.	1886–95	42 1 42 19 43 15S	160	18 × 24 19 × 24 19 × 26	5′ 1¼″	17,265 19,240 20,840	31
J-24	0-6-0	W. Worsdell ... W. Worsdell ... Reb. Raven	N.E.R.	1894–98	38 10 39 11S	160	18 × 24 18½ × 24	4′ 7¼″	19,140 20,220	41
J-25	0-6-0	W. Worsdell ... W. Worsdell ... Reb. Raven	N.E.R.	1898–02	39 11 40 17 41 14S	160	18½ × 26	4′ 7¼″	21,905	42
J-26	0-6-0	W. Worsdell ...	N.E.R.	1904–05	46 16	180	18½ × 26	4′ 7¼″	24,640	42
J-27	0-6-0	W. Worsdell ... Raven	N.E.R.	1906–23	47 0 49 10S	180	18½ × 26	4′ 7¼″	24,640	42
J-35/4 J-35/5	0-6-0	Reid	N.B.R.	1908–13 1906–8	50 15 51 0	180S	18½ × 26	5′ 0″	22,080	29 29

J-36	0-6-0	Holmes (1888 - 1900) Reb. Reid and Chalmers	N.B.R.	1913-22	41	19	165		18 × 26	5′ 0″	19,690	32
J-37	0-6-0	Reid	N.B.R.	1914-21	54	14	180S		19½ × 26	5′ 0″	25,210	29
J-38	0-6-0	Gresley	—	1926	58	19	180S		20 × 26	4′ 8″	28,415	43
J-39	0-6-0	Gresley	—	1926-41	57	17	180S		20 × 26	5′ 2″	25,665	30
J-50/1	0-6-0T	Gresley	—	1913-14	56	6	175		18½ × 26	4′ 8″	23,635	51
J-50/2	0-6-0T	Gresley	—	1914-24	57	0	175		18½ × 26	4′ 8″	23,635	51
J-50/3 J-50/4	0-6-0T	Gresley	—	1926-39	58	3	175		18½ × 26	4′ 8″	23,635	51 51
J-52/1 J-52/2	0-6-0ST	P. Stirling (1892-97) Reb. Gresley Ivatt	G.N.R.	1922-32 1897-09	51	14	170 170 175		18 × 26	4′ 8″	21,735 21,735 22,370	50 50
J-55	0-6-0T	P. Stirling (1891-2) ... Reb. Gresley	G.N.R.	1928-34	45	16	175 160		17½ × 26	4′ 8″	21,150 19,340	48
J-62	0-6-0ST	Pollitt	G.C.R.	1897	30	17	150	O	13 × 20	3′ 6″	10,260	47
J-63	0-6-0T	Robinson	G.C.R.	1906-14	37	9	150	O	13 × 20	3′ 6″	10,260	47
J-65	0-6-0T	J. Holden	G.E.R.	1889-93	36	11	160		14 × 20	4′ 0″	11,105	47
J-66	0-6-0T	J. Holden	G.E.R.	1886-88	40	6	160		16½ × 22	4′ 0″	16,970	48
J-67/1	0-6-0T	J. Holden	G.E.R.	1890-01	40	0	160		16½ × 22	4′ 0″	16,970	49
J-67/2	0-6-0T	J. and S. D. Holden ...	G.E.R.	1890-04	41	8	160		16½ × 22	4′ 0″	16,970	49
J-68	0-6-0T	S. D. Holden	G.E.R.	1912-23	42	9	180		16½ × 22	4′ 0″	19,090	50
J-69	0-6-0T	J. Holden	G.E.R.	1902-04	42	9	180		16½ × 22	4′ 0″	19,090	49
J-70	0-6-0T	J. Holden	G.E.R.	1903-21	27	1	180	O	12 × 15	3′ 1″	8,930	47
J-71	0-6-0T	T. W. Worsdell ...	N.E.R.	1886-95	37	12	140		16 × 22 18 × 22 16¾ × 22	4′ 7¼″	12,130 15,355 13,300	48
J-72	0-6-0T	W. Worsdell ...	N.E.R.	1898-1925	38	12	140		17 × 24 18 × 24	4′ 1¼″	16,760 18,790	50
J-73	0-6-0T	W. Worsdell ...	N.E.R.	1891-92	46	15	160		19 × 24	4′ 7¼″	21,320	48
J-75	0-6-0T	M. Stirling	H. & B.R.	1908	47	7	175		18 × 26	4′ 6″	23,205	48
J-77	0-6-0T	Fletcher and T. W. Worsdell (1874-84) Reb. W. Worsdell and Raven	N.E.R.	1899-21	43	0	160		17 × 22	4′ 1¼″	17,560	49
J-83	0-6-0T	Holmes	N.B.R.	1900-01	45	5	150		17 × 26	4′ 6″	17,745	49
J-88	0-6-0T	Holmes	N.B.R.	1904-19	38	14	130	O	15 × 22	3′ 9″	12,155	48
J-92	0-6-0CT	Ruston and Proctor* (1868)	G.E.R.	1891-4	40	8	140		16 × 22	4′ 0″	13,960	50

* Rebuilt by J. Holden.

Class	Type	Designer	Originating Pre-Grouping Owner (if any)	Building or Re-building Date	Weight of Loco.	Boiler Pressure	Cylinders	Driving Wheels	Tractive Effort at 85% B.P.	Page
					T. Cwt.	Lb. per sq. in.	Ins.		Lb.	
J-93	0-6-0T	W. Marriott	M. & G.N.J.R.	1897-05	37 14	150	O 16 × 20	3′ 7″	15,180	49
J-94	0-6-0ST	Riddles (M.O.S.) ...	—	1943-46	48 5	170	18 × 26	4′ 3″	23,870	45
K-1	2-6-0	K-4, Reb. Thompson	—	1945	66 17	225S	O 20 × 26	5′ 2″	32,080	18
K-2	2-6-0	Gresley	G.N.R.	1914-21	64 8	180S	O 20 × 26	5′ 8″	23,400	12
K-3	2-6-0	Gresley	G.N.R.	1920-37	72 12	180S	(3) 18½ × 26	5′ 8″	30,030	17
K-4	2-6-0	Gresley	—	1937-38	68 8	200S	(3) 18½ × 26	5′ 2″	36,600	18
K-5	2-6-0	K-3, Reb. Thompson	—	1945	71 5	225S	O 20 × 26	5′ 8″	29,250	17
L-1	2-6-4T	Thompson	—	1945-48	89 9	225S	O 20 × 26	5′ 2″	32,080	45
L-2	2-6-4T	Hally	Met. R.	1925	87 7	200S	O 19 × 26	5′ 6″	26,035	51
L-3	2-6-4T	Robinson	G.C.R.	1914-17	97 9	180S	21 × 26 20 × 26	5′ 1″	28,760 26,085	51
M-2	0-6-4T	Jones	Met. R.	1915-16	71 1	160S	20 × 26	5′ 9″	20.500	51
N-1	0-6-2T	Ivatt	G.N.R.	1907-12	64 14 65 17	175 170S	18 × 26	5′ 8″	18,430 17,900	53
N-2	0-6-2T	Gresley	G.N.R.	1920-29	*	170S	19 × 26	5′ 8″	19,945	54
N4/2 N4/4	0-6-2T	Parker	M.S. & L.R.	1889-92	61 10 61 19	160	18 × 26	5′ 1″	18,780	52 52
N-5/2	0-6-2T	Parker and Pollitt ...	M.S. & L.R.	1891-01	62 7	160	18 × 26	5′ 1″	18,780	52
N-5/3	0-6-2T	Pollitt (1898) ... Reb. Robinson	G.C.R.	1915	64 13	160	18½ × 26	5′ 1″	19,840	52
N-7	0-6-2T	Hill and Gresley ...	G.E.R.	1914-28	†	180S	18 × 24	4′ 10″	20,515	54
N-8	0-6-2T	T. W. Worsdell ... Reb. W. Worsdell	N.E.R.	1886-90	56 5	160	18 × 24	5′ 1¼″	17,265	53
		Reb. Raven ...	N.E.R.	1886-90	58 14	160S	19 × 24 19 × 26	5′ 1¼″	19,235 20,840	
N-9	0-6-2T	W. Worsdell ...	N.E.R.	1893-94	56 10	160	19 × 26	5′ 1¼″	20,840	53
N-10	0-6-2T	W. Worsdell ...	N.E.R.	1902-03	57 14	160	18½ × 26	4′ 7¼″	21,905	52
N-13	0-6-2T	M. Stirling	H. & B.R.	1913-14	61 9	175	18 × 26	4′ 6″	23,205	52
N-14	0-6-2T	Reid	N.B.R.	1909	62 19	175	18 × 26	4′ 6″	23,205	52
N-15/1 N-15/2	0-6-2T	Reid	N.B.R.	1910-24	60 18 62 1	175	18 × 26	4′ 6″	23,205	52

O–1	2–8–0	Robinson (1911-20) ...	—	1944–48	73	6	225S	O 20 ×26	4′ 8″	35,520	25
		Reb. Thompson									
O–2/1/2	2–8–0	Gresley	G.N.R.	1921–4	75	16					
O–2/3		Gresley	—	1923–43	78	13	180S	18½ ×26	4′ 8″	36,470	27
O–2 (100A boiler)		Reb. Thompson	—	1943–5	74	2					
O–3	2–8–0	Gresley	G.N.R.	1913–19	76	4	180S	O 21 ×28	4′ 8″	33,735	25
O–4/1, /2 /3, /6	2–8–0	Robinson	G.C.R.	1911–20	73	4	180S	O 21 ×26	4′ 8″	31,325	25
O–4/5	2–8–0	O–4 Reb. Gresley ...	—	1932–39	74	13	180S	O 21 ×26	4′ 8″	31,325	25
O–4/7	2–8–0	,, Reb Gresley ...	—	1939–44	73	17	180S	O 21 ×26	4′ 8″	31,325	25
O–4/8	2–8–0	,, Reb. Thompson	—	1944–8	72	10	180S	O 21 ×26	4′ 8″	31,325	25
O–7	2–8–0	Riddles (M.O.S.) ...	—	1943–45	70	5	225S	O 19 ×28	4′ 8½″	34,215	24
Q–1	0–8–0T	Q–4 Reb. Thompson	—	1942–43	69 / 73	18 / 13	180	O 19 ×26	4′ 8″	25,645	56
Q–4/1	0–8–0	Robinson	G.C.R.	1902–11	62	8	180	O 19 ×26	4′ 8″	25,645	24
Q4/2	0–8–0	Robinson	G.C.R.	1902–11	63 / 64	0 / 1	180S	O 19 ×26 / O 21 ×26	4′ 8″	25,645 / 31,325	24
Q–5/1	0–8–0	W. Worsdell ...	N.E.R.	1901–11	58	8	175	O 20 ×26	4′ 7½″	28,000	24
Q–5/2		Reb. Gresley		1931	60	4					24
Q–6	0–8–0	Raven	N.E.R.	1913–21	65	18	180S	O 20 ×26	4′ 7½″	28,800	25
Q–7	0–8–0	Raven	N.E.R.	1919–24	71	12	180S	(3) 18½ ×26	4′ 7½″	36,965	25
S–1/1	0–8–4T	Robinson	G.C.R.	1907–08	99	6	180S	(3) 18 ×26	4′ 8″	34,525	56
S–1/2	0–8–4T	S1/1 Reb. Gresley ...	—	1932	99	2	180S	(3) 18 ×26	4′ 8″	34,525	56
S–1/3	0–8–4T	Gresley	—	1932	99	1	180S	(3) 18 ×26	4′ 8″	34,525	56
T–1	4–8–0T	Raven	N.E.R.	1909–25	85	8	175SS	(3) 18 ×26	4′ 7½″	34,080	56
U–1	2–8–8–2T	Beyer-Garratt-Gresley	—	1925	178	1	180S	(6) 18½ ×26	4′ 8″	72,940	56
V–1	2–6–2T	Gresley	—	1930–39	84	0	180S	(3) 16 ×26	5′ 8″	22,465	45
V–2	2–6–2	Gresley	—	1936–44	93	2	220S	(3) 18½ ×26	6′ 2″	33,730	6
V–3	2–6–2T	Gresley	—	1939–40	86	16	200S	(3) 16 ×26	5′ 8″	24 960	45
V–4	2–6–2	Gresley	—	1941	70	8	250S	(3) 15 ×26	5′ 8″	27,420	12
W–1‡	4–6–4	Gresley	—	1937	107	17	250S	(3) 20 ×26	6′ 8″	41,435	6
Y–1/1§	0–4–0T	Sentinel Co. ...	—	1925–33	20	17	275S	6¾ × 9	2′ 6″	7,260 / 8,870¶	46
Y–1/2§	0–4–0T		—	1927–9	19	16					46
Y–1/3§	0–4–0T		—	1926	14	0					46
Y–1/4§	0–4–0T		—	1927	19	7					46

* For weights see p. 54.

† For weights see p. 54.

‡ Originally designed as 4-6-4 compound engine with water tube boiler, and rebuilt as 3-cylinder simple engine with a Stephenson-type boiler in 1937.

§ Geared Locomotives (single speed).

¶ With gear ratio 9 : 25 (remainder 11 : 25).

Class	Type	Designer	Originating Pre-Grouping Owner (if any)	Building or Re-building Date	Weight of Loco.	Boiler Pres-sure	Cylinders	Driving Wheels	Tractive Effort at 85% B.P.	Page
					T. Cwt.	Lb. per sq. in.	Ins.		Lb.	
Y-3‡	0-4-0T	Sentinel Co. ...	—	1927–31	20 16	275S	6¾ × 9	2' 6"	§4,705† ‡12,600† §5,960 ‡15,960	47
Y-4	0-4-0T	Hill	G.E.R.	1913–21	38 1	180	O 17 × 20	3' 10"	19,225	46
Y-6	0-4-0T	J. Holden	G.E.R.	1897	21 5	140	11 × 15	3' 1"	5,835	46
Y-7	0-4-0T	T. W. Worsdell ...	N.E.R.	1923	22 14	140	14 × 20	3' 6¼"	11,040	46
Y-8	0-4-0T	T. W. Worsdell ...	N.E.R.	1890	15 10	140	11 × 15	3' 0"	6,000	46
Y-9	0-4-0ST	Holmes	N.B.R.	1882–99	27 16	130	O 14 × 20	3' 8"	9,845	46
Y-10*	0-4-0T	Sentinel Co. ...	—	1930	23 19	275S	6¾ × 9	3' 2"	§7,965 ‡11,435	47
Z-4	0-4-2T	Manning-Wardle ...	G.N. of S.R.	1915	25 17	160	O 13 × 20	3' 6"	10,945	47
Z-5	0-4-2T	Manning-Wardle ...	G.N. of S.R.	1915	30 18	160	O 14 × 20	4' 0"	11,105	47

NOTES. O—Outside cylinders (2). T—Tank. ST—Saddle Tank. C—Crane engines.
* Geared Locomotives (two speeds). † With sprocket gears 15 : 19 (remainder 19 : 19).
§ High gear. ‡ Low gear.

PETROL FREIGHT

Class	Type	Designer	Date Built	Weight of Loco.	Horse Power	Page
				T. C.		
Y-11	0-4-0	Motor, Rail & Tram Car Co.	1921	8 0	40	47

SOME POINTS OF INTEREST

Ex-North Eastern 0-6-0 Locomotives

Of the remaining ex N.E. 0-6-0 locomotives, classes J21, J25, J26 and J27 have the same length and wheelbase, the two former having 4′ 3″ diameter boilers and the two latter 5′ 6″. The fireboxes of J26 and J27 are also larger, and the boilers originally fitted to J26 had shallower fireboxes than those of J27. J21 and J25 have identical boilers. J24 has a 4′ 3″ boiler shorter than that of J25, and the wheelbase is also shorter. For 22 years up to the introduction of J38, J26 and J27 were the only 0-6-0's in the country with boilers as large in diameter as 5′ 6″.

Note on Boiler Interchangeability

There are several types of boiler which are common to more than one ex-L.N.E.R. class. In some cases boilers are frequently interchanged between the classes, a locomotive under repair receiving the first boiler of that type which is available. In other cases the boilers are identical from the manufacturing standpoint, but the fittings vary on the different classes, and interchanges are not normally made. Groups of classes with similar boilers include : A2/1 and V2 ; A5 and D9 ; A6, A8 (except for superheater) and T1 ; B1, B2, B3, B17 (100A), O1, O2 (100A) and O4/8 ; B4, C4, O4 and S1 ; B5, B9 and Q4 (sup.) ; B7 and B8 ; B12/1 and J20 ; B16 and Q7 ; C12, J4, J50 and J55 ; C13 and C14 ; C15, C16 (except for superheater), J36, N14 and N15 ; D1, D2 (sup.), J2, J6 and N2 (with recent boiler) ; D2 (sat.), J1, J5 and N1 (this group differs only from the preceding in being saturated) ; D10, D11 and L3 ; D16/3 and J19 ; D29, D30, D32, D33 and D34 ; D40 (sat.) and D41 ; D49, J38/2 and J39 ; E4, F3 and J15 ; F1, F2, J10, N4 and N5 ; F5 and F6 ; G5 and J24 ; J21, J25, N8, N9 and N10 ; J35 and J37 ; J62 and J63 ; J65, J66 and J67 ; J68 and J69 ; J71 and J72 ; O2 and O3.

Note on Boilers of Ex-N.E.R. Locomotives

Although several ex-N.E.R. classes have boilers very similar in dimensions to standard L.N.E.R. classes (e.g. B16 and B1), it is not possible for the standard boilers to be fitted to the N.E. locomotives as the latter have their frames ½″ closer together than L.N.E.R. standard. Most of the N.E. boilers had the dome on the centre of the barrel, whereas most of the L.N.E.R. boilers have the dome to the rear of the barrel, a bracket for stays being attached near the centre of the barrel. Since 1937 new boilers with domes to the rear and standard stays have been built for the more modern N.E. classes, including A8, B16, J26 and J27.

Note on Ex-G.N.R. Locomotives

The standard 0-6-0 and 4-4-0 of the early Ivatt period became L.N.E.R. J4 and D4. They had identical 4′ 4″ diameter boilers, cylinders and other details. D2 was developed from D4, with a 4′ 8″ boiler and longer firebox ; the corresponding larger 0-6-0 was J5. Later all class D4 and most of J4 were rebuilt with 4′ 8″ boilers, but with fireboxes of the same length as before, becoming D3 and J3. J1 was a large-wheeled version of J5. Towards the end of the Ivatt regime, superheated developments of these classes, with piston valves, were introduced, D1 (from D2), J2 (from J1) and J6 (from J5). The tank version of J1 was N1 and the tank version of J2 was N2. As built N2 had Gresley twin-tube superheaters instead of the Robinson pattern of the other classes, but these locomotives are now receiving the Robinson apparatus.

Note on Ex-G.E.R. Locomotives

F3 was the tank version of E4, and is larger than the other G.E. 2-4-2T's, F4, F5 and F6 (the "Wordsell Gobblers"). The first F4's were built in 1886-8 and many more were built from 1903. F5 is a rebuild of F4 with higher pressure boiler, and F6 were the locomotives built new with the higher boiler pressure.

Of the G.E. 0-6-0T's, although the boilers are all of the same dimensions, J65 are much smaller locomotives than the rest. The other classes are generally similar, except that J68 and J69 have larger tanks and higher pressure. J69 are rebuilds from J67, and J68 new locomotives. J69 and many of J68 were originally passenger locomotives for the London suburban area.

Note on Classification of L.N.E.R. Locomotives

The L.N.E.R. locomotive classification scheme was based on that used on the former G.N.R. Each wheel arrangement was allotted a letter, and the classes of that arrangement were numbered in groups according to the pre-grouping ownership, in the order G.N., G.C., G.E., N.E., N.B., G.N.S. L.N.E.R. classes were at first usually added at the end of the list, but the new standard locomotives have been given the lowest number in most groups. Types 0-8-2T (R) and 2-2-4 (X) have now disappeared. Many classes are sub-divided into "parts," denoted thus : "D16/3." This division is not entirely consistent, as some classes with comparatively wide variations, such as "C1," are not sub-divided, but others, such as "O4," have some divisions dependent only on details such as brakes and whether or not the tender has a water scoop. In these lists, sub-divisions are denoted by "parts" where these exist, but elsewhere it is to be assumed that any variations between the locomotives in the class are not covered by the classification (e.g. "C1").

The ABC
LOCOSHED BOOK

SHED ALLOCATIONS OF BRITISH RAILWAYS STEAM, DIESEL, ELECTRIC AND GAS TURBINE LOCOMOTIVES,

SUMMER 1950

Nos 1-90774

Publisher's note: In photographically reprinting the Locoshed Book section, which was originally published as four separate books, certain basic information appears here once only instead of being repeated and thus the page numbers in this part do not run consecutively.

LONDON

NOTES ON THE USE OF THIS BOOK

In response to many requests it has been found possible to reprint one of the earlier year's Locoshed Books, but since the Ian Allan Locoshed Book had not appeared by 1948 it has not been possible to co-ordinate shed allocation information exactly to the locomotive details in the first part of this combined book. Thus some engines listed in part 1 may have been withdrawn by the time the shed allocation lists in part 2 were compiled. Conversely some engines built after 1948 do not appear in part 1 but are shown in part 2. Nevertheless the two parts of this combined book give the general picture of British Railways motive power in the period 1948/50.

Against each number is the BR code number of its home shed which can be identified from the key to BR shed codes listed on the following four pages. The locomotives carried the shed code on a small oval plate on the smokebox door. If no shed allocation is shown the locomotive was still on order or was awaiting allocation.

The numerical lists of locomotives are divided into classes, except in the case of Southern locomotives where classifications are shown for each locomotive. Named locomotives are denoted by an asterisk. Class details and engine names are shown in part 1 of this combined publication. Western Region locomotives classified by initials were from pre-grouping Welsh railways. A key to the initials is given on page 11 of part 1. A bold **S** against certain locomotives indicates that they were in departmental use; the locomotives concerned did not carry this letter except on the Southern Region.

These lists were checked to August 31, 1950 except for LMR locomotives numbered between 40001 and 58935 which were checked to September 9, 1950.

MOTIVE POWER DEPOTS, AND CODES

LONDON MIDLAND REGION

Heavy type thus, **Rugby,** indicates a main district depot. In addition to depots shown, there are several sub-depots, the engines attached to which bear the code of the main district depot.

1A **Willesden**
1B Camden
1C Watford
1D Devons Road

2A **Rugby**
2B Nuneaton
2C Warwick
2D Coventry

3A **Bescot**
3B Bushbury
3C Walsall
3D Aston
3E Monument Lane

4A **Bletchley**
4B Northampton

5A **Crewe North**
5B Crewe South
5C Stafford
5D Stoke
5E Alsager
5F Uttoxeter

6A **Chester**
6B Mold Junction
6C Birkenhead
6D Northgate
6E Wrexham
6F Bidston

7A **Llandudno Junc.**
7B Bangor
7C Holyhead
7D Rhyl

8A **Edge Hill**
8B Warrington
8C Speke Junction
8D Widnes
8E Brunswick
8E Warrington

9A **Longsight**
9B Stockport
9C Macclesfield
9D Buxton
9E Trafford Park
9F Heaton Mersey
9G Northwich

10A **Springs Branch**
10B Preston
10C Patricroft
10D Plodder Lane
10E Sutton Oak
10F Wigan (L.I.)

11A **Carnforth**
11B Barrow
11C Oxenholme
11D Tebay

12A **Carlisle (Upperby)**
12B Carlisle (Canal)
12C Penrith
12D Workington
12E Moor Row

14A **Cricklewood**
14B Kentish Town
14C St. Albans

15A **Wellingboro'**
15B Kettering
15C Leicester
15D Bedford

16A **Nottingham**
16C Kirkby
16D Mansfield

17A **Derby**
17B Burton
17C Coalville
17D Rowsley

18A **Toton**
18B Westhouses
18C Hasland
18D Staveley

19A **Sheffield**
19B Millhouses
19C Canklow

MOTIVE POWER DEPOTS AND CODES

20A **Leeds**
20B Stourton
20C Royston
20D Normanton
20E Manningham

21A **Saltley**
21B Bournville
21C Bromsgrove
21D Stratford-on-Avon

22A **Bristol**
22B Gloucester

23A **Skipton**
23B Hellifield
23C Lancaster

24A **Accrington**
24B Rose Grove
24C Lostock Hall
24D Lower Darwen

25A **Wakefield**
25B Huddersfield
25C Goole
25D Mirfield
25E Sowerby Bridge
25F Low Moor
25G Farnley Junction

26A **Newton Heath**
26B Agecroft
26C Bolton
26D Bury
26E Bacup
26F Lees
26G Belle Vue

27A **Bank Hall**
27B Aintree
27C Southport
27D Wigan (C)
27E Walton
27E Southport

28A **Blackpool**
28B Fleetwood

EASTERN REGION

30A **Stratford**
30B Hertford East
30C Bishops Stortford
30D Southend Victoria
30E Colchester
30F Parkeston

31A **Cambridge**
31B March
31C King's Lynn
31D South Lynn
31E Bury St. Edmunds

32A **Norwich**
32B Ipswich
32C Lowestoft
32D Yarmouth (South Town)
32E Yarmouth (Vauxhall)
32F Yarmouth Beach
32G Melton Constable

33A **Plaistow**
33B Tilbury
33C Shoeburyness

34A **Kings Cross**
34B Hornsey
34C Hatfield
34D Hitchin
34E Neasden

35A **New England**
35B Grantham
35C Peterborough (ex L.M.)

36A **Doncaster**
36B Mexborough
36C Frodingham
36D Barnsley
36E Retford

37A **Ardsley**
37B Copley Hill
37C Bradford

38A **Colwick**
38B Annesley
38C Leicester
38D Staveley
38E Woodford Halse

39A **Gorton**
39B Sheffield

40A **Lincoln**
40B Immingham
40C Louth
40D Tuxford
40E Langwith
40F Boston

MOTIVE POWER DEPOTS AND CODES

NORTH EASTERN REGION

50A **York**
50B Leeds (Neville Hill)
50C Selby
50D Starbeck
50E Scarborough
50F Malton
50G Whitby

51A **Darlington**
51B Newport
51C West Hartlepool
51D Middlesborough
51E Stockton
51F West Auckland
51G Haverton Hill
51H Kirkby Stephen
51J Northallerton
51K Saltburn

52A **Gateshead**
52B Heaton
52C Blaydon
52D Tweedmouth
52E Percy Main
52F North Blyth

53A **Hull (Dairycoates)**
53B Hull (Botanic Gardens)
53C Hull (Springhead)
53D Bridlington
53E Cudworth

54A **Sunderland**
54B Tyne Dock
54C Borough Gardens
54D Consett

SCOTTISH REGION

60A **Inverness**
60B Aviemore
60C Helmsdale
60D Wick
60E Forres

61A **Kittybrewster**
61B Ferryhill
61C Keith

62A **Thornton**
62B Dundee
62C Dunfermline

63A **Perth**
63B Stirling
63C Forfar
63D Fort William
63E Oban

64A **St. Margarets**
64B Haymarket
64C Dalry Road
64D Carstairs
64E Polmont
64F Bathgate
64G Hawick

65A **Eastfield**
65B St. Rollox
65C Parkhead
65D Dawsholme
65E Kipps
65F Grangemouth
65G Yoker
65H Helensburgh
65I Balloch

66A **Polmadie**
66B Motherwell
66C Hamilton
66D Greenock

67A **Corkerhill**
67B Hurlford
67C Ayr
67D Ardrossan

68A **Carlisle Kingmoor**
68B Dumfries
68C Stranraer
68D Beattock

SOUTHERN REGION

70A **Nine Elms**
70B Feltham
70C Guildford
70D Basingstoke
70E Reading

71A **Eastleigh**
71B Bournemouth
71C Dorchester
71D Fratton
71E Newport, I.O.W.

MOTIVE POWER DEPOTS AND CODES

SOUTHERN REGION

71F Ryde
71G Bath (S. & D.)
71H Templecombe
71I Southampton

72A **Exmouth Junction**
72B Salisbury
72C Yeovil
72D Plymouth
72E Barnstaple
72F Wadebridge

73A **Stewarts Lane**
73B Bricklayers' Arms
73C Hither Green
73D Gillingham
73E Faversham

74A **Ashford**
74B Ramsgate
74C Dover
74D Tonbridge
74E St. Leonards

75A **Brighton**
75B Redhill
75C Norwood
75D Horsham
75E Three Bridges
75F Tunbridge Wells
75G Eastbourne

WESTERN REGION

81A **Old Oak Common**
81B Slough
81C Southall
81D Reading
81E Didcot
81F Oxford

82A **Bristol (Bath Road)**
82B Bristol (S.P.M.)
82C Swindon
82D Westbury
82E Yeovil
82F Weymouth

83A **Newton Abbot**
83B Taunton
83C Exeter
83D Laira
83E St. Blazey
83F Truro
83G Penzance

84A **Wolverhampton (Stafford Rd.)**
84B Oxley
84C Banbury
84D Leamington
84E Tyseley
84F Stourbridge
84G Shrewsbury
84H Wellington
84J Croes Newydd
84K Chester

85A **Worcester**
85B Gloucester
85C Hereford
85D Kidderminster

86A **Newport (Ebbw Junction)**
86B Newport Pill
86C Cardiff (Canton)
86D Llantrisant
86E Severn Tunnel Junction
86F Tondu
86G Pontypool Road
86H Aberbeeg
86J Aberdare
86K Abergavenny

87A **Neath**
87B Duffryn Yard
87C Danygraig
87D Swansea East Dock
87E Landore
87F Llanelly
87G Carmarthen
87H Neyland
87J Goodwick
87K Swansea Victoria

88A **Cardiff Cathays**
88B Cardiff East Dock
88C Barry
88D Merthyr
88E Abercynon
88F Treherbert

89A **Oswestry**
89B Brecon
89C Machynlleth

BRITISH RAILWAYS LOCOMOTIVES

Nos. 1—9999

WITH SHED ALLOCATIONS

YTW
0-4-0T
1* 87C

WCP
0-6-0T
5* 82C

V.o.R.
2-6-2T
7 89C
8 89C
9 89C

CMDP
0-6-0T
28 85D
29 85D

RR
0-6-2T
31 88A
33 88B
35 88A
36 88B
37 88B
38 88A
39 88B
40 88A
41 88A
42 88A
43 88A
44 88A
55 88B
56 88A
57 88C
58 88C
59 88C
60 87C
63 88A
65 86J
66 88B
67 88B
68 88B
69 87B
70 87B
72 88B
73 88B
74 88B
75 87A
76 88D
77 88D
78 88D
79 88D
80 88D
81 88D
82 88D
83 88D

RR
0-6-0T
90 88B
91 88B
92 88B
93 88B
94 88B
95 88B
96 88B

Class 4073
4-6-0
111* 83D

Car. R.
0-6-2T
155 88B

TV
0-6-0T
193 88F
194 88F
195 88F

TV
0-6-2T
203 86C
204 86J
205 86C
207 88F
208 86C
209 86C
210 88F
211 88D
215 88F
216 88F
217 88D
218 88F
219 88E
220 86C
236 88E

BR
0-6-2T
240 88C
263 88C
267 88C
270 88C
271 88C
274 88C
276 88C

TV
0-6-2T
278 88F
279 88F
282 86J
284 86J
285 88F
286 88A
290 88F
292 88D
293 88A
295 88E
299 88F
303 88F
304 88E
305 88A
306 88C
307 88A
308 87D
309 87D
312 88C
316 88D
322 88C
335 86C
337 88E
343 88A
344 88A
345 88A
346 88A
347 88A
348 88A
349 86G
351 88E
352 88F
356 88E
357 86C

LMM
0-6-0T
359* 87C

TV
0-6-2T
360 88A
361 88C
362 86J
364 88A
365 88F
366 88F
367 88A
368 88F
370 88D
371 88A
372 88C
373 88C
374 86J
375 88D
376 88A
377 88A
378 88F
379 88C
380 88E
381 86C
382 88C
383 88A
384 88A
385 86G
386 88E
387 88C
388 88C
389 88C
390 88A
391 88A
393 88A
394 88C
397 88E
398 88D
399 88F

BM
0-6-2T
425 86C
431 86A
432 86A
433 88A
434 88A
435 86A
436 86A

AD
0-6-0T
666 86B
667 86B

Car. R.
0-6-0T
681 88B

682 88B
683 88B
684 88B

LMM
0–6–0T
803 87C

W. & L.
0–6–0T
822* 89A
823* 89A

Cam. R.
0–6–0
844 89A
849 89A
855 89A
864 89C
873 89A
887 89A
892 89C
893 89A
894 89C
895 89A
896 89A

Class 1854
0–6–0T
907 81E

Class 1901
0–6–0T
992 82C

Class 1000
4–6–0
1000* 81A
1001* 87H
1002* 82A
1003* 81A
1004* 83G
1005* 82A
1006* 83D
1007* 82A
1008* 81A
1009* 87H
1010* 81A
1011* 82A
1012* 81A
1013* 83F
1014* 82A
1015* 81A
1016* 84A
1017* 84A
1018* 83A
1019* 83A
1020* 87H
1021* 81A
1022* 83D
1023* 83D
1024* 84A
1025* 84A
1026* 81A
1027* 82D
1028* 82A
1029* 84A

Class 1101
0–4–0T
1101 87C
1102 87C
1103 87C
1104 87C
1105 87C
1106 87C

SHT
0-4-0T
1140 87D
1141 87C
1142 87C
1143 87C
1144 87D
1145 87C

SHT
0–6–0T
1146 87D
1147 87C

PM
0–4–0T
1150 87D
1151 87C
1152 87D
1153 87C

AD
2–6–2T
1205 86D
1206 85C

MSWJ
2–4–0
1334 81E
1335 81D
1336 81D
1338 83B

Class 1361
0–6–0T
1361 83D
1362 83A
1363 83D
1364 83D
1365 83D

Class 1366
0–6–0T
1366 82C
1367 82F
1368 82F
1369 82C
1370 82F
1371 82C

Class 1400
0–4–2T
1400 82C
1401 84C
1402 85B
1403 82C
1404 85B
1405 83C
1406 85B
1407 81D
1408 85A
1409 85B
1410 84A
1411 84C
1412 89A
1413 85B
1414 84F
1415 82A
1416 84J
1417 6C
1418 85A
1419 83E
1420 88A
1421 86D
1422 86G
1423 87J
1424 85B
1425 88A
1426 34E
1427 83A
1428 89A
1429 83C
1430 82A
1431 87J
1432 89A
1433 82C
1434 84K
1435 83C
1436 82C
1437 81B
1438 84F
1439 83A
1440 83C
1441 85B
1442 81B
1443 81C
1444 81D
1445 85C
1446 82C
1447 81D
1448 81F
1449 83C
1450 81F
1451 83C
1452 87J
1453 82F
1454 82F
1455 85C
1456 85B
1457 84J
1458 84C
1459 89A
1460 85C
1461 88A
1462 81C
1463 82A
1464 85B
1465 89C
1466 83A
1467 82F
1468 83C
1469 83C
1470 83A
1471 86D
1472 87G
1473 84J
1474 89C

Class 1500 †
0–6–0T
1500 81A
1501 81A
1502 81A
1503 81A
1504 81A
1505 81A
1506 86B
1507 86B
1508 86E
1509 86A

Class 1501
0–6–0T
1542 82C

Class 1600 †
0–6–0T
1600 88C
1601 87B
1602 87B
1603 89C
1604 89A
1605 81C
1606 87C
1607 87F
1608 83A
1609 87F
1610 88B
1611 87H
1612 85B
1613 87G
1614 87F
1615 88C
1616 85B
1617 81F

† See also page 21.

1618 87F
1619 84H
1620 88E
1621 84F
1622 87B
1623 85B
1624 84J
1625 85B
1626 83E
1627
1628
1629

Class 1854
0–6–0T
1705 88B
1709 86B

Class 1501
0–6–0T
1782 83F
1789 82F

Class 1854
0–6–0T
1855 87A
1858 87A
1861 81E
1862 86A
1870 86F

Class 1901
0–6–0T
1903 87G
1917 6C
1925 81C
1935 81F
1941 87F
1943 85B
1957 87F
1964 87H
1967 87F
1968 6C
1989 85B
1991 87F
1993 88C
1996 87H
2001 85A
2002 87F
2004 6C
2008 88E
2009 85B
2010 87H
2011 87H
2012 87F
2014 82C
2016 85A
2017 82C

Class 2021
0–6–0T
2021 86G
2023 82D
2025 85B
2026 85C
2027 87F
2030 84H
2031 82B
2032 89A
2033 86B
2034 85B
2035 86G
2038 83B
2040 85C
2042 87F
2043 85B
2044 85B
2048 88B
2050 83E
2051 85D
2053 82D
2054 89A
2055 87C
2056 87G
2060 82C
2061 84A
2063 86A
2066 88A
2067 6C
2068 89A
2069 87G
2070 82B
2072 82A
2073 86A
2075 89A
2076 81F
2079 87B
2080 85B
2081 87F
2082 87C
2083 87F
2085 87F
2086 88B
2088 83C
2089 6C
2090 84F
2092 6C
2093 85A
2094 86G
2095 84A
2097 83F
2098 87F
2099 85C
2100 85A
2101 85A
2104 6C
2106 6C
2107 84F
2108 6C
2109 84A
2111 87G
2112 81B
2115 85C
2117 86G
2121 85B
2122 86A
2123 88B
2126 87F
2127 83B
2129 6C
2131 85B
2134 87C
2135 82B
2136 86B
2138 85C
2140 88A
2141 88B
2144 85B
2146 85B
2147 88B
2148 83D
2150 87F
2151 87C
2152 6C
2153 85B
2154 86B
2155 85B
2156 6C
2159 86J
2160 85C

BPGV
0–6–0T
2162 87F
2165 87F
2166 87D
2167 87F
2168 87F
2176 87F

Class 2181
0–6–0T
2181 83A
2182 83E
2183 83A
2184 84J
2185 84F
2186 84F
2187 84F
2188 84J
2189 84F
2190 84J

BPGV
0–6–0T
2192* 87A
2193* 87F
2194* 83B
2195 82C
2196* 87F
2197* 87F
2198 87F

Class 2251
0–6–0
2200 89C
2201 89C
2202 81E
2203 84E
2204 89C
2205 85A
2206 89C
2207 85A
2208 81D
2209 84J
2210 89A
2211 83B
2212 83B
2213 83B
2214 83B
2215 82B
2216 87G
2217 87G
2218 86A
2219 89C
2220 82B
2221 81E
2222 81E
2223 89C
2224 82C
2225 82B
2226 81E
2227 86A
2228 84G
2229 84G
2230 83C
2231 84G
2232 84J
2233 84G
2234 84G
2235 84G
2236 87G
2237 85A
2238 84E
2239 86A
2240 81E
2241 85A
2242 85A
2243 85C
2244 89A
2245 81D
2246 84F
2247 85A
2248 85B
2249 81F
2250 82C
2251 82B
2252 81E
2253 82B
2254 85B
2255 89A
2256 84C
2257 84E
2258 83D
2259 84J
2260 89C

2261 83B
2262 84J
2263 85A
2264 81D
2265 82B
2266 83B
2267 83B
2268 83B
2269 82B
2270 84F
2271 87G
2272 87G
2273 87E
2274 85A
2275 83B
2276 81A
2277 85A
2278 85A
2279 84F
2280 86A
2281 85C
2282 81A
2283 89C
2284 87G
2285 81C
2286 85C
2287 89B
2288 87H
2289 81E
2290 85A
2291 85B
2292 89C
2293 82B
2294 85A
2295 84C
2296 84E
2297 84J
2298 89C
2299 81D

Class 2301
0–6–0

2322 82B
2323 89C
2327 89A
2339 85B
2340 82B
2343 89B
2349 85C
2350 85B
2351 89B
2354 89A
2385 86G
2386 89A
2401 89B
2407 86C
2408 89A
2409 89A
2411 87A
2414 86E
2426 82D
2431 87G
2444 82D
2445 82A
2449 89A
2452 89B
2458 85A
2460 86E
2462 82B
2468 89B
2474 87G
2482 89A
2483 89A
2484 89A
2513 84K
2515 85C
2516 89A
2532 81E
2534 82A
2537 86C
2538 89A
2541 85C
2543 89A
2551 85A
2556 89A
2568 82C
2572 89A
2573 81D
2578 82B
2579 81E

Class 1501
0–6–0T

2716 84J
2719 84J

Class 2721
0–6–0T

2722 87A
2743 85A
2744 84G
2754 88B
2760 88D

Class 2800
2–8–0

2800 86G
2801 86G
2802 86G
2803 87F
2804 86E
2805 84C
2806 86J
2807 85C
2808 86J
2809 83A
2810 84K
2811 86G
2812 84K
2813 86G
2814 83B
2815 86A
2816 84C
2817 86A
2818 82B
2819 86A
2820 86C
2821 86A
2822 84J
2823 85B
2824 87F
2825 84B
2826 81A
2827 81F
2828 86J
2829 86E
2830 84B
2831 86J
2832 84B
2833 84B
2834 86A
2835 81A
2836 86J
2837 86C
2838 86E
2839 82B
2840 84J
2841 84G
2842 86A
2843 81C
2844 82B
2845 81F
2846 82B
2847 84C
2848 84E
2849 84E
2850 87F
2851 86A
2852 84F
2853 84C
2854 84B
2855 87F
2856 84F
2857 84F
2858 81C
2859 82B
2860 81F
2861 86A
2862 86G
2863 84C
2864 86G
2865 86A
2866 86A
2867 84E
2868 81A
2869 84C
2870 86J
2871 84J
2872 87F
2873 83C
2874 84F
2875 83D
2876 86A
2877 86C
2878 84J
2879 86A
2880 86J
2881 83A
2882 84K
2883 84C
2884 86G
2885 84F
2886 84C
2887 86E
2888 86G
2889 86A
2890 84K
2891 86C
2892 86E
2893 86G
2894 86A
2895 81A
2896 86A
2897 84C
2898 84C
2899 84C

Class 2900
4–6–0

2906* 86C
2908* 82C
2912* 82F
2915* 84K
2920* 85C
2926* 84K
2927* 82C
2931* 82A
2932* 84E
2933* 84D
2934* 82C
2936* 86A
2937* 85C
2938* 85B
2939* 82A
2940* 86C
2943* 86C
2944* 85C
2945* 82C
2947* 82C
2948* 82A
2949* 82C
2950* 82A
2951* 85B
2952* 86E
2953* 84K
2954* 82C
2979* 86A
2981* 84C

Class R.O.D.
2–8–0

3010 87G
3011 87G
3012 86G
3014 82B
3015 87G
3016 84E
3017 81A

No.	Shed
3018	86G
3020	84C
3022	85A
3023	86G
3024	81E
3025	81D
3026	84J
3028	84J
3029	85A
3031	84B
3032	82B
3033	84B
3034	82B
3036	86C
3038	86G
3040	86G
3041	82B
3042	86G
3043	84C
3044	86G
3047	81D
3048	85A

Class 3100
2-6-2T

No.	Shed
3100	86F
3101	84E
3102	84A
3103	86A
3104	84A

Class 3150
2-6-2T

No.	Shed
3150	86E
3151	84E
3153	85B
3154	86E
3157	86E
3160	84A
3161	86E
3163	85B
3164	85B
3167	86E
3168	86E
3170	86E
3171	85B
3172	86E
3174	86E
3176	86E
3177	86E
3178	83D
3180	84E
3183	86E
3185	86E
3186	83D
3187	83D
3188	86E
3190	86E

Class 2251
0-6-0

No.	Shed
3200	89C
3201	89C
3202	89C
3203	84J
3204	85B
3205	85B
3206	84J
3207	89C
3208	89A
3209	85C
3210	81E
3211	81E
3212	81E
3213	85B
3214	85A
3215	82B
3216	84C
3217	84G
3218	84C
3219	85A

Class 3300
4-4-0

No.	Shed
3377	85A
3406*	85C
3444*	82C
3447*	85A
3449*	82C
3451*	82C
3453*	82C
3454*	81D

Class 5700
0-6-0T

No.	Shed
3600	83A
3601	85D
3602	84G
3603	83C
3604	82B
3605	86J
3606	83C
3607	85A
3608	81F
3609	85B
3610	86J
3611	87A
3612	86D
3613	84H
3614	82B
3615	84A
3616	86F
3617	86D
3618	81C
3619	84K
3620	81C
3621	87A
3622	81E
3623	82B
3624	84E
3625	84E
3626	6C
3627	86F
3628	86G
3629	83D
3630	84C
3631	84D
3632	82B
3633	87D
3634	86A
3635	83E
3636	86A
3637	87J
3638	89B
3639	83D
3640	86H
3641	87D
3642	87F
3643	82B
3644	86D
3645	82C
3646	84K
3647	86A
3648	81A
3649	84F
3650	84E
3651	86G
3652	86F
3653	84E
3654	87H
3655	86J
3656	86D
3657	84E
3658	84E
3659	83A
3660	84E
3661	87F
3662	86A
3663	86B
3664	84E
3665	84K
3666	82C
3667	84F
3668	86F
3669	83B
3670	86C
3671	82E
3672	88B
3673	84E
3674	86F
3675	83D
3676	82B
3677	83C
3678	87E
3679	87D
3680	86H
3681	88B
3682	82C
3683	86H
3684	82C
3685	81A
3686	83D
3687	84H
3688	81A
3689	84E
3690	86G
3691	86D
3692	86G
3693	84E
3694	84C
3695	86F
3696	82D
3697	81D
3698	87F
3699	86F
3700	86A
3701	87E
3702	84G
3703	86D
3704	81C
3705	83D
3706	89B
3707	88B
3708	86H
3709	81E
3710	81A
3711	86H
3712	86A
3713	87E
3714	86A
3715	81D
3716	86H
3717	86G
3718	87B
3719	87F
3720	82B
3721	81E
3722	81F
3723	81D
3724	82C
3725	85A
3726	86A
3727	81C
3728	85C
3729	86C
3730	86G
3731	82B
3732	84H
3733	82E
3734	88A
3735	82D
3736	81D
3737	82C
3738	81B
3739	82C
3740	84F
3741	87A
3742	6C
3743	84E

3744 84B
3745 84B
3746 82B
3747 86J
3748 82C
3749 84H
3750 81C
3751 84E
3752 87F
3753 86J
3754 81A
3755 86C
3756 84A
3757 87A
3758 82D
3759 82B
3760 84H
3761 87F
3762 84K
3763 82B
3764 82B
3765 82B
3766 87A
3767 89B
3768 87E
3769 84E
3770 89B
3771 87F
3772 86F
3773 82B
3774 87A
3775 84H
3776 86H
3777 87F
3778 84A
3779 86G
3780 82C
3781 87C
3782 84G
3783 88B
3784 82B
3785 87E
3786 84K
3787 83D
3788 84G
3789 85C
3790 83D
3791 87B
3792 84B
3793 84B
3794 83C
3795 82B
3796 86A
3797 87E
3798 86A
3799 81C

Class 2800
2–8–0

3800 86A
3801 86A
3802 84C
3803 81C
3804 86A
3805 86A
3806 86E
3807 86A
3808 86E
3809 86C
3810 86A
3811 87F
3812 86C
3813 81A
3814 86C
3815 86E
3816 86A
3817 86C
3818 86E
3819 84C
3820 84C
3821 84F
3822 86G
3823 86C
3824 86C
3825 84J
3826 86G
3827 84F
3828 86G
3829 84C
3830 86A
3831 84C
3832 83D
3833 86A
3834 83C
3835 81F
3836 86A
3837 84E
3838 86E
3839 85A
3840 81D
3841 81D
3842 82B
3843 86E
3844 86E
3845 81D
3846 81D
3847 81F
3848 85B
3849 84C
3850 86E
3851 87F
3852 81A
3853 81A
3854 81C
3855 81C
3856 81C
3857 81C
3858 84K
3859 84K
3860 84K
3861 84C
3862 86G
3863 84C
3864 83D
3865 84C
3866 81F

Class 4073
4–6–0

4000* 84A

Class 4000
4–6–0

4003* 87E
4007* 85A
4015* 82C

Class 4073
4–6–0

4016* 81A

Class 4000
4–6–0

4018* 84A
4020* 82A
4021* 81F
4022 82C
4023 87E
4028 82D
4031* 84A

Class 4073
4–6–0

4032* 83D

Class 4000
4–6–0

4033* 82A
4034* 82A
4035* 82A
4036* 82C

Class 4073
4–6–0

4037* 81A

Class 4000
4–6–0

4038* 82D
4039* 87E
4040* 84G
4041* 82A
4042* 82A
4043* 82A
4044* 84G
4045* 82D
4046* 84G
4047* 82A
4048* 87E
4049* 84A
4050* 87E
4051* 85A
4052* 84G
4053* 84A
4054* 83D
4055* 82C
4056* 82A
4057* 82C
4058* 84A
4059* 85B
4060* 84A
4061* 84G
4062* 82C

Class 4073
4–6–0

4073* 82A
4074* 87E
4075* 81A
4076* 84K
4077* 83A
4078* 87E
4079* 85B
4080* 82F
4081* 82C
4082* 85A
4083* 86C
4084* 82A
4085* 81D
4086* 85A
4087* 83D
4088* 83D
4089* 83D
4090* 83G
4091* 82A
4092* 85A
4093* 82A
4094* 86C
4095* 87E
4096* 82A
4097* 83D
4098* 83A
4099* 83A

Class 5100
2–6–2T

4100 85D
4101 84E
4102 84D
4103 84A
4104 84F
4105 84A
4106 84E
4107 84E
4108 84A
4109 83A
4110 84E
4111 84E
4112 84D
4113 83B
4114 85A
4115 84A
4116 84E
4117 83B
4118 84G
4119 86E
4120 6C
4121 86G

4122-4580

4122 6C
4123 6C
4124 6C
4125 6C
4126 6C
4127 6C
4128 6C
4129 6C
4130 86G
4131 86G
4132 87H
4133 83A
4134 87E
4135 86G
4136 83B
4137 86A
4138 86G
4139 85A
4140 85A
4141 85B
4142 82A
4143 82A
4144 86E
4145 86C
4146 84F
4147 84E
4148 86A
4149 84C
4150 84F
4151 82A
4152 82A
4153 85D
4154 84H
4155 82A
4156 86A
4157 84E
4158 86G
4159 84E
4160 88C
4161 88C
4162 88F
4163 88C
4164 87B
4165 84E
4166 84E
4167 83F
4168 86A
4169 87A
4170 84E
4171 84D
4172 84E
4173 84F
4174 85B
4175 85D
4176 83C
4177 88F
4178 87G
4179 83A

Class 4200
2–8–0T

4200 86E
4201 86B
4203 86A
4206 86A
4207 87E
4208 86D
4211 86B
4212 87B
4213 87F
4214 86H
4215 83E
4217 86H
4218 86F
4221 87A
4222 86C
4223 86H
4224 86C
4225 86A
4226 86B
4227 86C
4228 86J
4229 86B
4230 86A
4231 86C
4232 87A
4233 86B
4235 86B
4236 86F
4237 86B
4238 86H
4241 86F
4242 86A
4243 86E
4246 86B
4247 86A
4248 86A
4250 87E
4251 86F
4252 87A
4253 86B
4254 87F
4255 86C
4256 87B
4257 86J
4258 86B
4259 87A
4260 86F
4261 86D
4262 82B
4263 86A
4264 86J
4265 87B
4266 86C
4267 86H
4268 86A
4269 86B
4270 86C
4271 86G
4272 87A
4273 86F
4274 87A
4275 86C
4276 86F
4277 86E
4278 87F
4279 87A
4280 86B
4281 87F
4282 86E
4283 87F
4284 87A
4285 86C
4286 86E
4287 86C
4288 87A
4289 86A
4290 86H
4291 86B
4292 87B
4293 87A
4294 86A
4295 87A
4296 87D
4297 86J
4298 83E
4299 87C

Class 4300
2–6–0

4303 86G
4318 81E
4326 81E
4337 84A
4358 87H
4375 84J
4377 82D
4381 82C

Class 4400
2–6–2T

4400 84H
4401 84H
4403 84H
4404 86F
4405 83A
4406 84H
4407 83D
4408 86F
4409 83D
4410 83C

Class 4500
2–6–2T

4500 83G
4501 89C
4502 82C
4503 83E
4504 83F
4505 83E
4506 87H
4507 82F
4508 82D
4509 83G
4510 82D
4511 81F
4512 89C
4513 81F
4514 86H
4515 87H
4516 83E
4517 83D
4518 83D
4519 87H
4520 82F
4521 82C
4522 86H
4523 83F
4524 83D
4525 83G
4526 83E
4527 82F
4528 83D
4529 83E
4530 89C
4532 83A
4533 86G
4534 85B
4535 82A
4536 82A
4537 83G
4538 82C
4539 82A
4540 83C
4541 86G
4542 83D
4544 82C
4545 83G
4546 85A
4547 83A
4548 83G
4549 89C
4550 82C
4551 82C
4552 83E
4553 87H
4554 83F
4555 89C
4556 87H
4557 86F
4558 81F
4559 83E
4560 89C
4561 83F
4562 82F
4563 82A
4564 85B
4565 83E
4566 83G
4567 85B
4568 83E
4569 83E
4570 83E
4571 89C
4572 82D
4573 82D
4574 83G
4575 89C
4576 87H
4577 82A
4578 85D
4579 87H
4580 82A

4581 89C
4582 83A
4583 83D
4584 85D
4585 82C
4586 85D
4587 83A
4588 83F
4589 83F
4590 82C
4591 83D
4592 82C
4593 86G
4594 85D
4595 82A
4596 85A
4597 86H
4598 83E
4599 85D

Class 5700
0–6–0T

4600 85C
4601 88C
4602 84G
4603 82B
4604 83B
4605 84E
4606 81B
4607 82B
4608 81C
4609 81D
4610 81C
4611 86G
4612 82C
4613 85A
4614 85A
4615 81A
4616 88B
4617 84K
4618 88B
4619 82B
4620 86D
4621 87A
4622 86C
4623 84G
4624 82B
4625 85D
4626 82B
4627 85B
4628 85B
4629 85A
4630 88B
4631 84C
4632 88D
4633 86C
4634 86F
4635 88D
4636 82D
4637 86H
4638 84F
4639 86G
4640 87B
4641 85A
4642 86G
4643 86F
4644 81A
4645 81F
4646 84C
4647 82D
4648 84E
4649 81E
4650 81B
4651 82C
4652 86H
4653 83D
4654 87H
4655 82B
4656 83D
4657 85C
4658 83D
4659 85B
4660 82B
4661 81D
4662 86B
4663 83B
4664 85A
4665 81D
4666 81A
4667 88A
4668 86G
4669 86F
4670 81D
4671 86A
4672 84G
4673 81C
4674 86D
4675 86F
4676 81F
4677 86C
4678 85C
4679 83D
4680 81F
4681 87B
4682 86H
4683 84E
4684 87B
4685 86H
4686 86H
4687 84F
4688 82B
4689 82E
4690 88C
4691 81B
4692 88C
4693 83D
4694 87C
4695 81C
4696 84F
4697 82C
4698 81A
4699 81A

Class 4700
2–8–0

4700 81A
4701 81A
4702 81A
4703 83D
4704 6C
4705 81A
4706 82B
4707 81A
4708 84B

Class 4900
4–6–0

4900* 81A
4901* 86C
4902* 81F
4903* 81F
4904* 84G
4905* 84K
4906* 83F
4907* 82B
4908* 87H
4909* 82B
4910* 87G
4912* 86G
4913* 86C
4914* 82A
4915* 87G
4916* 82B
4917* 81C
4918* 84K
4919* 84G
4920* 81D
4921* 81F
4922* 87G
4923* 81A
4924* 84E
4925* 82C
4926* 82D
4927* 82D
4928* 81F
4929* 85B
4930* 82F
4931* 81D
4932* 86G
4933* 86G
4934* 82B
4935* 81E
4936* 83F
4937* 87G
4938* 81F
4939* 81D
4940* 83E
4941* 86A
4942* 82A
4943* 81D
4944* 81C
4945* 82C
4946* 83G
4947* 83G
4948* 82B
4949* 83B
4950* 83A
4951* 82A
4952* 86C
4953* 86C
4954* 82A
4955* 84B
4956* 82C
4957* 87H
4958* 81A
4959* 84E
4960* 84A
4961* 81A
4962* 81D
4963* 82D
4964* 84E
4965* 83G
4966* 83D
4967* 82B
4968* 83D
4969* 82B
4970* 83B
4971* 83B
4972* 83D
4973* 82C
4974* 86C
4975* 86C
4976* 84K
4977* 85B
4978* 81C
4979* 86C
4980* 84E
4981* 87G
4982* 87H
4983* 82C
4984* 87G
4985* 82A
4986* 82B
4987* 84K
4988* 82F
4989* 81D
4990* 82B
4991* 84B
4992* 83D
4993* 85A
4994* 81D
4995* 81D
4996* 85B
4997* 87H
4998* 81D
4999* 82B

Class 4073
4–6–0

5000* 82A
5001* 86C
5002* 87E
5003* 83B
5004* 81A
5005* 86C
5006* 86C
5007* 86C
5008* 84A
5009* 82C
5010* 84A
5011* 83A
5012* 83D

5013* 87E
5014* 81A
5015* 84A
5016* 87E
5017* 85A
5018* 82A
5019* 82A
5020* 86C
5021* 83D
5022* 84A
5023* 83D
5024* 83A
5025* 82A
5026* 83D
5027* 81A
5028* 83A
5029* 81A
5030* 86C
5031* 84A
5032* 84G
5033* 84K
5034* 83A
5035* 81A
5036* 81D
5037* 82A
5038* 81A
5039* 81A
5040* 81A
5041* 83A
5042* 85B
5043* 81A
5044* 81A
5045* 81A
5046* 86C
5047* 83A
5048* 82A
5049* 86C
5050* 84G
5051* 87E
5052* 86C
5053* 84A
5054* 86C
5055* 81A
5056* 81A
5057* 83D
5058* 83D
5059* 83C
5060* 83D
5061* 84G
5062* 83C
5063* 85A
5064* 84G
5065* 81A
5066* 81A
5067* 82A
5068* 82C
5069* 81A
5070* 84A
5071* 83A
5072* 87E
5073* 84G
5074* 82A
5075* 84K
5076* 82A
5077* 83B
5078* 83A
5079* 83A
5080* 86C
5081* 81A
5082* 82A
5083* 82C
5084* 82C
5085* 81A
5086* 84G
5087* 81A
5088* 84A
5089* 86C
5090* 83D
5091* 82C
5092* 85A
5093* 87E
5094* 82A
5095* 83D
5096* 82A
5097* 84G
5098* 83D
5099* 86C

Class 5100
2–6–2T

5101 84F
5102 84E
5103 84K
5104 84D
5105 84F
5106 84E
5107 84F
5108 83A
5109 84H
5110 85D
5112 85B
5113 83A
5114 85B
5122 84F
5125 84H
5129 84K
5132 83A
5134 84F
5136 84F
5137 84H
5138 84H
5139 84H
5140 83A
5141 84K
5142 83A
5143 84A
5144 84D
5147 84F
5148 83D
5150 83A
5151 84A
5152 84E
5153 83A
5154 84G
5155 84F
5156 84E
5157 83A
5158 83A
5159 88F
5160 84F
5161 84D
5162 87E
5163 84D
5164 84E
5165 84F
5166 84E
5167 84F
5168 84G
5169 82A
5170 84F
5171 84E
5172 83B
5173 85A
5174 84K
5175 84E
5176 6C
5177 84E
5178 84H
5179 84K
5180 84F
5181 84K
5182 84E
5183 88C
5184 84K
5185 84D
5186 84K
5187 84E
5188 84E
5189 84F
5190 84E
5191 84F
5192 84D
5193 84F
5194 84D
5195 88C
5196 84F
5197 84F
5198 84E
5199 84F

Class 4200
2–8–0T

5200 86B
5201 86A
5202 86F
5203 87F
5204 87F
5205 86E
5206 86A
5207 86H
5208 86A
5209 87F
5210 87D
5211 87E
5212 86A
5213 87F
5214 86E
5215 87F
5216 87B
5217 86A
5218 86A
5219 87E
5220 87B
5221 87D
5222 86A
5223 87F
5224 86A
5225 87A
5226 86C
5227 87D
5228 86E
5229 86A
5230 87F
5231 86B
5232 87D
5233 86A
5234 86A
5235 86B
5236 86H
5237 86J
5238 86A
5239 87A
5240 87F
5241 86D
5242 87A
5243 86A
5244 86B
5245 86J
5246 87D
5247 87F
5248 87F
5249 86C
5250 86B
5251 86A
5252 86B
5253 86E
5254 87A
5255 86A
5256 86A
5257 87B
5258 86J
5259 86A
5260 86B
5261 87F
5262 86E
5263 86J
5264 86A

Class 4300
2–6–0

5300 84F
5303 85A
5305 82F
5306 82D
5307 86C
5309 84B
5310 87H
5311 82A
5312 85B
5313 84B
5314 82F
5315 84J
5316 6C

5317 84C
5318 83D
5319 84J
5321 83C
5322 82C
5323 81F
5324 84C
5325 82A
5326 82D
5327 82A
5328 82F
5330 81E
5331 84K
5332 84C
5333 84E
5334 84J
5335 87F
5336 85B
5337 82F
5338 82F
5339 87G
5341 87E
5344 84K
5345 85B
5346 84E
5347 85B
5348 85C
5350 83A
5351 82B
5353 87H
5355 86G
5356 81C
5357 87H
5358 82B
5359 82F
5360 81C
5361 84C
5362 86E
5364 86A
5365 84J
5367 82C
5368 87H
5369 84E
5370 84E
5371 82C
5372 87H
5375 81D
5376 83D
5377 85C
5378 87F
5379 84B
5380 81E
5381 81E
5382 86C
5384 82F
5385 82D
5386 84B
5388 86C
5390 84B
5391 83A
5392 87H
5393 6C
5394 85B
5395 87J
5396 82C
5397 81E
5398 85B
5399 84K

Class 5400 0–6–0T

5400 87E
5401 81C
5402 82D
5403 82D
5404 84C
5405 81C
5406 82D
5407 84C
5408 87E
5409 81B
5410 81C
5411 88A
5412 83B
5413 81F
5414 81C
5415 81C
5416 81C
5417 84C
5418 81C
5419 82D
5420 81C
5421 88E
5422 82D
5423 82D
5424 84C

Class 4500 2–6–2T

5500 83F
5501 83B
5502 83E
5503 83B
5504 83B
5505 83A
5506 82A
5507 89C
5508 82D
5509 82D
5510 82C
5511 82A
5512 82A
5513 87H
5514 82A
5515 83F
5516 86G
5517 89C
5518 85B
5519 83E
5520 86H
5521 83B
5522 83B
5523 82A
5524 89C
5525 83C
5526 83F
5527 82A
5528 82A
5529 82E
5530 85B
5531 83E
5532 86G
5533 83B
5534 82C
5535 82A
5536 82A
5537 83F
5538 85B
5539 82A
5540 83D
5541 89C
5542 83B
5543 83B
5544 83A
5545 86A
5546 82A
5547 82A
5548 82A
5549 87H
5550 86A
5551 83A
5552 83A
5553 82A
5554 82D
5555 82A
5556 86F
5557 83A
5558 82A
5559 82A
5560 89C
5561 82A
5562 83F
5563 82C
5564 82A
5565 82E
5566 82C
5567 83D
5568 87H
5569 83D
5570 89C
5571 83B
5572 82A
5573 85A
5574 85B

Class 5600 0-6-2T

5600 88F
5601 88A
5602 86A
5603 88D
5604 87E
5605 88D
5606 84B
5607 88F
5608 88F
5609 88C
5610 88F
5611 88F
5612 87B
5613 88F
5614 88C
5615 88F
5616 87D
5617 88D
5618 88E
5619 88E
5620 86E
5621 88C
5622 88D
5623 88A
5624 84B
5625 86E
5626 86E
5627 88C
5628 87D
5629 87B
5630 88E
5631 87E
5632 88C
5633 86F
5634 84D
5635 88D
5636 88A
5637 88E
5638 86B
5639 87B
5640 88A
5641 88E
5642 84G
5643 88E
5644 88E
5645 86E
5646 87B
5647 84K
5648 88C
5649 86J
5650 88E
5651 84F
5652 88D
5653 88D
5654 88D
5655 88D
5656 87E
5657 84B
5658 84F
5659 88D
5660 88D
5661 87H
5662 88D
5663 88F
5664 88C
5665 88C
5666 88D
5667 88C
5668 88F
5669 88A
5670 88A
5671 88D
5672 88A
5673 84G
5674 88D
5675 87F

5676-5999

5676 88F
5677 88D
5678 88A
5679 86C
5680 88F
5681 88A
5682 88E
5683 88D
5684 84B
5685 86C
5686 88E
5687 88A
5688 88F
5689 82D
5690 84K
5691 88F
5692 88D
5693 88F
5694 88D
5695 88F
5696 88D
5697 88A
5698 88D
5699 88C

Class 5700 0-6-0T

5700 84E
5701 84A
5702 87F
5703 87A
5704 87D
5705 87F
5706 86E
5707 86F
5708 86D
5709 86A
5710 88B
5711 88D
5712 84E
5713 87B
5714 86B
5715 81B
5716 87J
5717 81B
5718 82D
5719 84F
5720 87A
5721 88D
5722 87F
5723 84K
5724 84C
5725 84K
5726 84F
5727 81C
5728 86G
5729 86E
5730 87C
5731 87B
5732 86A
5733 86H
5734 87B
5735 81E
5736 84E
5737 81B
5738 84E
5739 84A
5740 86B
5741 86A
5742 84J
5743 87D
5744 81E
5745 84E
5746 87A
5747 86B
5748 84B
5749 86C
5750 86B
5751 81C
5752 81E
5753 81C
5754 84F
5755 81C
5756 86F
5757 82D
5758 84H
5759 87E
5760 83C
5761 87B
5762 81D
5763 81D
5764 81A
5765 85C
5766 81D
5767 82E
5768 86G
5769 88D
5770 86J
5771 82D
5772 81D
5773 87B
5774 84J
5775 87C
5776 86C
5777 86H
5778 87A
5779 83F
5780 84A
5781 82D
5782 87F
5783 81B
5784 82B
5785 82D
5786 86C
5787 86J
5788 86D
5789 86H
5790 84E
5791 84K
5792 86G
5793 88D
5794 84F
5795 84F
5796 86J
5797 86F
5798 83A
5799 81C

Class 1400 0-4-2T

5800 82C
5801 89B
5802 82C
5803 89A
5804 82C
5805 82C
5806 89A
5807 85C
5808 85C
5809 82A
5810 84J
5811 84J
5812 89A
5813 82A
5814 85C
5815 85A
5816 85A
5817 85C
5818 86G
5819 87G

Class 4900 4-6-0

5900* 82D
5901* 81D
5902* 83C
5903* 81E
5904* 81F
5905* 87J
5906* 86A
5907* 84E
5908* 87J
5909* 84E
5910* 86C
5911* 86A
5912* 84K
5913* 87E
5914* 85A
5915* 83G
5916* 84E
5917* 85A
5918* 81A
5919* 82B
5920* 83A
5921* 84B
5922* 82C
5923* 84K
5924* 82D
5925* 82D
5926* 83E
5927* 84E
5928* 87J
5929* 87E
5930* 84C
5931* 81A
5932* 81A
5933* 81D
5934* 82C
5935* 81E
5936* 81A
5937* 81A
5938* 81A
5939* 81A
5940* 81A
5941* 81A
5942* 84A
5943* 82C
5944* 84A
5945* 84B
5946* 86C
5947* 81A
5948* 81D
5949* 82B
5950* 84E
5951* 85B
5952* 81A
5953* 86C
5954* 84D
5955* 87F
5956* 81D
5957* 81D
5958* 86C
5959* 81D
5960* 81F
5961* 82D
5962* 81A
5963* 87G
5964* 83D
5965* 81F
5966* 84K
5967* 84C
5968* 82F
5969* 83G
5970* 86C
5971* 82D
5972* 87G
5973* 81D
5974* 82D
5975* 86G
5976* 83C
5977* 86C
5978* 82F
5979* 81D
5980* 85B
5981* 84G
5982* 82B
5983* 81C
5984* 87G
5985* 82D
5986* 81A
5987* 81A
5988* 85B
5989* 81C
5990* 85B
5991* 84B
5992* 82B
5993* 84E
5994* 84G
5995* 84A
5996* 81A
5997* 84E
5998* 83D
5999* 83B

Class 6000
4–6–0

6000*	82A
6001*	81A
6002*	81A
6003*	81A
6004*	84A
6005*	84A
6006*	84A
6007*	81A
6008*	84A
6009*	81A
6010*	83D
6011*	84A
6012*	83D
6013*	81A
6014*	81A
6015*	81A
6016*	83D
6017*	81A
6018*	81A
6019*	81A
6020*	84A
6021*	81A
6022*	83D
6023*	83D
6024*	83D
6025*	83D
6026*	83D
6027*	83D
6028*	81A
6029*	83D

Class 6100
2–6–2T

6100	81D
6101	81D
6102	81C
6103	81D
6104	81B
6105	81D
6106	81B
6107	81B
6108	81B
6109	81F
6110	81C
6111	81F
6112	81E
6113	81B
6114	81B
6115	81B
6116	81B
6117	81A
6118	81E
6119	81B
6120	81A
6121	81A
6122	81F
6123	81B
6124	81B
6125	81C
6126	81C
6127	81B
6128	81C
6129	34E
6130	81D
6131	81B
6132	81E
6133	81B
6134	81E
6135	81A
6136	81B
6137	81A
6138	81F
6139	81C
6140	81B
6141	81A
6142	81A
6143	81B
6144	81A
6145	81D
6146	81B
6147	81C
6148	81C
6149	81A
6150	81B
6151	81B
6152	81B
6153	81D
6154	81B
6155	81A
6156	81C
6157	81B
6158	81A
6159	81A
6160	81B
6161	81B
6162	81D
6163	81D
6164	81B
6165	81C
6166	34E
6167	81E
6168	81A
6169	81C

Class 4300
2–6–0

6300	81F
6301	83C
6302	81D
6303	84J
6304	87G
6305	83B
6306	85A
6307	84G
6308	84K
6309	85B
6310	87G
6311	84J
6312	81D
6313	81F
6314	82D
6316	84J
6317	83B
6318	83G
6319	83D
6320	82C
6321	84A
6322	82C
6323	83B
6324	85A
6325	81C
6326	85C
6327	84J
6328	83B
6329	81E
6330	83E
6331	87G
6332	84F
6333	86G
6334	81D
6335	84B
6336	84E
6337	84K
6338	84G
6339	84K
6340	81E
6341	85B
6342	84C
6343	83B
6344	87G
6345	83A
6346	6C
6347	87H
6348	84G
6349	85C
6350	6C
6351	82A
6352	85C
6353	86C
6354	83G
6355	87H
6356	83E
6357	82C
6358	82C
6359	81E
6360	82C
6261	84B
6362	84B
6363	81D
6364	83B
6365	82D
6366	81D
6367	87G
6368	82D
6369	82D
6370	86G
6371	87H
6372	83B
6373	83F
6374	82C
6375	82D
6376	6C
6377	83B
6378	85A
6379	81D
6380	84K
6381	85B
6382	85D
6383	81D
6384	82C
6385	85B
6386	86E
6387	82C
6388	81C
6389	87H
6390	84C
6391	84A
6392	84K
6393	81D
6394	83B
6395	85C
6396	85A
6397	83C
6398	83B
6399	82D

Class 6400
0–6–0T

6400	86G
6401	88E
6402	88A
6403	86G
6404	84J
6405	84J
6406	83D
6407	83D
6408	88D
6409	86A
6410	86J
6411	88E
6412	87E
6413	86J
6414	83D
6415	86A
6416	88A
6417	83D
6418	84C
6419	83D
6420	83D
6421	83D
6422	84J
6423	88A
6424	86G
6425	87E
6426	86A
6427	88D
6428	86A
6429	86G
6430	86G
6431	87E
6432	86G
6433	88A
6434	88D
6435	88A
6436	88A
6437	86J
6438	88E
6439	86A

6600-6874

Class 5600
0–6–2T

No.	Shed
6600	84B
6601	82B
6602	87H
6603	88A
6604	87E
6605	86J
6606	84G
6607	88A
6608	88A
6609	84B
6610	84B
6611	84E
6612	88A
6613	87D
6614	88C
6615	88C
6616	87B
6617	84F
6618	88A
6619	88C
6620	88C
6621	86F
6622	86J
6623	87B
6624	84K
6625	84D
6626	88A
6627	88A
6628	86J
6629	87B
6630	84E
6631	85B
6632	84D
6633	84G
6634	88A
6635	88A
6636	86G
6637	88C
6638	84B
6639	86E
6640	84B
6641	88C
6642	86F
6643	88C
6644	87B
6645	84B
6646	84F
6647	88A
6648	88F
6649	86F
6650	87B
6651	86J
6652	86J
6653	88C
6654	86A
6655	88F
6656	82B
6657	84D
6658	88C
6659	88A
6660	88A
6661	88E
6662	87D
6663	86G
6664	88A
6665	88A
6666	86E
6667	84F
6668	88C
6669	88C
6670	82B
6671	82B
6672	86A
6673	86E
6674	84F
6675	86F
6676	86E
6677	84F
6678	84F
6679	87E
6680	87E
6681	85C
6682	88A
6683	84G
6684	88A
6685	86H
6686	87B
6687	86G
6688	87F
6689	86E
6690	82D
6691	87B
6692	86J
6693	86J
6694	84J
6695	87E
6696	84C
6697	84D
6698	84J
6699	82D

Class 5700†
0–6–0T

No.	Shed
6700	88B
6701	88B
6702	88B
6703	88B
6704	88B
6705	88B
6706	88B
6707	88B
6708	88B
6709	88B
6710	86B
6711	86B
6712	88C
6713	87C
6714	87D
6715	87B
6716	82C
6717	87B
6718	87B
6719	87B
6720	87B
6721	88B
6722	88C
6723	88C
6724	88C
6725	86B
6726	86B
6727	86B
6728	86B
6729	86B
6730	86B
6731	86B
6732	86B
6733	88C
6734	87C
6735	86B
6736	88C
6737	82C
6738	88C
6739	82C
6740	88C
6741	82C
6742	86G
6743	86B
6744	88B
6745	88C
6746	88C
6747	88C
6748	88C
6749	87B
6750	88C
6751	88B
6752	88C
6753	88C
6754	88C
6755	86B
6756	86B
6757	86B
6758	88C
6759	86B
6760	86B
6761	87B
6762	87C
6763	87C
6764	86B
6765	88B
6766	87C
6767	88B
6768	87B
6769	88C

Class 6800
4–6–0

No.	Shed
6800*	83G
6801*	83G
6802*	81D
6803*	84C
6804*	82D
6805*	82B
6806*	83G
6807*	85A
6808*	83G
6809*	83G
6810*	87F
6811*	82B
6812*	84A
6813*	83A
6814*	83A
6815*	83B
6816*	84C
6817*	83G
6818*	87G
6819*	84C
6820*	86A
6821*	86A
6822*	83A
6823*	87J
6824*	87F
6825*	83G
6826*	83G
6827*	82B
6828*	84F
6829*	83A
6830*	82B
6831*	6C
6832*	82B
6833*	84D
6834*	86A
6835*	84C
6836*	82B
6837*	82B
6838*	83G
6839*	84C
6840*	82B
6841*	6C
6842*	82B
6843*	84E
6844*	6C
6845*	82D
6846*	82B
6847*	84E
6848*	84A
6849*	82B
6850*	82B
6851*	85A
6852*	82B
6853*	84E
6854*	84C
6855*	83D
6856*	84B
6857*	84F
6858*	84E
6859*	6C
6860*	6C
6861*	82B
6862*	84B
6863*	82B
6864*	81D
6865*	81D
6866*	84E
6867*	82B
6868*	83B
6869*	83G
6870*	86A
6871*	86E
6872*	83F
6873*	83D
6874*	86A

† See also page 21

6875* 83B
6876* 82B
6877* 85A
6878* 6C
6879* 84B

Class 4900
4-6-0

6900* 81A
6901* 84A
6902* 82F
6903* 87E
6904* 84E
6905* 85C
6906* 84C
6907* 83D
6908* 82C
6909* 82B
6910* 81A
6911* 83G
6912* 82F
6913* 83D
6914* 82B
6915* 82C
6916* 85C
6917* 85B
6918* 87E
6919* 87G
6920* 84B
6921* 85B
6922* 82B
6923* 81E
6924* 84A
6925* 81F
6926* 81A
6927* 86A
6928* 86C
6929* 84C
6930* 85A
6931* 83F
6932* 81A
6933* 81F
6934* 83A
6935* 82D
6936* 85C
6937* 81F
6938* 85A
6939* 86C
6940* 85B
6941* 84K
6942* 84E
6943* 86C
6944* 81A
6945* 82F
6946* 86C
6947* 85A
6948* 86C
6949* 83D
6950* 85A
6951* 85C
6952* 81E
6953* 81A
6954* 82A
6955* 82D
6956* 84B
6957* 82B
6958* 82A

Class 6959
4-6-0

6959* 81A
6960* 81A
6961* 81C
6962* 81A
6963* 84G
6964* 84A
6965* 82A
6966* 82D
6967* 84B
6968* 81D
6969* 86C
6970* 81F
6971* 84E
6972* 82A
6973* 81A
6974* 81A
6975* 84B
6976* 84G
6977* 82A
6978* 82D
6979* 84C
6980* 84G
6981* 82A
6982* 82D
6983* 81A
6984* 85C
6985* 81A
6986* 82B
6987* 85B
6988* 82F
6989* 85C
6990* 81A
6991* 82D
6992* 85B
6993* 82F
6994* 83C
6995* 83B
6996* 81D
6997* 82A
6998* 86C
6999* 86C

Class 4073
4-6-0

7000* 83A
7001* 81A
7002* 87E
7003* 87E
7004* 81A
7005* 85A
7006* 85B
7007* 85A
7008* 81F
7009* 87E
7010* 81F
7011* 82A
7012* 87E
7013* 81A
7014* 82A
7015* 82C
7016* 86C
7017* 86C
7018* 87E
7019* 82A
7020* 86C
7021* 87G
7022* 86C
7023* 86C
7024* 81A
7025* 81A
7026* 84A
7027* 83D
7028* 87E
7029* 83A
7030* 81A
7031* 83D
7032* 81A
7033* 81A
7034* 82A
7035* 84G
7036*
7037*

Class 7200
2-8-2T

7200 83A
7201 86C
7202 88A
7203 86A
7204 87F
7205 88A
7206 86G
7207 84B
7208 84D
7209 83A
7210 86E
7211 87E
7212 86E
7213 86J
7214 86A
7215 86A
7216 86E
7217 86A
7218 84D
7219 86C
7220 83A
7221 86J
7222 85A
7223 86E
7224 86E
7225 87E
7226 84B
7227 84B
7228 87F
7229 86E
7230 86E
7231 86A
7232 86E
7233 86G
7234 86G
7235 86G
7236 85A
7237 84D
7238 84B
7239 86E
7240 85A
7241 86A
7242 86J
7243 84B
7244 87E
7245 86A
7246 86E
7247 86A
7248 85A
7249 86A
7250 83A
7251 86E
7252 86A
7253 86A

Class 4300
2-6-0

7300 82D
7301 85A
7302 82D
7303 85B
7304 83B
7305 84J
7306 87H
7307 85C
7308 85C
7309 82D
7310 84J
7311 84B
7312 85B
7313 84J
7314 85C
7315 84A
7316 83C
7317 84E
7318 81D
7319 84G
7320 81D
7321 82C

Class 7400
0-6-0T

7400 87G
7401 87G
7402 84F
7403 84J
7404 81F
7405 89A
7406 89C
7407 87G
7408 82F
7409 84J
7410 89A
7411 81F
7412 81F

7413 87H
7414 84J
7415 82C
7416 85C
7417 89C
7418 82C
7419 87G
7420 85C
7421 83B
7422 83F
7423 86J
7424 82C
7425 87G
7426 86G
7427 83A
7428 84F
7429 84F
7430 84F
7431 84J
7432 84F
7433 84J
7434 89A
7435 84F
7436 81F
7437 85A
7438 84E
7439 87K
7440 84J
7441 81B
7442 81B
7443 84J
7444 87G
7445 88A
7446 83E
7447 84J
7448 84F
7449 84F

Class 5700
0-6-0T

7700 85D
7701 87A
7702 84D
7703 86H
7704 87D
7705 84F
7706 87B
7707 85C
7708 81D
7709 83E
7710 81E
7711 82B
7712 86B
7713 84E
7714 6C
7715 83E
7716 83C
7717 88D
7718 82B
7719 82B
7720 86J
7721 86H
7722 88A
7723 85B
7724 86G
7725 86F
7726 82B
7727 82D
7728 82B
7729 82B
7730 81C
7731 81C
7732 81C
7733 87B
7734 81A
7735 84E
7736 86A
7737 87A
7738 88A
7739 87A
7740 86G
7741 85B
7742 87A
7743 87A
7744 87B
7745 87F
7746 86F
7747 87J
7748 86J
7749 82B
7750 85A
7751 88B
7752 86F
7753 86A
7754 84H
7755 87F
7756 87D
7757 87A
7758 84E
7759 84B
7760 81F
7761 83C
7762 83D
7763 84C
7764 86E
7765 87F
7766 88D
7767 87A
7768 86A
7769 87A
7770 86F
7771 86A
7772 88D
7773 86J
7774 86B
7775 86H
7776 87F
7777 81D
7778 86H
7779 82B
7780 82B
7781 86A
7782 82B
7783 82B
7784 82D
7785 87F
7786 87A
7787 87E
7788 81D
7789 86B
7790 82B
7791 81A
7792 82C
7793 82B
7794 82C
7795 82B
7796 84B
7797 84B
7798 86F
7799 87A

Class 7800
4-6-0

7800* 84E
7301* 83D
7802* 89C
7803* 89C
7804* 83D
7805* 84C
7806* 84C
7807* 89A
7808* 89A
7809* 83D
7810* 84D
7811* 84C
7812* 83A
7813* 83A
7814* 83D
7815* 85B
7816* 87H
7817* 84J
7818* 85B
7819* 89A
7820*
7821*
7822*
7823*
7824*
7825*
7826*
7827*
7828*
7829*

Class 6959
4-6-0

7900* 82B
7901* 82A
7902* 81A
7903* 81A
7904* 81A
7905* 83D
7906* 82B
7907* 82B
7908* 82B
7909* 83D
7910* 81C
7911* 81A
7912* 84E
7913* 84E
7914* 82C
7915* 84A
7916* 82C
7917* 82A
7918* 84E
7919* 81D
7920*
7921*
7922*
7923*
7924*
7925*
7926*
7927*
7928*
7929*

Class 8100
2–6–2T

8100 84D
8101 85D
8102 87H
8103 89A
8104 87A
8105 82B
8106 85A
8107 87H
8108 84E
8109 84D

Class 9400†
0–6–0T

8400 84C
8401 86C
8402 86H
8403 83A
8404 83D
8405 84C
8406 86A
8407 84C
8408 87C
8409 83G
8410 84E
8411 84A
8412 83F
8413 82B
8414 88B
8415 84E
8416 88B
8417 84B
8418 84F
8419 84F
8420 87A
8421 83C
8422
8423
8424
8425
8426
8427
8428

† See also page 21

No.	Shed
8429	
8430	
8431	
8432	
8433	
8434	
8435	
8436	
8437	
8438	
8439	
8440	
8441	
8442	
8443	
8444	
8445	
8446	
8447	
8448	
8449	
8450	86A
8451	88C
8452	84E
8453	86A
8454	84D
8455	88B
8456	83C
8457	88B
8458	88C
8459	84C
8460	88C
8461	88C
8462	84A
8463	
8464	
8465	
8466	
8467	
8468	
8469	
8470	
8471	
8472	
8473	
8474	
8475	
8476	
8477	
8478	
8479	
8480	
8481	
8482	
8483	
8484	
8485	
8486	
8487	
8488	
8489	
8490	
8491	
8492	
8493	
8494	
8495	
8496	
8497	
8498	
8499	

Class 5700
0–6–0T

No.	Shed
8700	84E
8701	85B
8702	82B
8703	82B
8704	84F
8705	84A
8706	87F
8707	81A
8708	87F
8709	83D
8710	86A
8711	86A
8712	86F
8713	82B
8714	82B
8715	87A
8716	86G
8717	85B
8718	85D
8719	83D
8720	87C
8721	86F
8722	82B
8723	86C
8724	86H
8725	6C
8726	84A
8727	85D
8728	86C
8729	84C
8730	82B
8731	85B
8732	87F
8733	82C
8734	84A
8735	88C
8736	88D
8737	82B
8738	87F
8739	86D
8740	86F
8741	82B
8742	84F
8743	88B
8744	82D
8745	82E
8746	82B
8747	82B
8748	86F
8749	87F
8750	81A
8751	81A
8752	81C
8753	81A
8754	81A
8755	86G
8756	81A
8757	81A
8758	81C
8759	81A
8760	81A
8761	81A
8762	81A
8763	81A
8764	81A
8765	81A
8766	82B
8767	81A
8768	81A
8769	81A
8770	81A
8771	81A
8772	81A
8773	81A
8774	81C
8775	87A
8776	86H
8777	86F
8778	86A
8779	82C
8780	88A
8781	85B
8782	87A
8783	83E
8784	84E
8785	87F
8786	86J
8787	84C
8788	86G
8789	87E
8790	82B
8791	84F
8792	84F
8793	82C
8794	86H
8795	82B
8796	86B
8797	84F
8798	84B
8799	86E

Class 9000
4–4–0

No.	Shed
9000	89C
9001	89A
9002	89C
9003	89A
9004	89C
9005	89C
9008	84E
9009	89C
9010	84E
9011	82C
9012	89C
9013	89C
9014	89C
9015	81E
9016	89A
9017	89C
9018	82C
9020	89A
9021	89C
9022	89A
9023	82C
9024	89C
9025	89C
9026	89A
9027	89C
9028	89A

Class 3252
4–4–0

No.	Shed
9083*	82C
9084*	89A
9089	82C

Class 4300
2–6–0

No.	Shed
9300	81C
9301	81C
9302	81A
9303	81D
9304	81A
9305	81A
9306	81A
9307	81D
9308	81A
9309	81A
9310	81C
9311	81C
9312	84B
9313	81D
9314	84B
9315	81A
9316	81F
9317	81F
9318	81D
9319	81D

Class 9400†
0–6–0T

No.	Shed
9400	82C
9401	81A
9402	81A
9403	81A
9404	81A
9405	81A
9406	81A
9407	81C
9408	84B
9409	81C
9410	81D
9411	81D
9412	81D
9413	81E
9414	81B
9415	81B
9416	81F

† See also page 21

9417	81E
9418	81A
9419	81A
9420	81D
9421	81B
9422	81A
9423	81D
9424	81B
9425	
9426	
9427	
9428	
9429	
9430	
9431	
9432	
9433	
9434	
9435	
9436	
9437	
9438	
9439	
9440	
9441	
9442	
9443	
9444	
9445	
9446	
9447	
9448	
9449	
9450	
9451	
9452	
9453	
9454	
9455	
9456	
9457	
9458	
9459	
9460	
9461	
9462	
9463	
9464	
9465	
9466	
9467	
9468	
9469	
9470	
9471	
9472	
9473	
9474	
9475	
9476	
9477	
9478	
9479	
9480	
9481	
9482	
9483	
9484	
9485	
9486	
9487	
9488	
9489	
9490	
9491	
9492	
9493	
9494	
9495	
9496	
9497	
9498	
9499	

Class 5700
0–6–0T

9600	82C
9601	82E
9602	87J
9603	87J
9604	82B
9605	82B
9606	82B
9607	86J
9608	84E
9609	86J
9610	84E
9611	81F
9612	82D
9613	84F
9614	84E
9615	82D
9616	86A
9617	87B
9618	88D
9619	85C
9620	82B
9621	84A
9622	88D
9623	83A
9624	84H
9625	87D
9626	82B
9627	87A
9628	82D
9629	86C
9630	84H
9631	88C
9632	86A
9633	83A
9634	87B
9635	84E
9636	84F
9637	86A
9638	88D
9639	84H
9640	81B
9641	81C
9642	82F
9643	88D
9644	86A
9645	87D
9646	83B
9647	83C
9648	86C
9649	86F
9650	86G
9651	6C
9652	87H
9653	81B
9654	81F
9655	83E
9656	84G
9657	84G
9658	81A
9659	81A
9660	86F
9661	81A
9662	86A
9663	83B
9664	86A
9665	82B
9666	87A
9667	86A
9668	83A
9669	84J
9670	83B
9671	83D
9672	84G
9673	83D
9674	86F
9675	88D
9676	88C
9677	88B
9678	6C
9679	88B
9680	84E
9681	86F
9682	84E
9700	81A
9701	81A
9702	81A
9703	81A
9704	81A
9705	81A
9706	81A
9707	81A
9708	81A
9709	81A
9710	81A
9711	83D
9712	86J
9713	86C
9714	84B
9715	84B
9716	83D
9717	83G
9718	83B
9719	84G
9720	82C
9721	82C
9722	81D
9723	86C
9724	84E
9725	81A
9726	81C
9727	85B
9728	84K
9729	82B
9730	84B
9731	86A
9732	82E
9733	84E
9734	87A
9735	87B
9736	87B
9737	87B
9738	87E
9739	84B
9740	84D
9741	84F
9742	84B
9743	87F
9744	87D
9745	86E
9746	86D
9747	84B
9748	84E
9749	81D
9750	87A
9751	81A
9752	84B
9753	84E
9754	81A
9755	83E
9756	87A
9757	83B
9758	81A
9759	86C
9760	87J
9761	87E
9762	82D
9763	81D
9764	82B
9765	83D
9766	87B
9767	84F
9768	84B
9769	84B
9770	83D
9771	82E
9772	82C
9773	82C
9774	84K
9775	87E
9776	88C
9777	87E
9778	83A
9779	87A
9780	86D
9781	81B
9782	84C
9783	87A
9784	81A
9785	87B

9786	87A
9787	87F
9788	87F
9789	81B
9790	82C
9791	81D
9792	87A
9793	84E
9794	84K
9795	82C
9796	86H
9797	86G
9798	84E
9799	87B

Diesel Railcars

1	81D
2	87E
3	86A
4	87E
5	85A
6	85A
7	85A
8	84F
10	81F
11	87E
12	87E
13	87E
14	84F
15	87G
16	87G
17	81C
18	86D
19	81D
20	82F
21	82B
22	81D
23	86A
24	82B
25	85B
26	84D
27	85A
28	85B
29	84D
30	86G
31	85A
32	85A
33	84F
34	81C
35	82B
36	82B
37	81D
38	81D

LOCOMOTIVES ON ORDER

Class 1500
0-6-0T

1510
1511
1512
1513
1514
1515
1516
1517
1518
1519
1520
1521
1522
1523
1524
1525
1526
1527
1528
1529

Class 1600
0-6-0T

1630
1631
1632
1633
1634
1635
1636
1637
1638
1639
1640
1641
1642
1643
1644
1645
1646
1647
1648
1649

Class 5700
0-6-0T

6770
6771
6772
6773
6774
6775
6776
6777
6778
6779

Class 9400
0-6-0T

3400
3401
3402
3403
3404
3405
3406
3407
3408
3409

BRITISH RALWAYS
INTERNAL COMBUSTION LOCOMOTIVES
Nos. 10000-18000

WITH SHED ALLOCATIONS

No.	Class	Shed

Diesel Electric
0–6–6–0
London Midland

10000 1A
10001 1A

Diesel Mech.
4–8–4
London Midland

10100

Diesel Electric
2–6–6–2
Southern

10201
10202
10203

Diesel Electric
0–4–4–0
London Midland

10800 4A

Diesel Mech.
0–6–0
Southern

11001 75C

Diesel Electric
0–6–0
London Midland

12000 5B
12001 5B
12002 5B
12003 8C
12004 1A
12005 1A
12006 18A
12007 8C
12008 8C
12009 1A
12010 1A
12011 8C
12012 8C
12013 8C
12014 8C
12015 8C
12016 8C
12017 8C
12018 5B
12019 1A
12020 8C
12021 1A
12022 1A
12023 1A
12024 12A
12025 12A
12026 12A
12027 12A
12028 12A
12029 1A
12030 1A
12031 1A
12032 1A
12033 5B
12034 5B
12035 5B
12036 5B
12037 5B
12038 18A
12039 21A
12040 21A
12041 21A
12042 21A
12043 21A
12044 21A
12045 18A
12046 18A
12047 18A
12048 18A
12049 5B
12050 5B
12051 5B
12052 5B
12053 5B
12054 5B
12055 5B
12056 18A
12057 18A
12058 1A
12059 21A
12060 21A
12061 21A
12062 21A
12063 14A
12064 14A
12065 14A
12066 14A
12067 14A
12068 14A
12069 18A
12070 18A
12071
12072
12073
12074
12075
12076
12077
12078
12079
12080
12081
12082

Diesel Electric
0–6–0
Eastern

15000 31B
15001 31B
15002 31B
15003 31B
15004 31B

Petrol Electric
0–4–0
Eastern

15097 51C
15098 30A
15099 30A

Diesel Electric
0–6–0
Western

15100 82B
15101 81A
15102 81A
15103 81A
15104 81A
15105 81A
15106 81A
15107 82B

Diesel Electric
0–6–0
Southern

15201 75C
15202 75C
15203 75C
15211 75C
15212 75C
15213 75C
15214 75C
15215 75C
15216 75C
15217 75C
15218 73C
15219 73C
15220 73C
15221 73C
15222 73C
15223 73C
15224 73C
15225 73C

Gas Turbine
A–I–A–A–I–A
Western

18000 81A

BRITISH RAILWAYS ELECTRIC LOCOMOTIVES

Nos. 20001-26510

WITH SHED ALLOCATIONS

No.	Class	Shed
Class CC		
Co-Co		
Southern		
20001		Durnsford Rd.
20002		Durnsford Rd-
20003		Durnsford Rd.
Class EM1		
Bo—Bo		
Eastern		
26000†		
26001		
26002		
26003		
26004		
26005		
26006		
26007		
26008		
26009		
26010		
26011		
26012		
26013		
26014		
26015		
26016		
26017		
26018		
26019		
26020		
26021		
26022		
26023		
26024		
26025		
26026		
26027		
26028		
26029		
26030		
26031		
26032		
26033		
26034		
26035		
26036		
26037		
26038		
26039		
26040		
26041		
26042		
26043		
26044		
26045		
26046		
26047		
26048		
26049		
26050		
26051		
26052		
26053		
26054		
26055		
26056		
26057		
Class ES1		
Bo—Bo		
North Eastern		
26500		52B
26501		52B
Class EB1		
Bo—Bo		
Eastern		
26510		30A

†On loan to Netherlands Rlys.

BRITISH RAILWAYS LOCOMOTIVES

Nos. 30007-36005

WITH SHED ALLOCATIONS

No.	Class	Shed	No.	Class	Shed	No.	Class	Shed	No.	Class	Shed
30007	T1	72D	30032	M7	71A	30045	M7	71D	30058	M7	72C
30020	T1	71D	30033	M7	71A	30046	M7	72A	30059	M7	71B
30021	M7	70C	30034	M7	72A	30047	M7	75D	30060	M7	70C
30022	M7	70C	30035	M7	72D	30048	M7	71A	30061	U.S.A.	71I
30023	M7	72B	30036	M7	72E	30049	M7	72A	30062	U.S.A.	71I
30024	M7	72A	30037	M7	72D	30050	M7	71D	30063	U.S.A.	71I
30025	M7	72A	30038	M7	70A	30051	M7	71B	30064	U.S.A.	71I
30026	M7	70C	30039	M7	72A	30052	M7	71B	30065	U.S.A.	71I
30027	M7	75D	30040	M7	71B	30053	M7	71A	30066	U.S.A.	71I
30028	M7	71B	30041	M7	72B	30054	M7	71D	30067	U.S.A.	71I
30029	M7	71A	30042	M7	72E	30055	M7	72A	30068	U.S.A.	71I
30030	M7	72A	30043	M7	70B	30056	M7	70C	30069	U.S.A.	71I
30031	M7	71A	30044	M7	72E	30057	M7	71B	30070	U.S.A.	71I

No.	Class	Shed	No.	Class	Shed	No.	Class	Shed	No.	Class	Shed
30071	U.S.A.	711	30172	L11	71D	30285	T9	71D	30379	M7	71B
30072	U.S.A.	711	30173	L11	71A	30286	T9	71A	30384	K10	70B
30073	U.S.A.	711	30174	L11	70B	30287	T9	71A	30389	K10	72C
30074	U.S.A.	711	30175	L11	71A	30288	T9	72B	30390	K10	70A
30082	B4	71A	30177	O2	71C	30289	T9	72B	30395	S11	71D
30083	B4	71A	30179	O2	71C	30300	T9	71A	30396	S11	71D
30084	B4	72D	30182	O2	72D	30301	T9	72B	30397	S11	71D
30086*	B4	71B	30183	O2	72D	30302	T9	70D	30398	S11	71B
30087	B4	71B	30192	O2	72A	30303	T9	71D	30399	S11	71C
30088	B4	72D	30193	O2	72A	30304	T9	71A	30400	S11	71D
30089*	B4	71A	30197	O2	71C	30305	T9	71D	30401	S11	71A
30093*	B4	71B	30199	O2	72A	30306	700	71A	30402	S11	71D
30094	B4	72D	30200	O2	72F	30307	T9	71C	30403	S11	71B
30096*	B4	74A	30203	O2	72F	30308	700	70C	30404	S11	71B
30102*	B4	72D	30204	O2	71B	30309	700	70B	30405	L11	70A
30104	M7	71B	30207	O2	72D	30310	T9	71D	30406	L11	70A
30105	M7	72A	30212	O2	71B	30311	T9	70B	30407	L11	72C
30106	M7	71B	30213	O2	71A	30312	T9	70C	30408	L11	72A
30107	M7	72D	30216	O2	72D	30313	T9	71A	30409	L11	72A
30108	M7	70C	30221	O2	70A	30314	T9	71D	30411	L11	71A
30109	M7	71A	30223	O2	71C	30315	700	72B	30412	L11	72C
30110	M7	70C	30224	O2	72A	30316	700	71A	30413	L11	71A
30111	M7	71B	30225	O2	71A	30317	700	72B	30414	L11	70B
30112	M7	71B	30229	O2	71C	30318	M7	71B	30415	L12	71C
30113	T9	71D	30230	O2	72A	30319	M7	70A	30416	L12	70C
30114	T9	71D	30231	O2	71C	30320	M7	72A	30417	L12	71D
30115	T9	71D	30232	O2	72A	30321	M7	72E	30418	L12	70D
30116	T9	71C	30233	O2	71A	30322	M7	70A	30419	L12	71D
30117	T9	72C	30236	O2	72D	30323	M7	72A	30420	L12	70C
30118	T9	71D	30238	G6	72B	30324	M7	70C	30421	L12	72B
30119	T9	70A	30241	M7	70A	30325	700	70C	30422	L12	71A
30120	T9	71D	30242	M7	71A	30326	700	70C	30423	L12	71A
30121	T9	71A	30243	M7	72B	30327	700	70C	30424	L12	71C
30122	T9	72B	30244	M7	70A	30328	M7	70C	30425	L12	70C
30123	M7	70A	30245	M7	72A	30330	H15	70B	30426	L12	71D
30124	M7	72A	30246	M7	70C	30331	H15	70B	30427	L12	71D
30125	M7	71A	30247	M7	72E	30332	H15	70A	30428	L12	70C
30127	M7	72B	30248	M7	70A	30333	H15	70A	30429	L12	71A
30128	M7	71A	30249	M7	70A	30334	H15	70A	30430	L12	71A
30129	M7	72C	30250	M7	72E	30335	H15	70A	30431	L12	71A
30130	M7	70A	30251	M7	71B	30336	T9	70C	30432	L12	71A
30131	M7	71B	30252	M7	72A	30337	T9	72C	30433	L12	71A
30132	M7	70A	30253	M7	72A	30338	T9	71C	30434	L12	71A
30133	M7	72A	30254	M7	70B	30339	700	70A	30436	L11	70C
30134	L11	72C	30255	M7	72A	30346	700	70B	30437	L11	71A
30148	L11	71A	30256	M7	72A	30349	G6	70C	30438	L11	70B
30154	L11	71A	30258	G6	70D	30350	700	71A	30441	L11	71D
30155	L11	71A	30259	G6	70A	30352	700	70B	30442	L11	71A
30156	L11	71A	30260	G6	71B	30353	G6	70A	30446	T14	70A
30157	L11	71A	30266	G6	70D	30355	700	72B	30448*	N15	72B
30158	L11	70C	30268	G6	70C	30356	M7	72D	30449*	N15	72B
30159	L11	71A	30270	G6	70C	30357	M7	71A	30450*	N15	72B
30160	G6	70A	30274	G6	71H	30367	T1	71A	30451*	N15	70D
30162	G6	71C	30277	G6	71H	30368	700	70D	30452*	N15	72B
30163	L11	70A	30280	T9	71D	30374	M7	72A	30453*	N15	72B
30164	L11	70B	30281	T9	70C	30375	M7	72D	30454*	N15	72B
30165	L11	70A	30282	T9	71A	30376	M7	72A	30455*	N15	72A
30170	L11	71D	30283	T9	72A	30377	M7	72A	30456*	N15	70D
30171	L11	71A	30284	T9	71C	30378	M7	71A	30457*	N15	72A

30458-30826

No.	Class	Shed	No.	Class	Shed	No.	Class	Shed	No.	Class	Shed
30458*	0458	70C	30520	H16	70B	30676	M7	70A	30748*	N15	72B
30461	T14	70A	30521	H15	71A	30687	700	70B	30749*	N15	71A
30463	D15	71A	30522	H15	71A	30688	700	70B	30750*	N15	71B
30464	D15	71A	30523	H15	71A	30689	700	70B	30751*	N15	71B
30465	D15	71A	30524	H15	71A	30690	700	72B	30752*	N15	71A
30466	D15	71A	30530	Q	71A	30691	700	72B	30753*	N15	72B
30467	D15	71A	30531	Q	71A	30692	700	70A	30754*	N15	71B
30468	D15	71A	30532	Q	71A	30693	700	70D	30755*	N15	70A
30469	D15	71A	30533	Q	75C	30694	700	70A	30756*	756	73A
30470	D15	71A	30534	Q	75C	30695	700	71B	30757*	757	72D
30471	D15	71A	30535	Q	71A	30696	700	70B	30758*	757	72D
30472	D15	71A	30536	Q	71A	30697	700	70B	30763*	N15	73A
30473	H15	71A	30537	Q	75C	30698	700	70B	30764*	N15	73A
30474	H15	71A	30538	Q	75C	30699	700	70A	30765*	N15	70A
30475	H15	71A	30539	Q	75C	30700	700	71A	30766*	N15	73A
30476	H15	70A	30540	Q	75E	30701	700	70A	30767*	N15	74C
30477	H15	71A	30541	Q	75E	30702	T9	72A	30768*	N15	74C
30478	H15	71A	30542	Q	71A	30703	T9	72A	30769*	N15	74C
30479	M7	71A	30543	Q	71A	30704	T9	72C	30770*	N15	74C
30480	M7	71D	30544	Q	71A	30705	T9	71A	30771*	N15	74C
30481	M7	70C	30545	Q	75D	30706	T9	72A	30772*	N15	71A
30482	H15	70A	30546	Q	75D	30707	T9	72A	30773*	N15	70A
30483	H15	71A	30547	Q	75C	30708	T9	71A	30774*	N15	73A
30484	H15	70A	30548	Q	71B	30709	T9	72B	30775*	N15	73A
30485	H15	70A	30549	Q	71B	30710	T9	70C	30776*	N15	73A
30486	H15	70A	30564	0395	72A	30711	T9	71A	30777*	N15	71A
30487	H15	70A	30565	0395	70C	30712	T9	70D	30778*	N15	73A
30488	H15	70A	30566	0395	71A	30713	T9	71A	30779*	N15	71A
30489	H15	71A	30567	0395	70B	30714	T9	72C	30780*	N15	70A
30490	H15	70A	30568	0395	70C	30715	T9	72A	30781*	N15	74C
30491	H15	71A	30569	0395	70B	30716	T9	72A	30782*	N15	70A
30492	G16	70B	30570	0395	70B	30717	T9	72A	30783*	N15	71A
30493	G16	70B	30571	0395	71A	30718	T9	70A	30784*	N15	71A
30494	G16	70B	30572	0395	70B	30719	T9	72B	30785*	N15	71A
30495	G16	70B	30573	0395	70B	30721	T9	71A	30786*	N15	73A
30496	S15	70B	30574	0395	70C	30722	T9	71A	30787*	N15	70A
30497	S15	70B	30575	0395	70C	30723	T9	72A	30788*	N15	71A
30498	S15	70B	30576	0395	70C	30724	T9	72B	30789*	N15	71A
30499	S15	70B	30577	0395	72B	30725	T9	72B	30790*	N15	71A
30500	S15	70B	30578	0395	70C	30726	T9	71D	30791*	N15	70A
30501	S15	70B	30579	0395	70B	30727	T9	72B	30792*	N15	70A
30502	S15	70B	30580	0395	70C	30728	T9	71B	30793*	N15	73A
30503	S15	70B	30581	0395	72A	30729	T9	71A	30794*	N15	73B
30504	S15	70B	30582	0415	72A	30730	T9	72B	30795*	N15	73B
30505	S15	70B	30583	0415	72A	30731	T9	71D	30796*	N15	73A
30506	S15	70B	30584	0415	72A	30732	T9	70B	30797*	N15	74A
30507	S15	70B	30585	0298	72F	30733	T9	71D	30798*	N15	73B
30508	S15	70B	30586	0298	72F	30736*	N15	71B	30799*	N15	73B
30509	S15	70B	30587	0298	72F	30737*	N15	71B	30800*	N15	73C
30510	S15	70B	30588	C14	71A	30738*	N15	70B	30801*	N15	74A
30511	S15	70B	30589	C14	71A	30739*	N15	72B	30802*	N15	74A
30512	S15	70B	30667	M7	70A	30740*	N15	71B	30803*	N15	74A
30513	S15	70B	30668	M7	72A	30741*	N15	71B	30804*	N15	74A
30514	S15	70B	30669	M7	72A	30742*	N15	70A	30805*	N15	74A
30515	S15	70B	30670	M7	72E	30743*	N15	71B	30806*	N15	74C
30516	H16	70B	30671	M7	72A	30744*	N15	72B	30823	S15	72A
30517	H16	70B	30673	M7	71A	30745*	N15	70A	30824	S15	72A
30518	H16	70B	30674	M7	71A	30746*	N15	71B	30825	S15	72A
30519	H16	70B	30675	M7	72B	30747*	N15	70A	30826	S15	72B

No.	Class	Shed
30827	S15	72B
30828	S15	72B
30829	S15	72B
30830	S15	72B
30831	S15	72B
30832	S15	72B
30833	S15	70B
30834	S15	70B
30835	S15	70B
30836	S15	70B
30837	S15	70B
30838	S15	70B
30839	S15	70B
30840	S15	70B
30841	S15	72A
30842	S15	72A
30843	S15	72A
30844	S15	72A
30845	S15	72A
30846	S15	72A
30847	S15	72A
30850*	LN	71A
30851*	LN	71A
30852*	LN	71A
30853*	LN	71A
30854*	LN	71A
30855*	LN	71A
30856*	LN	71A
30857*	LN	71A
30858*	LN	70A
30859*	LN	70A
30860*	LN	70A
30861*	LN	71B
30862*	LN	71B
30863*	LN	71B
30864*	LN	71B
30865*	LN	71B
30900*	V	74E
30901*	V	74E
30902*	V	74E
30903*	V	74E
30904*	V	74E
30905*	V	74E
30906*	V	74E
30907*	V	74E
30908*	V	73B
30909*	V	74E
30910*	V	74E
30911*	V	74B
30912*	V	74B
30913*	V	74B
30914*	V	74B
30915*	V	74B
30916*	V	74B
30917*	V	74B
30918*	V	74B
30919*	V	73B
30920*	V	73B
30921*	V	73B
30922*	V	73B
30923*	V	73B
30924*	V	74C
30925*	V	74C
30926*	V	74C
30927*	V	74C
30928*	V	73B
30929*	V	73B
30930*	V	73B
30931*	V	73B
30932*	V	73B
30933*	V	73B
30934*	V	73B
30935*	V	74E
30936*	V	73B
30937*	V	73B
30938*	V	73B
30939*	V	73B
30950	Z	71A
30951	Z	73D
30952	Z	71A
30953	Z	74A
30954	Z	72A
30955	Z	70A
30956	Z	71A
30957	Z	72B
31004	C	74B
31005	H	73A
31010	R1	74A
31016	H	75F
31018	C	73C
31019	E1	73A
31027	P	74C
31033	C	73B
31036	E	73B
31037	C	74E
31038	C	74E
31041	O1	74A
31044	O1	73B
31047	R1	74C (F)
31048	O1	74C
31054	C	73C
31057	D	70E
31059	C	73C
31061	C	73C
31063	C	74C
31064	O1	73B (NC)
31065	O1	74B
31066	O1	73B (NC)
31067	E1	73A
31068	C	73B
31069	R1	74A
31071	C	73B
31075	D	70E
31086	C	73D
31090	C	73D
31092	D	73D
31093	O1	74B
31102	C	73B
31107	R1	74C (F)
31108	O1	74C
31112	C	73D
31113	C	74C
31128	R1	74C (F)
31145	D1	73A
31147	R1	74C (F)
31150	C	73C
31154	R1	74C (F)
31157	E	73E
31158	H	74A
31159	E	73C
31160	E1	73B
31161	H	74A
31162	H	73B
31164	H	74D
31165	E1	73A
31166	E	73B
31174	R1	74E
31175	E	73B
31176	E	73B
31177	H	73A
31178	P	75A
31179	E1	73B
31182	H	75F
31184	H	73A
31191	C	74C
31193	H	74D
31218	C	74A
31219	C	74D
31221	C	73D
31223	C	73D
31225	C	73D
31227	C	73B
31229	C	73E
31234	C	73A
31239	H	74A
31242	C	73E
31243	C	74C
31244	C	74D
31245	C	73C
31246	D1	74D
31247	D1	74C
31248	O1	73C
31252	C	74B
31253	C	73B
31255	C	73D
31256	C	73D
31258	O1	73C
31259	H	74B
31260	C	74A
31261	H	73A
31263	H	73A
31265	H	74B
31266	H	73A
31267	C	73D
31268	C	73E
31269	H	74A
31270	C	73C
31271	C	74A
31272	C	74D
31273	E	73B
31274	H	74A
31275	E	73B
31276	H	74C
31277	C	74D
31278	H	73B
31279	H	74E
31280	C	73B
31287	C	73D
31291	C	74C
31293	C	73B
31294	C	73B
31295	H	73A
31297	C	73B
31298	C	74B
31305	H	74A
31306	H	74C
31307	H	73A
31308	H	73D
31309	H	73B
31310	H	74E
31311	H	73A
31315	E	73B
31317	C	73D
31319	H	74E
31320	H	74D
31321	H	73A
31322	H	74A
31323	P	74C
31324	H	73B
31325	P	71A
31326	H	73B
31327	H	74D
31328	H	74E
31329	H	73A
31335	R1	74E
31337	R1	74C (F)
31339	R1	74A
31340	R1	74C (F)
31369	O1	73E
31370	O1	74A
31373	O1	74C
31379	O1	74A
31381	O1	74C
31383	O1	74C
31390	O1	74B
31391	O1	73C

31395-31767

No.	Class	Shed
31395	O1	73B (NC)
31400	N	74A
31401	N	74A
31402	N	74A
31403	N	74A
31404	N	74A
31405	N	74A
31406	N	74A
31407	N	72A
31408	N	72A
31409	N	73A
31410	N	73A
31411	N	73A
31412	N	73A
31413	N	73A
31414	N	73A
31425	O1	74C
31430	O1	74C
31432	O1	73C
31434	O1	74C
31443	B1	70E
31461	C	74D
31470	D1	74C
31477	D	74A
31480	C	73C
31481	C	73E
31486	C	73C
31487	D1	73A
31488	D	73B
31489	D1	73E
31490	D	73B
31491	E	73B
31492	D1	73D
31493	D	74E
31494	D1	73D
31495	C	73E
31496	D	74D
31497	E1	73B
31498	C	73D
31500	H	73B
31501	D	73E
31502	D1	73E
31503	H	74C
31504	E1	73A
31505	D1	73E
31506	E1	73A
31507	E1	73B
31508	C	73B
31509	D1	74D
31510	C	73D
31511	E1	73B
31512	H	74C
31513	C	74A
31514	E	74A
31515	E	70E
31516	E	73D
31517	H	74D
31518	H	74C
31519	H	74B
31520	H	74A
31521	H	74B
31522	H	74B
31523	H	74D
31530	H	74C
31531	H	74C
31532	H	74B
31533	H	73B
31540	H	74C
31541	H	73B
31542	H	73B
31543	H	74B
31544	H	73B
31545	D1	74C
31546	H	73B
31547	E	73B
31548	H	74D
31549	D	74D
31550	H	74D
31551	H	70A
31552	H	70A
31553	H	70A
31554	H	70A
31555	P	73A
31556	P	75A
31557	P	74C
31558	P	74C
31572	C	74A
31573	C	73D
31574	D	74A
31575	C	73A
31576	C	73A
31577	D	74A
31578	C	73A
31579	C	73D
31580	C	74D
31581	C	73C
31582	C	73A
31583	C	73D
31584	C	73B
31585	C	73D
31586	D	73E
31587	E	74E
31588	C	73D
31589	C	74A
31590	C	74D
31591	D	73B
31592	C	74B
31593	C	74D
31595	J	74A
31596	J	74A
31597	J	74A
31598	J	74A
31602	T	70E
31604	T	70E
31610	U	70E
31611	U	70E
31612	U	72B
31613	U	70A
31614	U	70E
31615	U	70E
31616	U	73C
31617	U	73C
31618	U	72B
31619	U	70A
31620	U	70C
31621	U	70C
31622	U	71B
31623	U	73A
31624	U	70B
31625	U	70A
31626	U	72B
31627	U	70C
31628	U	70C
31629	U	70C
31630	U	70C
31631	U	73E
31632	U	71B
31633	U	70D
31634	U	72C
31635	U	70C
31636	U	72C
31637	U	70A
31638	U	73E
31639	U	73C
31658	R	73D
31659	R	73D
31660	R	73A
31661	R	73E
31662	R	73D
31663	R	73D
31665	R	73D
31666	R	73D
31667	R	74D
31670	R	74D
31671	R	74D
31673	R	74C
31674	R	73E
31675	R	74D
31681	C	73A
31682	C	73D
31683	C	73A
31684	C	74D
31685	S	74A
31686	C	74D
31687	C	73B
31688	C	73D
31689	C	73C
31690	C	74B
31691	C	73E
31692	C	73E
31693	C	73D
31694	C	73C
31695	C	73C
31696	R1	73E
31697	R1	73D
31698	R1	73E
31700	R1	74D
31703	R1	74D
31704	R1	74D
31705	R1	73E
31706	R1	73A
31708	R1	74C
31710	R1	74A
31711	C	74A
31712	C	73D
31713	C	73D
31714	C	73A
31715	C	73E
31716	C	73A
31717	C	73A
31718	C	73A
31719	C	73A
31720	C	73C
31721	C	74A
31722	C	73A
31723	C	73B
31724	C	73D
31725	C	73B
31727	D1	73E
31728	D	74D
31729	D	73D
31730	D	74D
31731	D	74D
31732	D	73C
31733	D	74D
31734	D	73E
31735	D1	74C
31736	D1	74A
31737	D	74C
31738	D	74E
31739	D1	73E
31740	D	70E
31741	D1	73E
31743	D1	73A
31744	D	70E
31745	D1	74D
31746	D	73B
31748	D	74A
31749	D1	73A
31750	D	70E
31753	L1	74C
31754	L1	74C
31755	L1	74C
31756	L1	74C
31757	L1	74C
31758	L1	73B
31759	L1	73B
31760	L	74D
31761	L	74D
31762	L	73A
31763	L	74A
31764	L	73A
31765	L	74D
31766	L	74E
31767	L	73A

No.	Class	Shed	No.	Class	Shed	No.	Class	Shed	No.	Class	Shed
31768	L	74E	31827	N	73B	31895	U1	75B	32067	B4X	70D
31769	L	74E	31828	N	71A	31896	U1	75B	32068	B4	75G
31770	L	74A	31829	N	72A	31897	U1	75B	32070	B4X	73B
31771	L	74A	31830	N	72A	31898	U1	75B	32071	B4X	75G
31772	L	74A	31831	N	72A	31899	U1	75B	32072	B4X	75G
31773	L	74A	31832	N	72A	31900	U1	75B	32073	B4X	75G
31774	L	74A	31833	N	72A	31901	U1	73B	32075	I3	75F
31775	L	74A	31834	N	72A	31902	U1	73B	32076	I3	75A
31776	L	74B	31835	N	72A	31903	U1	73A	32077	I3	75G
31777	L	74B	31836	N	72B	31904	U1	73A	32078	I3	75E
31778	L	74D	31837	N	72A	31905	U1	73A	32079	I3	75E
31779	L	74D	31838	N	72A	31906	U1	73A	32081	I3	75G
31780	L	74B	31839	N	72A	31907	U1	73A	32082	I3	75F
31781	L	74B	31840	N	72A	31908	U1	73A	32083	I3	75G
31782	L1	73B	31841	N	72A	31909	U1	73A	32084	I3	85E
31783	L1	73B	31842	N	72E	31910	U1	73A	32086	I3	75A
31784	L1	73B	31843	N	75B	31911	W	73C	32087	I3	75F
31785	L1	73B	31844	N	75B	31912	W	73A	32088	I3	75A
31786	L1	73B	31845	N	72A	31913	W	73C	32089	I3	75G
31787	L1	73B	31846	N	72B	31914	W	73A	32090	I3	75F
31788	L1	73B	31847	N	72A	31915	W	73A	32091	I3	75E
31789	L1	73B	31848	N	75B	31916	W	75C	32094	E1/R	72D
31790	U	72C	31849	N	75B	31917	W	75C	32095	E1/R	72E
31791	U	72C	31850	N	73E	31918	W	75C	32096	E1/R	72E
31792	U	72C	31851	N	75B	31919	W	75C	32100	E2	73A
31793	U	73A	31852	N	75B	31920	W	75C	32101	E2	73A
31794	U	70E	31853	N	72A	31921	W	73C	32102	E2	73A
31795	U	71B	31854	N	73E	31922	W	73C	32103	E2	73A
31796	U	70E	31855	N	72A	31923	W	73C	32104	E2	73A
31797	U	70E	31856	N	72A	31924	W	73C	32105	E2	73A
31798	U	70C	31857	N	75B	31925	W	73C	32106	E2	73A
31799	U	70E	31858	N	75B	32002	I1X	75E	32107	E2	73A
31800	U	70C	31859	N	73A	32005	I1X	75A	32108	E2	74C
31801	U	70C	31860	N	74A	32008	I1X	73B	32109	E2	74C
31802	U	70C	31861	N	74A			(NC)	32113	E1	73B
31803	U	73A	31862	N	75B	32009	I1X	75G	32124	E1/R	72A
31804	U	70C	31863	N	75B	32021	I3	75F	32128	E1	73A
31805	U	71D	31864	N	75B	32022	I3	75F	32129	E1	71D
31806	U	73E	31865	N	75B	32023	I3	75F	32133	E1	71A
31807	U	70A	31866	N	71A	32026	I3	75F	32135	E1/R	72A
31808	U	73E	31867	N	71A	32027	I3	75F	32138	E1	70A
31809	U	71D	31868	N	73E	32028	I3	75F	32139	E1	75A
31810	N	73A	31869	N	72A	32029	I3	75F	32142	E1	75A
31811	N	73A	31870	N	71D	32030	I3	75G	32145	E1	74D
31812	N	73A	31871	N	72D	32037*	H1	75A	32147	E1	71A
31813	N	73A	31872	N	72B			(N)	32151	E1	73B
31814	N	73A	31873	N	72B	32038*	H1	75A	32156	E1	71I
31815	N	73A	31874	N	72A			(N)	32160	E1	70D
31816	N	73A	31875	N	72A	32039*	H1	75A	32165	E3	73B
31817	N	73A	31876	N1	73C	32043	B4X	75G	32166	E3	73B
31818	N	73A	31877	N1	73C	32045	B4X	70D	32167	E3	74D
31819	N	74C	31878	N1	73C	32050	B4X	73B	32168	E3	73B
31820	N	74C	31879	N1	73C	32052	B4X	70D	32169	E3	74D
31821	N	74C	31880	N1	73C	32054	B4	75G	32170	E3	73B
31822	N1	73C	31890	U1	75A	32055	B4X	75G	32300	C3	71D
31823	N	74C	31891	U1	75A	32056	B4X	73B	32301	C3	71D
31824	N	73B	31892	U1	75A	32060	B4X	75G	32302	C3	75D
31825	N	73B	31893	U1	75A	32062	B4	75G	32303	C3	71D
31826	N	73B	31894	U1	75A	32063	B4	75G	32306	C3	71D

32325-32646

No.	Class	Shed
32325	J1	75F
32326	J2	75F
32327*	N15X	70D
32328*	N15X	70D
32329*	N15X	70D
32330*	N15X	70D
32331*	N15X	70D
32332*	N15X	70D
32333*	N15X	70D
32337*	K	75A (N)
32338	K	71D
32339	K	75A
32340	K	71D
32341	K	75A
32342	K	75A
32343	K	75A
32344	K	75A
32345	K	75A
32346	K	75A
32347	K	75A
32348	K	75G
32349	K	75A
32350	K	75E
32351	K	75E
32352	K	75E
32353	K	75E
32359	D1/M	74C
32364	D3	75D
32365	D3	75D
32368	D3	75A
32372	D3	75A
32376	D3	75A
32378	D3	74E
32379	D3	75D
32380	D3	75D
32384	D3	75D
32385	D3	75G
32386	D3	75A
32388	D3	74E
32390	D3	75F
32391	D3	74E
32393	D3	75A
32394	D3	75G
32399	E5	75D
32400	E5	75A
32401	E5X	75D
32402	E5	75G
32404	E5	75G
32405	E5	75G
32406	E5	75G
32407	E6X	75C
32408	E6	73B
32409	E6	75C
32410	E6	73B
32411	E6X	75C
32412	E6	73B
32413	E6	73B
32414	E6	75C
32415	E6	73B
32416	E6	75C
32417	E6	75C
32418	E6	75C
32421*	H2	75A
32422*	H2	75A
32424*	H2	75A
32425*	H2	75A (N)
32426*	H2	75A (N)
32434	C2X	75G
32437	C2X	75A (N)
32438	C2X	75A
32440	C2X	75C
32441	C2X	75E
32442	C2X	73B
32443	C2X	75A
32444	C2X	75C
32445	C2X	75E
32446	C2X	73B
32447	C2X	75C
32448	C2X	73B
32449	C2X	75B
32450	C2X	75B
32451	C2X	75E
32453	E3	73B
32454	E3	74D
32455	E3	75A
32456	E3	74D
32458	E3	73B
32459	E3	73B
32460	E3	73B
32461	E3	73B
32462	E3	73B
32463	E4	73B
32464	E4	75D
32465	E4	75E
32466	E4X	75C
32467	E4	73B
32468	E4	70A
32469	E4	73B
32470	E4	75A
32471	E4	75A
32472	E4	73B
32473	E4	75C
32474	E4	73B
32475	E4	75A (N)
32476	E4	75C
32477	E4X	75C
32478	E4X	75C
32479	E4	75C
32480	E4	75E
32481	E4	73B
32482	E4	75D
32484	E4	75E
32485	E4	75G
32486	E4	75A
32487	E4	71D
32488	E4	74D
32489	E4X	75C
32490	E4	70C
32491	E4	71A
32492	E4	71A
32493	E4	70A
32494	E4	75A (N)
32495	E4	75C
32496	E4	75E
32497	E4	75E
32498	E4	75C
32499	E4	73B
32500	E4	70A
32501	E4	75D
32502	E4	75C
32503	E4	74D
32504	E4	75A (N)
32505	E4	75A
32506	E4	75C
32507	E4	75B
32508	E4	75A (N)
32509	E4	75A
32510	E4	71A
32511	E4	75D
32512	E4	75F
32513	E4	75A
32514	E4	75A
32515	E4	75D
32516	E4	75E
32517	E4	75B
32518	E4	75G
32519	E4	75E
32520	E4	75E
32521	C2X	75D
32522	C2X	75E
32523	C2X	75A
32524	C2X	73B
32525	C2X	73B
32526	C2X	75C
32527	C2X	75E
32528	C2X	75A
32529	C2X	75E
32532	C2X	75E
32534	C2X	75G
32535	C2X	75C
32536	C2X	75C
32537	C2X	75D
32538	C2X	75G
32539	C2X	75A
32540	C2X	75B
32541	C2X	75B
32543	C2X	75A
32544	C2X	75D
32545	C2X	75E
32546	C2X	75C
32547	C2X	75C
32548	C2X	75D
32549	C2X	73B
32550	C2X	75B
32551	C2X	73B
32552	C2X	75E
32553	C2X	75E
32554	C2X	73B
32556	E4	75D
32557	E4	71A
32558	E4	71A
32559	E4	71A
32560	E4	75B
32561	E4	75B
32562	E4	71A
32563	E4	71A
32564	E4	73B
32565	E4	73B
32566	E4	75A
32568	E5	75D
32570	E5X	75D
32571	E5	75E
32573	E5	75A
32574	E5	75G
32575	E5	75A
32576	E5X	75A
32577	E4	75A
32578	E4	75C
32579	E4	71A
32580	E4	74D
32581	E4	74D
32582	E4	75F
32583	E5	75A
32584	E5	75E
32585	E5	73B (NC)
32586	E5X	75D
32587	E5	73B (NC)
32588	E5	75G
32590	E5	73B
32591	E5	75G
32592	E5	75B
32593	E5	75G
32594	E5	75A
32595	I1X	75A
32596	I1X	73B (NC)
32602	I1X	73B
32603	I1X	75G
32606	E1	71I
32608	E1/R	72E
32610	E1/R	72E
32636	A1X	75A (N)
32640	A1X	74A
32644	A1X	74A
32646	A1X	71D

No.	Class	Shed	No.	Class	Shed	No.	Class	Shed	No.	Class	Shed
32647	A1X	75A	33036	Q1	74D	34046*	WC	72A	34096*	WC	74B
		(N)	33037	Q1	74D	34047*	WC	72A	34097*	WC	74B
32655	A1X	71D	33038	Q1	74D	34048*	WC	72A	34098*	WC	74B
32659	A1X	74A	33039	Q1	74E	34049*	BB	70A	34099*	WC	74B
32661	A1X	71D	33040	Q1	74E	34050*	BB	70A	34100*	WC	74B
32662	A1X	71D	34001*	WC	72A	34051*	BB	70A	34101*	WC	73A
32670	A1X	74A	34002*	WC	72A	34052*	BB	70A	34102*	WC	73A
32677	A1X	71D	34003*	WC	72A	34053*	BB	70A	34103*	WC	73A
32678	A1X	74A	34004*	WC	72A	34054*	BB	70A	34104*	WC	73A
32689	E1	75A	34005*	WC	72A	34055*	BB	70A	34105*	WC	71B
32691	E1	71D	34006*	WC	72A	34056*	BB	70A	34106*	WC	71B
32694	E1	71D	34007*	WC	72A	34057*	BB	70A	34107*	WC	71B
32695	E1/R	72A	34008*	WC	72A	34058*	BB	70A	34108*	WC	71B
32696	E1/R	72E	34009*	WC	72A	34059*	BB	70A	34109*	BB	71B
32697	E1/R	72A	34010*	WC	72A	34060*	BB	70A	34110*	BB	
33001	Q1	70C	34011*	WC	72D	34061*	BB	70A	35001*	MN	72A
33002	Q1	70C	34012*	WC	72D	34062*	BB	70A	35002*	MN	72A
33003	Q1	70C	34013*	WC	72D	34063*	BB	70A	35003*	MN	72A
33004	Q1	70C	34014*	WC	72A	34064*	BB	70A	35004*	MN	72A
33005	Q1	70C	34015*	WC	72A	34065*	BB	70A	35005*	MN	70A
33006	Q1	70B	34016*	WC	72A	34066*	BB	73A	35006*	MN	72B
33007	Q1	70B	34017*	WC	72A	34067*	BB	73A	35007*	MN	72B
33008	Q1	70B	34018*	WC	72A	34068*	BB	73A	35008*	MN	72B
33009	Q1	70B	34019*	WC	72A	34069*	BB	73A	35009*	MN	72B
33010	Q1	70B	34020*	WC	72A	34070*	BB	73A	35010*	MN	70A
33011	Q1	70B	34021*	WC	72D	34071*	BB	73A	35011*	MN	70A
33012	Q1	70B	34022*	WC	72B	34072*	BB	74C	35012*	MN	70A
33013	Q1	70B	34023*	WC	72B	34073*	BB	74C	35013*	MN	70A
33014	Q1	70C	34024*	WC	72A	34074*	BB	74C	35014*	MN	70A
33015	Q1	70C	34025*	WC	72A	34075*	BB	74C	35015*	MN	70A
33016	Q1	70C	34026*	WC	72A	34076*	BB	73A	35016*	MN	70A
33017	Q1	71A	34027*	WC	72A	34077*	BB	74B	35017*	MN	70A
33018	Q1	71A	34028*	WC	72A	34078*	BB	74B	35018*	MN	70A
33019	Q1	71A	34029*	WC	72A	34079*	BB	74B	35019*	MN	70A
33020	Q1	71A	34030*	WC	72A	34080*	BB	74B	35020*	MN	70A
33021	Q1	71A	34031*	WC	72A	34081*	BB	74B	35021*	MN	72A
33022	Q1	71A	34032*	WC	72B	34082*	BB	74B	35022*	MN	72A
33023	Q1	71A	34033*	WC	73A	34083*	BB	73A	35023*	MN	72A
33024	Q1	71A	34034*	WC	73A	34084*	BB	73A	35024*	MN	72A
33025	Q1	71A	34035*	WC	73A	34085*	BB	73A	35025*	MN	73A
33026	Q1	74D	34036*	WC	75A	34086*	BB	74B	35026*	MN	73A
33027	Q1	74D	34037*	WC	75A	34087*	BB	74B	35027*	MN	73A
33028	Q1	74D	34038*	WC	75A	34088*	BB	74B	35028*	MN	73A
33029	Q1	74D	34039*	WC	75A	34089*	BB	74B	35029*	MN	74C
33030	Q1	74D	34040*	WC	75A	34090*	BB	74B	35030*	MN	74C
33031	Q1	74D	34041*	WC	75A	34091*	WC	73A	36001	Lead	
33032	Q1	74D	34042*	WC	72B	34092*	WC	73A	36002	Lead	
33033	Q1	74D	34043*	WC	72B	34093*	WC	71B	36003	Lead	
33034	Q1	74D	34044*	WC	72A	34094*	WC	71B	36004	Lead	
33035	Q1	74D	34045*	WC	72A	34095*	WC	71B	36005	Lead	

Isle of Wight Locomotives

No.	Class	Shed	No.	Class	Shed	No.	Class	Shed	No.	Class	Shed
			W15*	O2	71F	W23*	O2	71F	W30*	O2	71E
			W16*	O2	71F	W24*	O2	71F	W31*	O2	71E
			W17*	O2	71F	W25*	O2	71F	W32*	O2	71E
W1*	E1	71E	W18*	O2	71F	W26*	O2	71E	W33*	O2	71E
W2*	E1	71E	W19*	O2	71F	W27*	O2	71E	W34*	O2	71E
W3*	E1	71E	W20*	O2	71F	W28*	O2	71E	W35*	O2	71E
W4*	E1	71E	W21*	O2	71F	W29*	O2	71E	W36*	O2	71E
W14*	O2	71F	W22*	O2	71F						

SOUTHERN REGION SERVICE LOCOS.

No.	Old No.	Class	Station
†49 S	—	Shunter	Broad Clyst Sleep. Depot
*74 S	—	Bo-Bo	Durnsford R. Power Stn.
*75 S	—	Bo	Waterloo & City Rly.
77 S	0745	C14	Redbridge Sleep. Depot
†343 S	—	Shunter	Eastleigh Carr. Works
†346 S	—	Inspection Car	Engin'r's Dept.
‡377 S	2635	AIX	Brighton Wks.
§400 S	—	0-4-0	S'hamptonDks.
515 S	L.B.S.C. 650 I.W. 9	AIX	Lancing Carr. Wks.
600 S	—	0-4-0 diesel	
680 S	L.B.S.C. 654 SEC. 751.	A I	,,
701 S	2284	D I	Fratton**
DS 1169	—	0-4-0 Diesel	Engineer's Dt.
DS 1173	2217	0-4-0 Diesel	Engineer's Dt.
DS 3152	30272	G 6	Meldon Quarry

Electric
** Ex-oil Pumping Engine
‡ Repainted 1947 in Stroudley livery
§ Fowler Diesel
† Petrol

BRITISH RAILWAYS LOCOMOTIVES

Nos. 40001-58935

WITH SHED ALLOCATIONS

Cl. "3MT"
2-6-2T

40001	8A
40002	2C
40003	8A
40004	1A
40005	84G
40006	1A
40007	8A
40008	84G
40009	1A
40010	1C
40011	3C
40012	26F
40013	26A
40014	26F
40015	26A
40016	11D
40017	1A
40018	1A
40019	3C
40020	1C
40021	23B
40022	14C
40023	14A
40024	14C
40025	14A
40026	14C
40027	14B
40028	14B
40029	14B
40030	14A
40031	14B
40032	14B
40033	14B
40034	14B
40035	14B
40036	14B
40037	14B
40038	14B
40039	14C
40040	22B
40041	11A
40042	8B
40043	1C
40044	1A
40045	3C
40046	1A
40047	3B
40048	84G
40049	3B
40050	1A
40051	3D
40052	1A
40053	3B
40054	1A
40055	1A
40056	26F
40057	26F
40058	84G
40059	26F
40060	26F
40061	26F
40062	26F
40063	26A
40064	23B
40065	26A
40066	3B
40067	11D
40068	11A
40069	20E
40070	11A
40071	9B
40072	1A
40073	1A
40074	20C
40075	20A
40076	2C
40077	9A
40078	2C
40079	14B
40080	10E
40081	1A
40082	19B
40083	7A
40084	10E
40085	6E
40086	5F
40087	1A
40088	5D
40089	9F
40090	20A
40091	14A
40092	14B
40093	9E
40094	9E
40095	9F
40096	14B
40097	21A
40098	14A
40099	14B
40100	14B
40101	6C
40102	6C
40103	6E
40104	6C
40105	21B
40106	9B
40107	9A
40108	10E
40109	1A
40110	6C
40111	14B
40112	14B
40113	9F
40114	14B
40115	21A
40116	22B
40117	21A
40118	9E
40119	14B
40120	16A
40121	6C
40122	5D
40123	7A
40124	7B
40125	8D
40126	5D
40127	6E
40128	5D
40129	6C
40130	7A
40131	6C
40132	6C
40133	7A
40134	7B
40135	1A
40136	9A
40137	7A
40138	9B
40139	19B
40140	16A
40141	15D
40142	14B
40143	7B
40144	6A
40145	15C
40146	15C
40147	20C
40148	14B
40149	14B
40150	66C
40151	66C
40152	65D
40153	65D
40154	65D
40155	14A
40156	6E
40157	5D
40158	65D
40159	66B
40160	14B
40161	14B
40162	23B
40163	22A
40164	22A
40165	15D
40166	14B
40167	14B
40168	21B
40169	20A
40170	68B
40171	21A
40172	14A
40173	15C
40174	22A
40175	21A
40176	65D
40177	65D
40178	16A
40179	20D
40180	8E
40181	20C
40182	15C
40183	23B
40184	23B
40185	65D
40186	65D
40187	65D
40188	65D
40189	65D
40190	27C
40191	27C
40192	27C
40193	20C
40194	27C
40195	27C
40196	27C
40197	27C
40198	27C
40199	27D
40200	66B
40201	2B
40202	2B
40203	2C
40204	1A
40205	2B

40206-40670

40206	1A
40207	6C
40208	2B
40209	7A

Cl. "2P" 4-4-0

40322	5C
40323	20A
40324	7D
40325	17B
40326	20A
40332	5A
40337	18C
40351	20A
40353	15A
40356	12A
40359	18C
40362	20A
40364	17B
40370	18A
40377	7D
40383	17A
40395	17B
40396	7D
40397	8E
40401	16B
40402	5A
40404	17A
40405	5C
40406	20D
40407	17A
40409	18C
40410	35C
40411	17A
40412	4B
40413	2B
40414	23A
40415	16A
40416	17A
40417	16A
40418	17A
40419	16A
40420	4B
40421	4B
40422	23A
40423	22A
40424	16D
40425	5A
40426	17A
40430	6A
40432	17B
40433	7D
40434	10C
40436	17B
40438	2B
40439	21B
40443	5C
40444	20C
40447	2B
40448	12A
40450	10C
40452	16A
40453	17B
40454	16D
40455	20E
40458	16A
40461	5C
40462	3C
40463	21B
40464	8E
40470	23B
40471	5C
40472	18C
40477	14B
40478	16A
40480	20D
40482	35C
40484	23A
40485	15C
40486	21A
40487	19B
40488	23C
40489	20E
40491	18C
40493	19B
40495	7D
40497	35C
40499	17D
40501	3C
40502	19B
40503	18C
40504	16A
40505	71G
40507	5C
40508	2B
40509	71H
40511	21A
40513	17A
40514	20A
40518	19B
40519	17B
40520	17D
40521	20C
40522	8E
40523	22B
40524	7B
40525	17B
40526	17B
40527	5A
40528	2B
40529	8E
40530	22B
40531	9D
40532	35C
40534	4B
40535	16A
40536	15C
40537	18C
40538	15C
40539	9A
40540	16A
40541	15C
40542	15C
40543	15C
40546	16A
40547	14B
40548	18C
40549	19B
40550	15B
40551	15D
40552	16A
40553	16A
40556	18C
40557	18C
40558	35C
40559	35C
40560	16A
40562	20E
40563	71H
40564	71H
40565	10B
40566	67B
40567	20E
40568	71G
40569	71G
40570	67B
40571	67B
40572	67B
40573	67B
40574	67C
40575	67C
40576	68B
40577	68B
40578	67D
40579	67D
40580	27D
40581	27A
40582	27A
40583	8E
40584	27A
40585	27A
40586	25C
40587	27D
40588	24D
40589	25C
40590	67C
40592	64D
40593	67B
40594	67A
40595	67A
40596	67A
40597	67B
40598	67A
40599	67A
40600	68C
40601	71G
40602	68A
40603	61A
40604	67A
40605	67B
40606	67D
40607	67D
40608	67D
40609	67D
40610	67C
40611	68C
40612	67B
40613	68A
40614	68B
40615	68A
40616	68C
40617	67B
40618	67B
40619	67B
40620	67A
40621	67A
40622	61A
40623	68C
40624	67D
40625	67D
40626	67D
40627	67A
40628	10C
40629	7D
40630	20D
40631	10B
40632	17A
40633	17B
40634	71H
40635	10C
40636	67A
40637	67A
40638	67C
40640	67C
40641	67A
40642	67A
40643	67B
40644	67B
40645	67B
40646	7D
40647	67C
40648	67C
40649	67A
40650	61A
40651	67A
40652	12A
40653	4B
40654	11B
40655	9D
40656	12D
40657	4B
40658	6A
40659	5A
40660	5A
40661	67B
40662	67B
40663	67B
40664	67C
40665	67B
40666	67B
40667	67D
40668	67D
40669	67D
40670	67C

40671	7D
40672	1C
40673	12B
40674	9A
40675	7D
40676	24A
40677	24A
40678	27D
40679	8E
40680	24A
40681	24A
40682	26E
40683	8E
40684	27D
40685	25C
40686	67B
40687	67B
40688	67B
40689	67B
40690	27E
40691	26E
40692	9D
40693	9A
40694	12D
40695	12D
40696	71G
40697	71G
40698	71G
40699	12A
40700	71G

Cl. "3P" 4-4-0

40726	19C
40728	19A
40729	19A
40741	71H
40743	20A
40747	20A
40758	20A
40762	15D

Cl. "4P" 4-4-0

40900	9E
40901	64D
40902	68B
40903	64D
40904	68B
40905	67A
40906	67A
40907	64D
40908	67C
40909	67A
40910	9E
40911	64C
40912	68B
40913	63B
40914	67A
40915	67A
40916	66A
40917	21B
40918	65B
40919	67A
40920	67C
40921	63A
40922	63A
40923	63A
40924	63B
40925	7A
40926	8E
40927	17A
40928	21A
40929	16A
40930	14B
40931	23C
40932	14B
40933	7A
40934	35C
40935	22A
40936	9E
40937	27E
40938	63A
40939	63A
41000	17A
41001	22B
41003	17A
41004	20E
41005	23C
41006	15C
41007	15D
41009	15D
41011	15C
41012	15B
41014	19B
41015	16A
41016	19B
41019	16A
41020	14B
41021	19B
41023	17A
41025	22B
41028	22A
41030	22A
41032	16A
41035	21A
41037	19B
41038	15D
41040	20A
41041	15C
41043	17A
41044	15D
41045	23C
41046	21A
41047	22B
41048	20A
41049	17D
41050	14B
41051	14B
41052	9E
41053	15B
41054	14B
41055	9E
41056	23C
41057	17A
41058	22B
41059	17A
41060	17A
41061	21B
41062	19B
41063	15B
41064	21B
41065	23C
41066	9E
41067	20E
41068	20A
41069	20E
41070	15D
41071	14B
41072	19B
41073	21B
41074	22B
41075	15C
41076	9E
41077	14B
41078	22B
41079	19B
41080	20E
41081	23C
41082	16A
41083	35C
41084	17A
41085	26C
41086	7A
41087	15B
41088	17A
41089	15C
41090	2A
41091	15D
41092	68C
41093	7A
41094	15D
41095	15C
41096	16A
41097	22B
41098	6A
41099	68C
41100	26B
41101	27D
41102	27C
41103	26C
41104	26C
41105	2A
41106	6A
41107	6A
41108	6A
41109	68B
41110	67B
41111	3E
41112	5A
41113	9A
41114	7A
41115	5A
41116	3E
41117	14B
41118	8E
41119	7A
41120	6A
41121	6A
41122	2A
41123	7A
41124	7A
41125	63A
41126	65B
41127	68C
41128	65B
41129	68A
41130	64D
41131	66A
41132	67C
41133	67C
41134	61B
41135	68B
41136	64D
41137	20A
41138	67C
41139	68A
41140	68A
41141	68A
41142	68A
41143	68A
41144	20A
41145	64D
41146	68A
41147	64D
41148	66D
41149	66D
41150	7A
41151	3E
41152	2A
41153	6A
41154	9E
41155	67C
41156	8E
41157	6A
41158	6A
41159	9A
41160	5A
41161	7A
41162	8E
41163	6A
41164	6A
41165	2A
41166	8E
41167	5A
41168	9A
41169	6A
41170	6A
41171	68B
41172	3E
41173	8E
41174	2A
41175	68B

41176-41909

41176 61B
41177 64C
41178 64C
41179 68B
41180 64D
41181 9E
41182 66D
41183 67C
41184 61B
41185 28A
41186 26C
41187 27A
41188 24A
41189 26B
41190 26C
41191 26B
41192 28A
41193 27A
41194 27E
41195 28A
41196 26B
41197 20E
41198 15D
41199 14B

Cl. "2MT" 2-6-2T

41200 32B
41201 86K
41202 86K
41203 86K
41204 86K
41205 23B
41206 23B
41207 14A
41208 14A
41209 15D
41210 7D
41211 7D
41212 10D
41213 10D
41214 10D
41215 10D
41216 10D
41217 10D
41218 4B
41219 4B
41220 1C
41221 11B
41222 4A
41223 7B
41224 7B
41225 3B
41226 3C
41227 2C
41228 2C
41229 5A
41230 17B
41231 7D
41232 7A
41233 7B
41234 2B
41235 2B
41236 2B
41237 2B
41238 2B
41239 2C
41240 71G
41241 71G
41242 71G
41243 71G
41244 15A
41245 19B
41246 19B
41247 17A
41248 14B
41249 14B
41250 25A
41251 25A
41252 25A
41253 25A
41254 25A
41255 25G
41256 25G
41257 25G
41258 25G
41259 25G
41260 28B
41261 28B
41262 28B
41263 28B
41264 28B
41265 20E
41266 20E
41267 20A
41268 15C
41269 15D
41270 15D
41271 15D
41272
41273
41274
41275
41276
41277
41278
41279
41280
41281
41282
41283
41284
41285
41286
41287
41288
41289
41290
41291
41292
41293
41294
41295
41296
41297
41298
41299

Cl. "0F" 0-4-0T

41516 17B
41518 18C
41523 17B

Cl. "0F" 0-4-0T

41528 18D
41529 18D
41530 22B
41531 18C
41532 18C
41533 18D
41534 18D
41535 17A
41536 17B
41537 22B

Cl. "1F" 0-6-0T

41660 19A
41661 14B
41664 14B
41666 20B
41671 14B
41672 14B
41682 16A
41686 16A
41690 26G
41695 14A
41699 21A
41702 26G
41706 22A
41708 18D
41710 18D
41711 18D
41712 14A
41713 14B
41720 22B
41724 14B
41725 84G
41726 17A
41727 22B
41734 6C
41739 20B
41745 20A
41747 17A
41748 17B
41749 18D
41752 18D
41753 18D
41754 17A
41763 18D
41767 23A
41769 87K
41770 17B
41773 17A
41777 18D
41779 17A
41780 6C
41781 19A
41793 20D
41794 20B
41795 17A
41797 19C
41803 18D
41804 18D
41805 19C
41811 14A
41813 18C
41814 26G
41820 23A
41824 87K
41826 14B
41829 18C
41833 17A
41835 19C
41838 20B
41839 17B
41844 20D
41846 16A
41847 17A
41852 87K
41853 6C
41854 14C
41855 23A
41856 21A
41857 19A
41859 20B
41860 87K
41865 17B
41869 20B
41874 18C
41875 17D
41878 17B
41879 21A
41885 16D
41889 17A
41890 20B

Cl. "2P" 0-4-4T

41900 23C
41901 23C
41902 23C
41903 17A
41904 23C
41905 9A
41906 9A
41907 9A
41908 1C
41909 1C

Cl. "2P" 4-4-2T

41911 18A
41915 33A
41916 15A
41917 16A
41919 16A
41921 16A
41922 16A
41925 16A
41926 16A

Cl. "3P" 4-4-2T

41928 33A
41929 33A
41930 33A
41931 33A
41932 33B
41933 33B
41934 33B
41935 33B
41936 33A
41937 33A
41938 15C
41939 33A
41940 16D
41941 33A
41942 33A
41943 16D
41944 33A
41945 33A
41946 33B
41947 16D
41948 33A
41949 33B
41950 33A
41951 33A
41952 33B
41953 33B
41954 33B
41955 33B
41956 33A
41957 33B
41958 16D
41959 33B
41960 33C
41961 16D
41962 16D
41963 33C
41964 33C
41965 33A
41966 33C
41967 33A
41968 33A
41969 33A
41970 33A
41971 23A
41972 23A
41973 23A
41974 23A
41975 33A
41976 33A
41977 33A
41978 33A

Cl. "3F" 0-6-2T

41980 33B
41981 33A
41982 33A
41983 33A
41984 33A
41985 33A
41986 33A
41987 33A
41988 33A
41989 33A
41990 33A
41991 33C
41992 33C
41993 33A

Cl. "4MT" 2-6-4T

42050 21B
42051
42052
42053
42054
42055
42056
42057
42058
42059
42060
42061
42062
42063
42064
42065
42066
42067
42068
42069
42070
42071
42072
42073
42074
42075
42076
42077
42078
42079
42080
42081
42082
42083
42084
42085
42086
42087
42088
42089
42090
42091
42092
42093
42094
42095
42096 75F
42097 75F
42098 75F
42099 71F
42100 71F
42101 71F
42102
42103
42104
42105
42106
42107 25F
42108 25F
42109 25F
42110 25F
42111 25F
42112 25F
42113 25F
42114 25F
42115 25F
42116 25F
42117 1A
42118 1A
42119 1C
42120 1C
42121 1C
42122 67A
42123 67A
42124 67A
42125 66B
42126 66B
42127 66B
42128 66C
42129 66C
42130 66C
42131 67C
42132 14C
42133 14B
42134 14C
42135 23C
42136 23C
42137 15C
42138 14B
42139 14B
42140 16A
42141 21A
42142 20C
42143 20C
42144 23C
42145 20C
42146 20E
42147 24D
42148 29A
42149 25E
42150 25E
42151 25E
42152 25D
42153 24A
42154 24D
42155 2A
42156 7B
42157 7B
42158 24C
42159 1C
42160 14C
42161 14C
42162 64D
42163 64D
42164 66C
42165 66C
42166 66C
42167 66A
42168 66A
42169 66A
42170 66A
42171 66A
42172 66A
42173 64D
42174 64D
42175 66D
42176 66D
42177 17A
42178 1C
42179 11B
42180 23D
42181 15C
42182 15C
42183 15C
42184 16A
42185 16A
42186 21B
42187 24B
42188 25F
42189 25F
42190 67A
42191 67A
42192 67A
42193 67A
42194 67A
42195 67A
42196 67A
42197 67A
42198 63B
42199 63B
42200 66A
42201 66A
42202 66A
42203 66A
42204 66A
42205 66A
42206 66A
42207 66A
42208 66B
42209 67D
42210 67D
42211 67D

42212	67D	42274	66A	42336	17B	42398	9A
42213	66A	42275	66A	42337	21A	42399	9A
42214	66A	42276	66A	42338	21B	42400	66D
42215	66A	42277	66A	42339	16A	42401	11B
42216	66A	42278	26A	42340	17A	42402	11B
42217	64D	42279	26A	42341	17A	42403	11D
42218	33B	42280	26A	42342	21B	42404	11D
42219	33B	42281	26A	42343	5D	42405	25D
42220	33B	42282	26A	42344	5D	42406	25D
42221	33B	42283	26A	42345	5C	42407	25D
42222	33B	42284	26A	42346	5C	42408	25B
42223	33B	42285	26A	42347	5C	42409	25B
42224	33B	42286	26A	42348	4A	42410	25B
42225	33A	42287	26A	42349	5D	42411	25C
42226	33A	42288	26A	42350	9A	42412	25B
42227	33A	42289	26A	42351	9A	42413	25B
42228	16A	42290	26A	42352	9B	42414	25B
42229	16A	42291	27C	42353	9B	42415	66D
42230	33C	42292	27C	42354	9B	42416	66D
42231	33A	42293	27C	42355	9C	42417	66D
42232	33A	42294	27C	42356	9C	42418	66D
42233	5D	42295	24A	42357	9C	42419	66D
42234	5D	42296	24C	42358	5F	42420	66D
42235	5D	42297	27D	42359	11B	42421	66D
42236	5D	42298	24C	42360	9C	42422	66D
42237	14B	42299	27D	42361	16A	42423	66D
42238	66A	42300	14C	42362	9C	42424	11D
42239	66A	42301	11C	42363	9C	42425	6A
42240	66A	42302	14C	42364	5D	42426	8A
42241	66A	42303	4A	42365	9D	42427	9A
42242	66A	42304	1C	42366	9D	42428	11A
42243	66A	42305	87K	42367	9D	42429	11A
42244	66A	42306	9D	42368	9D	42430	9A
42245	66A	42307	87K	42369	9C	42431	5D
42246	66A	42308	5A	42370	9D	42432	11A
42247	66A	42309	5E	42371	9D	42433	24A
42248	33A	42310	25B	42372	11B	42434	24C
42249	33A	42311	25B	42373	16A	42435	24C
42250	33A	42312	25B	42374	33A	42436	24C
42251	33A	42313	11C	42375	5D	42437	24A
42252	33A	42314	11C	42376	5D	42438	24B
42253	33A	42315	9D	42377	20E	42439	24D
42254	33A	42316	1A	42378	1C	42440	5D
42255	33A	42317	11C	42379	9B	42441	3D
42256	33A	42318	9D	42380	20E	42442	10A
42257	33A	42319	9C	42381	9C	42443	5D
42258	7B	42320	5C	42382	9C	42444	3C
42259	7B	42321	11B	42383	14B	42445	5D
42260	7B	42322	9A	42384	25B	42446	4A
42261	7B	42323	5D	42385	87K	42447	5E
42262	3E	42324	25D	42386	9C	42448	3C
42263	3E	42325	14B	42387	87K	42449	5D
42264	3E	42326	21A	42388	87K	42450	6A
42265	3E	42327	21B	42389	1C	42451	6A
42266	10A	42328	33A	42390	87K	42452	3C
42267	3E	42329	14B	42391	5C	42453	10A
42268	64C	42330	15C	42392	11B	42454	10A
42269	64C	42331	15C	42393	11B	42455	6A
42270	64C	42332	9B	42394	87K	42456	10A
42271	64C	42333	16A	42395	11B	42457	11C
42272	64C	42334	14C	42396	11D	42458	5D
42273	64C	42335	14C	42397	9A	42459	8A

42460	7B
42461	9A
42462	11B
42463	9B
42464	11C
42465	10A
42466	3C
42467	9A
42468	1C
42469	3E
42470	3D
42471	5E
42472	26C
42473	26D
42474	26D
42475	24B
42476	26D
42477	26A
42478	9A
42479	5D
42480	24C
42481	24C
42482	3C
42483	24D
42484	24D
42485	24D
42486	26A
42487	2A
42488	3C
42489	3E
42490	24D
42491	24C
42492	24C
42493	11B
42494	5D
42500	33C
42501	33C
42502	33C
42503	33C
42504	33C
42505	33C
42506	33C
42507	33C
42508	33C
42509	33C
42510	33C
42511	33C
42512	33C
42513	33C
42514	33C
42515	33C
42516	33C
42517	33C
42518	33C
42519	33C
42520	33C
42521	33C
42522	33C
42523	33C
42524	33C
42525	33C
42526	33C
42527	33C
42528	33C
42529	33C
42530	33A
42531	33A
42532	33A
42533	33A
42534	33A
42535	33A
42536	33A
42537	27D
42538	3D
42539	10A
42540	6A
42541	2A
42542	9A
42543	5D
42544	11A
42545	26C
42546	24B
42547	24B
42548	24A
42549	24A
42550	26A
42551	26A
42552	3D
42553	25D
42554	27D
42555	24B
42556	24C
42557	27D
42558	24D
42559	24D
42560	10C
42561	10C
42562	3C
42563	10A
42564	8A
42565	26C
42566	4A
42567	5D
42568	6A
42569	27D
42570	8A
42571	11B
42572	10A
42573	11A
42574	10C
42575	9A
42576	2A
42577	2A
42578	3D
42579	3E
42580	9A
42581	11B
42582	5D
42583	8A
42584	6A
42585	2A
42586	3C
42587	6A
42588	7B
42589	1C
42590	1C
42591	4A
42592	27D
42593	1C
42594	9A
42595	6A
42596	8A
42597	8A
42598	1C
42599	9A
42600	4A
42601	11A
42602	8A
42603	5D
42604	3C
42605	5D
42606	8B
42607	8B
42608	9A
42609	5D
42610	10A
42611	5E
42612	8A
42613	11C
42614	27D
42615	11A
42616	3D
42617	7B
42618	26A
42619	26E
42620	26E
42621	26A
42622	26A
42623	26A
42624	26A
42625	26A
42626	26A
42627	3C
42628	7B
42629	26D
42630	26A
42631	27D
42632	27D
42633	26C
42634	24A
42635	26A
42636	28A
42637	28A
42638	28A
42639	25E
42640	27D
42641	27D
42642	27D
42643	24A
42644	27D
42645	26B
42646	26B
42647	26B
42648	26B
42649	26E
42650	26E
42651	26E
42652	26C
42653	26C
42654	26C
42655	26C
42656	26C
42657	26C
42658	8A
42659	4A
42660	7B
42661	24A
42662	10C
42663	5F
42664	5D
42665	5F
42666	4A
42667	5D
42668	5D
42669	4A
42670	5D
42671	2C
42672	5D
42673	2A
42674	2C
42675	26G
42676	5D
42677	5A
42678	33A
42679	33A
42680	16A
42681	33A
42682	20E
42683	5D
42684	33A
42685	20E
42686	16A
42687	33A
42688	66A
42689	66A
42690	66A
42691	66A
42692	66A
42693	66A
42694	66A
42695	66A
42696	66A
42697	66D
42698	66A
42699	66A

Cl. "5MT" 2-6-0

42700	25D
42701	26A
42702	26A
42703	26A
42704	26A
42705	26A
42706	24B
42707	26A
42708	26A

42709-42956

42709	26A
42710	26A
42711	26A
42712	25D
42713	26A
42714	26A
42715	26A
42716	24A
42717	24A
42718	24A
42719	25D
42720	68A
42721	26B
42722	26B
42723	26B
42724	26B
42725	26B
42726	25F
42727	25F
42728	25F
42729	28B
42730	25G
42731	25G
42732	25F
42733	24B
42734	26B
42735	66C
42736	65F
42737	65F
42738	63C
42739	67C
42740	66C
42741	66C
42742	63A
42743	63A
42744	67B
42745	67B
42746	65B
42747	1A
42748	68A
42749	68A
42750	26A
42751	68A
42752	68A
42753	26B
42754	21A
42755	26B
42756	17B
42757	68A
42758	21A
42759	14A
42760	17D
42761	17B
42762	20E
42763	17B
42764	21A
42765	26G
42766	26A
42767	17B
42768	17D
42769	17B
42770	23B
42771	14A
42772	9A
42773	5B
42774	14A
42775	9A
42776	9A
42777	2B
42778	9A
42779	3A
42780	68A
42781	2B
42782	3D
42783	2B
42784	23B
42785	5B
42786	1A
42787	1A
42788	9A
42789	26A
42790	21A
42791	17B
42792	15C
42793	68A
42794	14A
42795	20A
42796	26B
42797	19A
42798	20A
42799	17B
42800	63C
42801	63C
42802	68A
42803	68A
42804	64C
42805	67C
42806	67C
42807	64C
42808	67C
42809	67C
42810	5B
42811	5B
42812	1A
42813	2B
42814	2B
42815	5B
42816	20A
42817	1A
42818	21A
42819	26B
42820	26A
42821	24B
42822	21A
42823	16A
42824	21A
42825	21A
42826	21A
42827	21A
42828	25F
42829	21A
42830	64C
42831	68A
42832	68A
42833	68A
42834	68A
42835	68A
42836	68A
42837	68A
42838	26B
42839	14A
42840	28B
42841	28B
42842	28B
42843	24A
42844	28B
42845	26A
42846	17B
42847	17A
42848	9A
42849	8C
42850	66C
42851	3A
42852	8C
42853	3A
42854	9A
42855	14A
42856	5B
42857	21A
42858	9A
42859	9B
42860	26B
42861	25B
42862	25B
42863	25B
42864	26B
42865	25F
42866	25B
42867	28B
42868	26B
42869	25B
42870	1A
42871	26A
42872	17A
42873	17D
42874	17D
42875	68A
42876	68A
42877	68A
42878	26A
42879	67C
42880	66C
42881	68A
42882	68A
42883	68A
42884	68A
42885	1A
42886	9A
42887	9A
42888	2B
42889	9A
42890	21A
42891	3A
42892	8C
42893	23C
42894	3A
42895	23C
42896	17B
42897	17A
42898	26G
42899	68A
42900	21A
42901	26A
42902	17D
42903	21A
42904	19A
42905	68A
42906	68A
42907	68A
42908	68B
42909	68B
42910	67B
42911	67A
42912	67B
42913	68A
42914	67A
42915	68B
42916	67A
42917	67A
42918	68B
42919	68B
42920	5B
42921	3D
42922	17B
42923	9A
42924	9A
42925	9A
42926	5B
42927	67C
42928	23C
42929	3A
42930	9A
42931	1A
42932	2B
42933	2B
42934	9B
42935	9A
42936	9A
42937	9A
42938	9A
42939	5B
42940	1A
42941	2B
42942	9D
42943	9D
42944	2B
42945	6B
42946	3D
42947	3D
42948	3D
42949	8E
42950	5B
42951	3D
42952	5B
42953	6C
42954	3D
42955	5B
42956	5B

42957	3D
42958	3D
42959	6B
42960	2B
42961	6C
42962	8C
42963	3D
42964	8C
42965	8C
42966	3D
42967	6C
42968	5B
42969	6C
42970	6C
42971	8C
42972	5B
42973	3D
42974	3D
42975	6B
42976	6B
42977	8C
42978	9A
42979	9A
42980	5B
42981	6C
42982	8C
42983	5B
42984	5B

Cl. "4MT" 2-6-0

43000	4A
43001	4A
43002	4A
43003	4A
43004	4A
43005	4A
43006	12D
43007	12D
43008	12D
43009	12D
43010	17A
43011	21A
43012	22A
43013	71G
43014	21A
43015	19A
43016	20A
43017	71G
43018	16A
43019	16A
43020	2B
43021	2B
43022	2B
43023	2B
43024	2B
43025	2B
43026	10E
43027	10E
43028	10E
43029	10E
43030	20A
43031	17A
43032	19A
43033	16A
43034	23C
43035	23C
43036	71G
43037	19A
43038	19A
43039	20A
43040	16A
43041	19A
43042	19A
43043	21A
43044	21A
43045	15C
43046	22A
43047	22A
43048	21A
43049	17A
43050	51A
43051	51A
43052	50E
43053	53A
43054	51A
43055	51A
43056	
43057	
43058	
43059	
43060	
43061	
43062	
43063	
43064	
43065	
43066	
43067	
43068	
43069	
43070	52B
43071	51A
43072	51A
43073	
43074	
43075	
43076	
43077	
43078	
43079	
43080	
43081	
43082	
43083	
43084	
43085	
43086	
43087	
43088	
43089	
43090	
43091	
43092	
43093	
43094	
43095	
43096	
43097	
43098	
43099	
43100	
43101	
43102	
43103	
43104	
43105	
43106	
43107	
43108	
43109	
43110	
43111	

Cl. "3F" 0-6-0

43137	17A
43174	15D
43178	20E
43180	19C
43181	19C
43183	15C
43185	17A
43186	18A
43187	23C
43188	17B
43189	5B
43191	17A
43192	16A
43193	15A
43194	71H
43200	17A
43201	21A
43203	21B
43204	71H
43205	15C
43207	5B
43208	19C
43210	21A
43211	18C
43212	18C
43213	22B
43214	21A
43216	71H
43218	71H
43219	18C
43222	15D
43223	21A
43224	18D
43225	21A
43226	17A
43228	71H
43231	3E
43232	15C
43233	20C
43234	18D
43235	18B
43237	8B
43239	16D
43240	16A
43241	19A
43242	18A
43243	19C
43244	17B
43245	14C
43246	21A
43247	17B
43248	71H
43249	16A
43250	20C
43251	18A
43252	18D
43253	18B
43254	18B
43256	17B
43257	21A
43258	22B
43259	17A
43261	14A
43263	21B
43266	18B
43267	20B
43268	9D
43271	9D
43273	17D
43274	9D
43275	9A
43277	21D
43278	9D
43281	9B
43282	8B
43283	8B
43284	21A
43286	17B
43287	18A
43290	17D
43292	18D
43293	23C
43294	18D
43295	23A
43296	9D
43298	18D
43299	18D
43300	16A
43301	20D
43305	18A
43306	17B
43307	14A
43308	3D
43309	18D
43310	18D
43312	17A
43313	14A
43314	8B
43315	17A
43317	18B
43318	17A
43319	35C

43321	21A
43323	17A
43324	17A
43325	19C
43326	15C
43327	18A
43329	8B
43330	23C
43331	18B
43332	20C
43333	15C
43334	19A
43335	19A
43336	21A
43337	22B
43339	21A
43340	17B
43341	19B
43342	17D
43344	22B
43351	20E
43355	21B
43356	71H
43357	84G
43359	21B
43361	17A
43364	17A
43367	15A
43368	17A
43369	16A
43370	17D
43371	16A
43373	22B
43374	21A
43378	16A
43379	18B
43381	21D
43386	18D
43387	9D
43388	17B
43389	8B
43392	20B
43394	84G
43395	17B
43396	7D
43398	8B
43399	16A
43400	14A
43401	16A
43402	17A
43405	18A
43406	17A
43410	3C
43411	15C
43419	71H
43427	22A
43428	15D
43429	17C
43431	16D
43433	21A
43435	21A
43436	22A
43440	14A
43441	21A
43443	21A
43444	22A
43446	20C
43448	14A
43449	20B
43453	18A
43454	15C
43456	20B
43457	9A
43459	17A
43462	22A
43463	19A
43464	22A
43468	16C
43469	17A
43474	15D
43476	20B
43482	17A
43484	21A
43490	21A
43491	21A
43494	16C
43496	17A
43497	20D
43499	18A
43502	3C
43506	22B
43507	21A
43509	20D
43510	17A
43514	20D
43515	18D
43520	21D
43521	21D
43522	16D
43523	21D
43524	18D
43529	16D
43531	21A
43538	16A
43540	21A
43544	21A
43546	18D
43548	17A
43550	17A
43553	20C
43558	16A
43562	9D
43565	14A
43568	21D
43570	84G
43572	17A
43574	17A
43575	18D
43578	17A
43579	20B
43580	18B
43581	84G
43582	17B
43583	21B
43584	17A
43585	23B
43586	23B
43587	19C
43593	71H
43594	21A
43595	19A
43596	16C
43598	17A
43599	18A
43600	84G
43604	19A
43605	19A
43607	19A
43608	17B
43612	26G
43615	8B
43618	8B
43619	17B
43620	21A
43621	21A
43622	18C
43623	17B
43624	21A
43627	21A
43629	14A
43630	26G
43631	18A
43633	3C
43634	16D
43636	19A
43637	16A
43638	26G
43639	20D
43644	21A
43645	22B
43650	18A
43651	35C
43652	17B
43653	15C
43656	20D
43657	8B
43658	17A
43660	19C
43661	19A
43662	19A
43664	19C
43665	20A
43667	21C
43668	21B
43669	19C
43673	21A
43674	21A
43675	21B
43676	15C
43678	20B
43679	84G
43680	21A
43681	20B
43682	17C
43683	19A
43684	21A
43686	21C
43687	21B
43690	21A
43693	21D
43698	21A
43705	20B
43709	17B
43710	15C
43711	16A
43712	22A
43714	20D
43715	19A
43717	9A
43721	15D
43723	16A
43724	16A
43727	16D
43728	15C
43729	16A
43731	19A
43734	22A
43735	17A
43737	20B
43742	20E
43745	17A
43747	19C
43748	15C
43749	19A
43751	18D
43753	15C
43754	22B
43755	19A
43756	26G
43757	84G
43759	21A
43760	84G
43762	21A
43763	17A
43765	20C
43766	15D
43767	21D
43770	20E
43771	18C
43773	16C
43775	19A
43776	17A
43777	15D
43778	18A
43779	17C
43781	20B
43782	14C
43784	23A
43785	15D
43786	3C
43787	3C
43789	20C
43790	15C
43791	21A
43792	71H
43793	18A
43795	18A
43797	15A

43798	18A
43799	18A
43800	21A
43801	14A
43802	18C
43803	18A
43804	18A
43805	18A
43806	15C
43807	15C
43808	15A
43809	17C
43810	18A
43811	9F
43812	21A
43814	19C
43815	17B
43817	18A
43819	18A
43820	18A
43821	18A
43822	21D
43823	18A
43824	18A
43825	18A
43826	18A
43827	18A
43828	18A
43829	15C
43832	18A
43833	18A

Cl. "4F" 0-6-0

43835	17C
43836	9F
43837	17B
43838	17A
43839	17A
43840	17A
43841	4A
43842	9D
43843	21A
43844	19A
43845	21A
43846	22B
43847	22A
43848	65B
43849	65B
43850	18B
43851	20B
43852	20B
43853	22A
43854	35C
43855	21A
43856	18C
43857	18D
43858	21A
43859	18A
43860	18B
43861	15A
43862	18D
43863	35C
43864	35C
43865	17C
43866	18B
43867	18B
43868	68A
43869	21A
43870	15C
43871	20B
43872	17C
43873	21D
43874	16D
43875	71G
43876	15C
43877	7A
43878	20B
43879	21A
43880	18B
43881	17D
43882	17C
43883	65F
43884	66B
43885	18B
43886	18D
43887	22B
43888	15D
43889	15B
43890	23C
43891	21A
43892	17B
43893	23A
43894	17C
43895	16C
43896	9E
43897	24D
43898	15B
43899	67A
43900	18A
43901	14A
43902	68A
43903	16C
43904	23A
43905	14A
43906	19C
43907	16C
43908	9E
43909	14B
43910	15D
43911	21A
43912	21A
43913	23A
43914	18D
43915	5D
43916	17B
43917	23A
43918	17D
43919	17B
43920	18D
43921	17C
43922	68A
43923	15D
43924	22B
43925	17D
43926	22A
43927	26G
43928	22A
43929	17D
43930	15A
43931	20A
43932	22B
43933	23C
43934	14A
43935	14B
43936	18C
43937	15C
43938	17B
43939	21A
43940	21A
43941	21A
43942	20C
43943	18A
43944	23A
43945	9F
43946	21A
43947	14A
43948	17B
43949	21A
43950	19C
43951	21A
43952	26G
43953	20A
43954	16A
43955	17A
43956	16A
43957	35C
43958	16A
43959	18C
43960	23A
43961	18A
43962	14A
43963	20B
43964	14B
43965	17B
43966	18B
43967	15D
43968	21A
43969	22A
43970	18A
43971	15D
43972	17B
43973	68A
43974	18A
43975	15A
43976	17B
43977	15C
43978	22B
43979	18A
43980	35C
43981	35C
43982	14A
43983	16D
43984	23A
43985	18A
43986	21A
43987	20B
43988	18A
43989	20B
43990	18A
43991	17B
43992	18B
43993	18D
43994	18A
43995	18A
43996	68A
43997	16D
43998	18B
43999	23A
44000	23A
44001	68A
44002	17B
44003	20C
44004	16D
44005	16C
44006	18D
44007	23A
44008	68A
44009	68A
44010	21A
44011	63B
44012	18A
44013	19C
44014	18B
44015	19C
44016	68A
44017	17D
44018	17D
44019	26G
44020	20B
44021	16C
44022	26G
44023	21A
44024	17D
44025	26G
44026	21A
44027	3B
44028	14A
44029	14A
44030	16A
44031	17A
44032	23C
44033	15A
44034	15C
44035	22B
44036	19C
44037	15A
44038	24B
44039	16A
44040	26G
44041	23A
44042	23B
44043	15B
44044	20A
44045	22B
44046	17D
44047	17B
44048	17B

44049	21A
44050	17D
44051	14A
44052	14B
44053	35C
44054	18C
44055	16A
44056	25D
44057	3E
44058	2A
44059	11B
44060	11A
44061	3D
44062	25C
44063	5E
44064	12D
44065	6B
44066	18D
44067	5D
44068	5D
44069	5D
44070	18D
44071	19C
44072	4B
44073	6B
44074	9B
44075	11A
44076	4B
44077	5D
44078	3C
44079	5E
44080	9F
44081	12A
44082	16C
44083	11D
44084	21A
44085	17C
44086	12C
44087	22B
44088	21A
44089	19C
44090	9F
44091	18A
44092	21A
44093	5D
44094	20B
44095	16A
44096	71G
44097	35C
44098	20D
44099	20D
44100	17B
44101	17A
44102	71H
44103	17C
44104	18D
44105	25C
44106	18A
44107	18C
44108	21A
44109	17C
44110	35C
44111	19C
44112	21A
44113	16A
44114	26G
44115	3C
44116	1A
44117	35C
44118	5D
44119	26G
44120	5D
44121	12A
44122	18D
44123	15C
44124	17B
44125	5E
44126	5B
44127	19C
44128	19C
44129	18D
44130	18B
44131	14A
44132	16A
44133	18A
44134	17D
44135	22A
44136	18A
44137	21A
44138	21B
44139	14A
44140	16C
44141	20C
44142	17A
44143	17B
44144	9F
44145	21A
44146	71H
44147	18D
44148	17C
44149	23B
44150	21A
44151	20D
44152	35C
44153	20B
44154	18D
44155	35C
44156	17C
44157	18A
44158	16A
44159	67A
44160	15C
44161	20C
44162	18C
44163	17D
44164	17A
44165	21A
44166	17B
44167	22B
44168	17D
44169	22A
44170	17B
44171	17B
44172	17D
44173	19C
44174	17D
44175	22B
44176	21A
44177	17A
44178	9F
44179	21A
44180	17C
44181	68A
44182	18D
44183	68A
44184	21A
44185	21A
44186	21D
44187	21A
44188	18B
44189	68A
44190	21A
44191	18B
44192	11A
44193	63A
44194	63A
44195	14A
44196	66A
44197	23A
44198	67A
44199	68A
44200	21A
44201	23C
44202	16C
44203	21A
44204	21D
44205	16C
44206	16C
44207	20A
44208	1A
44209	17D
44210	14B
44211	19A
44212	19A
44213	21A
44214	17A
44215	16A
44216	20E
44217	20D
44218	35C
44219	3D
44220	25C
44221	24B
44222	23A
44223	16A
44224	21A
44225	24D
44226	17B
44227	17C
44228	33A
44229	18B
44230	16A
44231	15C
44232	19C
44233	18A
44234	65B
44235	71G
44236	9E
44237	10D
44238	35C
44239	35C
44240	24D
44241	19C
44242	15A
44243	14B
44244	18C
44245	20B
44246	17D
44247	16A
44248	21A
44249	15A
44250	18A
44251	63A
44252	17C
44253	63A
44254	63A
44255	65B
44256	65B
44257	63A
44258	63A
44259	14A
44260	17C
44261	10D
44262	17D
44263	21A
44264	16A
44265	17B
44266	22A
44267	22A
44268	16C
44269	22A
44270	17B
44271	9A
44272	22B
44273	35C
44274	18C
44275	17B
44276	23B
44277	23A
44278	15B
44279	17C
44280	23C
44281	65B
44282	23B
44283	63B
44284	19A
44285	19A
44286	9F
44287	15C
44288	18C
44289	21A
44290	19C
44291	24D
44292	11D
44293	35C
44294	18C
44295	17B
44296	35C

44297	14A
44298	14B
44299	18D
44300	5B
44301	5B
44302	3D
44303	9A
44304	14A
44305	7B
44306	11B
44307	5F
44308	9A
44309	5D
44310	5D
44311	26A
44312	67B
44313	16A
44314	63A
44315	68A
44316	17B
44317	21A
44318	63A
44319	67B
44320	65F
44321	18B
44322	63B
44323	67B
44324	68A
44325	67B
44326	68A
44327	17D
44328	63A
44329	67A
44330	63B
44331	63B
44332	17B
44333	21B
44334	19A
44335	22A
44336	20D
44337	20D
44338	20D
44339	9D
44340	9B
44341	5E
44342	5E
44343	5D
44344	5E
44345	3C
44346	12A
44347	11B
44348	1D
44349	9A
44350	3D
44351	11B
44352	2B
44353	5D
44354	2A
44355	71G
44356	10D
44357	9A
44358	5D
44359	5E
44360	3C
44361	3E
44362	21A
44363	5D
44364	12D
44365	12D
44366	21B
44367	6B
44368	11B
44369	5D
44370	1D
44371	18A
44372	1A
44373	5D
44374	11A
44375	5D
44376	18A
44377	5D
44378	5D
44379	10E
44380	5D
44381	1A
44382	9D
44383	5D
44384	10D
44385	11A
44386	5B
44387	4B
44388	5D
44389	7A
44390	12A
44391	5D
44392	2A
44393	5D
44394	16D
44395	2A
44396	5D
44397	14B
44398	24D
44399	11A
44400	20E
44401	16A
44402	17A
44403	15C
44404	20A
44405	23C
44406	21A
44407	9F
44408	16A
44409	17A
44410	18C
44411	22A
44412	16A
44413	21A
44414	16A
44415	16D
44416	16D
44417	71H
44418	21A
44419	17A
44420	17A
44421	9F
44422	71G
44423	15C
44424	22A
44425	16A
44426	19A
44427	21A
44428	17B
44429	17D
44430	18B
44431	20A
44432	17A
44433	17B
44434	17B
44435	17B
44436	17B
44437	19A
44438	5D
44439	3B
44440	14B
44441	1C
44442	1A
44443	1C
44444	9B
44445	7B
44446	20C
44447	4A
44448	5D
44449	12D
44450	5E
44451	1A
44452	5B
44453	5E
44454	10D
44455	5D
44456	2A
44457	19C
44458	35C
44459	11D
44460	24A
44461	12E
44462	27B
44463	16C
44464	24B
44465	15B
44466	22A
44467	20B
44468	23A
44469	11D
44470	16C
44471	25D
44472	16A
44473	10D
44474	25D
44475	21A
44476	35C
44477	19C
44478	5D
44479	24A
44480	16A
44481	27B
44482	18B
44483	24D
44484	5D
44485	25C
44486	24A
44487	11B
44488	3C
44489	5D
44490	3D
44491	4B
44492	3B
44493	6B
44494	9G
44495	12D
44496	5D
44497	1A
44498	5D
44499	5D
44500	5D
44501	20A
44502	5D
44503	5D
44504	5F
44505	12D
44506	3E
44507	5D
44508	5D
44509	35C
44510	11A
44511	11B
44512	3C
44513	5D
44514	3E
44515	21A
44516	21A
44517	3D
44518	35C
44519	35C
44520	21A
44521	35C
44522	35C
44523	71G
44524	21A
44525	21A
44526	17B
44527	17B
44528	17B
44529	14A
44530	33A
44531	14B
44532	14B
44533	16A
44534	22A
44535	71G
44536	22A
44537	22A
44538	21A
44539	17C
44540	17D
44541	27B
44542	17A
44543	26A
44544	24B

44545	21A
44546	16A
44547	16C
44548	5D
44549	12E
44550	19A
44551	17B
44552	16C
44553	22A
44554	17C
44555	20E
44556	19A
44557	71G
44558	71G
44559	71G
44560	71G
44561	71G
44562	20D
44563	14B
44564	17D
44565	17A
44566	17A
44567	21A
44568	19A
44569	22A
44570	20E
44571	21A
44572	17C
44573	19A
44574	15A
44575	15A
44576	19C
44577	16A
44578	16A
44579	23B
44580	21A
44581	14A
44582	17B
44583	15C
44584	20A
44585	16A
44586	20D
44587	21D
44588	17D
44589	16C
44590	18D
44591	21A
44592	3E
44593	12D
44594	11B
44595	5E
44596	5D
44597	17B
44598	16A
44599	17B
44600	17B
44601	17A
44602	17A
44603	20D
44604	20D
44605	18B
44606	21D

Cl. "5MT" 4-6-0

44658	14B
44659	21A
44660	21A
44661	21A
44662	20A
44663	15C
44664	19B
44665	19B
44666	21A
44667	17A
44668	68A
44669	68A
44670	68A
44671	68A
44672	68A
44673	68A
44674	68A
44675	68A
44676	68A
44677	68A
44678	5A
44679	5A
44680	5A
44681	5A
44682	5A
44683	5A
44684	5A
44685	5A
44686	
44687	
44688	27A
44689	
44690	
44691	
44692	
44693	
44694	
44695	
44696	
44697	
44698	63A
44699	63A
44700	64D
44701	64D
44702	65B
44703	65B
44704	63A
44705	63A
44706	67A
44707	66A
44708	10B
44709	11A
44710	2A
44711	2A
44712	2A
44713	2A
44714	2A
44715	2A
44716	2A
44717	21A
44718	68A
44719	68A
44720	68A
44721	68A
44722	68A
44723	68A
44724	68A
44725	68A
44726	68A
44727	68A
44728	27C
44729	27C
44730	28A
44731	28A
44732	28A
44733	28A
44734	26A
44735	26A
44736	26A
44737	27C
44738	7A
44739	7A
44740	7A
44741	7A
44742	7A
44743	22A
44744	22A
44745	22A
44746	22A
44747	22A
44748	9A
44749	9A
44750	9A
44751	9A
44752	9A
44753	20A
44754	20A
44755	20A
44756	20A
44757	20A
44758	5A
44759	9A
44760	9A
44761	5A
44762	5A
44763	5A
44764	5A
44765	5A
44766	5A
44767	27A
44768	8A
44769	8A
44770	5A
44771	5A
44772	8A
44773	16A
44774	20A
44775	20A
44776	17A
44777	14B
44778	28A
44779	28A
44780	25B
44781	26B
44782	26B
44783	60A
44784	60A
44785	60A
44786	65B
44787	66A
44788	60A
44789	60A
44790	66A
44791	65C
44792	66A
44793	66A
44794	66A
44795	68A
44796	63A
44797	63A
44798	60A
44799	60A
44800	6B
44801	63A
44802	19A
44803	26G
44804	21A
44805	21A
44806	15C
44807	9A
44808	7C
44809	17A
44810	21A
44811	21B
44812	15C
44813	21A
44814	21A
44815	17A
44816	14B
44817	14B
44818	17A
44819	17A
44820	17A
44821	20A
44822	14B
44823	26B
44824	25B
44825	16A
44826	71G
44827	19A
44828	20A
44829	3E
44830	71G
44831	2A
44832	9A
44833	1A
44834	9A
44835	84G
44836	2A
44837	9A
44838	9A
44839	71G
44340	6A
44841	16A

44842 21A
44843 20A
44844 6A
44845 19A
44846 14B
44847 17A
44848 17A
44849 20A
44850 20A
44851 17A
44852 21B
44853 20A
44854 20A
44855 22A
44856 20A
44857 20A
44858 19A
44859 19B
44860 2A
44861 16A
44862 2A
44863 2A
44864 4A
44865 4A
44866 2A
44867 2A
44868 7C
44869 12A
44870 2A
44871 12A
44872 3D
44873 3C
44874 10B
44875 1A
44876 12A
44877 68A
44878 68A
44879 63A
44880 65B
44881 65B
44882 68A
44883 68A
44884 68A
44885 63A
44886 68A
44887 27C
44888 26A
44889 26A
44890 26A
44891 26A
44892 10B
44893 26A
44894 26A
44895 26A
44896 25G
44897 8B
44898 68A
44899 68A
44900 68A
44901 68A
44902 68A
44903 68A
44904 11A
44905 11B
44906 8A
44907 8A
44908 84G
44909 2A
44910 2A
44911 1A
44912 25F
44913 7B
44914 3A
44915 2A
44916 4A
44917 17A
44918 16A
44919 21A
44920 21A
44921 26G
44922 65B
44923 65B
44924 63A
44925 63A
44926 27C
44927 28A
44928 28A
44929 28A
44930 28A
44931 63A
44932 28A
44933 26A
44934 26A
44935 9A
44936 12A
44937 9A
44938 9E
44939 12A
44940 26A
44941 8A
44942 3D
44943 20A
44944 19A
44945 71G
44946 27A
44947 28A
44948 28B
44949 25B
44950 28A
44951 25F
44952 64D
44953 64D
44954 62B
44955 64D
44956 65B
44957 65B
44958 63A
44959 63A
44960 63A
44961 63A
44962 19B
44963 19B
44964 19B
44965 19B
44966 21A
44967 65B
44968 67A
44969 66B
44970 65B
44971 7A
44972 63A
44973 63A
44974 63A
44975 63A
44976 63A
44977 63A
44978 63A
44979 63A
44980 63A
44981 14B
44982 27A
44983 20A
44984 14B
44985 14B
44986 19B
44987 26A
44988 28A
44989 27C
44990 25F
44991 60A
44992 60A
44993 68A
44994 68A
44995 65B
44996 65B
44997 63A
44998 63A
44999 63A
45000 2A
45001 8B
45002 2A
45003 2A
45004 2A
45005 8A
45006 5B
45007 63A
45008 66B
45009 66B
45010 65A
45011 63A
45012 60A
45013 5B
45014 12B
45015 3E
45016 63B
45017 8A
45018 60B
45019 10A
45020 2A
45021 4B
45022 64C
45023 64C
45024 1A
45025 1A
45026 10C
45027 1A
45028 7C
45029 64C
45030 5B
45031 26G
45032 8B
45033 2A
45034 2A
45035 8B
45036 64A
45037 10C
45038 5B
45039 11A
45040 20A
45041 1A
45042 10C
45043 28A
45044 5B
45045 6A
45046 11B
45047 67A
45048 5B
45049 67A
45050 11A
45051 3D
45052 3D
45053 60A
45054 11B
45055 10C
45056 19A
45057 4A
45058 3D
45059 16A
45060 5B
45061 27C
45062 25G
45063 25G
45064 1A
45065 12A
45066 60A
45067 5B
45068 27A
45069 3C
45070 7C
45071 1A
45072 8B
45073 5B
45074 19A
45075 25G
45076 25G
45077 28A
45078 25G
45079 26A
45080 25G
45081 68A
45082 68A
45083 68A
45084 68A
45085 64A
45086 63A
45087 64D
45088 15C
45089 1A

45090 60A
45091 4B
45092 2A
45093 5B
45094 3D
45095 6A
45096 12B
45097 1A
45098 60A
45099 25B
45100 68A
45101 25A
45102 26A
45103 26A
45104 26A
45105 26A
45106 12A
45107 28A
45108 5B
45109 8B
45110 7C
45111 7C
45112 84G
45113 7C
45114 5D
45115 65B
45116 65B
45117 64D
45118 63A
45119 63A
45120 60A
45121 66B
45122 60A
45123 60A
45124 60A
45125 63A
45126 68A
45127 63A
45128 19A
45129 12A
45130 4A
45131 5B
45132 6B
45133 12A
45134 5B
45135 10C
45136 60A
45137 10C
45138 60A
45139 12A
45140 1A
45141 10A
45142 10C
45143 84G
45144 7B
45145 84G
45146 1A
45147 10C
45148 5B
45149 8B
45150 2A
45151 66B
45152 66B
45153 65B
45154* 65B
45155 65B
45156* 65B
45157* 65B
45158* 65B
45159 65B
45160 60A
45161 64D
45162 63A
45163 67A
45164 63A
45165 63A
45166 63A
45167 63A
45168 67A
45169 63A
45170 63A
45171 63A
45172 63A
45173 63A
45174 67A
45175 63A
45176 66B
45177 65B
45178 65B
45179 60A
45180 84G
45181 8A
45182 10C
45183 84G
45184 64C
45185 5B
45186 21A
45187 2A
45188 10C
45189 5B
45190 84G
45191 4B
45192 60A
45193 11A
45194 67A
45195 5B
45196 8B
45197 12A
45198 5B
45199 10C
45200 27C
45201 25F
45202 26A
45203 26A
45204 25A
45205 25A
45206 25A
45207 25F
45208 25F
45209 25A
45210 26A
45211 26A
45212 28B
45213 63A
45214 28A
45215 25B
45216 27A
45217 5A
45218 25G
45219 26A
45220 26A
45221 25A
45222 26A
45223 26A
45224 26A
45225 19A
45226 27A
45227 27A
45228 27A
45229 27A
45230 12A
45231 10C
45232 26A
45233 26A
45234 26A
45235 10A
45236 21B
45237 25B
45238 25B
45239 5B
45240 5B
45241 7A
45242 8A
45243 8A
45244 12A
45245 84G
45246 12A
45247 6A
45248 8A
45249 7C
45250 2A
45251 67A
45252 8B
45253 14B
45254 5B
45255 8B
45256 8A
45257 5D
45258 12A
45259 10C
45260 19B
45261 25A
45262 19A
45263 15C
45264 19B
45265 21A
45266 63A
45267 14B
45268 21A
45269 21A
45270 5B
45271 5B
45272 20A
45273 21A
45274 21B
45275 6B
45276 8A
45277 14B
45278 5D
45279 14B
45280 15C
45281 84G
45282 2A
45283 84G
45284 26G
45285 14B
45286 6B
45287 3B
45288 6B
45289 9A
45290 10C
45291 11B
45292 7A
45293 12A
45294 5B
45295 12A
45296 12A
45297 19B
45298 84G
45299 12A
45300 5B
45301 5B
45302 10C
45303 8A
45304 10C
45305 8B
45306 11A
45307 9A
45308 3C
45309 63A
45310 3A
45311 12A
45312 10C
45313 10A
45314 4A
45315 6B
45316 4A
45317 11B
45318 84G
45319 60A
45320 60A
45321 8B
45322 3D
45323 12A
45324 5D
45325 5D
45326 5D
45327 10C
45328 8B
45329 10C
45330 84G
45331 4B
45332 10B
45333 11A
45334 27C
45335 27A
45336 27A
45337 10B

45338	26B
45339	25A
45340	25B
45341	25G
45342	15C
45343	11A
45344	3C
45345	12A
45346	7C
45347	8A
45348	12A
45349	3D
45350	8A
45351	12A
45352	8A
45353	1A
45354	8B
45355	65B
45356	65B
45357	63A
45358	63B
45359	63B
45360	60A
45361	60A
45362	64C
45363	68A
45364	68A
45365	63A
45366	63A
45367	24A
45368	12A
45369	5B
45370	8B
45371	12A
45372	2A
45373	10C
45374	2A
45375	2A
45376	7C
45377	10C
45378	10C
45379	2A
45380	8A
45381	5D
45382	7C
45383	11B
45384	84G
45385	6A
45386	11B
45387	9A
45388	12A
45389	63A
45390	3E
45391	2A
45392	11A
45393	8A
45394	2A
45395	3C
45396	24A
45397	3D
45398	8A
45399	8A
45400	84G
45401	10C
45402	6B
45403	10C
45404	2A
45405	3B
45406	84G
45407	19A
45408	10C
45409	12A
45410	10C
45411	10C
45412	12A
45413	10A
45414	12A
45415	27C
45416	12A
45417	3A
45418	3E
45419	2A
45420	10C
45421	10C
45422	84G
45423	65B
45424	10C
45425	10A
45426	10C
45427	11A
45428	10C
45429	2A
45430	2A
45431	2A
45432	68A
45433	3A
45434	3B
45435	27C
45436	84G
45437	3B
45438	10C
45439	12A
45440	71G
45441	2A
45442	10C
45443	65B
45444	10C
45445	12A
45446	3D
45447	21A
45448	3D
45449	10A
45450	26G
45451	12A
45452	63A
45453	60A
45454	12B
45455	68A
45456	63A
45457	63A
45458	63A
45459	63A
45460	63A
45461	60A
45462	66B
45463	63A
45464	63A
45465	63A
45466	63A
45467	63A
45468	65B
45469	63A
45470	63A
45471	65B
45472	63A
45473	63A
45474	63A
45475	63A
45476	60A
45477	60A
45478	60A
45479	60A
45480	65B
45481	65B
45482	65B
45483	63A
45484	66A
45485	66A
45486	66A
45487	66A
45488	63A
45489	67A
45490	67A
45491	67A
45492	63A
45493	2A
45494	12A
45495	10C
45496	63A
45497	63A
45498	66B
45499	65B

Cl. "5XP" "Patriot" 4-6-0

45500*	9A
45501*	9A
45502*	5A
45503*	5A
45504*	5A
45505*	12A
45506*	5A
45507*	5A
45508	10B
45509	1A
45510	5A
45511*	5A
45512*	12A
45513	5A
45514*	1B
45515*	8A
45516*	10B
45517	12A
45518*	12A
45519*	10B
45520*	9A
45521*	8B
45522*	1B
45523*	5A
45524*	3B
45525*	12A
45526*	12A
45527*	8A
45528	5A
45529*	5A
45530*	9A
45531*	8A
45532*	1B
45533*	8A
45534*	7C
45535*	5A
45536*	9A
45537*	10B
45538*	8A
45539*	9A
45540*	9A
45541*	1B
45542	12A
45543*	5A
45544	10B
45545*	3B
45546*	5A
45547	10B
45548*	5A
45549	12A
45550	12A
45551	12A

Cl. "5XP" "Jubilee" 4-6-0

45552*	12A
45553*	9E
45554*	16A
45555*	12A
45556*	9A
45557*	14B
45558*	5A
45559*	10C
45560*	67A
45561*	22A
45562*	20A
45563*	10C
45564*	63A
45565*	20A
45566*	20A
45567*	8A
45568*	20A
45569*	20A
45570*	22A
45571*	28A
45572*	22A
45573*	20A
45574*	28A

45575* 63A
45576* 67A
45577* 68A
45578* 12A
45579* 66A
45580* 68A
45581* 68A
45582* 68A
45583* 66A
45584* 66A
45585* 17A
45586* 5A
45587* 20A
45588* 28A
45589* 20A
45590* 19B
45591* 1A
45592* 5A
45593* 9A
45594* 19B
45595* 12A
45596* 25B
45597* 20A
45598* 14B
45599* 10B
45600* 10C
45601* 1B
45602* 17A
45603* 9A
45604* 20A
45605* 20A
45606* 5A
45607* 19B
45608* 20A
45609* 14B
45610* 17A
45611* 16A
45612* 14B
45613* 8A
45614* 14B
45615* 14B
45616* 14B
45617* 9A
45618* 9E
45619* 20A
45620* 16A
45621* 19B
45622* 9E
45623* 8A
45624* 12A
45625* 1A
45626* 20A
45627* 14B
45628* 9E
45629* 9E
45630* 12A
45631* 9A
45632* 9A
45633* 9A
45634* 5A
45635* 26A
45636* 16A
45637* 8A
45638* 9A
45639* 17A
45640* 16A
45641* 14B
45642* 26A
45643* 67A
45644* 63A
45645* 67A
45646* 67A
45647* 5A
45648* 14B
45649* 14B
45650* 14B
45651* 20A
45652* 9E
45653* 28A
45654* 14B
45655* 9A
45656* 17A
45657* 14B
45658* 20A
45659* 20A
45660* 22A
45661* 26A
45662* 22A
45663* 22A
45664* 19B
45665* 14B
45666* 5A
45667* 17A
45668* 10C
45669* 1B
45670* 8A
45671* 26A
45672* 1B
45673* 8A
45674* 5A
45675* 20A
45676* 1B
45677* 12A
45678* 5A
45679* 19B
45680* 9A
45681* 8A
45682* 22A
45683* 19B
45684* 5A
45685* 22A
45686* 5A
45687* 12A
45688* 9A
45689* 5A
45690* 22A
45691* 66A
45692* 66A
45693* 67A
45694* 20A
45695* 28A
45696* 17A
45697* 28A
45698* 27A
45699* 22A
45700* 26A
45701* 26A
45702* 25G
45703* 3B
45704* 25G
45705* 25G
45706* 26A
45707* 28A
45708* 25G
45709* 9A
45710* 26A
45711* 25G
45712* 26A
45713* 68A
45714* 68A
45715* 68A
45716* 68A
45717* 27A
45718* 3B
45719* 26A
45720* 10C
45721* 8A
45722* 3B
45723* 9A
45724* 3B
45725* 19B
45726* 3B
45727* 68A
45728* 68A
45729* 68A
45730* 68A
45731* 68A
45732* 68A
45733* 3B
45734* 9A
45735* 1B
45736* 1B
45737* 8A
45738* 5A
45739* 20A
45740* 9A
45741* 3B
45742* 3B

Cl. "6P" "Royal Scot" 4-6-0

46100* 1B
46101* 1B
46102* 66A
46103* 20A
46104* 66A
46105* 66A
46106* 8A
46107* 66A
46108* 20A
46109* 20A
46110* 12A
46111* 8A
46112* 7C
46113* 5A
46114* 9A
46115* 9A
46116* 1B
46117* 20A
46118* 1B
46119* 7C
46120* 9A
46121* 66A
46122* 9A
46123* 8A
46124* 8A
46125* 8A
46126* 1B
46127* 7C
46128* 5A
46129* 9A
46130* 5A
46131* 9A
46132* 7C
46133* 20A
46134* 8A
46135* 8A
46136* 12A
46137* 8A
46138* 8A
46139* 1B
46140* 1B
46141* 1B
46142* 1B
46143* 9A
46144* 8A
46145* 9A
46146* 5A
46147* 12A
46148* 1B
46149* 9A
46150* 9A
46151* 1B
46152* 1B
46153* 8A
46154* 1B
46155* 5A
46156* 8A
46157* 5A
46158* 7C
46159* 1B
46160* 9A
46161* 7C
46162* 1B
46163* 12A
46164* 8A
46165* 7C
46166* 7C
46167* 9A
46168* 1B
46169* 9A
46170* 1B

Cl. "7P" "Princess Royal" 4-6-2

46200* 8A
46201* 8A
46202 1B
46203* 8A
46204* 5A
46205* 8A
46206* 5A
46207* 5A
46208* 5A
46209* 5A
46210* 5A
46211* 5A
46212* 5A

Cl. "7P" "Princess Coronation" 4-6-2

46220* 66A
46221* 66A
46222* 66A
46223* 66A
46224* 66A
46225* 12A
46226* 12A
46227* 66A
46228* 12A
46229* 12A
46230* 66A
46231* 66A
46232* 66A
46233* 5A
46234* 5A
46235* 5A
46236* 5A
46237* 1B
46238* 1B
46239* 1B
46240* 1B
46241* 1B
46242* 1B
46243* 5A
46244* 1B
46245* 1B
46246* 5A
46247* 1B
46248* 5A
46249* 1B
46250* 1B
46251* 1B
46252* 1B
46253* 1B
46254* 12A
46255* 12A
46256* 1B
46257* 1B

Cl. "2MT" 2-6-0

46400 15B
46401 15B
46402 15B
46403 15B
46404 15B
46405 25C
46406 27A
46407 25C
46408 25C
46409 25C
46410 28A
46411 28A
46412 28A
46413 28A
46414 27A
46415 27A
46416 27A
46417 27A
46418 26A
46419 26A
46420 8D
46421 8D
46422 8D
46423 8D
46424 8D
46425 3A
46426 3A
46427 3A
46428 9F
46429 10B
46430 10B
46431 1A
46432 1A
46433 1A
46434 9F
46435 28A
46436 27E
46437 25C
46438 25A
46439 25A
46440 23A
46441 23C
46442 23A
46443 17A
46444 17A
46445 2D
46446 2D
46447 12D
46448 12D
46449 12C
46450 19A
46451 19A
46452 20E
46453 20E
46454 17A
46455 12C
46456 12D
46457 5A
46458 5A
46459 2A
46460 64A
46461 64A
46462 64A
46463 62B
46464 62B
46465
46466
46467
46468
46469
46470
46471
46472
46473
46474
46475
46476
46477
46478
46479
46480
46481
46482
46483
46484
46485
46486
46487
46488
46489
46490
46491
46492
46493
46494
46495
46496
46497
46498
46499
46500
46501
46502

Cl. "1P" 2-4-2T

46601 4A
46603 8B
46604 7A
46616 9D
46620 87K
46628 10E
46643 10E
46654 8B
46656 68D
46658 10E
46666 4B
46680 5A
46683 2C
46688 8B
46701 8B
46712 3C
46727 10E
46749 2C
46757 3C

Cl. "2P" 2-4-2T

46762 10B

Cl. "2MT" 0-6-2T

46899 7B
46900 3E
46906 7B
46912 3E
46922 3E

Cl. "0F" 0-4-0T

47000 17B
47001 27A
47002 27A
47003 18C
47004 18C
47005
47006
47007
47008
47009

Cl. "2F" 0-6-0T

47160 6C
47161 28B
47162 64A
47163 64C
47164 6C
47165 28B
47166 6C
47167 66D
47168 66D
47169 66D

"Sentinel" 0-4-0T

47180 10E
47181 10E
47182 67C
47183 84G
47184 6E
47190 22A
47191 71G

47200-47445

Cl. "3F" 0-6-0T

No.	Shed
47200	14B
47201	23C
47202	14B
47203	14A
47204	14A
47205	14A
47206	14A
47207	14A
47208	14A
47209	14A
47210	14A
47211	14A
47212	14A
47213	14A
47214	14A
47215	14A
47216	14A
47217	14A
47218	14A
47219	14A
47220	14A
47221	14A
47222	20E
47223	15D
47224	14A
47225	14A
47226	14A
47227	14A
47228	14A
47229	14B
47230	87K
47231	17B
47232	87K
47233	17B
47234	21C
47235	19A
47236	19A
47237	22B
47238	15A
47239	20D
47240	14A
47241	14B
47242	14B
47243	14A
47244	14B
47245	14B
47246	14B
47247	18A
47248	14A
47249	20B
47250	17A
47251	14A
47252	15D
47253	17B
47254	20A
47255	20E
47256	87K
47257	17B
47258	87K
47259	87K
47260	14B
47261	14C
47262	14B
47263	18D
47264	15A
47265	15A
47266	5B
47267	9A
47268	8B
47269	35C
47270	35C
47271	20B
47272	18C
47273	15A
47274	15C
47275	71G
47276	21A
47277	16A
47278	18C
47279	15A
47280	5B
47281	5D
47282	14B
47283	14B
47284	8C
47285	2B
47286	2B
47287	11B
47288	4A
47289	9B
47290	12D
47291	10B
47292	12D
47293	10B
47294	8A
47295	12A
47296	10B
47297	6A
47298	4A
47299	4B
47300	33A
47301	21A
47302	1D
47303	21C
47304	1D
47305	21C
47306	1D
47307	1D
47308	21C
47309	8A
47310	1D
47311	33A
47312	1D
47313	21A
47314	1D
47315	1D
47316	71G
47317	11A
47318	4B
47319	10B
47320	8A
47321	7C
47322	11B
47323	11B
47324	6C
47325	8A
47326	12A
47327	12A
47328	33A
47329	67A
47330	5B
47331	66A
47332	66A
47333	15A
47334	20D
47335	20D
47336	26G
47337	12E
47338	5D
47339	11A
47340	12A
47341	9A
47342	1A
47343	9A
47344	5B
47345	9A
47346	9B
47347	9A
47348	1D
47349	1D
47350	1D
47351	33A
47352	8B
47353	8A
47354	1B
47355	1C
47356	1B
47357	8A
47358	1B
47359	1B
47360	2A
47361	1A
47362	8C
47363	3D
47364	3D
47365	3D
47366	3D
47367	2B
47368	7C
47369	9A
47370	5D
47371	6B
47372	6B
47373	8C
47374	6A
47375	6A
47376	8B
47377	12A
47378	2A
47379	2A
47380	1A
47381	23C
47382	3A
47383	6A
47384	5B
47385	8A
47386	24B
47387	8B
47388	8C
47389	6A
47390	12E
47391	12A
47392	8A
47393	10E
47394	7A
47395	9A
47396	3A
47397	3B
47398	3B
47399	3B
47400	9A
47401	10D
47402	8A
47403	12A
47404	8A
47405	20D
47406	11A
47407	8A
47408	12A
47409	11A
47410	11A
47411	1D
47412	1A
47413	3C
47414	5B
47415	12A
47416	8A
47417	17A
47418	20A
47419	20E
47420	20A
47421	20C
47422	16A
47423	18C
47424	18D
47425	21C
47426	18D
47427	23A
47428	14B
47429	14B
47430	1A
47431	5B
47432	19A
47433	14A
47434	14A
47435	14A
47436	18A
47437	15B
47438	16A
47439	8C
47440	26G
47441	15C
47442	15C
47443	20B
47444	10E
47445	5E

No.	Shed
47446	15A
47447	17D
47448	20C
47449	17C
47450	5B
47451	10E
47452	4A
47453	10E
47454	18A
47455	18D
47457	17D
47458	33A
47459	17D
47460	17D
47461	17D
47462	20C
47463	20B
47464	17B
47465	71G
47466	18B
47467	1B
47468	23C
47469	23C
47470	23C
47471	23C
47472	6C
47473	3B
47474	1A
47475	1A
47476	7C
47477	87K
47478	87K
47479	87K
47480	87K
47481	87K
47482	1D
47483	1D
47484	33A
47485	16A
47486	1D
47487	1D
47488	1D
47489	1D
47490	1D
47491	1A
47492	1D
47493	1D
47494	1D
47495	1D
47496	71G
47497	1D
47498	1D
47499	1D
47500	1D
47501	1D
47502	18D
47503	11C
47504	6A
47505	1A
47506	1D
47507	6C
47508	25E
47509	25E
47510	25A
47511	1D
47512	33A
47513	19A
47514	1D
47515	1D
47516	1D
47517	1D
47518	1D
47519	3A
47520	1A
47521	4A
47522	1B
47523	5B
47524	5B
47525	12E
47526	5B
47527	1B
47528	9A
47529	1B
47530	6C
47531	1A
47532	23C
47533	15C
47534	15C
47535	18C
47536	66A
47537	66A
47538	20B
47539	16A
47540	66A
47541	66A
47542	71G
47543	15A
47544	22A
47545	18A
47546	19C
47547	19C
47548	19A
47549	15D
47550	22A
47551	18A
47552	16A
47554	15A
47555	18A
47556	12A
47557	71G
47558	1D
47559	1D
47560	1D
47561	1D
47562	23A
47563	19A
47564	1D
47565	21C
47566	35C
47567	25G
47568	25G
47569	25G
47570	25G
47571	25G
47572	25A
47573	25A
47574	26B
47575	24B
47576	24B
47577	26A
47578	26B
47579	26B
47580	25A
47581	20C
47582	25A
47583	26B
47584	26B
47585	26B
47586	26A
47587	5D
47588	5C
47589	20B
47590	5B
47591	8B
47592	C. Wks.
47593	12D
47594	2B
47595	5B
47596	5D
47597	8A
47598	5C
47599	5D
47600	6A
47601	9B
47602	5E
47603	8B
47604	12E
47605	11A
47606	5C
47607	22B
47608	5E
47609	5D
47610	5D
47611	19A
47612	4B
47614	12A
47615	6B
47616	5E
47618	12A
47619	22B
47620	22B
47621	35C
47622	35C
47623	16A
47624	19A
47625	18D
47626	18D
47627	6C
47628	6C
47629	16A
47630	18A
47631	16A
47632	16A
47633	5B
47634	20C
47635	22B
47636	15A
47637	16A
47638	21A
47639	23C
47640	20B
47641	17B
47642	15A
47643	17B
47644	14B
47645	14B
47646	6B
47647	5D
47648	5D
47649	5C
47650	6B
47651	8C
47652	8B
47653	5C
47654	8B
47655	87K
47656	6B
47657	8B
47658	5D
47659	35C
47660	17A
47661	5B
47662	5B
47664	12A
47665	5C
47666	12A
47667	1B
47668	1B
47669	1B
47670	5B
47671	1B
47672	6C
47673	9A
47674	6C
47675	1A
47676	1A
47677	2A
47678	22A
47679	17D
47680	5B
47681	87K

Cl. "1F" 0-4-2T

No.	Shed
47862	C. Wks.
47865	C. Wks.

Cl. "6F" 0-8-2T

No.	Shed
47877	10A
47881	10A
47884	10A
47896	10A

Cl. "7F" 0-8-4T

47931	8A
47937	8A
47939	8A

Beyer-Garratt 2-6-0+0-6-2

47967	18A
47968	18C
47969	18A
47970	18A
47971	18C
47972	18A
47973	18C
47974	18A
47975	18A
47976	18A
47977	18A
47978	18A
47979	18A
47980	18C
47981	18A
47982	18A
47983	18C
47984	18C
47985	18A
47986	18A
47987	18A
47988	18A
47989	18A
47990	18C
47991	18A
47992	18C
47993	18C
47994	18A
47995	18A
47996	18A
47997	18C
47998	18A
47999	18A

Cl. "8F" 2-8-0

48000	16C
48001	23C
48002	18D
48003	16A
48004	16C
48005	23A
48006	16C
48007	18A
48008	17C
48009	16C
48010	15A
48011	1A
48012	2C
48016	2B
48017	6B
48018	2C
48020	2B
48024	15A
48026	19C
48027	21A
48029	16C
48033	18A
48035	15A
48036	2B
48037	18A
48039	2A
48045	9G
48046	9G
48050	15A
48053	18D
48054	9D
48055	19C
48056	18B
48057	18B
48060	18B
48061	2B
48062	20C
48063	18B
48064	16A
48065	19C
48067	20A
48069	15B
48070	20A
48073	16C
48074	12B
48075	18A
48076	18B
48077	2B
48078	20C
48079	17A
48080	20C
48081	16C
48082	15A
48083	18B
48084	20D
48085	2A
48088	16D
48089	9F
48090	9D
48092	16C
48093	20C
48094	6B
48095	20C
48096	16C
48097	16C
48098	16C
48099	9F
48100	16C
48101	16C
48102	16A
48103	20C
48104	20A
48105	23B
48106	6C
48107	17C
48108	16C
48109	14A
48110	26G
48111	18D
48112	18A
48113	20C
48114	16C
48115	18B
48116	19A
48117	18A
48118	18B
48119	16D
48120	3A
48121	17A
48122	1A
48123	20B
48124	15B
48125	18B
48126	20A
48127	9F
48128	15A
48129	1A
48130	20D
48131	20D
48132	14A
48133	18A
48134	9F
48135	9G
48136	18B
48137	16C
48138	16C
48139	16C
48140	19C
48141	15B
48142	6B
48143	15B
48144	18A
48145	23A
48146	20D
48147	1A
48148	23C
48149	15A
48150	15A
48151	15A
48152	18B
48153	17A
48154	9F
48155	9F
48156	16D
48157	20A
48158	20A
48159	20A
48160	20D
48161	23C
48162	20C
48163	14A
48164	20D
48165	2A
48166	9D
48167	15A
48168	18A
48169	20C
48170	16A
48171	1A
48172	1A
48173	2A
48174	1A
48175	3A
48176	18A
48177	15D
48178	18A
48179	19A
48180	15A
48181	15A
48182	18A
48183	15A
48184	18B
48185	18B
48186	18B
48187	18A
48188	26G
48189	23B
48190	9F
48191	15A
48192	15A
48193	16C
48194	18A
48195	18D
48196	18A
48197	18A
48198	15A
48199	18A
48200	18A
48201	18A
48202	18A
48203	18A
48204	18A
48205	18A
48206	16A
48207	84G
48208	9F
48209	19C
48210	18D
48211	15C
48212	18B
48213	18D
48214	16C
48215	16C
48216	19A
48217	16A
48218	16A
48219	19A
48220	9F
48221	18A
48222	15A
48223	16C
48224	16C
48225	16C
48246	6B
48247	6C
48248	5B
48249	5B
48250	5B
48251	5B
48252	5B
48253	5B

48254	5B
48255	5B
48256	5B
48257	5B
48258	9G
48259	5B
48260	5B
48261	5B
48262	5B
48263	5B
48264	15A
48265	17C
48266	20D
48267	16C
48268	16C
48269	15A
48270	16C
48271	20D
48272	16C
48273	18A
48274	20D
48275	9F
48276	20B
48277	20B
48278	1A
48279	16A
48280	18B
48281	15A
48282	16C
48283	20A
48284	19A
48285	15B
48286	5B
48287	5B
48288	5B
48289	5B
48290	5B
48291	5B
48292	5B
48293	16A
48294	5B
48295	5B
48296	5B
48297	5B
48301	15B
48302	17A
48303	18A
48304	18A
48305	15A
48306	15C
48307	84G
48308	84G
48309	1A
48310	1A
48311	20B
48312	1A
48313	18A
48314	19A
48315	9F
48316	9F
48317	21A
48318	3A
48319	24B
48320	2A
48321	68A
48322	9D
48323	12B
48324	18A
48325	3A
48326	9D
48327	1A
48328	84G
48329	9F
48330	26G
48331	18A
48332	18D
48333	18B
48334	15A
48335	3A
48336	21A
48337	20C
48338	15A
48339	21A
48340	1A
48341	18D
48342	6B
48343	2A
48344	6C
48345	2B
48346	18D
48347	84G
48348	26G
48349	26G
48350	18A
48351	21A
48352	20D
48353	18B
48354	1A
48355	15B
48356	15B
48357	20D
48358	18B
48359	15A
48360	15A
48361	18A
48362	18A
48363	15A
48364	15A
48365	15A
48366	8B
48367	18A
48368	1A
48369	84G
48370	18A
48371	15A
48372	2A
48373	84G
48374	15A
48375	3A
48376	20C
48377	20C
48378	15A
48379	16C
48380	16A
48381	16A
48382	16C
48383	16C
48384	18A
48385	15A
48386	15A
48387	18A
48388	21A
48389	9A
48390	17A
48391	18B
48392	16C
48393	16C
48394	20D
48395	20D
48396	20D
48397	15C
48398	2A
48399	20A
48400	18A
48401	21A
48402	16A
48403	16C
48404	17A
48405	16C
48406	9F
48407	19C
48408	16C
48409	16C
48410	14A
48411	9E
48412	20C
48413	16C
48414	14A
48415	14A
48416	1A
48417	21A
48418	18A
48419	20C
48420	21A
48421	9D
48422	4B
48423	4B
48424	21A
48425	9A
48426	4B
48427	2A
48428	9A
48429	9A
48430	18B
48431	20C
48432	17A
48433	1A
48434	19C
48435	24B
48436	8B
48437	2A
48438	1A
48439	20C
48440	9E
48441	18D
48442	16C
48443	20C
48444	6B
48445	4B
48446	6B
48447	6B
48448	6C
48449	25C
48450	19C
48451	9D
48452	6B
48453	26C
48454	20A
48455	6C
48456	25G
48457	8A
48458	6B
48459	6B
48460	18D
48461	18A
48462	8D
48463	18A
48464	68A
48465	9D
48466	8B
48467	6B
48468	26C
48469	8B
48470	6B
48471	15B
48472	68A
48473	8B
48474	84G
48475	17C
48476	1A
48477	6B
48478	84G
48479	2A
48490	18A
48491	6C
48492	15A
48493	18D
48494	18B
48495	18B
48500	9A
48501	9A
48502	25A
48503	9F
48504	25A
48505	2A
48506	25A
48507	20D
48508	20D
48509	2A
48510	8A
48511	25A
48512	8A
48513	8A
48514	25A
48515	27B
48516	9A
48517	15C
48518	3A

48519	9D
48520	8C
48521	8C
48522	8C
48523	27B
48524	27B
48525	27B
48526	2B
48527	9F
48528	8C
48529	8C
48530	16C
48531	26G
48532	20C
48533	15A
48534	18B
48535	18B
48536	68A
48537	20A
48538	18D
48539	18D
48540	20C
48541	14A
48542	20C
48543	17C
48544	12B
48545	18D
48546	18D
48547	20D
48548	19C
48549	18B
48550	4B
48551	1A
48552	16C
48553	18A
48554	8D
48555	9G
48556	3A
48557	1A
48558	8D
48559	2A
48600	1A
48601	1A
48602	1A
48603	1A
48604	18D
48605	1A
48606	18A
48607	18A
48608	23B
48609	23A
48610	1A
48611	15B
48612	68A
48613	9G
48614	16A
48615	18A
48616	23B
48617	15A
48618	18A
48619	15A
48620	18B
48621	16D
48622	20B
48623	18B
48624	1A
48625	15A
48626	1A
48627	15A
48628	1A
48629	1A
48630	8C
48631	8C
48632	1A
48633	1A
48634	1A
48635	16A
48636	18A
48637	18A
48638	18A
48639	16A
48640	17A
48641	20B
48642	19A
48643	16D
48644	15A
48645	15B
48646	19C
48647	17A
48648	1A
48649	1A
48650	18B
48651	15A
48652	20B
48653	16A
48654	17A
48655	18A
48656	1A
48657	1A
48658	1A
48659	1A
48660	1A
48661	18B
48662	18A
48663	18D
48664	8B
48665	1A
48666	16A
48667	9G
48668	15A
48669	21A
48670	20D
48671	15A
48672	18A
48673	6C
48674	3A
48675	16A
48676	9F
48677	17A
48678	15A
48679	1A
48680	9E
48681	18A
48682	9F
48683	9F
48684	6C
48685	18A
48686	3A
48687	21A
48688	84G
48689	8B
48690	18A
48691	6C
48692	15A
48693	4B
48694	18A
48695	15A
48696	16A
48697	9G
48698	9E
48699	15A
48700	21A
48701	16D
48702	20D
48703	20B
48704	15B
48705	26A
48706	9G
48707	26A
48708	8D
48709	15C
48710	26C
48711	26C
48712	9D
48713	27B
48714	26A
48715	26A
48716	2B
48717	9G
48718	9G
48719	26A
48720	25D
48721	18B
48722	26A
48723	2B
48724	26B
48725	26B
48726	26A
48727	26A
48728	15C
48729	2A
48730	26A
48731	9D
48732	26B
48733	26A
48734	9D
48735	26A
48736	2A
48737	9D
48738	25C
48739	26A
48740	9D
48741	9D
48742	9D
48743	8C
48744	6B
48745	9D
48746	9D
48747	8C
48748	8C
48749	9D
48750	6B
48751	25D
48752	26A
48753	8D
48754	26A
48755	25D
48756	9G
48757	5B
48758	1A
48759	15B
48760	26B
48761	26A
48762	26C
48763	21A
48764	8D
48765	26C
48766	26B
48767	26C
48768	25C
48769	26A
48770	6B
48771	8D
48772	8D

Cl. "6F" and "7F" 0-8-0

48893	87K
48895	10A
48898	8A
48899	86K
48901	84G
48902	3B
48905	3A
48907	3A
48914	4B
48915	1C
48917	3A
48920	10C
48921	86K
48922	5C
48926	10C
48927	2B
48930	10A
48932	8A
48933	8A
48936	4B
48940	3B
48942	8C
48943	8A
48944	8C
48945	84G
48950	3A
48951	4A

48952	4A
48953	4A
48964	4A
49002	9B
49005	4A
49006	86K
49007	4A
49008	8B
49009	3A
49010	9B
49014	4A
49017	3D
49018	10A
49020	8D
49021	1A
49022	3A
49023	10A
49024	10A
49025	3A
49027	10C
49028	86K
49030	10A
49031	3C
49033	87K
49034	10A
49035	87K
49037	3B
49044	3B
49045	3A
49046	86K
49047	5C
49048	3C
49049	4A
49050	10A
49051	86K
49057	9D
49061	4A
49062	1A
49063	3A
49064	86K
49066	3C
49068	2B
49070	4A
49071	3A
49073	8D
49074	8C
49077	3A
49078	1A
49079	8D
49081	3A
49082	10A
49087	10C
49088	4A
49089	3A
49090	10A
49092	10A
49093	3A
49094	10C
49096	3A
49098	9B
49099	3A
49101	10D
49104	10B
49105	8C
49106	3A
49108	9B
49109	11A
49112	11A
49113	86K
49114	3A
49115	5C
49116	8D
49117	1A
49119	8B
49120	8C
49121	86K
49122	1A
49125	8C
49126	8A
49129	10A
49130	11A
49132	9D
49134	10B
49137	8A
49138	84G
49139	1A
49140	3D
49141	10B
49142	3A
49143	8C
49144	4A
49145	1C
49146	86K
49147	10D
49148	87K
49149	8B
49150	10B
49151	11A
49153	4B
49154	4A
49155	4A
49156	9B
49157	1C
49158	5C
49160	10A
49161	86K
49162	3B
49163	1A
49164	1A
49167	3B
49168	86K
49171	3C
49172	8C
49173	4A
49174	86K
49177	87K
49178	10C
49180	3A
49181	2B
49186	2B
49187	9B
49189	3A
49191	10B
49193	3C
49196	3B
49198	3C
49199	10C
49200	10B
49202	3A
49203	4B
49204	3B
49205	10E
49208	3C
49209	10C
49210	5B
49212	8C
49213	3C
49214	9D
49216	3A
49218	8C
49219	8C
49222	3C
49223	3A
49224	8A
49226	86K
49228	10A
49229	5C
49230	5B
49234	10C
49239	8A
49240	3B
49241	11A
49243	86K
49244	8C
49245	3A
49246	3A
49247	8B
49249	8C
49252	11A
49253	8C
49254	10C
49257	11A
49258	3C
49260	87K
49261	3D
49262	10E
49264	10A
49265	3A
49266	3A
49267	10B
49268	10A
49270	4B
49271	4B
49275	1A
49276	84G
49277	1A
49278	6B
49281	9B
49282	3A
49287	4A
49288	4A
49289	4A
49292	4A
49293	8C
49296	1A
49300	3C
49301	8A
49302	8C
49304	2B
49306	10A
49307	4A
49308	3A
49310	10A
49311	10A
49312	10E
49313	3A
49314	11A
49315	10D
49316	86K
49318	2B
49319	5B
49321	4B
49322	3C
49323	1C
49326	3C
49327	3A
49328	3A
49330	2D
49331	10A
49334	3A
49335	10C
49339	2B
49340	10C
49341	10A
49342	1A
49343	8D
49344	1A
49345	86K
49346	3B
49347	9D
49348	9D
49350	2B
49352	10A
49354	3A
49355	8A
49356	1A
49357	4B
49358	87K
49359	3A
49361	3A
49364	3C
49366	4B
49367	3A
49368	2B
49370	3D
49371	3A
49373	3C
49375	1C
49376	87K
49377	10E
49378	10A
49381	10A
49382	10B
49385	2B

49386	10C
49387	9D
49388	3C
49389	10E
49390	10B
49391	4A
49392	2A
49393	1C
49394	10A

Cl. "7F" "G2" 0-8-0

49395	8C
49396	2B
49397	2B
49398	2A
49399	8A
49400	10C
49401	3C
49402	10A
49403	86K
49404	8A
49405	2D
49406	4A
49407	5B
49408	2A
49409	86K
49410	5C
49411	2A
49412	8A
49413	2A
49414	2B
49415	2A
49416	2A
49417	4A
49418	2B
49419	8A
49420	8C
49421	10C
49422	86K
49423	2A
49424	2B
49425	2A
49426	10C
49427	4A
49428	9A
49429	2B
49430	2C
49431	2A
49432	2B
49433	2A
49434	2B
49435	2B
49436	2B
49437	8A
49438	11A
49439	9A
49440	84G
49441	2D
49442	2D
49443	4A
49444	2D
49445	8A
49446	2D
49447	2A
49448	4A
49449	8A
49450	9D
49451	2B
49452	2A
49453	2B
49454	9D

Cl. "7F" 0-8-0

49502	26B
49503	27B
49505	27B
49506	27B
49508	26D
49509	26F
49510	26C
49511	26B
49515	27B
49523	27B
49524	27B
49531	26A
49532	26B
49535	27B
49536	26A
49538	26B
49540	25E
49544	26B
49545	26A
49547	27B
49548	26F
49552	27B
49554	26A
49555	26B
49557	26D
49558	26A
49560	26A
49563	27B
49566	27B
49568	27D
49570	26B
49571	27B
49578	26B
49580	26A
49582	27B
49585	27D
49586	27B
49587	27D
49590	26F
49591	26D
49592	27B
49593	26F
49594	26D
49595	27B
49598	25D
49600	27B
49602	25D
49603	27B
49608	26A
49609	27B
49610	27D
49612	26A
49617	27B
49618	25D
49620	25D
49623	27B
49624	27B
49625	25A
49627	26B
49631	27B-
49635	27B
49637	26A
49638	26B
49640	26C
49641	27B
49648	25B
49649	27B
49650	26A
49651	26A
49657	26A
49659	25D
49660	25D
49661	25D
49662	25D
49663	25D
49664	26C
49666	26D
49667	26D
49668	26F
49671	27B
49672	26C
49673	26A
49674	26A

Cl. "5P" 4-6-0

50455	28A

Cl. "2P" and "3P" 2-4-2T

50621	20D
50622	20A
50623	20E
50625	23B
50630	20E
50633	20E
50634	20E
50636	20E
50639	10B
50640	28B
50642	28B
50643	11B
50644	10D
50646	28B
50647	26C
50648	27B
50650	25A
50651	26E
50652	26E
50653	24B
50654	24B
50655	27B
50656	25A
50660	26C
50671	20E
50676	10B
50678	7D
50681	20E
50686	23B
50687	7D
50689	20E
50695	10B
50697	8B
50703	8B
50705	8B
50712	25A
50714	20E
50715	25A
50720	28B
50721	28A
50725	28A
50731	25B
50735	25B
50736	25B
50746	28A
50749	28A
50752	28A
50757	28A
50762	25A
50764	25A
50765	25E
50766	28B
50777	28A
50778	28B
50781	28B
50788	25A
50795	20E
50799	25A
50802	28B
50806	25F
50807	26C
50812	28B
50815	26C
50818	26C
50829	26C
50831	26C
50840	28B
50842	20E
50850	28B
50852	24C
50855	26A

50859 26A
50865 26C
50869 25A
50872 26C
50873 25A
50886 25A
50887 25B
50892 25A
50897† Rugby Test P.
50898 25A
50909 25F
50925 25E

Cl. "0F" 0-4-0T

51202 71G
51204 5B
51206 27A
51207 25C
51212 22A
51216 27A
51217† 17B
51218 10B
51221 5B
51222 25C
51227 27A
51229 27A
51230 26B
51231 27A
51232 27A
51234 27A
51235 17A
51237 27A
51240 27A
51241 25C
51244 25C
51246 27A
51253 27A

Cl. "2F" 0-6-0T

51307 27A
51313 6C
51316 10E
51319 10E
51321 28B
51323 25C
51336 24B
51338 26A
51343 27B
51345 24C
51348 25E
51353 8A
51358 25D
51361 25C
51371 27A
51375 27A
51376 26D
51379 25C
51381 25E
51390 26B
51396 27A
51397 10E
51404 25F
51408 25B
51410 24A
51412 C. Wks.
51413 27B
51415 24D
51419 26D
51423 24C
51424 26A
51425 26A
51429 26A
51432 25C
51436 26A
51439 8C
51441 6C
51444 C. Wks.
51445 8A
51446 C. Wks.
51447 25A
51453 25D
51457 26A
51458 26A
51460 27B
51462 27B
51464 26B
51470 26A
51471 10E
51472 26A
51474 27D
51477 28B
51479 25E
51481 28B
51484 26G
51486 26D
51488 25E
51489 26D
51490 27C
51491 10E
51496 26A
51497 24B
51498 28B
51499 24D
51500 26B
51503 25E
51504 26D
51506 24D
51510 26A
51511 26C
51512 26B
51513 26C
51514 24A
51516 25C
51519 26C
51521 25C
51524 25B
51526 24C
51530 27B

Cl. "1F" 0-6-0T

51535 27A
51536 27A
51537 27A
51544 27B
51546 27A

Cl. "2F" 0-6-0

52016 10C
52021 10A
52022 10C
52024 10C
52030 10C
52031 10C
52034 10C
52037 25C
52041 25A
52043 25A
52044 25A
52045 10A
52051 10A
52053 10A
52056 25C
52059 10C
52064 10C

Cl. "3F" 0-6-0

52088 8B
52089 20D
52091 10E
52092 25F
52093 27B
52094 26A
52095 20C
52098 10A
52099 26F
52100 8C
52102 26A
52104 25F
52105 10B
52107 10A
52108 20C
52111 8A
52112 27B
52118 8A
52119 7B
52120 25A
52121 16A
52123 16A
52124 25D
52125 7D
52126 10A
52129 26D
52132 26A
52133 25C
52135 16A
52136 26C
52137 26A
52138 28A
52139 26A
52140 26B
52141 2B
52143 8C
52150 25A
52154 25A
52156 26A
52157 28A
52159 26D
52160 24C
52161 27C
52162 27C
52163 8C
52164 26D
52165 26D
52166 25D
52167 7D
52169 27D
52171 24C
52172 7D
52174 28A
52175 8C
52176 7B
52177 10E
52179 27B
52182 28A
52183 27C
52186 25A
52189 25E
52191 25D
52194 28A
52196 27B
52197 27D
52201 12E
52203 24D
52207 26A
52208 6C
52212 26C
52215 28A
52216 24C
52217 25E
52218 27B
52219 26B
52220 24C
52225 6C
52230 7B
52231 26C
52232 6C
52233 7D
52235 25A
52236 26C
52237 25F
52238 24C
52239 26A
52240 28A
52243 25E
52244 27B
52245 26D
52246 26D
52248 26F

† Not included in L.M.R. stock.

52250	10A
52252	20C
52255	25D
52258	20C
52260	24D
52262	24D
52266	26A
52268	24D
52269	7B
52270	6C
52271	27E
52272	24C
52273	25C
52275	28A
52278	27C
52279	26B
52280	10E
52284	25A
52285	12E
52288	27D
52289	24D
52290	28B
52293	26B
52296	24C
52299	26E
52300	26A
52304	26A
52305	25A
52309	25F
52311	26C
52312	27B
52317	24C
52319	25A
52321	8A
52322	2B
52328	27E
52330	8A
52331	25D
52333	27E
52334	28A
52336	24C
52338	7D
52341	10A
52343	26A
52345	25A
52348	26C
52349	10E
52350	26C
52351	25A
52353	25A
52355	26A
52356	7D
52357	28A
52358	26A
52360	27D
52362	27B
52363	24D
52365	26F
52366	10E
52368	24C
52369	25A
52376	25E
52378	26F
52379	27D
52381	27B
52382	26D
52386	25A
52387	26F
52388	25D
52389	26F
52390	27D
52393	10E
52397	10E
52399	24C
52400	25E
52404	26C
52405	27B
52407	7B
52408	25D
52410	25F
52411	25F
52412	27B
52413	27D
52414	84G
52415	28A
52416	26E
52418	12E
52427	25F
52428	84G
52429	2B
52430	28A
52431	24D
52432	6C
52433	25A
52435	25A
52437	27E
52438	8C
52440	26E
52441	24D
52443	26E
52444	24D
52445	24D
52446	26C
52447	28A
52448	25D
52449	10E
52450	27D
52452	25E
52453	7D
52455	26A
52456	24C
52458	28B
52459	28A
52460	24D
52461	25F
52464	26F
52465	2B
52466	28A
52494	12E
52499	12E
52501	12D
52508	12D
52509	12D
52510	12E
52515	25D
52517	26A
52521	25A
52522	24C
52523	24C
52524	24C
52525	84G
52526	24D
52527	24C
52529	24D

Cl. "3F" 0-6-0

52549	27D
52551	84G
52554	26D
52557	27B
52558	26A
52559	20C
52561	25A
52569	26A
52572	28A
52575	25E
52576	25A
52579	24D
52580	26D
52581	26D
52582	27C
52583	26A
52587	25E
52588	28B
52590	25F
52592	25C
52598	8B
52608	8B
52615	26D
52616	25E
52619	10B

Cl. "6F" 0-8-0

52727	27D
52822	27D
52831	27D

Cl. "7F" 0-8-0

52857	25F
52870	27D
52906	27D
52910	27D
52916	27D
52945	27D

Cl. "7F" 2-8-0

53800	71G
53801	71G
53802	71G
53803	71G
53804	71G
53805	71G
53806	71G
53807	71G
53808	71G
53809	71G
53810	71G

Cl. "2P" 4-4-0

54398*	60D
54399*	60D
54404*	60D

Cl. "3P" 4-4-0

54438	64D
54439	60A
54440	66D
54441	66B
54443	68B
54444	68B
54445	60D
54446	64D
54447	63A
54448	63A
54449	64D
54450	63C
54451	64C
54452	64C
54453	66B
54454	63C
54455	60B
54456	67B
54457	66D
54458	63A
54459	63A
54460	66B

Cl. "3P" 4-4-0

54461	64D
54462	66B
54463	60A
54464	66B
54465	66B
54466	60B
54467	63A
54468	66D
54469	63A
54470	60A
54471	60A
54472	60A

54473	60E
54474	65B
54475	65B
54476	63A
54477	64D
54478	64C
54479	66D
54480	60C
54481	60E
54482	60E
54483	65F
54484	60A
54485	63A
54486	63C
54487	60A
54488	60B
54489	63A
54490	64D
54491	60A
54492	66D
54493	60B
54494	63A
54495	60C
54496	60A
54497	66D
54498	66D
54499	63A
54500	63A
54501	63A
54502	63A
54503	63A
54504	67B
54505	64D
54506	66D
54507	68B
54508	66D

Cl. "4MT" 4-6-0

54630	66B
54634	66B
54635	66B
54636	66B
54638	66C
54639	66C
54640	66B
54647	66B
54648	66B
54649	66B
54650	66B
54654	66B

Cl. "1P" 0-4-4T

55051	60C
55053	60C

Cl. "2P" 0-4-4T

55119	65F
55121	65B
55122	63B
55124	68B
55125	68C
55126	63B
55132	67C
55134	66B
55135	67A
55136	63C
55138	66B
55139	64C
55140	67A
55141	66A
55142	68D
55143	67A
55144	63A
55145	63B
55146	66C
55160	60A
55161	63C
55162	63C
55164	68B
55165	64C
55166	64C
55167	66A
55168	65D
55169	63C
55170	66A
55171	63A
55172	63C
55173	62B
55174	60B
55175	63A
55176	63A
55177	64C
55178	68D
55179	66A
55181	68D
55182	67A
55185	63C
55186	62B
55187	63E
55188	66B
55189	64C
55191	66B
55192	62B
55193	63C
55194	63C
55195	63C
55196	63E
55197	66A
55198	63E
55199	60A
55200	63C
55201	66A
55202	64C
55203	67B
55204	65B
55206	67A
55207	66A
55208	63A
55209	63A
55210	64C
55211	67A
55212	63A
55213	63A
55214	63C
55215	63E
55216	63A
55217	62B
55218	63A
55219	67A
55220	68D
55221	66C
55222	63B
55223	62B
55224	66A
55225	67A
55226	62B
55227	62B
55228	66A
55229	64C
55230	63C
55231	62B
55232	68D
55233	68D
55234	68D
55235	67A
55236	67B
55237	68D
55238	65F
55239	68D
55240	67C
55260	67B
55261	64D
55262	67C
55263	63E
55264	67C
55265	66A
55266	67A
55267	66A
55268	66A
55269	67A

Cl. "4P" 4-6-2T

55350	68D
55352	68D
55353	68D
55359	68D
55360	68D
55361	68D

Cl. "0F" 0-4-0T

56011	60A
56020	17B
56025	St. R. Wks.
56027	84G
56028	66D
56029	65D
56030	65G
56031	66D
56032	C. Wks.
56035	66D
56038	60A
56039	65G

Cl. "2F" 0-6-0T

56151	65B
56152	65F
56153	66A
56154	66A
56155	66B
56156	66D
56157	66D
56158	65G
56159	66A
56160	66A
56161	65G
56162	66A
56163	66D
56164	65F
56165	66D
56166	66D
56167	66A
56168	65G
56169	65D
56170	65G
56171	65D
56172	66B
56173	66D

Cl. "3F" 0-6-0T

56230	65F
56231	68A
56232	63B
56233	65B
56234	68C
56235	68A
56236	67B
56237	66C
56238	65G
56239	66A
56240	61B
56241	66B
56242	66C
56243	65F
56244	66A
56245	66B
56246	63A
56247	66B
56248	68A
56249	67A
56250	65G
56251	61B
56252	65B
56253	64C
56254	63B
56255	66C

No.	Shed
56256	66C
56257	67C
56258	66B
56259	67D
56260	66A
56261	66A
56262	60A
56263	66A
56264	66B
56265	66B
56266	68A
56267	65F
56268	66B
56269	66B
56271	66B
56272	67C
56273	67C
56274	67C
56275	65F
56276	66B
56277	66B
56278	61B
56279	67D
56280	66A
56281	66A
56282	67D
56283	64C
56284	66C
56285	66B
56286	66C
56287	66C
56288	66D
56289	65B
56290	63A
56291	60A
56292	66A
56293	60A
56294	66A
56295	66A
56296	66C
56297	65G
56298	66A
56299	60A
56300	65F
56301	60E
56302	65D
56303	66C
56304	66A
56305	66A
56306	66A
56307	66A
56308	66A
56309	66C
56310	65B
56311	67D
56312	64C
56313	64C
56314	66A
56315	65G
56316	68A
56317	68A
56318	66A
56319	66C
56320	66C
56321	66C
56322	66A
56323	62B
56324	66A
56325	62B
56326	61B
56327	68A
56328	63A
56329	67A
56330	65B
56331	63A
56332	68A
56333	68A
56334	66B
56335	66B
56336	65F
56337	66B
56338	66B
56339	65G
56340	68A
56341	60A
56342	66A
56343	63B
56344	65D
56345	66B
56346	66A
56347	63A
56348	61B
56349	66A
56350	67A
56352	63A
56353	63A
56354	68A
56355	68A
56356	66B
56357	66B
56358	66B
56359	63A
56360	66C
56361	67A
56362	66C
56363	67C
56364	67D
56365	63B
56366	63B
56367	67C
56368	67B
56369	67A
56370	65B
56371	66C
56372	68C
56373	68A
56374	68A
56375	65F
56376	65F

Cl. "2F" 0-6-0

No.	Shed
57230	66A
57232	63B
57233	63B
57234	67C
57235	67C
57236	67B
57237	66C
57238	66A
57239	66A
57240	65B
57241	67A
57242	66C
57243	63B
57244	66C
57245	65D
57246	63B
57247	66B
57249	67A
57250	66C
57251	65B
57252	63B
57253	65B
57254	63E
57255	67A
57256	66B
57257	63B
57258	65D
57259	65G
57260	66C
57261	65B
57262	67C
57263	67D
57264	63B
57265	65F
57266	67A
57267	66B
57268	66A
57269	65B
57270	66B
57271	66A
57272	66B
57273	65D
57274	67D
57275	66A
57276	67D
57277	67B
57278	66B
57279	67C
57280	66C
57282	67D
57283	63B
57284	67C
57285	65F
57287	65F
57288	66A
57289	66B
57291	66B
57292	66A
57295	67C
57296	65D
57299	66B
57300	67A
57302	68B
57303	66B
57306	65D
57307	66C
57309	67A
57311	65B
57312	67C
57314	65D
57315	67C
57317	66A
57318	65B
57319	66A
57320	66A
57321	66A
57322	65D
57323	64D
57324	63C
57325	66B
57326	66B
57328	66B
57329	68B
57331	67B
57332	66B
57334	65F
57335	66B
57336	65D
57337	68B
57338	65F
57339	63A
57340	64D
57341	65D
57344	68B
57345	63A
57346	65D
57347	66A
57348	67D
57349	68B
57350	65B
57352	65B
57353	67B
57354	67C
57355	67D
57356	67D
57357	67D
57359	67A
57360	66A
57361	66A
57362	68B
57363	66B
57364	67C
57365	66A
57366	65F
57367	66A
57368	63C
57369	66D
57370	66A
57372	65D
57373	65D
57375	68C
57377	66B
57378	68B
57379	66B
57383	67B
57384	66C

57385 64D
57386 64D
57387 66A
57388 66A
57389 66A
57391 68B
57392 67C
57394 65D
57395 66C
57396 63E
57397 68B
57398 66C
57404 66B
57405 68B
57407 66C
57410 66C
57411 65B
57412 66A
57413 66C
57414 66B
57416 66B
57417 66B
57418 66B
57419 66B
57423 63B
57424 63B
57425 63B
57426 65D
57429 65D
57430 66C
57431 66C
57432 66A
57433 66A
57434 65B
57435 66B
57436 66B
57437 66B
57438 64D
57439 66A
57441 63C
57443 66A
57444 66A
57445 68C
57446 66A
57447 66A
57448 66A
57450 63A
57451 64D
57453 65B
57454 65B
57455 65B
57456 65D
57457 65B
57458 68C
57459 66A
57460 63B
57461 66B
57462 66B
57463 66A
57464 66A
57465 66A
57468 63B
57470 65D
57472 65D
57473 63A

Cl. "3F" 0-6-0

57550 64C
57552 66D
57553 64C
57554 65B
57555 66A
57556 66D
57557 65B
57558 65B
57559 64C
57560 67A
57562 67A
57563 68B
57564 66A
57565 64C
57566 67A
57568 62B
57569 67C
57570 67B
57571 67B
57572 67B
57573 67B
57575 67A
57576 64C
57577 67D
57579 67D
57580 67A
57581 66A
57582 66B
57583 64D
57585 60D
57586 60B
57587 60C
57588 66B
57589 67A
57590 67D
57591 60A
57592 65D
57593 66B
57594 67C
57595 66B
57596 67A
57597 60A
57599 66B
57600 68B
57601 68B
57602 68B
57603 64D
57604 64D
57605 65D
57607 65D
57608 64D
57609 66C
57611 67C
57612 65D
57613 64D
57614 67C
57615 67C
57617 65B
57618 64D
57619 66A
57620 60E
57621 68B
57622 66A
57623 68B
57625 66A
57626 64D
57627 67D
57628 67C
57630 66A
57631 65B
57632 68A
57633 67C
57634 60A
57635 64D
57637 67B
57638 66B
57640 67C
57642 60A
57643 67B
57644 67C
57645 64C
57650 67B
57651 67B
57652 65D
57653 62B
57654 64C
57655 64D
57658 67C
57659 66B
57661 66A
57663 66C
57665 66C
57666 66B
57667 65F
57668 66B
57669 67D
57670 64D
57671 67B
57672 67B
57673 67D
57674 66A
57679 64D
57681 66B
57682 66D
57684 67C
57686 65B
57688 67B
57689 65F
57690 66A
57691 65F
57695 67A
57697 67C
57698 67A

Cl. "4F" 4-6-0

57951 60A
57954 60A
57955 60A
57956 60A

Cl. "1P" 2-4-0

New No.	*Old No.*	
58020	20155	16A

Cl. "1P" 0-4-4T

New No.	*Old No.*	
58034	1251	22B
58038	1261	33A
58040	1273	15D
58042	1278	9D
58043	1287	33A
58045	1295	15A
58046	1298	71H
58047	1303	71H
58050	1324	16A
58051	1330	15D
58052	1337	20C
58053	1340	15A
58054	1341	15D
58056	1344	16A

New No.	Old No.	
58058	1350	17A
58059	1353	15D
58060	1357	20A
58061	1358	23A
58062	1360	33A
58063	1365	22B
58065	1367	33A
58066	1368	20C
58067	1370	19B
58068	1371	19B
58069	1373	20E
58070	1375	20E
58071	1377	19B
58072	1379	15C
58073	1382	15C
58075	1390	20C
58076	1396	19B
58077	1397	23A
58080	1411	17B
58083	1420	2A
58084	1421	9D
58085	1422	15A
58086	1423	71H
58087	1424	17B
58088	1425	71H
58089	1426	33A
58090	1429	20C
58091	1430	15D

Cl. "1P" 2-4-0T

58092	26428	9D

0-10-0

58100	22290	21C

Cl. "2F" 0-6-0

58110	22630	17A
58114	22900	19C
58115	22901	11B
58116	22902	3C
58117	22904	3D
58118	22907	2B
58119	22911	3B
58120	22912	11B
58121	22913	11B
58122	22915	3C
58123	22918	3C
58124	22920	3E
58125	22921	17A
58126	22924	21B
58127	22926	19C
58128	22929	9F
58129	22931	33B
58130	22932	17B

New No.	Old No.	
58131	22933	14B
58132	22934	17A
58133	22935	16A
58135	22944	16A
58136	22945	20B
58137	22946	16C
58138	22947	21B
58139	22950	19A
58140	22951	19A
58142	22954	15C
58143	22955	21B
58144	22958	17A
58145	22959	17B
58146	22963	18A
58147	22965	19C
58148	22967	17A
58149	22968	15D
58151	22970	19A
58152	22971	3B
58153	22974	18A
58154	22975	20E
58156	22977	20C
58157	22978	3C
58158	22982	14B
58159	22983	18A
58160	22984	17B
58161	2987	14A
58162	2988	15B
58163	2989	17C
58164	2990	15B
58165	2992	19A
58166	2993	18B
58167	2994	21A
58168	2995	18B
58169	2996	18A
58170	2997	19C
58171	2998	18A
58172	2999	15B
58173	23000	18A
58174	23001	17C
58175	23002	19A
58176	23003	18A
58177	23005	3E
58178	23006	3E
58179	23007	3E
58180	23008	3D
58181	23009	2A
58182	23010	3D
58183	23011	15B
58184	23012	33A
58185	23013	3D
58186	23014	17B
58187	23018	11B
58188	3023	20C
58189	3027	17D
58190	3031	19A
58191	3035	33A
58192	3037	18A
58193	3038	15B
58194	3039	15B
58195	3042	15B

New No.	Old No.		New No.	Old No.	
58196	3044	18B	58272	3493	1C
58197	3045	18A	58273	3503	3E
58198	3047	19C	58274	3508	14A
58199	3048	11B	58276	3512	19A
58200	3049	14A	58277	3516	3A
58201	3051	16A	58278	3517	2D
58203	3054	17A	58279	3525	3D
58204	3058	19C	58280	3526	1A
58206	3062	22B	58281	3527	4B
58207	3064	17B	58282	3533	19D
58209	3071	19B	58283	3536	1A
58211	3074	84G	58285	3539	1A
58212	3078	20B	58286	3543	1A
58213	3084	84G	58287	3545	3B
58214	3090	15B	58288	3551	3C
58215	3094	14B	58289	3559	33A
58216	3095	17A	58290	3561	2C
58217	3096	2D	58291	3564	11B
58218	3098	4B	58293	3571	2D
58219	3099	17D	58295	3603	3D
58220	3101	19A	58296	3617	18A
58221	3103	17B	58298	3648	15C
58224	3113	17D	58299	3655	11B
58225	3118	19A	58300	3688	15C
58226	3119	17D	58302	3691	1A
58228	3127	17D	58303	3696	1A
58229	3130	14B	58304	3703	17B
58230	3134	21A	58305	3707	15D
58231	3138	21A	58306	3725	2D
58232	3140	19A	58307	3726	3E
58233	3144	19C	58308	3738	2C
58234	3149	14B	58309	3739	11B
58235	3150	14A	58310	3764	14C
58236	3151	17B	58321	28091	C. Wks.
58237	3154	20C	58322	28093	84G
58238	3156	19C	58323	28100	C. Wks.
58239	3157	15D	58326	28106	C. Wks.
58240	3161	2B	58327	28107	84G
58241	3164	15D	58328	28115	C. Wks.
58242	3166	15C	58330	28128	84G
58244	3171	19C	58332	28141	C. Wks.
58245	3173	20B	58333	28152	84G
58246	3175	17A	58335	28166	11B
58247	3176	17C	58336	28172	C. Wks.
58248	3177	16A	58340	28205	11B
58249	3190	15C	58343	28227	C. Wks.
58252	3262	16A	58346	28239	11B
58254	3270	17D	58347	28245	C. Wks.
58257	3372	3A	58349	28247	11B
58258	3377	17B	58350	28251	11B
58259	3385	33A	58352	28256	11B
58260	3420	20C	58354	28263	11B
58261	3423	21A	58360	28312	11B
58262	3425	17B	58362	28318	12D
58264	3445	17C	58363	28333	8D
58265	3451	20C	58364	28335	7A
58267	3477	17B	58365	28337	7A
58268	3479	18A	58368	28345	3B
58269	3485	2A	58373	28403	8D
58271	3492	21A	58375	28408	7B

58376-58935

New No.	Old No.	
58376	28417	12A
58377	28428	9B
58378	28430	3B
58381	28450	7B
58382	28451	5D
58383	28457	8D
58388	28487	5A
58389	28492	12C
58392	28505	7D
58393	28507	8D
58394	28509	10E
58396	28512	12D
58398	28515	10A
58400	28525	5D
58409	28548	12C
58410	28549	10E
58412	28553	12C
58413	28555	8D
58415	28559	8D
58418	28580	12D
58419	28583	12A
58420	28585	7D
58421	28589	12D
58426	28611	9B
58427	28616	5D
58429	28619	5A
58430	28622	8D

Cl. "2F" 0-6-0T

58850	27505	17D
58851	27509	6C
58852	27510	1D
58853	27512	1D
58854	27513	6C
58855	27514	1D
58856	27515	17D
58857	27517	6C
58858	27520	1D
58859	27522	1D
58860	27527	17D
58861	27528	6C
58862	27530	17D
58863	27532	6C

Crane Engine 0-4-2ST

New No.	Old No.	
58865	27217	1D

Cl. "2F" 0-6-2T

58880	27553	86K
58881	27561	84G
58887	27596	8A
58888	27602	86K
58889	27603	7D
58891	27621	86K
58892	27625	87K
58895	27654	86K
58897	27674	4A
58899	7692	86K
58900	7699	10E
58902	7710	86K
58903	7711	7B
58904	7720	84G
58908	7737	4A
58910	7741	87K
58911	7746	8A
58912	7751	86K
58913	7752	86K
58915	7757	86K
58916	7759	86K
58919	7773	86K
58921	7782	8A
58924	7791	7D
58925	7794	86K
58926	7799	4A
58928	7803	3E
58932	7822	7D
58933	7829	86K
58935	7833	86K

Diesel Rail-cars (Leyland)

(Numbered in coach stock series)

29950	66C
29951	66C
29952	66C

SERVICE LOCOMOTIVES

Ex L.N.W. 0-6-0ST

CD3, CD6, CD7, CD8† — Wolverton

† Named *Earlestown*

3323 Crewe

Ex M.R. 0-4-0ST

41509 Derby

Ex L. & Y. 0-6-0ST

51304, 51305, 51324, 51368, 51394 — Horwich

Diesel 0-4-0

ED1 Beeston
ED2 Beeston
ED3 Castleton
ED4 Castleton
ED5 Castleton
ED6 Beeston

Battery 0-4-0

41550 W. India Dock, London

One unnumbered
Oakamoor

BRITISH RAILWAYS LOCOMOTIVES
Nos. 60001—90774

WITH SHED ALLOCATIONS

A4
4–6–2

60001* 52A
60002* 52A
60003* 34A
60004* 64B
60005* 52A
60006* 34A
60007* 34A
60008* 34A
60009* 64B
60010* 34A
60011* 64B
60012* 64B
60013* 34A
60014* 34A
60015* 35B
60016* 52A
60017* 34A
60018* 52A
60019* 52A
60020* 52A
60021* 34A
60022* 34A
60023* 52A
60024* 64B
60025* 34A
60026* 35B
60027* 64B
60028* 34A
60029* 34A
60030* 34A
60031* 64B
60032* 34A
60033* 34A
60034* 34A

A3
4–6–2

60035* 64B
60036* 50B
60037* 64B
60038* 52A
60039* 34A
60040* 52A
60041* 64B
60042* 52A
60043* 64B
60044* 37B
60045* 52A
60046* 37B
60047* 36A
60048* 38C
60049* 38C
60050* 34E
60051* 34E
60052* 38C
60053* 35B
60054* 38C
60055* 36A
60056* 37B
60057* 64B
60058* 36A
60059* 34A
60060* 52A
60061* 36A
60062* 37B
60063* 34A
60064* 36A
60065* 34A
60066* 36A
60067* 34A
60068* 12B
60069* 52B
60070* 51A
60071* 52A
60072* 52B
60073* 52B
60074* 50B
60075* 52A
60076* 51A
60077* 52B
60078* 52A
60079* 12B
60080* 52B
60081* 50B
60082* 52A
60083* 52B
60084* 50B
60085* 52B
60086* 50B
60087* 64B
60088* 52B
60089* 34A
60090* 64B
60091* 52B
60092* 52B
60093* 12B
60094* 64B
60095* 12B
60096* 64B
60097* 64B
60098* 64B
60099* 64B
60100* 64B
60101* 64B
60102* 38C
60103* 38C
60104* 38C
60105* 34A
60106* 35B
60107* 38C
60108* 34A
60109* 34A
60110* 34A
60111* 34E
60112* 37B

A1
4–6–2

60113* 35A
60114* 37B
60115* 52A
60116* 52B
60117* 37B
60118* 37B
60119* 37B
60120* 37B
60121* 50A
60122* 34A
60123* 37B
60124* 52A
60125* 37B
60126* 52B
60127* 52B
60128* 34A
60129* 52A
60130* 34A
60131* 34A
60132* 52A
60133* 37B
60134* 37B
60135* 52A
60136* 34A
60137* 52A
60138* 50A
60139* 34A
60140* 50A
60141* 37B
60142* 52A
60143* 52A
60144* 34A
60145* 52A
60146* 50A
60147* 52A
60148* 34A
60149* 34A
60150* 52A
60151* 52A
60152* 64B
60153* 50A
60154* 52A
60155* 52A
60156* 34A
60157* 34A
60158* 34A
60159* 64B
60160* 64B
60161* 64B
60162* 64B

A2
4–6–2

60500* 35A
60501* 50A
60502* 50A
60503* 50A
60504* 35A
60505* 35A
60506* 35A
60507* 64B
60508* 35A
60509* 64B
60510* 64B
60511* 52B
60512* 52B
60513* 35A
60514* 35A
60515* 52B
60516* 52B
60517* 52B
60518* 52A
60519* 64B
60520* 35A
60521* 52A
60522* 50A
60523* 35A
60524* 50A
60525* 61B
60526* 50A

60527* 62B
60528* 62B
60529* 64B
60530* 64B
60531* 61B
60532* 64B
60533* 35A
60534* 64B
60535* 64B
60536* 64B
60537* 61B
60538* 52A
60539* 52B

W1
4-6-4

60700 34A

V2
2-6-2

60800* 34A
60801 52B
60802 52B
60803 35A
60804 62B
60805 52B
60806 52B
60807 52B
60808 52B
60809* 52B
60810 52B
60811 52B
60812 52B
60813 34A
60814 34A
60815 38E
60816 64B
60817 38E
60818 38E
60819 61B
60820 38E
60821 34A
60822 61B
60823 34A
60824 61B
60825 64A
60826 38E
60827 61B
60828 35A
60829 35A
60830 38E
60831 38E
60832 38E
60833 52B
60834 64B
60835* 52B
60836 64A
60837 50A
60838 62B
60839 50A
60840 62B
60841 35A
60842 35A
60843 50A
60844 62B
60845 38E
60846 36A
60847* 50A
60848 64A
60849 36A
60850 35A
60851 61B
60852 36A
60853 38E
60854 35A
60855 35A
60856 50A
60857 36A
60858 35A
60859 35A
60860* 52B
60861 36A
60862 34A
60863 35A
60864 50A
60865 35A
60866 35A
60867 36A
60868 52B
60869 35A
60870 36A
60871 35A
60872* 36A
60873* 34A
60874 35A
60875 36A
60876 35A
60877 36A
60878 35A
60879 35A
60880 36A
60881 36A
60882 64B
60883 52A
60884 52A
60885 52A
60886 52B
60887 52B
60888 61B
60889 36A
60890 36A
60891 52B
60892 34A
60893 35A
60894 64A
60895 52B
60896 36A
60897 35A
60898 61B
60899 35A
60900 34A
60901 50A
60902 36A
60903 34A
60904 50A
60905 35A
60906 35A
60907 50A
60908 35A
60909 34A
60910 52B
60911 35A
60912 35A
60913 35A
60914 34A
60915 34A
60916 35A
60917 36A
60918 50A
60919 61B
60920 62B
60921 36A
60922 34A
60923 52A
60924 35A
60925 50A
60926 52A
60927 64B
60928 36A
60929 50A
60930 36A
60931 62B
60932 52D
60933 50A
60934 50A
60935 36A
60936 35A
60937 62B
60938 35A
60939 52B
60940 52A
60941 50A
60942 52B
60943 36A
60944 52B
60945 52B
60946 50A
60947 52B
60948 36A
60949 52B
60950 35A
60951 64B
60952 52B
60953 64A
60954 50A
60955 61B
60956 36A
60957 52B
60958 62B
60959 64B
60960 50A
60961 50A
60962 50A
60963 50A
60964 52A
60965 52A
60966 35A
60967 52A
60968 50A
60969 62B
60970 61B
60971 62B
60972 64B
60973 61B
60974 50A
60975 50A
60976 50A
60977 50A
60978 50A
60979 50A
60980 64A
60981 50A
60982 50A
60983 34A

B1
4-6-0

61000* 30A
61001* 30A
61002* 64A
61003* 30F
61004* 30F
61005* 30F
61006* 30F
61007* 64B
61008* 30A
61009* 30A
61010* 53B
61011* 52A
61012* 52A
61013* 52A
61014* 52A
61015* 50A
61016* 50A
61017* 51E
61018* 51E
61019* 52D
61020* 50A
61021* 51A
61022* 51A
61023* 51A
61024* 52D
61025* 52D
61026* 36A
61027* 35A
61028* 34E
61029* 37A
61030* 51E
61031* 37A
61032* 51E
61033* 37A
61034* 51E

61035* 50B
61036* 36A
61037* 51E
61038* 50A
61039* 51A
61040* 32A
61041 32A
61042 32A
61043 32A
61044 32A
61045 32A
61046 32A
61047 32A
61048 32A
61049 32A
61050 32A
61051 32A
61052 32A
61053 32B
61054 32B
61055 32B
61056 32B
61058 32B
61059 32B
61060 53A
61061 64A
61062 50B
61063 38B
61064 65A
61065 50B
61066 38B
61067 64A
61068 53A
61069 50B
61070 35A
61071 50A
61072 62A
61073 35A
61074 53A
61075 35A
61076 64B
61077 34E
61078 38A
61079 40B
61080 53A
61081 64B
61082 40B
61083 34E
61084 50A
61085 37A
61086 36A
61087 36A
61088 38C
61089 30A
61090 34D
61091 34D
61092 38C
61093 34D
61094 34D
61095 34D
61096 37A
61097 34D
61098 30A
61099 34D
61100 52A
61101 62B
61102 62B
61103 62A
61104 30A
61105 34D
61106 38C
61107 36A
61108 38C
61109 30A
61110 38A
61111 38A
61112 40A
61113 34A
61114 39A
61115 50A
61116 65A
61117 65A
61118 62A
61119 30A
61120 36A
61121 31A
61122 38A
61123 38A
61124 36A
61125 36A
61126 36A
61127 36A
61128 36A
61129 34A
61130 30A
61131 38A
61132 61B
61133 61B
61134 61A
61135 30F
61136 34A
61137 34A
61138 34A
61139 34A
61140 34E
61141 38C
61142 40B
61143 35A
61144 30A
61145 39B
61146 62A
61147 62B
61148 62A
61149 30F
61150 39B
61151 39B
61152 39B
61153 39B
61154 39B
61155 39A
61156 39A
61157 39A
61158 39A
61159 39A
61160 39A
61161 39A
61162 39A
61163 34E
61164 34E
61165 36B
61166 36B
61167 36B
61168 36B
61169 39B
61170 36A
61171 30A
61172 65A
61173 51A
61174 36B
61175 30A
61176 51A
61177 30A
61178 64B
61179 39B
61180 65A
61181 39B
61182 39A
61183 39B
61184 39A
61185 38C
61186 38C
61187 38C
61188 38C
61189* 51E
61190 40B
61191 40B
61192 30A
61193 36A
61194 36B
61195 40B
61196 36A
61197 65A
61198 51A
61199 52D
61200 34A
61201 32B
61202 40B
61203 34A
61204 40B
61205 30A
61206 35A
61207 35A
61208 36E
61209 38B
61210 35A
61211 36E
61212 36E
61213 36E
61214 51E
61215* 53B
61216 50B
61217 12B
61218 50B
61219 12B
61220 51E
61221* 64B
61222 12B
61223 39A
61224 51A
61225 39A
61226 30F
61227 30A
61228 39A
61229 37C
61230 37C
61231 36E
61232 30F
61233 30A
61234 30A
61235 30A
61236 30A
61237* 50B
61238* 52A
61239 50A
61240* 50B
61241* 52D
61242* 64A
61243* 65A
61244* 64B
61245* 64B
61246* 36A
61247* 36A
61248* 36A
61249* 36A
61250* 36A
61251* 34A
61252 32B
61253 32B
61254 32B
61255 51A
61256 50B
61257 50B
61258 50B
61259 50B
61260 65A
61261 65A
61262 62A
61263 62B
61264 30F
61265 36A
61266 34A
61267 37C
61268 37C
61269 40A
61270 32A
61271 32A
61272 32A
61273 51A
61274 51A
61275 51A
61276 51A
61277 64A
61278 62B
61279 40A
61280 40A
61281 40A
61282 30A
61283 38A

No.	Shed
61284	40B
61285	31A
61286	31A
61287	31A
61288	50A
61289	51A
61290	51E
61291	51A
61292	62B
61293	62B
61294	37C
61295	37B
61296	37C
61297	37A
61298	38C
61299	38C
61300	31A
61301	31A
61302	31A
61303	51E
61304	53B
61305	53B
61306	53B
61307	61A
61308	61C
61309	37A
61310	37A
61311	39B
61312	39B
61313	39B
61314	39B
61315	39B
61316	39B
61317	39B
61318	40B
61319	54C
61320	54C
61321	54C
61322	52D
61323	61A
61324	61A
61325	40B
61326	26A
61327	39B
61328	40B
61329	40A
61330	35A
61331	35A
61332	32A
61333	31A
61334	31A
61335	30A
61336	30A
61337	50A
61338	50B
61339	50B
61340	65A
61341	64A
61342	65A
61343	61A
61344	65A
61345	61A
61346	61C
61347	61C
61348	61A
61349	61A
61350	61A
61351	61A
61352	61A
61353	61C
61354	64A
61355	64A
61356	64A
61357	64A
61358	64A
61359	64A
61360	30A
61361	30A
61362	30A
61363	30A
61364	40A
61365	40B
61366	40B
61367	38A
61368	38A
61369	38A
61370	

61371–61399: To be built

No.	Shed
61400	61A
61401	61A
61402	62B
61403	62B
61404	61A
61405	40A
61406	40B
61407	40B
61408	40B
61409	40B

B16
4-6-0

No.	Shed
61410	50B
61411	50B
61412	50B
61413	50B
61414	50B
61415	50B
61416	50A
61417	50A
61418	50A
61419	50A
61420	50A
61421	50A
61422	50A
61423	50A
61424	50A
61425	50B
61426	50A
61427	50B
61428	50B
61429	50B
61430	50A
61431	50B
61432	50B
61433	50B
61434	50A
61435	50A
61436	50A
61437	50A
61438	50A
61439	50A
61440	50B
61441	50A
61442	50B
61443	50A
61444	50A
61445	50B
61446	50B
61447	50B
61448	50A
61449	50A
61450	50A
61451	50A
61452	50A
61453	50A
61454	50A
61455	50A
61456	50A
61457	50A
61458	50A
61459	50A
61460	50A
61461	50A
61462	50A
61463	50A
61464	50A
61465	50A
61466	50A
61467	50A
61468	50A
61469	50B
61470	50B
61471	50B
61472	50A
61473	50A
61474	50A
61475	50A
61476	50A
61477	50A
61478	50B

B4
4-6-0

No.	Shed
61482*	37A

B12
4-6-0

No.	Shed
61501	61C
61502	61C
61503	61C
61505	61A
61507	61A
61508	61A
61511	61A
61512	30E
61513	61A
61514	30A
61515	30A
61516	30A
61519	30A
61520	32F
61521	61A
61523	30E
61524	61A
61525	30A
61526	61A
61528	61A
61530	32F
61532	61A
61533	31D
61535	32B
61537	31D
61538	35B
61539	61A
61540	31D
61541	35B
61542	30A
61543	61A
61545	32F
61546	30A
61547	31D
61549	30A
61550	30A

61552 61A
61553 35B
61554 35B
61555 30E
61556 30E
61557 30E
61558 30E
61559 30A
61560 61A
61561 32B
61562 32B
61563 61A
61564 32B
61565 35B
61566 32B
61567 30A
61568 30A
61569 32B
61570 32B
61571 30A
61572 30A
61573 30A
61574 30A
61575 30A
61576 30A
61577 32B
61578 30A
61579 30A
61580 30A

B2 & B17
4–6–0

61600* 32B
61601* 32B
61602* 30A
61603* 30E
61604* 32B
61605* 30A
61606* 30A
61607* 30E
61608* 30A
61609* 32A
61610* 30A
61611* 30A
61612* 30A
61613* 30A
61614* 30E
61615* 30E
61616* 30E
61617* 31A
61618* 32B
61619* 31A
61620* 31A
61621* 31A
61622* 31A
61623* 31A
61624* 31A
61625* 31A
61626* 31B
61627* 31A
61628* 31A
61629* 32A
61630* 31B
61631* 31A
61632* 30E
61633* 31B
61634* 32B
61635* 31B
61636* 31A
61637* 31A
61638* 31A
61639* 30E
61640* 31A
61641* 31B
61642* 31A
61643* 31A
61644* 30E
61645* 32B
61646* 31B
61647* 32B
61648* 30A
61649* 32B
61650* 38E
61651* 38E
61652* 38A
61653* 38A
61654* 30A
61655* 30A
61656* 31B
61657* 38A
61658* 30A
61659* 32A
61660* 31B
61661* 32D
61662* 38A
61663* 31A
61664* 38E
61665* 32D
61666* 31B
61667* 38E
61668* 32B
61669* 32B
61670* 32A
61671* 31A
61672* 31B

B13
4–6–0

61699S Rugby Plant

V4
2–6–2

61700* 65A
61701 65A

K2
2–6–0

61720 40B
61721 30A
61722 40B
61723 38A
61724 40B
61725 40F
61726 38A
61727 40B
61728 40B
61729 35A
61730 35A
61731 40F
61732 38A
61733 40B
61734 30A
61735 35A
61736 35A
61737 30A
61738 31D
61739 35A
61740 35A
61741 38A
61742 31D
61743 31D
61744 40F
61745 30A
61746 30A
61747 35A
61748 31D
61749 38A
61750 40F
61751 38A
61752 30A
61753 30A
61754 30A
61755 40F
61756 40F
61757 31D
61758 38A
61759 30A
61760 40F
61761 30A
61762 40F
61763 38A
61764* 65A
61765 30A
61766 31D
61767 30A
61768 38A
61769 38A
61770 40F
61771 38A
61772* 65C
61773 38A
61774* 65A
61775* 65A
61776 65A
61777 30A
61778 30A
61779 65A
61780 30A
61781* 65A
61782* 63D
61783* 63D
61784 65A
61785 65A
61786 65A
61787* 63D
61788* 63D
61789* 63D
61790* 63D
61791* 63D
61792 65A
61793 65A
61794* 65A

K3 & K1
2–6–0

61800 40B
61801 30A
61802 40B
61803 40B
61804 35A
61805 30A
61806 40B
61807 40A
61808 39A
61809 39A
61810 30A
61811 35A
61812 38A
61813 53A
61814 53A
61815 30A
61816 38A
61817 30A
61818 52B
61819 53A
61820 30A
61821 38A
61822 40A
61823 64A
61824 38A
61825 40B
61826 38A
61827 40B
61828 39A
61829 39A
61830 30A
61831 30A
61832 39A
61833 38A
61834 30A
61835 30A
61836 40B
61837 40B
61838 40B
61839 39A
61840 30A

61841	35A
61842	40B
61843	35A
61844	31B
61845	40B
61846	31B
61847	31B
61848	39A
61849	30A
61850	35A
61851	12B
61852	39A
61853	35A
61854	12B
61855	64A
61856	39A
61857	64A
61858	12B
61859	40A
61860	31B
61861	36A
61862	35A
61863	35A
61864	31B
61865	39A
61866	31B
61867	35A
61868	35A
61869	31B
61870	39A
61871	53A
61872	53A
61873	31B
61874	53A
61875	52B
61876	64A
61877	39A
61878	64A
61879	64A
61880	30A
61881	64A
61882	12B
61883	53A
61884	52B
61885	64A
61886	31B
61887	31B
61888	31B
61889	31B
61890	35A
61891	40B
61892	53A
61893	31B
61894	40A
61895	31B
61896	39A
61897	64A
61898	12B
61899	53A
61900	64A
61901	52B
61902	53A
61903	53A
61904	52B
61905	40B
61906	52B
61907	36A
61908	39A
61909	64A
61910	39A
61911	64A
61912	40B
61913	39A
61914	39A
61915	35A
61916	64A
61917	52B
61918	36A
61919	39A
61920	53A
61921	32A
61922	53A
61923	53A
61924	64A
61925	40A
61926	32C
61927	53A
61928	64A
61929	35A
61930	52B
61931	64A
61932	53A
61933	64A
61934	53A
61935	53A
61936	12B
61937	12B
61938	31B
61939	32A
61940	31B
61941	53A
61942	32A
61943	38B
61944	40A
61945	53A
61946	31B
61947	32A
61948	31B
61949	32C
61950	39A
61951	35A
61952	52B
61953	32A
61954	35A
61955	64A
61956	39A
61957	32A
61958	32C
61959	32C
61960	40A
61961	31B
61962	52B
61963	40B
61964	40A
61965	53A
61966	40A
61967	35A
61968	64A
61969	52B
61970	32A
61971	32A
61972	35A
61973	32C
61974	38B
61975	38B
61976	38B
61977	38B
61978	36A
61979	38B
61980	38B
61981	32A
61982	40A
61983	64A
61984	52B
61985	52B
61986	52B
61987	52B
61988	64A
61989	32A
61990	64A
61991	64A
61992	64A

K4 & K1
2–6–0

61993*	65A
61994*	65A
61995*	63D
61996*	63D
61997*	65A
61998*	65A

D3
4–4–0

62000	35B

K1
2–6–0

62001	51E
62002	52B
62003	52B
62004	51A
62005	52B
62006	51A
62007	52B
62008	51A
62009	51A
62010	52B
62011	31B
62012	31B
62013	31B
62014	31B
62015	31B
62016	31B
62017	31B
62018	31B
62019	31B
62020	31B
62021	52C
62022	52C
62023	52C
62024	52C
62025	52C
62026	52C
62027	52C
62028	52C
62029	52C
62030	52C
62031	31B
62032	31B
62033	31B
62034	31B
62035	31B
62036	31B
62037	31B
62038	31B
62039	31B
62040	31B
62041	51E
62042	51E
62043	51E
62044	51A
62045	51A
62046	51A
62047	51A
62048	51A
62049	51A
62050	51A
62051	31B
62052	31B
62053	31B
62054	31B
62055	31B
62056	51A
62057	51A
62058	51A
62059	51A
62060	51E
62061	51A
62062	51A
62063	51E
62064	51E
62065	51E
62066	31B
62067	31B
62068	31B
62069	31B
62070	31B

D3
4-4-0

62132 40C
62148 38A

D2
4-4-0

62154 40F
62172 38A
62181 40F

D1
4-4-0

62 09 63B

D41
4-4-0

62225 61A
62227 61C
62228 61A
62229 61A
62230 61A
62231 61C
62232 61A
62241 61A
62242 61C
62243 61C
62246 61C
62247 61C
62248 61C
62249 61C
62251 61C
62252 61C
62255 61C
62256 61C

D40
4-4-0

62260 61A
62261 61A
62262 61C
62264 61C
62265 61A
62267 61C
62268 61A
62269 61C
62270 61A
62271 61C
62272 61A
62273* 61A
62274* 61A
62275* 61A
62276* 61A
62277* 61A
62278* 61A
62279* 61A

D31
4-4-0

62281 12B
62283 64F

D20
4-4-0

62340 50C
62341 50C
62342 50D
62343 50D
62344 52D
62345 53B
62347 51J
62348 50C
62349 52D (A)
62351 52D (A)
62352 52D (A)
62353 53D
62354 52D (A)
62355 53D
62357 52D (A)
62358 52D (A)
62359 51J
62360 52D (A)
62361 50C
62362 52D (A)
62363 50C
62365 53D
62366 50C
62369 50A
62370 50D
62371 52D (A)
62372 51C
62373 50D
62374 50C
62375 53D
62376 50C
62378 50C
62379 51C
62380 52D (A)
62381 50C
62382 50C
62383 53B
62384 50D
62386 50C
62387 52D (A)
62388 51J
62389 50D
62391 51J
62392 50D
62395 50C
62396 53B
62397 50D

D29
4-4-0

62405* 64B
62410* 62A
62411* 62A

D30
4-4-0

62417* 64G
62418* 62A
62419* 62A
62420* 64G
62421* 64A
62422* 64G
62423* 64G
62424* 64A
62425* 64G
62426* 63B
62427* 62B
62428* 64G
62429* 62A
62430* 62A
62431* 62A
62432* 64G
62434* 62B
62435* 64A
62436* 62B
62437* 64B
62438* 62B
62439* 64F
62440* 64G
62441* 62C
62442* 62A

D32
4-4-0

62451 64A

D33
4-4-0

62457 62B
62459 62C
62460 65A
62461 63B
62462 65A
62464 62C
62466 62B

D34
4-4-0

62467* 62A
62468* 62A
62469* 65A
62470* 65A
62471* 64A
62472* 65A
62474* 65A
62475* 62A
62477* 65A
62478* 62A
62479* 65A
62480* 65A
62482* 65A
62483* 64A
62484* 64A
62485* 62B
62487* 64A
62488* 64A
62489* 65A
62490* 64A
62492* 62A
62493* 65A
62494* 64A
62495* 64F
62496* 65A
62497* 65A
62498* 65A

D15 & D16
4-4-0

62501 31C
62502 31C
62503 31E
62505 31C
62506 31C
62507 31C
62508 31E
62509 32G
62510 32A
62511 32D
62513 31C
62514 31C
62515 32G
62516 31A
62517 32D
62518 31C
62519 32G
62520 32G
62521 32D
62522 32A
62523 32G
62524 32D
62525 31A
62526 32B
62527 31A
62528 32G
62529 31B
62530 31A
62531 31A
62532 9E
62533 32G
62534 31D
62535 9E

62536 9E
62538 32G
62539 31B
62540 32A
62541 32A
62542 31B
62543 31D
62544 32D
62545 32A
62546* 32D
62547 31B
62548 31B
62549 31A
62551 31A
62552 32A
62553 32A
62554 32A
62555 32A
62556 32A
62557 31A
62558 31D
62559 31C
62561 32F
62562 32G
62564 32F
62565 30A
62566 31E
62567 31A
62568 9E
62569 31C
62570 32A
62571 31A
62572 30E
62573 31D
62574 31A
62575 31C
62576 32D
62577 32A
62578 32G
62579 31B
62580 32D
62581 32A
62582 31C
62584 32A
62585 32A
62586 32D
62587 9E
62588 9E
62589 31B
62590 32B
62592 32F
62593 32A
62596 32F
62597 32D
62598 30E
62599 9E
62601 31C
62603 31B
62604 32D
62605 31B
62606 32A
62607 31E
62608 30E
62609 9E
62610 32A
62611 32D
62612 32A
62613 32D
62614 31C
62615 31E
62616 32A
62617 32A
62618 31A
62619 32A
62620 32G

D10
4–4–0

62650* 9G
62651* 9E
62652* 9G
62653* 9E
62654* 9E
62655* 9G
62656* 9E
62657* 9E
62658* 9E
62659* 9E

D11
4–4–0

62660* 40B
62661* 40B
62662* 40B
62663* 9F
62664* 40B
62665* 9F
62666* 40B
62667* 40B
62668* 40B
62669* 40B
62670* 9E
62671* 65A
62672* 65A
62673* 65A
62674* 65A
62675* 65A
62676* 65A
62677* 64B
62678* 64B
62679* 64B
62680* 65A
62681* 65A
62682* 65A
62683* 64B
62684* 65A
62685* 64B
62686* 65A
62687* 65A
62688* 65A
62689* 65A
62690* 64B
62691* 64B
62692* 64B
62693* 64B
62694* 64B

D49
4–4–0

62700* 53B
62701* 53D
62702* 64A
62703* 53B
62704* 62A
62705* 64B
62706* 64B
62707* 53D
62708* 62A
62709* 64B
62710* 53B
62711* 64A
62712* 64A
62713* 62B
62714* 63A
62715* 64A
62716* 62A
62717* 62A
62718* 62B
62719* 64B
62720* 53B
62721* 64A
62722* 53B
62723* 53B
62724* 53B
62725* 63A
62726* 50A
62727* 50A
62728* 62B
62729* 62A
62730* 12B
62731* 12B
62732* 12B
62733* 64B
62734* 12B
62735* 12B
62736* 50A
62737* 53B
62738* 50D
62739* 50B
62740* 50A
62741* 53B
62742* 50A
62743* 53B
62744* 50A
62745* 50A
62746* 50B
62747* 52C
62748* 50B
62749* 50D
62750* 53D
62751* 50E
62752* 50D
62753* 50D
62754* 53B
62755* 50D
62756* 50B
62757* 53B
62758* 50D
62759* 50A
62760* 50A
62761* 50A
62762* 50D
62763* 50D
62764* 50E
62765* 50D
62766* 53D
62767* 53B
62768* 50D
62769* 50E
62770* 50E
62771* 52C
62772* 50D
62773* 50D
62774* 50F (P)
62775* 50B

E4
2–4–0

62780 32A
62781 31A
62782 32A
62783 31A
62784 31A
62785 31A
62786 31E
62787 32A
62788 31A
62789 32A
62790 31A
62791 30A
62792 32A
62793 32A
62794 31A
62795 31E
62796 32A
62797 32A

C1
4–4–2

62822 35B

C4
4–4–2

62900 40F
62901 40F
62908 40A

62909	40B
62918	40A
62919	40B

Q4
0–8–0

63201	36D
63202	37A
63203	36D
63204	37A
63205	37A
63217	37A
63220	36D
63221	37A
63223	37A
63225	37A
63226	37A
63227	37A
63229	36D
63234	37A
63235	36D
63236	37A
63240	37A
63243	37A

Q5
0–8–0

63251	54C
63257	54C
63259	54C
63261	54C
63267	54C
63270	50A (N)
63271	54C
63274	51B
63280	50C
63282	51D
63283	51D
63284	54C
63285	50C
63287	54C
63303	54C
63311	51G
63314	51G
63319	50C
63326	54C
63328	51D
63333	51D
63336	50C

Q6
0–8–0

63340	51G
63341	51B
63342	54C
63343	51B
63344	51B
63345	51B
63346	54D
63347	51B
63348	50C
63349	51D
63350	54C
63351	51D
63352	54B
63353	52C
63354	54C
63355	51C
63356	52C
63357	54D
63358	54C
63359	54D
63360	51B
63361	54D
63362	50B
63363	54B
63364	51D
63365	54D
63366	54C
63367	51G
63368	51D
63369	51D
63370	51B
63371	51B
63372	54D
63373	51D
63374	51G
63375	51D
63376	52C
63377	54C
63378	50C
63379	54B
63380	51D
63381	52C
63382	50C
63383	51C
63384	54C
63385	52C
63386	54C
63387	50C
63388	51B
63389	51B
63390	52C
63391	52C
63392	51C
63393	51D
63394	52C
63395	50C
63396	51C
63397	51C
63398	52C
63399	52C
63400	54C
63401	51C
63402	54C
63403	52C
63404	54D
63405	51G
63406	50C
63407	51G
63408	50C
63409	51D
63410	51C
63411	51D
63412	52C
63413	52C
63414	51C
63415	51C
63416	51G
63417	51D
63418	54D
63419	51C
63420	51D
63421	51C
63422	51C
63423	51G
63424	51C
63425	51G
63426	51B
63427	51C
63428	52C
63429	50C
63430	51B
63431	50C
63432	52C
63433	54D
63434	54C
63435	51C
63436	50C
63437	54B
63438	51C
63439	54D
63440	50C
63441	52C
63442	51D
63443	51G
63444	52C
63445	51B
63446	51G
63447	51B
63448	50C
63449	50C
63450	50B
63451	50C
63452	51C
63453	51G
63454	51C
63455	54D
63456	50C
63457	51C
63458	54C
63459	51D

Q7
0–8–0

63460	54B
63461	54B
63462	54B
63463	54B
63464	54B
63465	54B
63466	54B
63467	54B
63468	54B
63469	54B
63470	54B
63471	54B
63472	54B
63473	54B
63474	54B

O3
2–8–0

63475	36E
63476	36A
63477	36A
63478	36A
63479	36A
63480	36A
63481	36A
63482	36E
63483	36A
63484	36A
63485	36A
63486	36A
63488	36A
63491	36A
63493	36A

O1 & O4
2–8–0

63570	40D
63571	38B
63572	36C
63573	38A
63574	39B
63575	39A
63576	36C
63577	40E
63578	38B
63579	38B
63580	38B
63581	39B
63582	39A
63583	39B
63584	36C
63585	40E
63586	40B
63587	36C
63588	40D
63589	38B
63590	39A
63591	39A
63592	39A
63593	40B
63594	38B
63595	36C
63596	38B

63597	40E
63598	39A
63599	38A
63600	39A
63601	36C
63602	36C
63603	53A
63604	39B
63605	39B
63606	36C
63607	40B
63608	36E
63609	39B
63610	38B
63611	36B
63612	36B
63613	38D
63614	38B
63615	40E
63616	40B
63617	36C
63618	38B
63619	39A
63620	53E
63621	40B
63622	39B
63623	36D
63624	40B
63625	40E
63626	36C
63627	36B
63628	53A
63629	39B
63630	39A
63631	39A
63632	40E
63633	39A
63634	40D
63635	38B
63636	38A
63637	36E
63638	39A
63639	38B
63640	36C
63641	39A
63642	36C
63643	36C
63644	40E
63645	36C
63646	38B
63647	40B
63648	40E
63649	36C
63650	39A
63651	40B
63652	39A
63653	36C
63654	36E
63655	36C
63656	40E
63657	40B
63658	40E
63659	36C
63660	36C
63661	39B
63662	38B
63663	39A
63664	53A
63665	40E
63666	40E
63667	53E
63668	36B
63669	36C
63670	39A
63671	36C
63672	36B
63673	53A
63674	38B
63675	39B
63676	53A
63677	40E
63678	39A
63679	40E
63680	39B
63681	38B
63682	36B
63683	40E
63684	36C
63685	39B
63686	39A
63687	38B
63688	36E
63689	38B
63690	36C
63691	40D
63692	40B
63693	40B
63694	38D
63695	39A
63696	36C
63697	36D
63698	40B
63699	38B
63700	38B
63701	31B
63702	38D
63703	40E
63704	31B
63705	39A
63706	38B
63707	40E
63708	39A
63709	40E
63710	39B
63711	39A
63712	53A
63713	39A
63714	39B
63715	40E
63716	38B
63717	40E
63718	36C
63719	39A
63720	38D
63721	38B
63722	38B
63723	38B
63724	40E
63725	39A
63726	36C
63727	36D
63728	36C
63729	38A
63730	31B
63731	36C
63732	53A
63733	39B
63734	39B
63735	38A
63736	36E
63737	39B
63738	40B
63739	38B
63740	53A
63741	40E
63742	38B
63743	38B
63744	36C
63745	36C
63746	38B
63747	36C
63748	38B
63749	38D
63750	40E
63751	53E
63752	38B
63753	53A
63754	53A
63755	53A
63756	38A
63757	40E
63758	40E
63759	40E
63760	53A
63761	38A
63762	38A
63763	36E
63764	53A
63765	40E
63766	39B
63767	38B
63768	39A
63769	53A
63770	53A
63771	39B
63772	53A
63773	39A
63774	36B
63775	36B
63776	40E
63777	39A
63778	36C
63779	36B
63780	39A
63781	38A
63782	36E
63783	39B
63784	39A
63785	36E
63786	39A
63787	38A
63788	36C
63789	39A
63790	39B
63791	36B
63792	38B
63793	36C
63794	39A
63795	38B
63796	39A
63797	39B
63798	38B
63799	38B
63800	40E
63801	38A
63802	40B
63803	38B
63804	38A
63805	39A
63806	38B
63807	40E
63808	38B
63809	40E
63812	53A
63813	36B
63816	53A
63817	39A
63818	36C
63819	40B
63821	39B
63822	39B
63823	53A
63824	36C
63827	38B
63828	53A
63829	38A
63832	36C
63833	40E
63835	53A
63836	40B
63837	40E
63838	38B
63839	39A
63840	40E
63841	38B
63842	40E
63843	53E
63845	53A
63846	39B
63847	36C
63848	39A
63849	53E
63850	39B
63851	38A
63852	40D
63853	38B
63854	39A
63855	53A

63856	53A
63857	53A
63858	38B
63859	38D
63860	39B
63861	40D
63862	39A
63863	38B
63864	39A
63865	39A
63867	38B
63868	38B
63869	38B
63870	40E
63872	39A
63873	38B
63874	53A
63876	39A
63877	36E
63878	40B
63879	38B
63880	39A
63881	53A
63882	39B
63883	36D
63884	40E
63885	40D
63886	39A
63887	39A
63888	39B
63889	39B
63890	39A
63891	39A
63893	38B
63894	38A
63895	39A
63897	31B
63898	36B
63899	39A
63900	40E
63901	38B
63902	40E
63904	36D
63905	36E
63906	36C
63907	36E
63908	36E
63911	36C
63912	38B
63913	36D
63914	36E
63915	39A
63917	36C
63920	36C

O2
2–8–0

63922	36C
63923	35A
63924	36B
63925	36A
63926	36A
63927	36B
63928	36A
63929	35B
63930	35B
63931	35B
63932	35B
63933	35A
63934	36C
63935	35A
63936	35B
63937	36C
63938	35B
63939	36C
63940	35B
63941	36A
63942	36A
63943	36A
63944	36C
63945	36A
63946	36A
63947	36A
63948	35A
63949	35B
63950	35B
63951	36A
63952	36A
63953	36A
63954	36A
63955	36A
63956	36A
63957	36A
63958	36A
63959	36A
63960	35B
63961	36A
63962	36A
63963	36C
63964	36A
63965	35B
63966	35B
63967	36A
63968	36A
63969	36B
63970	36B
63971	36B
63972	36B
63973	36A
63974	36A
63975	36B
63976	36B
63977	36B
63978	36B
63979	36B
63980	36B
63981	36B
63982	36B
63983	36B
63984	36B
63985	36B
63986	36A
63987	36A

J3 & J4
0–6–0

64105	34D
64112	35A
64114	34D
64115	40F
64116	37A
64117	34D
64118	35A
64119	37A
64120	35A
64121	35A
64122	34D
64123	35A
64124	36A
64125	36E
64128	35A
64129	37A
64131	35A
64132	40F
64133	36E
64135	35A
64137	40F
64140	34D
64141	36E
64142	37A
64148	36E
64150	36E
64151	35A
64153	34D
64158	35A
64160	35A
64162	35A

J6
0–6–0

64170	37C
64171	35A
64172	35B
64173	37B
64174	37A
64175	34D
64176	35A
64177	35A
64178	35B
64179	36A
64180	40F
64181	40F
64182	37A
64183	36A
64184	35A
64185	36A
64186	35A
64187	35A
64188	34B
64189	35A
64190	40F
64191	35A
64192	35A
64193	36A
64194	38A
64195	36A
64196	40F
64197	38A
64198	40F
64199	38A
64200	38A
64201	40F
64202	38A
64203	37C
64204	40F
64205	37C
64206	35B
64207	35A
64208	37A
64209	36A
64210	40F
64211	35A
64212	38A
64213	38A
64214	37A
64215	38A
64216	35A
64217	35A
64218	36A
64219	36A
64220	35A
64221	35A
64222	38A
64223	38A
64224	38A
64225	35A
64226	37C
64227	35B
64228	35A
64229	40F
64230	38A
64231	38A
64232	36A
64233	38A
64234	34B
64235	35A
64236	36A
64237	35B
64238	35A
64239	34B
64240	34D
64241	36E
64242	40F
64243	36A
64244	40F
64245	35A
64246	35A
64247	40F
64248	40F
64249	35A
64250	37B
64251	34B
64252	35A
64253	38A
64254	35A

64255	36A
64256	34B
64257	35A
64258	36A
64259	36A
64260	37B
64261	36A
64262	36A
64263	36A
64264	36A
64265	35A
64266	35A
64267	37A
64268	37C
64269	38A
64270	36A
64271	37C
64272	37A
64273	35A
64274	37C
64275	35A
64276	40F
64277	37A
64278	35A
64279	36A

J11
0–6–0

64280	36E
64281	40E
64282	36E
64283	36B
64284	40B
64285	36A
64286	40D
64287	36E
64288	36B
64289	40E
64290	36D
64291	39B
64292	38B
64293	40D
64294	39A
64295	36E
64296	36B
64297	40E
64298	39A
64299	40D
64300	38B
64301	38A
64302	36B
64303	40A
64304	8E
64305	40B
64306	36E
64307	40B
64308	36C
64309	36C
64310	40E
64311	39A
64312	40B
64313	34E
64314	40B
64315	40A
64316	39A
64317	38D
64318	38B
64319	36B
64320	40C
64321	40E
64322	39A
64323	40B
64324	38E
64325	40B
64326	39A
64327	38E
64328	40C
64329	34E
64330	38E
64331	38D
64332	39A
64333	39A
64334	36B
64335	36E
64336	39B
64337	40D
64338	6E
64339	36C
64340	36E
64341	36E
64342	39A
64343	36D
64344	40D
64345	38D
64346	39A
64347	36E
64348	36E
64349	36A
64350	40A
64351	40A
64352	36B
64353	40D
64354	38B
64355	40B
64356	36B
64357	39A
64358	40E
64359	40A
64360	39B
64361	38B
64362	36D
64363	39A
64364	38E
64365	40A
64366	36D
64367	9G
64368	39A
64369	38E
64370	38B
64371	40A
64372	40B
64373	39B
64374	36B
64375	38E
64376	8E
64377	36B
64378	40E
64379	40E
64380	36E
64381	6E
64382	39A
64383	39A
64384	38D
64385	36E
64386	38D
64387	39B
64388	38E
64389	40E
64390	38E
64391	36D
64392	40D
64393	36E
64394	34E
64395	36C
64396	38D
64397	27E
64398	36D
64399	36D
64400	36B
64401	39A
64402	36E
64403	36B
64404	36B
64405	8E
64406	8E
64407	36C
64408	38E
64409	39A
64410	36A
64411	40B
64412	39B
64413	36E
64414	40E
64415	39A
64416	36E
64417	8E
64418	40E
64419	39B
64420	8E
64421	36E
64422	36E
64423	36E
64424	40D
64425	36D
64426	40E
64427	40E
64428	38D
64429	36C
64430	40A
64431	38B
64432	36B
64433	38D
64434	39A
64435	39A
64436	36D
64437	39A
64438	38E
64439	40B
64440	39A
64441	39B
64442	36B
64443	39B
64444	38D
64445	39B
64446	40B
64447	39B
64448	36D
64449	36B
64450	39A
64451	36E
64452	36D
64453	9G

J35
0–6–0

64460	65E
64461	63B
64462	64A
64463	64G
64464	62A
64466	62A
64468	64F
64470	65E
64471	63B
64472	65E
64473	65E
64474	62A
64475	62C
64476	62C
64477	62A
64478	12B
64479	64A
64480	62C
64482	62B
64483	62C
64484	64E
64485	62B
64486	64A
64487	62C
64488	62A
64489	64A
64490	64E
64491	64F
64492	64A
64493	62C
64494	64G
64495	62A
64496	62C
64497	63B
64498	65E
64499	12B
64500	62A
64501	63B
64502	64E

64504 64F
64505 62C
64506 64A
64507 65E
64509 64G
64510 64F
64511 12B
64512 64A
64513 62C
64514 62A
64515 64A
64516 62A
64517 64A
64518 64A
64519 64A
64520 63B
64521 62A
64522 62A
64523 64A
64524 64A
64525 62C
64526 12B
64527 64A
64528 64E
64529 64F
64530 62B
64531 65E
64532 64A
64533 64A
64534 65E
64535 64A

J37
0–6–0

64536 64C
64537 64E
64538 64A
64539 64G
64540 65A
64541 65A
64542 63B
64543 64A
64544 63B
64545 62C
64546 62A
64547 64A
64548 65C
64549 62A
64550 62A
64551 64E
64552 64A
64553 64E
64554 62C
64555 64A
64556 62C
64557 64A
64558 65A
64559 65C
64560 62C
64561 62C
64562 64A
64563 65C
64564 62A
64565 62A
64566 64A
64567 62C
64568 62C
64569 63B
64570 64E
64571 64E
64572 64A
64573 65C
64574 62C
64575 62B
64576 64A
64577 64A
64578 65A
64579 65A
64580 65A
64581 65A
64582 64A
64583 65A
64584 65C
64585 63B
64586 64A
64587 62B
64588 64E
64589 64E
64590 62C
64591 64C
64592 64E
64593 64E
64594 64A
64595 64A
64596 62A
64597 62A
64598 62B
64599 64A
64600 62A
64601 65A
64602 62A
64603 64A
64604 62C
64605 64A
64606 64A
64607 64A
64608 64A
64609 65C
64610 65C
64611 65A
64612 62A
64613 64E
64614 64A
64615 62B
64616 62A
64617 62C
64618 62A
64619 62B
64620 62B
64621 65C
64622 65A
64623 65A
64624 64A
64625 64A
64626 65C
64627 62B
64628 65A
64629 62A
64630 62C
64631 62B
64632 65A
64633 65A
64634 62B
64635 62A
64636 64A
64637 64A
64638 65A
64639 65A

J19
0–6–0

64640 31C
64641 31B
64642 31C
64643 31B
64644 32A
64645 31D
64646 31D
64647 31B
64648 31B
64649 31D
64650 30A
64651 30A
64652 30A
64653 31D
64654 31C
64655 31B
64656 31B
64657 30A
64658 31D
64659 31B
64660 30A
64661 31B
64662 30A
64663 30A
64664 30A
64665 30A
64666 31B
64667 31B
64668 31C
64669 31B
64670 30A
64671 31B
64672 31C
64673 31D
64674 32A

J20
0–6–0

64675 30A
64676 30A
64677 30A
64678 31A
64679 31A
64680 30A
64681 30A
64682 30A
64683 31A
64684 31A
64685 30A
64686 30A
64687 31A
64688 31B
64689 31B
64690 30A
64691 30A
64692 31B
64693 31B
64694 31B
64695 30A
64696 30A
64697 31B
64698 31B
64699 31B

J39
0–6–0

64700 52C
64701 52A
64702 40A
64703 52C
64704 52A
64705 52C
64706 50D
64707 52A
64708 30A
64709 52B
64710 51A
64711 52D
64712 39A
64713 36A
64714 39A
64715 40A
64716 38A
64717 39A
64718 39A
64719 38A
64720 38A
64721 36A
64722 40A
64723 9E
64724 32A
64725 40A
64726 32A
64727 9F
64728 40A
64729 38A
64730 40A
64731 32A
64732 14A
64733 9F
64734 40A

64735	38A
64736	40A
64737	36A
64738	40A
64739	38A
64740	39A
64741	39A
64742	39A
64743	39A
64744	39A
64745	39A
64746	39B
64747	38A
64748	39A
64749	37A
64750	38A
64751	37A
64752	32B
64753	39B
64754	37A
64755	39A
64756	51F
64757	38A
64758	36A
64759	36E
64760	37A
64761	32A
64762	38A
64763	38A
64764	30A
64765	30A
64766	30A
64767	30A
64768	30A
64769	30A
64770	30F
64771	30A
64772	30A
64773	30A
64774	30A
64775	30A
64776	30A
64777	30F
64778	51F
64779	30F
64780	30A
64781	30A
64782	30A
64783	30A
64784	32A
64785	32B
64786	62B
64787	30F
64788	30F
64789	40A
64790	62B
64791	50B
64792	62B
64793	32B
64794	64A
64795	61B
64796	37A
64797	32A
64798	38E
64799	37A
64800	32B
64801	37A
64802	32A
64803	32B
64804	40A
64805	38A
64806	37A
64807	38A
64808	39B
64809	39B
64810	39A
64811	37A
64812	52C
64813	52D
64814	52C
64815	52DA
64816	52C
64817	52B
64818	50D
64819	50B
64820	32B
64821	51D
64822	62B
64823	9E
64824	39A
64825	37A
64826	32B
64827	38A
64828	38A
64829	32B
64830	36E
64831	38A
64832	38A
64833	32A
64834	32B
64835	36A
64836	37A
64837	38A
64838	38E
64839	37A
64840	37A
64841	32B
64842	52C
64643	52D
64844	52D
64845	50D
64846	54C
64847	51D
64848	51F
64849	52C
64850	50B
64851	52C (A)
64852	52C
64853	52A
64854	52D
64855	50D
64856	52B
64857	50D
64858	52C
64859	50D
64860	50D
64861	50D
64862	51C
64863	50B
64864	53A
64865	52B
64866	50D
64867	53A
64868	52D (A)
64869	52A
64870	53A
64871	52A
64872	37A
64873	30F
64874	30A
64875	12B
64876	30A
64877	12B
64878	39B
64879	39A
64880	12B
64881	40A
64882	32A
64883	40A
64884	12B
64885	36A
64886	40A
64887	40A
64888	12B
64889	32A
64890	39B
64891	36A
64892	62B
64893	36A
64894	32B
64895	12B
64896	37A
64897	53A
64898	36E
64899	12B
64900	32B
64901	9E
64902	36A
64903	39B
64904	40A
64905	32B
64906	36E
64907	37A
64908	36E
64909	36A
64910	36A
64911	37A
64912	12B
64913	32A
64914	53A
64915	52B
64916	51C
64917	52D
64918	14A
64919	50E
64920	50B
64921	50B
64922	50D
64923	52B
64924	52D (A)
64925	52D
64926	53A
64927	53A
64928	53A
64929	54C
64930	12B
64931	53A
64932	12B
64933	51A
64934	50B
64935	50E
64936	54C
64937	40A
64938	50D
64939	53A
64940	52C
64941	53A
64942	50D
64943	50B
64944	50D
64945	52B
64946	64A
64947	52B
64948	12B
64949	50B
64950	62B
64951	36A
64952	36A
64953	30F
64954	9E
64955	38A
64956	36E
64957	32B
64958	32B
64959	32A
64960	39B
64961	36E
64962	39A
64963	64A
64964	12B
64965	38A
64966	14A
64967	36A
64968	32A
64969	39B
64970	36E
64971	40A
64972	39A
64973	39B
64974	38A
64975	61B
64976	36A
64977	36A
64978	51C
64979	37A
64980	38A
64981	38A
64982	52D

64983 38A
64984 36A
64985 37A
64986 64A
64987 36E
64988 38A

J1
0–6–0

65002 35A
65003 34D
65004 35A
65005 35A
65006 35A
65007 38A
65008 38A
65009 38A
65010 34D
65013 34D
65014 38A

J2
0–6–0

65015 38C
65016 40F
65017 40F
65018 38A
65019 38A
65020 40F
65021 38C
65022 38A
65023 38A

J21
0–6–0

65025 52C
65028 51H
65030 51J
65033 51A
65035 52F (R)
65038 51A
65039 50C
65040 51H
65041 50B
65042 50C
65043 50A
65047 51H
65057 51F
65061 51F
65062 50B
65064 51F (W)
65067 50B
65068 51A
65070 36E
65075 50A
65076 50B
65077 51F
65078 51F
65080 52F (SB)
65082 52C
65088 51F
65089 51H
65090 51A
65091 51F
65092 51F
65095 36A
65097 51F
65098 51A
65099 52C
65100 51H
65102 51F
65103 51H
65105 50C
65110 51A
65111 52C (R)
65117 36A
65118 50B
65119 51A
65122 50B

J10
0–6–0

65126 8E
65128 10F
65130 27E
65131 9G
65132 9F
65133 27E
65134 9G
65135 9F
65136 8E
65137 9E
65138 9G
65139 9G
65140 9G
65141 9E
65142 8E
65143 6D
65144 9F
65145 9F
65146 9F
65147 9G
65148 9F
65149 8E
65151 9G
65153 8E
65154 9E
65155 8E
65156 9G
65157 9F
65158 9G
65159 10F
65160 9F
65161 9E
65162 10F
65163 8E
65164 10F
65165 9G
65166 9G
65167 6D
65168 9E
65169 9G
65170 10F
65171 9G
65172 8E
65173 10F
65175 10F
65176 10F
65177 27E
65178 9F
65179 9E
65180 27E
65181 9F
65182 8E
65183 9E
65184 9E
65185 9F
65186 9E
65187 9G
65188 9F
65189 10F
65190 9G
65191 9G
65192 27E
65193 9F
65194 9F
65196 10F
65197 9F
65198 9F
65199 10F
65200 9F
65201 9E
65202 9G
65203 10F
65204 9E
65205 9G
65208 9G
65209 9F

J36
0–6–0

65210 65E
65211 64F
65213 61B
65214 65E
65216* 12B
65217* 65E
65218 62A
65221 65A
65222* 64E
65224* 64A
65225 64F
65226* 65E
65227 65I
65228 65A
65229 64F
65230 64F
65231 64F
65232 64G
65233* 64E
65234 64F
65235* 64F
65236* 65E
65237 63D
65238 65E
65239 62C
65240 64B
65241 64E
65242 64G
65243* 64B
65244 64E
65245 65E
65246 64E
65247 61A
65248 64F
65249 65E
65250 64F
65251 64A
65252 62C
65253* 62C
65254 64F
65255 65E
65257 64E
65258 64A
65259 64G
65260 65E
65261 64F
65264 65E
65265 64F
65266 65E
65267 64A
65268* 64E
65270 65A
65271 64C
65273 65A
65274 65C
65275 64E
65276 64F
65277 64F
65278 64F
65279 64G
65280 64F
65281 62C
65282 64F
65283 65C
65285 65E
65286 64A
65287 65E
65288 64A
65290 64E
65291 62A
65292 64A
65293 12B
65295 52C (H)
65296 65A
65297 61B
65298 65C
65300 63D

65303 64F
65304 12B
65305 64A
65306 64E
65307 62C
65308 65A
65309 62B
65310 64A
65311 64A
65312 12B
65313 63D
65314 64F
65315 65I
65316 64A
65317 64G
65318 64F
65319 62B
65320 62C
65321 12B
65322 62C
65323 62C
65324 65C
65325 65E
65327 64F
65329 64D
65330 62B
65331 52C (R)
65333 62B
65334 64A
65335 65C
65338 64E
65339 65I
65340 64G
65341 64F
65342 64F
65343 52C
65344 64F
65345 62A
65346 64F

J15
0-6-0

65350 31A
65354 30F
65355 32C
65356 31A
65359 31C
65361 30A
65362 31E
65366 31B
65369 30E
65370 30A
65373 32A
65374 32C
65377 32B
65378 31C
65382 32B
65384 30A
65388 30A
65389 32C
65390 32A
65391 31A
65396 32B
65398 32A
65401 32C
65402 30E
65404 32A
65405 31A
65406 31A
65407 32B
65408 32B
65413 31A
65417 32A
65420 31E
65422 32A
65423 32B
65424 30E
65425 31A
65426 32A
65427 30E
65429 32B
65430 32B
65431 30E
65432 30E
65433 32C
65434 30F
65435 32C
65437 31C
65438 31A
65439 31B
65440 30A
65441 30E
65442 31E
65443 30E
65444 30E
65445 30E
65446 30E
65447 32B
65448 30E
65449 30A
65450 30A
65451 31A
65452 30A
65453 30A
65454 30E
65455 30A
65456 30E
65457 31A
65458 30F
65459 32B
65460 32A
65461 31A
65462 32C
65463 30A
65464 30A
65465 30E
65466 30A
65467 32B
65468 30E
65469 32A
65470 32B
65471 32A
65472 32A
65473 30E
65474 31A
65475 31A
65476 30A
65477 31A
65478 32C
65479 32A

J5
0-6-0

65480 38A
65481 38A
65482 38A
65483 38A
65484 38A
65485 38A
65486 38A
65487 38A
65488 38A
65489 38A
65490 38A
65491 38A
65492 38A
65493 38A
65494 38B
65495 38C
65496 38A
65497 38A
65498 38A
65499 38A

J17
0-6-0

65500 30A
65501 31A
65502 31A
65503 31A
65504 31D
65505 31B
65506 31A
65507 32A
65508 30A
65509 32G
65510 32B
65511 30A
65512 32A
65513 32A
65514 32A
65515 31B
65516 32G
65517 31A
65518 31B
65519 31C
65520 31A
65521 31B
65522 30E
65523 30A
65524 32A
65525 31A
65526 31D
65527 31C
65528 30A
65529 31A
65530 31C
65531 30E
65532 31A
65533 31D
65534 32A
65535 31A
65536 30A
65537 31A
65538 31A
65539 30E
65540 30A
65541 30A
65542 31C
65543 30A
65544 31C
65545 31D
65546 31A
65547 31A
65548 31C
65549 31C
65551 32G
65552 32G
65553 32A
65554 31B
65555 31B
65556 31B
65557 32G
65558 32F
65559 32F
65560 32B
65561 31A
65562 31D
65563 31A
65564 30E
65565 31A
65566 32C
65567 32G
65568 32A
65569 32A
65570 32A
65571 31B
65572 31C
65573 31A
65574 32A
65575 31A
65576 31B
65577 31B
65578 32A
65579 31D
65580 31D
65581 32F
65582 31D
65583 31B
65584 31B
65585 31A
65586 32G

65587 31A
65588 31D
65589 31A

J24
0-6-0

65600 50F
65601 51B
65604 51B
65611 54C
65614 62B
65615 54C
65617 64A
65619 50A
65621 50G
65622 62B
65623 64A
65624 50G
65627 50G
65628 50G
65631 50F
65636 50F
65640 50F
65642 50F
65644 50F

J25
0-6-0

65645 51J
65647 53A
65648 51A
65650 51A
65651 53A
65653 51H
65654 53A
65655 51H
65656 50A
65657 54C
65659 51F
65660 51G
65661 54C
65662 51F
65663 53A
65664 51A
65666 54B
65667 53C
65670 54B
65671 51F
65672 51A
65673 51H
65675 51F
65676 54C
65677 51A
65679 50A
65680 54C
65683 51F
65685 54C
65686 54C
65687 51D
65688 51A
65689 51E
65690 53A
65691 51A
65692 51A
65693 51J
65694 54B
65695 51H
65696 51A
65697 52D
65698 53A
65699 53A
65700 50A
65702 51A
65705 53C
65706 51F
65708 50A
65710 51D
65712 53A
65713 53A
65714 53E
65716 54B
65717 51H
65718 51E
65720 51A
65723 50A
65725 51J
65726 51D
65727 52D
65728 53C

J26
0-6-0

65730 51B
65731 51B
65732 51B
65733 51D
65734 51B
65735 51B
65736 51B
65737 51B
65738 51B
65739 51B
65740 51B
65741 51B
65742 51B
65743 51B
65744 51B
65745 51B
65746 51B
65747 51C
65748 51C
65749 51B
65750 51B
65751 51B
65752 51B
65753 51B
65754 51B
65755 51B
65756 51B
65757 51B
65758 51B
65759 51B
65760 51B
65761 51B
65762 51B
65763 51B
65764 51D
65765 51B
65766 51B
65767 51B
65768 51B
65769 51B
65770 51B
65771 51D
65772 51B
65773 51B
65774 51B
65775 51D
65776 51D
65777 51B
65778 51B
65779 51D

J27
0-6-0

65780 52E
65781 52F (SB)
65782 51C
65783 52F
65784 52E
65785 54A
65786 52F
65787 51G
65788 52B
65789 52F
65790 51C
65791 52E
65792 52E
65793 50C
65794 52E
65795 52E
65796 52E
65797 52F
65798 54A
65799 52F
65800 52B
65801 52F
65802 52E
65803 51C
65804 52F
65805 51G
65806 52E
65807 52B
65808 52F (SB)
65809 52E
65810 52F (SB)
65811 52F
65812 52E
65813 52E
65814 52E
65815 52E
65816 51C
65817 54A
65818 51C
65819 52F
65820 51C
65821 52E
65822 52E
65823 54A
65824 52F (SB)
65825 52E
65826 52E
65827 50C
65828 52F
65829 52F (SB)
65830 51G
65831 52E
65832 54A
65833 54A
65834 52F (SB)
65835 54A
65836 54A
65837 52E
65838 52E
65839 52E
65840 54A
65841 54A
65842 52B
65843 54A
65844 50C
65845 50A
65846 51C
65847 54A
65848 50C
65849 50A
65850 54A
65851 52F
65852 52E
65853 51G
65854 54A
65855 51G
65856 54A
65857 51K
65858 52E
65859 51G
65860 51E
65861 50A
65862 52B
65863 52B
65864 52B
65865 51G
65866 51C
65867 52F
65868 51E
65869 52B
65870 52F
65871 54A
65872 54A
65873 52B

65874	50C
65875	50C
65876	52F
65877	52F
65878	54A
65879	52F
65880	52F
65881	50C
65882	50C
65883	50A
65884	54A
65885	50A
65886	52B
65887	51E
65888	50A
65889	52B
65890	50A
65891	50C
65892	52F
65893	52B
65894	50A

J38
0–6–0

65900	62C
65901	62A
65902	62A
65903	62A
65904	62A
65905	62C
65906	64A
65907	62A
65908	62A
65909	64E
65910	62A
65911	62A
65912	64A
65913	62A
65914	64A
65915	64A
65916	62C
65917	64E
65918	64A
65919	64A
65920	64A
65921	62A
65922	62C
65923	62C
65924	62C
65925	62A
65926	62C
65927	64A
65928	62C
65929	64A
65930	62C
65931	62A
65932	62A
65933	62C
65934	62C

F2
2–4–2T

67111	34A

F3
2–4–2T

67127	32C
67128	32B
67139	32A

F4
2–4–2T

67151	61A
67152	32G
67153	31B
67154	32D
67155	50F
67156	32C
67157	61A
67158	32C
67162	32G
67163	32C
67164	61A
67165	32C
67166	32C
67167	32C
67171	53A
67174	32C
67175	53A
67176	32A
67177	32C
67178	32A
67182	32C
67184	32C
67186	32C
67187	31B

F5
2–4–2T

67188	30E
67189	30E
67190	30E
67191	30E
67192	30A
67193	30A
67194	30E
67195	30E
67196	30E
67197	30A
67198	30A
67199	32D
67200	30A
67201	32C
67202	30A
67203	30A
67204	30E
67205	30A
67206	30A
67207	30A
67208	30A
67209	30A
67210	30A
67211	30A
67212	30A
67213	30A
67214	30A
67215	30E
67216	32C
67217	30E
67218	32D
67219	30E

F6
2–4–2T

67220	32B
67221	31C
67222	31A
67223	32F
67224	32G
67225	32G
67226	32F
67227	31C
67228	32G
67229	32A
67230	32B
67231	32C
67232	32A
67233	32F
67234	32F
67235	32F
67236	31E
67237	31E
67238	31E
67239	32B

G5
0–4–4T

67240	50B
67241	52C
67242	51E
67243	54A
67244	52F (SB)
67245	52C (H)
67246	52F (SB)
67247	54A
67248	52D
67249	52C (H)
67250	50C
67251	54A
67252	54A
67253	50D (P)
67254	53B
67255	52C
67256	53B
67257	54A
67258	54A (D)
67259	52C
67260	54A
67261	52F (SB)
67262	50B
67263	54A (D)
67264	54A
67265	52C (H)
67266	50B
67267	54A
67268	52C (H)
67269	30A
67270	54A
67271	51C
67272	51A
67273	50F
67274	50B
67275	50F
67276	54A
67277	52C
67278	51E
67279	30A
67280	53B
67281	51D (G)
67282	53B
67283	54A
67284	50D
67286	50C
67287	61A
67288	54B
67289	50D
67290	50B
67291	51C
67292	61C
67293	50B
67294	51F
67295	52F (SB)
67296	52F (R)
67297	54A
67298	54A (D)
67300	54A
67301	53B
67302	50G
67303	52D
67304	52D
67305	51E
67307	54A (D)
67308	50B
67309	52A
67310	54A
67311	53B
67312	51F
67313	52C (H)
67314	51C
67315	52C (A)
67316	51C
67317	51E
67318	51E
67319	50B
67320	52A

67321	53B
67322	30A
67323	52C
67324	51J
67325	52A
67326	52F (SB)
67327	61A
67328	54A
67329	52A
67330	50F
67331	51C
67332	50F
67333	51A
67334	52F (SB)
67335	50G
67336	54A
67337	50B (I)
67338	51D
67339	52C
67340	53B
67341	52F (SB)
67342	51A
67343	51C
67344	51J
67345	51F
67346	51J (L)
67347	52F (SB)
67348	54A
67349	50F

C12
4-4-2T

67350	40F
67352	40C
67353	37B
67354	53B
67356	34A
67357	35A
67360	31A
67361	35A
67362	35C
67363	38B
67364	40C
67365	35A
67366	9E
67367	31A
67368	35A
67369	9E
67371	53B
67372	37B
67373	35A
67374	34A
67375	31A
67376	34B
67379	40C
67380	35B
67381	40C
67382	35B
67383	40C
67384	40C
67385	31A
67386	37A
67387	38B
67389	40A
67390	35A
67391	53B
67392	53B
67393	53B
67394	53B
67395	53B
67397	53B
67398	40C

C13
4-4-2T

67400	6D
67401	39A
67402	39A
67403	39A
67404	39B
67405	39A
67406	39B
67407	39A
67408	39A
67409	36D
67410	39A
67411	36D
67412	39A
67413	6D
67414	6D
67415	39A
67416	39A
67417	39A
67418	34E
67419	39A
67420	34E
67421	39A
67422	39A
67423	39A
67424	39A
67425	39A
67426	39A
67427	39A
67428	6E
67429	6E
67430	6E
67431	39A
67432	6E
67433	6D
67434	36D
67435	6E
67436	6D
67437	39A
67438	39A
67439	39A

C14
4-4-2T

67440	37A
67441	37A
67442	6E
67443	37A
67444	37A
67445	37A
67446	37A
67447	37C
67448	37C
67449	6E
67450	37C
67451	37A

C15
4-4-2T

67452	62A
67453	62C
67454	65C
67455	61B
67456	65A
67457	64G
67458	12B
67459	64G
67460	65A
67461	62B
67462	63B
67463	64E
67464	64E
67465	64G
67466	62C
67467	65A
67468	64E
67469	62C
67470	65C
67471	62B
67472	64G
67473	64E
67474	12B
67475	65E
67476	62A
67477	64G
67478	61B
67479	65C
67480	65C
67481	12B

C16
4-4-2T

67482	65A
67483	62B
67484	62B
67485	65A
67486	62B
67487	65C
67488	65A
67489	62B
67490	62B
67491	62B
67492	64A
67493	62B
67494	64A
67495	64A
67496	64A
67497	64A
67498	62B
67499	62B
67500	65A
67501	65A
67502	62B

V1 & V3
2-6-2T

67600	65A
67601	65I
67602	65A
67603	65A
67604	65C
67605	64A
67606	64A
67607	64A
67608	64A
67609	64A
67610	64B
67611	65C
67612	65C
67613	65H
67614	65H
67615	64B
67616	65H
67617	64A
67618	65A
67619	65C
67620	64B
67621	65C
67622	65C
67623	65C
67624	64A
67625	65H
67626	65C
67627	65E
67628	65C
67629	64A
67630	64A
67631	65H
67632	65H
67633	65C
67634	52A
67635	52B
67636	52C
67637	52B
67638	51D
67639	51D
67640	52B
67641	52B
67642	52B
67643	65C
67644	65A
67645	52B
67646	52B
67647	51D
67648	65C

67649	64A
67650	63B
67651	52B
67652	52B
67653	52C
67654	52B
67655	65C
67656	52C
67657	52C
67658	52C
67659	64A
67660	65E
67661	65C
67662	65C
67663	32A
67664	32A
67665	65E
67666	64A
67667	61A
67668	64A
67669	62C
67670	64A
67671	61A
67672	62C
67673	51D
67674	65E
67675	63B
67676	65C
67677	32A
67678	65C
67679	32A
67680	65A
67681	65C
67682	51E
67683	52A
67684	51D
67685	51D
67686	51D
67687	52A
67688	52A
67689	52A
67690	52A
67691	51D

L1
2-6-4T

67701	30A
67702	32B
67703	32B
67704	32B
67705	32B
67706	32B
67707	34E
67708	32B
67709	32B
67710	32B
67711	32B
67712	30A
67713	30A
67714	34E
67715	34E
67716	32B
67717	34E
67718	34E
67719	32B
67720	34E
67721	30A
67722	30A
67723	30A
67724	30A
67725	30A
67726	30A
67727	30A
67728	30A
67729	30A
67730	30A
67731	30A
67732	30A
67733	30A
67734	30A
67735	30A
67736	30A
67737	30A
67738	30A
67739	30A
67740	34D
67741	34D
67742	51A
67743	34D
67744	34D
67745	34D
67746	34D
67747	34E
67748	34E
67749	34E
67750	51A
67751	34E
67752	34E
67753	34E
67754	51A
67755	51D
67756	34E
67757	34E
67758	34E
67759	51D
67760	34E
67761	34E
67762	34E
67763	51D
67764	51D
67765	51D
67766	51D
67767	34E
67768	34E
67769	34E
67770	34E
67771	34E
67772	34E
67773	34E
67774	34E
67775	34E
67776	34E
67777	51A
67778	34E
67779	34E
67780	34E
67781	34E
67782	34E
67783	34E
67784	34E
67785	34E
67786	34E
67787	32B
67788	32A
67789	32A
67790	34D
67791	34D
67792	34A
67793	34A
67794	32A
67795	32A
67796	34A
67797	34A
67798	32A
67799	
67800	

J94
0-6-0ST

68006	6F
68007	51B
68008	51A
68009	40B
68010	52C
68011	51B
68012	39A
68013	40B
68014	52B
68015	51A
68016	54A
68017	50A
68018	40B
68019	52C
68020	40B
68021	52C
68022	40B
68023	51B
68024	52C
68025	51A
68026	40B
68027	51A
68028	40B
68029	52C
68030	40B
68031	50A
68032	50A
68033	40B
68034	40B
68035	52C
68036	52C
68037	51B
68038	52C
68039	51A
68040	50A
68041	52C
68042	51C
68043	51A
68044	50A
68045	51A
68046	50A
68047	51A
68048	52C
68049	51B
68050	51A
68051	51A
68052	51A
68053	51C
68054	51C
68055	51C
68056	51C
68057	51C
68058	52C
68059	52C (H)
68060	51B
68061	50A
68062	51B
68063	6E
68064	9E
68065	6F
68066	6F
68067	39A
68068	40B
68069	40B
68070	40B
68071	39A
68072	40B
68073	40B
68074	40B
68075	40B
68076	40B
68077	40B
68078	40B
68079	39A
68080	40B

Y6
0-4-0T

68082	31C
68083	31C

Y7
0-4-0T

68088S	30A
68089	52D

Y8
0-4-0T

68091	50A

Y9
0–4–0ST

68092 64A
68093 64A
68094 65E
68095 64A
68096 64A
68097 64A
68098 64A
68099 64A
68100 62B
68101 62C
68102 64A
68103 65A
68104 64E
68105 64A
68106 65E
68107 62B
68108 60A
68109 65A
68110 62B
68111 64A
68112 65G
68113 64E
68114 62B
68115 64A
68116 65E
68117 65E
68118 65A
68119 64A
68120 65E
68121 65E
68122 64A
68123 62B
68124 65A

Y4
0–4–0T

68125 30A
68126 30A
68127 30A
68128 30A
68129S 30A

Y1
0–4–0T

68130S 32C
68131S 32C
68132S 36A†
68133S 35A
68136S 51A‡
68137 53A
68138 64G
68139 53A
68140 53A
68141 52A
68142 51F
68143 50C
68144 51E
68145 51F
68146 52A
68147 50F
68148 53D
68149 51F
68150 50F
68151 53B
68152S 50A
68153S 51A§

Y3
0–4–0T

68154 52A
68155 53D
68156 50C
68157 50F (P)
68158 50C
68159 51J
68160 52A
68161 50C
68162 40B
68163 6E
68164 6E
68165S 36A
68166S 40F
68168S 32C
68169 39A
68171 40F
68172 34E
68173S 32C
68174 30A
68175 34D
68176 39B
68177S 32C
68178S 32C
68179 40B
68180 52A
68181 54B
68182 51F
68183 54B
68184 39B
68185 35A

Y10
0–4–0T

68186 32D

Z4
0–4–2T

68190 61A
68191 61A

Z5
0–4–2T

68192 61A
68193 61A

J62
0–6–0ST

68200 6E

J63
0–6–0T

68204 40B
68205 40B
68206 40B
68207 40B
68208 40B
68209 40B
68210 40B

J65
0–6–0T

68211 32B
68214 32F

J70
0–6–0T

68216 32B
68217 31C
68219 32D
68220 31C
68221 32B
68222 31C
68223 31C
68224 32B
68225 31C
68226 30E

J71
0–6–0T

68230 50A
68231 51A
68232 53A
68233 51C
68234 52B
68235 51A
68236 51A
68238 50A (N)
68239 51A
68240 50A
68242 53A
68244 51C
68245 52B
68246 50A
68247 52B
68248 51C
68249 51F
68250 50A
68251 52A
68252 53A
68253 50A
68254 51F
68255 51F
68256 52B
68258 51C
68259 51A
68260 51D
68262 52B
68263 51C
68264 52B
68265 52C
68266 54B
68267 52B
68268 50C
68269 51F
68270 52A
68271 52B
68272 54B
68273 52B
68275 50A
68276 51C
68277 53A
68278 52B
68279 51A
68280 50A
68281 51A
68282 50A
68283 52A
68284 52D
68286 50A
68287 54C
68288 53A
68289 54C
68290 51C
68291 51C
68292 50A (N)
68293 50A
68294 50A (N)
68295 51C
68296 53A
68297 50A

† Operates at Ranskill Wagon Works
‡ Operates at Faverdale Wagon Works
§ Geneva P.W. depot

68298 53A
68299 54C
68300 51A
68301 51C
68302 51C
68303 51D
68304 53A
68305 51E
68306 51C
68307 51D
68308 51A
68309 52A
68310 50A
68311 53A
68312 51D
68313 50A
68314 52A
68316 53A

J55
0-6-0T

68319S 36A

J88
0-6-0T

68320 64A
68321 62A
68322 62A
68323 62A
68324 64E
68325 64A
68326 65A
68327 65A
68328 64B
68329 65E
68330 65A
68331 65E
68332 62A
68333 65A
68334 64A
68335 62A
68336 65A
68337 62A
68338 64A
68339 64B
68340 64A
68341 62A
68342 64A
68343 65E
68344 65E
68345 62C
68346 62C
68347 65A
68348 64A
68349 65A
68350 64E
68351 62C
68352 64A
68353 62A
68354 64E

J73
0-6-0T

68355 51C
68356 50C
68357 50C
68358 51C
68359 51C
68360 53C (AD)
68361 53C (AD)
68362 50C
68363 53C (AD)
68364 51C

J66
0-6-0T

68370S 30A
68371 38D
68372 31A
68373 32B
68374 32B
68375 32B
68376 40A
68377 32G
68378 31D
68379 38D
68380 30A
68381 32A
68382 38D
68383 31A
68385 40A
68387 35A
68388 32A

J77
0-6-0T

68391 51F
68392 50D
68393 50D
68395 50B
68397 52F
68398 52F
68399 50C
68401 53B
68402 53C (AD)
68404 50D
68405 52F
68406 50B
68407 51E
68408 51A
68409 51D
68410 51A
68412 51E
68413 53C (AD)
68414 51D
68417 52F
68420 51E
68421 52D
68422 51D
68423 51A
68424 52F (SB)
68425 51D
68426 52F
68427 52F
68428 52F (SB)
68429 53C (AD)
68430 52B
68431 52F (SB)
68432 51A
68433 50C
68434 50D
68435 53C (AD)
68436 50A
68437 52D
68438 50D
68440 53C (AD)

J83
0-6-0T

68442 65E
68443 65E
68444 65E
68445 65E
68446 62B
68447 65A
68448 64A
68449 64A
68450 64A
68451 62A
68452 62B
68453 62A
68454 64A
68455 62B
68456 62A
68457 64B
68458 62A
68459 62A
68460 64B
68461 65E
68463 64A
68464 64A
68465 62C
68466 62B
68467 62A
68468 65A
68469 64A
68470 62B
68471 64E
68472 64A
68473 64B
68474 64A
68475 65A
68476 65A
68477 64A
68478 64B
68479 65A
68480 65A
68481 64B

J67 & J69
0-6-0T

68490 31C
68491 30A
68492 64A
68493 31C
68494 31C
68495 32A
68496 30A
68497 31E
68498 32B
68499 12B
68500 30A
68501 32A
68502 31C
68503 65C
68504 62A
68505 64A
68507 30A
68508 30A
68509 31A
68510 30A
68511 64A
68512 34D
68513 30A
68514 31C
68515 31C
68516 31A
68517 30A
68518 32B
68519 30A
68520 30A
68521 30A
68522 30E
68523 30A
68524 64E
68525 64A
68526 30A
68527 30A
68528 40F
68529 40A
68530 31A
68531 6E
68532 30A
68533 64E
68534 30A
68535 62A
68536 32G
68537 40A
68538 30A
68540 9E
68541 34D
68542 31D
68543 40F
68544 64E

68545 31C
68546 30A
68547 8D
68548 30A
68549 30A
68550 62A
68551 65A
68552 65A
68553 40A
68554 30A
68555 62A
68556 30F
68557 30F
68558 40A
68559 8E
68560 40F
68561 30F
68562 64A
68563 30A
68565 34C
68566 31D
68567 65C
68568 61B
68569 30A
68570 32A
68571 30A
68572 34C
68573 30A
68574 30A
68575 30A
68576 30A
68577 30A
68578 30E
69579 31A
68581 40F
68583 9E
68584 27E
68585 27E
68586 32A
68587 40A
68588 30A
68589 30A
68590 30A
68591 30A
68592 30A
68593 32B
68594 30A
68595 9E
68596 30F
68597 31D
68598 9E
68599 40A
68600 31D
68601 30A
68602 32A
68603 32A
68605 34D
68606 30A
68607 30A
68608 30A
68609 31A
68610 40A
68611 32C
68612 30A
68613 30A
68616 30E
68617 30A
68618 40A
68619 30A
68621 30A
68623 64A
68625 32D
68626 30A
68628 32D
68629 30E
68630 30E
68631 30A
68632 35A
68633 30A
68635 62C
68636 30A

J68
0–6–0T

68638 30A
68639 30A
68640 32C
68641 32A
68642 30A
68643 30F
68644 30A
68645 31A
68646 30A
68647 30A
68648 30A
68649 30A
68650 30A
68651 32F
68652 30A
68653 30F
68654 31B
68655 40F
68656 31C
68657 40F
68658 40F
68659 40F
68660 30A
68661 30A
68662 30A
68663 30A
68664 31B
68665 30A
68666 30A

J92
0–6–0CT

68667S 30A
68668S 30A
68669S 30A

J72
0–6–0T

68670 53C (AD)
68671 6F
68672 50B
68673 53C (AD)
68674 52A
68675 52A
68676 53C (AD)
68677 50B
68678 54A
68679 51A
68680 52A
68681 50B
68682 52B
68683 51C
68684 51C
68685 51C
68686 53C (AD)
68687 52B
68688 51D
68689 51D
68690 51D
68691 51F
68692 51C
68693 52A
68694 51C
68695 50A
68696 51F
68697 51C
68698 54A
68699 50A
68700 61A
68701 6F
68702 52A
68703 51C
68704 54A
68705 54C
68706 54B
68707 51A
68708 54C
68709 65A
68710 61A
68711 51C
68712 51D
68713 51D
68714 6F
68715 50A
68716 51C
68717 61A
68718 54A
68719 61A
68720 52A
68721 51D
68722 50A
68723 52A
68724 53C (AD)
68725 52B
68726 50A
68727 6F
68728 54C
68729 54B
68730 54C
68731 54B
68732 52A
68733 65A
68734 51C
68735 50A
68736 54C
68737 54C
68738 52B
68739 50A
68740 51D
68741 50A
68742 52B
68743 53C (AD)
68744 52A
68745 50A
68746 53C (AD)
68747 53C (AD)
68748 53A
68749 61A
68750 61A
68751 53C (AD)
68752 53C (AD)
68753 53C (AD)
68754 51D

J52
0–6–0ST

68757 34B
68758 34B
68759 34B
68760 34B
68761 34B
68762 38A
68763 36A
68764 34A
68765 35A
68766 36E
68767 38A
68768 38A
68769 36A
68770 34A
68771 34A
68772 34A
68773 34B
68774 34B
68775 36A
68776 34B
68777 34B
68778 34B
68779 38A
68780 34A
68781 34B
68782S 36A
68783 34B
68784 34B
68785 34B
68786 36A
68787 34B

68788	34B
68789	35A
68790	37A
68791	34B
68792	38A
68793	34B
68794	34B
68795	34B
68796	34B
68797	34A
68798	35A
68799	34A
68800	36A
68801	35B
68802	34A
68803	34A
68804	36A
68805	34A
68806	36A
68807	38A
68808	34B
68809	34A
68810	38A
68811	34B
68812	38A
68813	36A
68814	38A
68815	34B
68817	35A
68818	34A
68819	35A
68820	35A
68821	35A
68822	34A
68823	35A
68824	35A
68825	34B
68826	34B
68827	34B
68828	34A
68829	34B
68830	34A
68831	34A
68832	34A
68833	34B
68834	34B
68835	36A
68836	36A
68837	36A
68838	34A
68839	38A
68840	35A
68841	36A
68842	36A
68843	36A
68844	35A
68846	35A
68847	36A
68848	37A
68849	36A
68850	35A
68851	34B
68852	35A
68853	34B
68854	34A
68855	34A
68856	34B
68857	36A
68858	36A
68859	38A
68860	36A
68861	34A
68862	34A
68863	38A
68864	34A
68865	36A
68866	35A
68867	36A
68868	35A
68869	36A
68870	36A
68871	37A
68872	37A
68873	34A
68874	34A
68875	38A
68876	35A
68877	35B
68878	34A
68879	35A
68880	35A
63881	34A
68882	38A
68883	34B
68884	34A
68885	36A
68886	36A
68887	38A
68888	34A
68889	34A

J50
0–6–0T

68890	36B
68891	38A
68892	37C
68893	36A
68894	38A
68895	37C
68896	37A
68897	37C
68898	37C
68899	32A
68900	37A
68901	37A
68902	37C
68903	37A
68904	37A
68905	32A
68906	37C
68907	37A
68908	37C
68909	37A
68910	37A
68911	37B
68912	37C
68913	37B
68914	37A
68915	37A
68916	37A
68917	36A
68918	36A
68919	37A
68920	38A
68921	37A
68922	37C
68923	37C
68924	32A
68925	37B
68926	36A
68927	38B
68928	39B
68929	38B
68930	37A
68931	37A
68932	37C
68933	37C
68934	37C
68935	38A
68936	36A
68937	37B
68938	37A
68939	37A
68940	37C
68941	37C
68942	37C
68943	37C
68944	37C
68945	36A
68946	36B
68947	37A
68948	37A
68949	37A
68950	30A
68951	37A
68952	64A
68953	65A
68954	65A
68955	65A
68956	65A
68957	65A
68958	65A
68959	37C
68960	36B
68961	36A
68962	36C
68963	30A
68964	36C
68965	30A
68966	37A
68967	30A
68968	36C
68969	37C
68970	36C
68971	36C
68972	38A
68973	36C
68974	36B
68975	38B
68976	38B
68977	30A
68978	37B
68979	36C
68980	36A
68981	38C
68982	38A
68983	39B
68984	37B
68985	36A
68986	36A
68987	36A
68988	37B
68989	36A
68990	39B
68991	36A

J72
0–6–0T

69001	53C (AD)
69002	53C (AD)
69003	53C (AD)
69004	51A
69005	52A
69006	51D
69007	51F
69008	54B
69009	53C (AD)
69010	53A
69011	53A
69012	32B
69013	32B
69014	36A
69015	39B
69016	50E
69017	54C
69018	54A
69019	51D
69020	50A

L3
2–6–4T

69050	38E
69051	36C
69052	9G
69055	34E
69056	34E
69060	34E
69061	34E
69062	9G
69064	35A
69065	34E
69067	34E
69069	38E

N10
0-6-2T

69090 52A
69091 52A
69092 52A
69093 53A
69094 53A
69095 52C
69096 53A
69097 52A (B)
69098 53A
69099 53A
69100 52A (B)
69101 51J
69102 53A
69104 53A
69105 53A
69106 53A
69107 53A
69108 53A
69109 52A

N13
0-6-2T

69111 53C (AD)
69112 53C
69113 53C
69114 50B
69115 50B
69116 53C
69117 50B
69118 50B
69119 53C

N14
0-6-2T

69120 65A
69124 65A
69125 61A

N15
0-6-2T

69126 65A
69127 65A
69128 61B
69129 61B
69130 64A
69131 65A
69132 62A
69133 64A
69134 64A
69135 62C
69136 62C
69137 64E
69138 65A
69139 12B
69140 64A
69141 64A
69142 64F
69143 65C
69144 64A
69145 65E
69146 64A
69147 64A
69148 64A
69149 64A
69150 62A
69151 65C
69152 64A
69153 62A
69154 62C
69155 12B
69156 64F
69157 65C
69158 64F
69159 64F
69160 62C
69161 65C
69162 64E
69163 65A
69164 62C
69165 65A
69166 65A
69167 64A
69168 64A
69169 64B
69170 65A
69171 65C
69172 64A
69173 64A
69174 12B
69175 64A
69176 65A
69177 65A
69178 65A
69179 65A
69180 65A
69181 65A
69182 65A
69183 65A
69184 65A
69185 12B
69186 64A
69187 64C
69188 65A
69189 65A
69190 65C
69191 65A
69192 62C
69193 65C
69194 65C
69195 65C
69196 65E
69197 12B
69198 65C
69199 65C
69200 64E
69201 61B
69202 62C
69203 65A
69204 62C
69205 65A
69206 65E
69207 65E
69208 65A
69209 65C
69210 65C
69211 62A
69212 65C
69213 65C
69214 65C
69215 12B
69216 64F
69217 65C
69218 12B
69219 64A
69220 64B
69221 62C
69222 65A
69223 62A
69224 62A

N4
0-6-2T

69225 39B
69227 39B
69228 39B
69229 39B
69230 39B
69231 39B
69232 39B
69233 39B
69234 39B
69235 39B
69236 39B
69239 39B
69240 39B
69242 39B
69244 39B
69245 39B
69246 39B

N5
0-6-2T

69250 39A
69252 9E
69253 40A
69254 8E
69255 9E
69256 40F
69257 34E
69258 8E
69259 34E
69260 39A
69261 40F
69262 9G
69263 38E
69264 36B
69265 27E
69266 37B
69267 6E
69268 36D
69269 38E
69270 39A
69271 37B
69272 8E
69273 36E
69274 6D
69275 40A
69276 9F
69277 36E
69278 36D
69279 38D
69280 40F
69281 6D
69282 36E
69283 34E
69284 40E
69285 36D
69286 38E
69287 40A
69288 8E
69289 6F
69290 6E
69291 36D
69292 38D
69293 9G
69294 36E
69295 38D
69296 39A
69297 36B
69298 27E
69299 39A
69300 34E
69301 38D
69302 34E
69303 36D
69304 9E
69305 40B
69306 40C
69307 39A
69308 39A
69309 40B
69310 38E
69311 40A
69312 38A
69313 36E
69314 36B
69315 34E
69316 36B
69317 9F
69318 34E
69319 40E
69320 36D
69321 36E
69322 40B
69323 40E

69324	38A
69325	36D
69326	9E
69327	40E
69328	9F
69329	6E
69330	6E
69331	9F
69332	9F
69333	39A
69334	36D
69335	9G
69336	9E
69337	35A
69338	39A
69339	8E
69340	6E
69341	34E
69342	8E
69343	9E
69344	27E
69345	36D
69346	6E
69347	39A
69348	36D
69349	6E
69350	34E
69351	38D
69352	6E
69353	39A
69354	36E
69355	36D
69356	27E
69357	36D
69358	34E
69359	9F
69360	38E
69361	9E
69362	6E
69363	38D
69364	9E
69365	36D
69366	6E
69367	36D
69368	36D
69369	34E
69370	9E
N8 0–6–2T	
69371	52B
69372	52B
69377	53A
69378	54B
69379	53A
69380	52B
69381	53A
69382	53A
69385	53A
69386	53A
69387	52B
69389	53A
69390	52B
69391	54C
69392	53A
69393	53A
69394	54D
69395	54D
69398	53A
69400	54B
69401	53A
N9 0–6–2T	
69410	54B
69413	54A
69418	54A
69423	54A
69424	54A
69425	54A
69426	51A
69427	54A
69429	54B
N1 0–6–2T	
69430	37B
69431	34B
69432	34B
69433	34B
69434	34B
69435	34B
69436	37B
69437	37B
69439	34B
69440	37B
69441	34B
69442	34B
69443	37C
69444	37B
69445	34B
69446	37B
69447	37C
69448	37C
69449	37C
69450	34B
69451	34B
69452	37A
69453	34B
69454	37C
69455	34B
69456	34B
69457	34B
69458	34B
69459	37C
69460	34B
69461	37A
69462	34B
69463	34B
69464	37C
69465	34B
69466	34B
69467	34B
69468	34B
69469	34B
69470	34B
69471	37B
69472	37B
69473	37B
69474	37C
69475	34B
69476	34B
69477	34B
69478	37C
69479	37C
69480	34B
69481	34B
69482	37C
69483	37C
69484	34C
69485	37C
N2 0–6–2T	
69490	34A
69491	34A
69492	34A
69493	34C
69494	34C
69495	34A
69496	34A
69497	34A
69498	34A
69499	34A
69500	65C
69501	38A
69502	34A
69503	65E
69504	34C
69505	34B
69506	34A
69507	65C
69508	65E
69509	65E
69510	65C
69511	65C
69512	34A
69513	34B
69514	65C
69515	34D
69516	34B
69517	34A
69518	65E
69519	34A
69520	34A
69521	34A
69522	34B
69523	34A
69524	34A
69525	34A
69526	34A
69527	34A
69528	34A
69529	34A
69530	34B
69531	34B
69532	34A
69533	34B
69534	34C
69535	34A
69536	34A
69537	34C
69538	34A
69539	34A
69540	34A
69541	34A
69542	34A
69543	34A
69544	34A
69545	34A
69546	34A
69547	34B
69548	34A
69549	34A
69550	38A
69551	34C
69552	38A
69553	65C
69554	34C
69555	38A
69556	34B
69557	34D
69558	34C
69559	34C
69560	38E
69561	34A
69562	65C
69563	65E
69564	65C
69565	65C
69566	34B
69567	34B
69568	34A
69569	34A
69570	34A
69571	34A
69572	34A
69573	34A
69574	34A
69575	34A
69576	34A
69577	34A
69578	34A
69579	34A
69580	34C
69581	34A
69582	34C
69583	34A
69584	34A
69585	34A

69586 34C
69587 34C
69588 34C
69589 34A
69590 34A
69591 34A
69592 34A
69593 34A
69594 34C
69595 65C
69596 65E

N7
0–6–2T

69600 30A
69601 30A
69602 30A
69603 30A
69604 30A
69605 30A
69606 30A
69607 30A
69608 30A
69609 30A
69610 30A
69611 30A
69612 30F
69613 34C
69614 30F
69615 34C
69616 30A
69617 30A
69618 30A
69619 30A
69620 34C
69621 30F
69622 30A
69623 30A
69624 30A
69625 30A
69626 30A
69627 30A
69628 30A
69629 30A
69630 30A
69631 30A
69632 34C
69633 30A
69634 30A
69635 30F
69636 30A
69637 30A
69638 30A
69639 34C
69640 34C
69641 30A
69642 30A
69643 30A
69644 34C
69645 30A
69646 30A
69647 30A
69648 30A
69649 30A
69650 30A
69651 30A
69652 30A
69653 30A
69654 30A
69655 30A
69656 30A
69657 30A
69658 30A
69659 30A
69660 30A
69661 30A
69662 30A
69663 30A
69664 30A
69665 30A
69666 30A
69667 30A
69668 30A
69669 30A
69670 30A
69671 30A
69672 30A
69673 30A
69674 30A
69675 30A
69676 30A
69677 30F
69678 30A
69679 32G
69680 30A
69681 30A
69682 30A
69683 30A
69684 30A
69685 30A
69686 30A
69687 30A
69688 30A
69689 34E
69690 34E
69691 34C
69692 34E
69693 30A
69694 34E
69695 34C
69696 34C
69697 30A
69698 34E
69699 30A
69700 30A
69701 30E
69702 30A
69703 32B
69704 30A
69705 30A
69706 32A
69707 32A
69708 32A
69709 32A
69710 30A
69711 32B
69712 30A
69713 30A
69714 30A
69715 30A
69716 30A
69717 30A
69718 30A
69719 30A
69720 30A
69721 30A
69722 30A
69723 30A
69724 30A
69725 30A
69726 30E
69727 30A
69728 30A
69729 30A
69730 30A
69731 30A
69732 30A
69733 30A

A7
4–62T

69770 53A
69771 53A
69772 53A
69773 53A
69774 53C
69775 53A
69776 53C
69777 53A
69778 53A
69779 53A
69780 53A
69781 51E
69782 53A
69783 53A
69784 53A
69785 53C
69786 53A
69787 51E
69788 53A
69789 53C

A6
4–6–2T

69791 50D
69793 50D
69794 50D
69796 53B
69797 50D
69798 53B

A5
4–6–2T

69800 40B
69801 38A
69802 51K
69803 35B
69804 40A
69805 34E
69806 38A
69807 38A
69808 40F
69809 38A
69810 38A
69811 51K
69812 40E
69813 40A
69814 38A
69815 40E
69816 35B
69817 38A
69818 40E
69819 40F
69820 40A
69821 38A
69822 34E
69823 38A
69824 35B
69825 38A
69826 38A
69827 34E
69828 34E
69829 34E
69830 51A
69831 51K
69832 51A
69833 51A
69834 51K
69835 51A
69836 51A
69837 51A
69838 51A
69839 51A
69840 51A
69841 51A
69842 51K

A8
4–6–2T

69850 54A
69851 51F
69852 51C
69853 54A
69854 53B
69855 53B
69856 51F
69857 54A
69858 50G
69859 53B
69860 50G

69861	50G
69862	51C
69863	51C
69864	50G
69865	50G
69866	53B
69867	50C
69868	51F
69869	51K
69870	51F
69871	51C
69872	51F
69873	53B
69874	54A
69875	51F
69876	53B
69877	50E
69878	53B
69879	50C
69880	53B
69881	50E
69882	50E
69883	51E
69884	51K
69885	50E
69886	50E
69887	54A
69888	50G
69889	51K
69890	50G
69891	51K
69892	51K
69893	51C
69894	53B

S1
0–8–4T

69900	36B
69901	36B
69902	36C
69903	36C
69904	36B
69905	36B

T1
4–8–0T

69910	51B
69911	51B
69912	53A
69913	51B
69914	53A
69915	53A
69916	51B
69917	51B
69918	51E
69919	51B
69920	53A
69921	51B
69922	53A

Q1
0–8–0T

69925	65A
69926	31B
69927	65A
69928	40E
69929	40E
69930	36C
69931	50C
69932	36C
69933	50C
69934	36C
69935	36C
69936	36C
69937	36C

U1
2–8–8–2

69999	21C

WD
2–8–0

NOTE: Former W.D. and L.N.E.R. numbers are given in the second column as not all these engines have yet received B.R. numbers.

B.R. No.	*Old No.*	
90000	63000	38A
90001	63001	52D
90002	63002	38A
90003	63003	31B
90004	63004	62A
90005	63005	31B
90006	63006	53A
90007	63007	53C
90008	63008	53A
90009	63009	53A
90010	63010	53C
90011	63011	53C
90012	63012	51E
90013	63013	31B
90014	63014	51B
90015	63015	31B
90016	63016	51B
90017	63017	62B
90018	63018	31B
90019	63019	62A
90020	63020	65A
90021	63021	53A
90022	63022	53A
90023	63023	31B
90024	63024	31B
90025	63025	38A
90026	63026	54B
90027	63027	51B
90028	63028	35A
90029	63029	30E
90030	63030	52D
90031	63031	35A
90032	63032	40B
90033	63033	38E
90034	63034	35A
90035	63035	31B
90036	63036	38A
90037	63037	31B
90038	63038	64A
90039	63039	38E
90040	63040	38E
90041	63041	61B
90042	63042	31B
90043	63043	38A
90044	63044	66B
90045	63045	51B
90046	63046	38E
90047	63047	53C
90048	63048	51E
90049	63049	62A
90050	63050	38A
90051	63051	38E
90052	63052	53C
90053	63053	31B
90054	63054	51B
90055	63055	31B
90056	63056	50A
90057	63057	53A
90058	63058	62A
90059	63059	35A
90060	63060	31B
90061	63061	51A
90062	63062	35A

B.R. No.	Old No.	
90063	63063	35A
90064	63064	31B
90065	63065	38E
90066	63066	31B
90067	63067	51E
90068	63068	51B
90069	63069	50A
90070	63070	35A
90071	63071	62B
90072	63072	52D
90073	63073	38A
90074	63074	51B
90075	63075	40B
90076	63076	51B
90077	63077	62B
90078	63078	51A
90079	63079	35A
90080	63080	38E
90081	63081	51B
90082	63082	51E
90083	63083	31B
90084	63084	38A
90085	63085	30E
90086	63086	51E
90087	63087	31B
90088	63088	35A
90089	63089	51B
90090	63090	51B
90091	63091	51B
90092	63092	51E
90093	63093	35A
90094	63094	53C
90095	63095	38E
90096	63096	35A
90097	63097	61B
90098	63098	51B
90099	63099	50A
90100	63100	50A
90101	77000	81A
90102	77001	87K
90103	77003	38A
90104	77004	36B
90105	77005	81A
90106	77006	35A
90107	77007	73C
90108	77008	36B
90109	77010	24B
90110	77012	84G
90111	77013	38A
90112	77014	26F
90113	77015	84G
90114	77016	64A
90115	77017	38D
90116	77018	53C
90117	77019	62C
90118	77020	31B
90119	77022	31B
90120	77023	36B
90121	77024	61B
90122	77025	24B
90123	77026	84G

B.R. No.	Old No.	
90124	77027	25A
90125	77028	66B
90126	77029	24B
90127	77030	73C
90128	77031	62A
90129	77032	38A
90130	77034	35A
90131	77035	31B
90132	77036	51B
90133	77037	40B
90134	77039	65F
90135	77040	6C
90136	77041	38A
90137	77042	38E
90138	77044	24B
90139	77047	38A
90140	77048	25G
90141	77049	84B
99142	77150	73C
90143	77151	6C
90144	77152	36B
90145	77155	62A
90146	77157	36B
90147	77160	65A
90148	77161	83D
90149	77162	65A
90150	77163	36B
90151	77164	35A
90152	77165	66B
90153	77166	36B
90154	77167	36B
90155	77169	51E
90156	77170	35A
90157	77171	25A
90158	77173	35A
90159	77174	24B
90160	77175	53C
90161	77176	36B
90162	77178	40B
90163	77179	25A
90164	77180	73B
90165	77181	35A
90166	77182	36B
90167	77184	86A
90168	77185	62A
90169	77186	35A
90170	77187	62A
90171	77192	24B
90172	77195	51E
90173	77196	87K
90174	77198	65A
90175	77199	31B
90176	77200	82B
90177	77201	62A
90178	77202	24D
90179	77203	85B
90180	77204	35A
90181	77205	25B
90182	77206	62A
90183	77207	24B
90184	77208	51E

B.R. No.	Old No.	
90185	77209	38E
90186	77210	87K
90187	77212	25A
90188	77214	87K
90189	77215	36B
90190	77218	36B
90191	77221	35A
90192	77222	65A
90193	77225	65A
90194	77226	73B
90195	77227	36B
90196	77228	36B
90197	77229	25A
90198	77230	62B
90199	77231	62C
90200	77232	50A
90201	77234	86E
90202	77235	38A
90203	77237	61B
90204	77239	25G
90205	77241	87K
90206	77242	24A
90207	77247	82B
90208	77248	35A
90209	77249	36B
90210	77252	54B
90211	77253	36B
90212	77255	25A
90213	77256	73C
90214	77257	84K
90215	77258	38A
90216	77259	73B
90217	77260	53C
90218	77261	38E
90219	77302	65F
90220	77303	36B
90221	77305	31B
90222	77306	65A
90223	77307	36B
90224	77309	31B
90225	77310	87K
90226	77311	73B
90227	77312	24B
90228	77313	25C
90229	77314	36B
90230	77315	51B
90231	77317	24B
90232	77319	36B
90233	77320	53C
90234	77321	73B
90235	77323	50A
90236	77324	65F
90237	77325	25A
90238	77326	82B
90239	77327	35A
90240	77328	51E
90241	77329	24B
90242	77330	25A
90243	77332	25A
90244	77334	35A
90245	77335	25G

B.R. No.	Old No.	
90246	77338	36B
90247	77340	75A
90248	77342	64A
90249	77348	25A
90250	77350	36B
90251	77351	38A
90252	77352	36B
90253	77353	35A
90254	77355	73B
90255	77356	36B
90256	77358	35A
90257	77359	70B
90258	77362	24B
90259	77364	35A
90260	77365	61B
90261	77368	86A
90262	77371	25C
90263	77372	38E
90264	77374	24B
90265	77375	65A
90266	77378	24D
90267	77379	73C
90268	77380	86G
90269	77381	38D
90270	77386	36B
90271	77388	86C
90272	77390	54B
90273	77392	51B
90274	77393	24B
90275	77394	31B
90276	77395	38D
90277	77398	25E
90278	77399	62C
90279	77401	35A
90280	77402	36B
90281	77404	25C
90282	77406	62A
90283	77407	24B
90284	77408	85A
90285	77411	36B
90286	77413	36B
90287	77414	35A
90288	77415	35A
90289	77416	64A
90290	77418	36B
90291	77419	64A
90292	77421	25A
90293	77424	62C
90294	77425	31B
90295	77426	24C
90296	77428	36B
90297	77429	87K
90298	77431	65A
90299	77432	38D
90300	77433	62A
90301	77434	36B
90302	77436	31B
90303	77439	38A
90304	77440	30E
90305	77441	35A
90306	77442	62C

B.R. No.	Old No.	
90307	77443	87K
90308	77444	25B
90309	77445	54B
90310	77447	25A
90311	77449	36B
90312	70801	82C
90313	70802	65A
90314	70807	24B
90315	70808	87F
90316	70809	25G
90317	70811	75B
90318	70814	25G
90319	70817	62A
90320	70825	24C
90321	70829	25E
90322	70833	25G
90323	70834	38A
90324	70836	82C
90325	70838	25G
90326	70839	25G
90327	70843	81E
90328	70845	24C
90329	70849	25A
90330	70850	38A
90331	70851	24C
90332	70853	25B
90333	70857	25A
90334	70859	25A
90335	70860	24C
90336	70864	25G
90337	70865	25A
90338	70866	26A
90339	70867	25A
90340	70871	36B
90341	70874	25A
90342	70875	25A
90343	70876	82D
90344	70877	51E
90345	70878	25B
90346	77263	35A
90347	77270	25B
90348	77271	24B
90349	77274	35A
90350	77278	62A
90351	77280	25G
90352	77283	54B
90353	77285	25A
90354	77286	75A
90355	77288	86E
90356	77289	82B
90357	77291	24D
90358	77292	38A
90359	77294	87K
90360	77296	75B
90361	77297	25A
90362	77299	25A
90363	78510	25A
90364	78512	26D
90365	78514	38E
90366	78521	84G
90367	78522	24C

B.R. No.	Old No.	
90368	78525	38A
90369	78526	38A
90370	78560	25A
90371	78561	24B
90372	78563	25G
90373	78564	51B
90374	78568	24D
90375	78569	73B
90376	78572	64A
90377	78575	51E
90378	78578	53C
90379	78580	25A
90380	78581	25A
90381	78583	25A
90382	78585	53A
90383	78587	36B
90384	78588	31B
90385	78590	25E
90386	78592	66B
90387	78594	24B
90388	78595	26A
90389	78596	73C
90390	78597	73C
90391	78598	38A
90392	78599	31B
90393	78600	31B
90394	78601	38D
90395	78602	25G
90396	78604	25A
90397	78605	25A
90398	78606	24C
90399	78607	24B
90400	78609	36B
90401	78610	36B
90402	78612	24A
90403	78614	38D
90404	78615	25A
90405	78616	51E
90406	78621	25E
90407	78624	25G
90408	78531	73B
90409	78532	53A
90410	78537	36B
90411	78538	38A
90412	78541	25A
90413	78542	85B
90414	78543	25A
90415	78544	25A
90416	78546	24A
90417	78551	25A
90418	78553	38D
90419	78554	26D
90420	78556	24B
90421	78559	36B
90422	63101	31B
90423	63102	51A
90424	63103	50A
90425	63104	31B
90426	63105	51B
90427	63106	52D
90428	63107	35A

B.R. No.	Old No.	
90429	63108	53C
90430	63109	54B
90431	63110	30E
90432	63111	50A
90433	63112	31B
90434	63113	51B
90435	63114	52D
90436	63115	64A
90437	63116	38A
90438	63117	35A
90439	63118	35A
90440	63119	65D
90441	63120	65A
90442	63121	31B
90443	63122	30E
90444	63123	62B
90445	63124	54B
90446	63125	51B
90447	63126	35A
90448	63127	38A
90449	63128	51A
90450	63129	53A
90451	63130	51B
90452	63131	51B
90453	63132	31B
90454	63133	35A
90455	63134	61B
90456	63135	40B
90457	63136	51B
90458	63137	54B
90459	63138	51B
90460	63139	40B
90461	63140	51B
90462	63141	51B
90463	63142	62B
90464	63143	68A
90465	63144	51B
90466	63145	38A
90467	63146	51A
90468	63147	64A
90469	63148	64A
90470	63149	53C
90471	63150	30E
90472	63151	62A
90473	63152	31B
90474	63153	31B
90475	63154	51B
90476	63155	31B
90477	63156	30E
90478	63157	53C
90479	63158	52D
90480	63159	31B
90481	63160	51B
90482	63161	54B
90483	63162	53A
90484	63163	38A
90485	63164	54B
90486	63165	38E
90487	63166	51B
90488	63167	51B
90489	63168	62A

B.R. No.	Old No.	
90490	63169	35A
90491	63170	38A
90492	63171	38A
90493	63172	64A
90494	63173	35A
90495	63174	35A
90496	63175	64A
90497	63176	53C
90498	63177	62A
90499	63178	38A
90500	63179	51B
90501	63180	35A
90502	63181	31B
90503	63182	51B
90504	63183	38E
90505	63184	68A
90506	63185	31B
90507	63186	38E
90508	63187	30E
90509	63188	38E
90510	63189	31B
90511	63190	50A
90512	63191	35A
90513	63192	62C
90514	63193	35A
90515	63194	62B
90516	63195	38E
90517	63196	51B
90518	63197	50A
90519	63198	31B
90520	63199	38E
90521	77050	36B
90522	77051	30E
90523	77052	63A
90524	77053	85C
90525	77054	26A
90526	77055	38D
90527	77056	25B
90528	77057	35A
90529	77058	81F
90530	77059	63A
90531	77060	25E
90532	77061	38A
90533	77062	73B
90534	77063	62A
90535	77064	84G
90536	77066	65F
90537	77067	36B
90538	77068	36B
90539	77070	62A
90540	77071	31B
90541	77072	24C
90542	77073	62C
90543	77074	25D
90544	77075	38A
90545	77076	65A
90546	77077	87K
90547	77078	62A
90548	77079	84G
90549	77080	65D
90550	77081	36B

B.R. No.	Old No.	
90551	77085	38A
90552	77086	73B
90553	77087	62C
90554	77088	35A
90555	77089	64A
90556	77090	73C
90557	77092	24B
90558	77094	73B
90559	77095	35A
90560	77096	62C
90561	77097	84G
90562	77098	70B
90563	77099	86G
90564	77101	73B
90565	77102	86A
90566	77103	73C
90567	77104	53A
90568	77106	87K
90569	77107	62C
90570	77108	70B
90571	77111	53C
90572	77115	84K
90573	77116	82B
90574	77118	38A
90575	77119	62C
90576	77120	24B
90577	77121	35A
90578	77122	25D
90579	77123	87K
90580	77124	31B
90581	77126	25A
90582	77127	31B
90583	77128	36B
90584	77129	24B
90585	77130	66B
90586	77135	53C
90587	77138	36B
90588	77141	25G
90589	77142	82C
90590	77144	36B
90591	77145	25G
90592	77147	24B
90593	77148	25E
90594	77149	36B
90595	77451	24C
90596	77452	36B
90597	77453	36B
90598	77454	36B
90599	77455	24B
90600	77456	62B
90601	77457	31B
90602	77458	31B
90603	77459	51E
90604	77460	70B
90605	77461	51B
90606	77462	38D
90607	77463	25A
90608	77464	31B
90609	77465	50A
90610	77466	24A
90611	77467	54B

B.R. No.	Old No.	
90612	77468	36B
90613	77469	35A
90614	77470	62A
90615	77471	25A
90616	77476	65F
90617	77479	25A
90618	77480	36B
90619	77481	25B
90620	77482	25A
90621	77484	24B
90622	77485	25D
90623	77488	51E
90624	77489	25A
90625	77492	51B
90626	77494	26F
90627	77497	54B
90628	77499	66B
90629	77503	38A
90630	77508	82D
90631	78626	25A
90632	78629	24A
90633	78632	25A
90634	78637	38D
90635	78638	25A
90636	78643	38A
90637	78644	25A
90638	78650	38E
90639	78652	25A
90640	78658	24C
90641	78666	75B
90642	78671	25D
90643	78672	25A
90644	78675	25A
90645	78681	25G
90646	78682	40B
90647	78683	40B
90648	78684	38A
90649	78685	25G
90650	78688	25B
90651	78689	25A
90652	78695	25A
90653	78700	36B
90654	78704	25A
90655	78705	25B
90656	78714	25A
90657	78715	35A
90658	78717	24C
90659	79178	35A
90660	79181	31B
90661	79182	53C
90662	79184	38A
90663	79186	53A
90664	79190	25G
90665	79194	35A
90666	79195	25G
90667	79196	25A
90668	79198	31B
90669	79199	73C
90670	79202	50A
90671	79203	73C
90672	79204	38A

B.R. No.	Old No.	
90673	79205	25A
90674	79206	52D
90675	79207	63A
90676	79208	38A
90677	79209	53C
90678	79210	73C
90679	79213	25A
90680	79214	25B
90681	79215	24C
90682	79219	25A
90683	79220	35A
90684	79221	25G
90685	79224	84D
90686	79225	84K
90687	79226	24B
90688	79227	53C
90689	79228	24C
90690	79229	62A
90691	79232	85B
90692	79233	25A
90693	79234	66B
90694	79235	25B
90695	79239	53A
90696	79242	36B
90697	79243	38A
90698	79244	25G
90699	79254	25G
90700	79259	36B
90701	79261	82D
90702	79262	73C
90703	79263	38A
90704	79264	52D
90705	79265	62C
90706	79266	26A
90707	79268	25E
90708	79269	26A
90709	79271	36B
90710	79272	25A
90711	79273	25G
90712	79274	87K
90713	79275	24A
90714	79276	36B
90715	79278	85A
90716	79279	86E
90717	79280	38A
90718	79281	73C
90719	79282	25A
90720	79283	26F
90721	79294†	
90722	79298	25A
90723	79301	25D
90724	79302	25E
90725	79303	25A
90726	79304†	
90727	79306	62B
90728	79307	25E
90729	79309	25A
90730	79310	35A
90731	79311	25E
90732	79312	30E

WD 2-10-0

90750	73774	66B
90751	73775	68A
90752	73776	66B
90753	73777	64D
90754	73778	66B
90755	73779	65F
90756	73780	66B
90757	73781	65F
90758	73782	66B
90759	73783	65F
90760	73784	66B
90761	73785	66B
90762	73786	66B
90763	73787	68A
90764	73788	Rugby Plan:
90765	73789	65F
90766	73790	66B
90767	73791	68A
90768	73792	64D
90769	73793	68A
90770	73794	66B
90771	73795	66B
90772	73796	66B
90773	73798	68A
90774	73799*	68A

†Not in service.

First published 1948-1950
This edition 1973
Second impression 1975

ISBN 0 7110 0401 3

Published by Ian Allan Limited

Printed by Ian Allan (Printing) Ltd., Shepperton, Middlesex, TW17 8AN